Tragic Drama and the Family

Tragic Drama and the Family

PSYCHOANALYTIC STUDIES

FROM AESCHYLUS

TO BECKETT

BENNETT SIMON, M.D.

Yale University Press
New Haven and London

Designed by Nancy Ovedovitz and set in Aldus type by
Keystone Typesetting Co. Printed in the United States of
America by Braun-Brumfield, Inc., Ann Arbor, Michigan.

Library of Congress Cataloging-in-Publication Data
Simon, Bennett, 1933–
Tragic drama and the family : psychoanalytic studies from
Aeschylus to Beckett / Bennett Simon.
 p. cm.
 Includes index.
 ISBN 0-300-04132-2
 1. Tragedy—History and criticism. 2. Family in literature.
3. Psychoanalysis in literature. I. Title.
PN1899.F27S55   1988
809.2′512—dc19   88-3200
                                                     CIP

The paper in this book meets the guidelines for permanence
and durability of the Committee on Production Guidelines for
Book Longevity of the Council on Library Resources.

10   9   8   7   6   5   4   3   2   1

To Robbie, who has taught me so much about family

CONTENTS

ACKNOWLEDGMENTS

M y interest in tragic drama goes far back in my life, but the idea of a book on the subject is of more recent origin. Writing the section on tragedy in my first book (*Mind and Madness in Ancient Greece*) proved very interesting and opened up for me many more questions than I addressed there. Many critics, both those who approved and those who disapproved of that book as a whole, singled out the sections on tragedy as containing something new. This book took root in the summer of 1980, when a friend, colleague, and Socratic midwife, Herman Sinaiko, asked me to participate with him in a panel on "Psychoanalysis and the Humanities" for the fiftieth anniversary celebration of the Chicago Institute for Psychoanalysis. A number of discussions on land and sea culminated in the decision to focus on "Tragic Drama and Psychoanalysis," and the panel took place in November of 1981.

The project grew and led to my teaching a course for Harvard under-graduates, "Tragic Drama and Human Conflict," which became an important vehicle for developing and trying out my ideas. Yale University Press and Gladys Topkis, Senior Editor, gave encouragement for a book on the topic, and the Rockefeller Foundation generously provided the month of March 1984 at the Study Center in Bellagio, Italy. There, in my walks and talks with my wife, Roberta Apfel, and my time sitting in Santa Caterina, the magnificent monk's cell in the woods overlooking Lake Como, the book underwent a major transformation. Originally conceived as a study of the methodology of psychoanalysis and literary criticism in relation to tragic drama, it took shape in its present form—a study of how and why tragic drama is so much concerned with the family. Critical insights into the relationship between the content of O'Neill's *Long Day's Journey into Night* and the form of the dialogue crystalized, and these insights led me, almost automatically, to the study of Beckett and to a number of serendipitous discoveries. My reading of O'Neill and Beckett led to a rethinking and reworking of my ideas about Greek tragedy and Shakespearean tragedy, and to a view of tragic drama as concerned with the problem of how the family at war with itself can propagate itself. Thereafter, in my teaching and writing, these ideas took on a life of their own and gradually became more refined and better articulated.

Along the way, I had several opportunities to present work in progress, for which I am most grateful—critical comments by discussants and audience proved extremely valuable. A panel at the 1980 American Philological Association meeting on "Oedipus—Myth, Complex and Tragedy," with presentations by Marylin Arthur, Richard Caldwell, and Charles Ducey; a symposium on Greek tragedy organized by Charles Segal at Brown University in the fall of 1980; two presentations at the Hebrew University in Jerusalem, in the English Department in 1981 and at the Center for Literary Studies in 1985 (Lawrence Besserman, Emily and Sanford Budick, Ruth Nevo, Shlomith Rimon-Kenan and Shimon and Tirzah Sandbank were and have remained extremely helpful); at the New York Psychoanalytic Society in the spring of 1983 (arranged by Arnold Richards, with Francis Baudry and Frank Kermode as discussants); at the Department of Classics at Miami University in Oxford, Ohio (Judith De-Luce and Peter Rose); at the Kanzer Study Group at Yale with the aid of Sidney Blatt; at a panel on creativity sponsored by the Guild for Continuing Education in November 1986 (I presented my work on Eugene O'Neill, with Margaret Brenman-Gibson, Arnold Modell, George Pollock, and Ana-Marie Rizzuto as co-panelists); at the Harvard Center for Literary Studies, chaired by Gregory Nagy; at The Washington Psychoanalytic Society, with Joseph Smith as discussant and Stanley Palombo as convener; at the New York Hospital in Westchester and Beth Israel and Cambridge Hospitals in Boston; and at the Colloquia in the History of Psychiatry series on "The Concept of Maturity in Literature" at Harvard Medical School.

Charles Segal was most helpful at an early stage, and his writings have been indispensable at every stage. Froma Zeitlin, both in her published works and in her careful critical reading of several manuscripts and proposals, was also helpful, demonstrating her friendship by a willingness to say, "You're wrong." On specific topics, Ruth Nevo, as editor, critic, and Shakespearean scholar, provided extraordinary assistance and support. Lynne Layton and Barbara Schapiro read an early draft on Beckett, and Lynne Layton later provided detailed criticism of my work on Beckett and *King Lear*. Deirdre Bair, Linda Ben-Zvi, and Kristin Morrison helped me considerably through the thickets of the life and work of Samuel Beckett. Arnold Modell read a manuscript on Beckett and James Grotstein's knowledge of Bion was invaluable. Francis Baudry has heard me out, read several manuscripts, and aided my thinking by his work on methodology. Stanley Cavell, both in his extensive writings on tragedy, including Shakespeare and Beckett, and in discussion, has been of substantial help over the past few years. Paul Schwaber's obiter dicta and his detailed reading of the entire manuscript were immensely helpful and affirming, as was Kenneth Levin, who also read the entire manuscript. Others who were helpful at various stages include William Grossman, Phillip Holzman, Amy Kass, Jerome Neu, Stanley Palombo, Amelie Rorty, and Patricia Spacks.

During the years 1983–86, the corps of teaching assistants for "Lit and Arts A-35" provided invaluable feedback and critique at many levels. Susan Pollak, head section person, has been a steady supporter, critical listener, and critical reader. Patricia Rosebush, Susan Wadsworth, and Rick Weissbourd were also there from the beginning. Julia Dubnoff, Juliet Faithfull, Jan Fogelquist, Nadia Medina, and Cynthia Willet have made extremely helpful, tactful comments on what has been clear and what has been muddled. During 1987, Wera Hildebrand, John Looper, and Lawrence Rhu taught and helped with clarification and error detection. Undergraduates who took the course have also contributed to my continuous scrutiny and reformulation with their questions, papers, examinations, and responses to the material. The course and the book were so organically intertwined that I also wish to thank Marjorie Garber, Joyce Toomre, and Emily Vermeule for their "leap of faith" and substantial help in formulating and making the course possible.

Institutional support of several sorts has been most important. John Nemiah, former chairman of psychiatry at Beth Israel Hospital, was most encouraging, and Fred Frankel, the current chairman, allowed me a partial leave during the year 1986–87. The Harvard University libraries provided virtually everything I needed and could have wished for. The Folger Library, a delightful place to commune with Shakespeare, was most hospitable. The library of the Boston Psychoanalytic Society and Institute, and its gifted librarian, Ann Menashi, once again provided me with much needed support. The Boston Psychoanalytic Society has similarly continued to nurture interdisciplinary work, both my own and that of numerous other members and students.

At the concrete level of transforming the manuscript into a book, Gladys Topkis and the staff at the Yale Press, especially Stephanie Jones, have been steady, wise, and judicious. They have added more than grace notes to the score.

Personal support and encouragement has come from family members of several generations. Again, I want to register my gratitude to my sister, Diana Simon Maine, for instructing and inspiring me in the classics and for introducing me to the magical world of serious theater. My children and step-children, Amy, Celia, Jonathan, Michael, and Molly, have cheered and critiqued my teaching and writing. Jonathan's guidance in the art of using a Macintosh was indispensable for the writing. My late mother-in-law, Polly Apfel, was most delighted to know of my work, and in her last months she meditated in her jottings and her conversations on the import of my work on "family," a topic of utmost interest for her. My father-in-law, Kalman Apfel, continues to take great pride in the writings of his children and their spouses. My mother, who took such pride and pleasure in my first book, did not live to see this work completed, but she had preserved, with my sister's help, an essay I wrote at the age of sixteen and had long forgotten: "Euripides' *Electra*: A Modern Psychological Study." The spirit and memory of my father, as well as of Nancy Simon, have also been important in sustaining this work.

To my wife I owe an enormous debt for her ongoing support, interest, and ability in helping the amorphous to take shape and the already formed to undergo necessary metamorphosis. Her skill and tact are much appreciated. She has been steadily there during the years of my attempts to assimilate experiences of sadness and loss and to help myself and others understand their inevitability in human life.

Finally, in this book so much concerned with the role of ancestors and progeny, I want to record my enormous debt to those teachers and scholarly ancestors, in literature, drama, and psychoanalysis, who have worked in these vineyards before me and prepared the ground for my own labors. I note the recent loss of Eric Havelock, mentor of many years. There are numerous others whose work I may well have replicated by virtue of not knowing of them. I see this work as part of an ongoing tradition of the study and interpretation of tragic qualities in human life, especially as embodied in the great tragic dramas. I feel privileged to be part of this chain of knowledge and inquiry, and I leave it to the reader to decide whether I have made a useful contribution to the propagation of knowledge in these areas.

I am grateful to the following publishers for permission to utilize excerpts of plays and translations to enhance my work: Cornell University Press, for P. Pucci's *The Violence of the Pity in Euripides'* Medea; Grove Press (and Faber and Faber and Les Éditions de Minuit) for Beckett's *Endgame* and *Not I;* Harper and Row for *The Odyssey of Homer,* translated by Richmond Lattimore; Harvard University Press, reprinted by permission of the publishers and the Loeb Classical Library from Aeschylus, Vol. 2, translated by H. W. Smyth, Cambridge, Massachusetts, 1926; Macmillan Publishing Company for permission for Yeats' *On Bailie's Strand* from *Collected Plays of W. B. Yeats*. Copyright 1934, 1952 by Macmillan Publishing Company. Copyrights renewed: 1962 by Bertha Georgie Yeats, and 1980 by Anne Yeats (Permission also of A. P. Watt Ltd. on behalf of Michael B. Yeats and Macmillan London Ltd.); University of Chicago Press for: *Agamemnon*, © 1953; © 1947 by Richmond Lattimore and for *The Libation Bearers* and *The Eumenides* also by Richmond Lattimore; Euripides' *Medea*, © University of Chicago, 1955, translated by Rex Warner, first published 1944, reprinted 1946 by John Lane, The Bodley Head, Ltd., London; [all from *The Complete Greek Tragedies*, ed. Grene and Lattimore]; University of Michigan Press for material from *Aristophanes: The Frogs*, translated by R. Lattimore, © 1969.

INTRODUCTION

Claudius: But now my cousin Hamlet, and my son—.
Hamlet: A little more than kin, and less than kind.

Tragic drama and the study of the family are inextricably intertwined—
that is the thesis of this book. I begin with Aristotle's observation that the
best tragic dramas deal with famous mythological houses, families, in
which terrible deeds took place. The tragedies he described depict tensions—indeed warfare—within the family. Murder, suicide, incest, betrayal, abandonment are—as a contemporary sitcom has it—"all in the
family."

> Initially, our poets accepted any chance plots; but now the best tragedies are
> constructed about a few families, for example, about Alcmaeon, Oedipus, Ores-
> tes, Meleager, Thyestes, Telephon, and any others who were destined to experi-
> ence, or to commit, terrifying acts. For, as we have indicated, artistically consid-
> ered, the best tragedy arises from this kind of plot.   (*Poetics*, XIII)

Plot structures that emphasize deeds done by one family member to
another, Aristotle continues, are most effective in achieving the full impact
of pity and terror. Indeed, recognition, *anagnorisis*—the movement from
ignorance to acknowledgment of the other—is one of the crucial features of
dramatic structure, and it is most powerful when it involves the recognition
of kin (*Poetics*, XIII, XIV). Even plays that are not explicitly familial but
are, for example, political or historical tend to focus on politics as if it were a
family affair. This is clearly the case with Aeschylus' *Persians*, but it is also
true of Shakespeare's history plays that have tragic dimensions, as well as
those explicitly labeled as tragedies (e.g., *Richard II* or even *Julius Caesar*).

1

I argue that one of the most important continuities between ancient and modern drama is, in fact, the focus on the family. While it is not correct to define tragedy as "the genre that deals with the family," since that description also applies to novels both ancient and modern, comedies, and romances, there is a characteristic way in which tragedy deals with the family. This involves, first, a sense of terrible warfare within the family, and second, the sense that problems cannot be solved by displacing the issues to outside the family (i.e., by fighting outsiders) or by changing conditions around the family. Further, in the tragic characterization, the family is at risk of destroying itself, either by literally destroying its own progeny or by making propagation impossible, for example, because of intractable warfare between husband and wife. The continuation of the family that is actively destroying itself is a dominant motif in Greek tragedy, in Shakespeare, and in much modern tragedy, whether the family is the royal house of Agamemnon or Hamlet or the bourgeois houses of Ibsen's characters.

The threat to continuity is expressed not only literally, when the children of the house are murdered, but also in the recurrent motif of the curse on birth. "Best is never to have been born," laments the chorus of Sophocles' *Oedipus at Colonus* (1224–25), and that lament is amplified as Lear, mad in the storm, commands that all seed should be spilled upon the ground (3.2.6–9):

And thou, all-shaking thunder,
Strike flat the thick rotundity o'th' world,
Crack Nature's molds, all germains spill at once,
That makes ingrateful man.

In much modern drama, whether tragic or tragic-grotesque, in the works of O'Neill, Beckett, Pinter, Ionesco, Albee, and Shepard, we find the recurrent motifs of the death of children, the wish never to have been born, and even doubt about whether a particular child *has* been born (e.g., *Who's Afraid of Virginia Woolf?*).

Related to a curse on generation we find a dread of the progression of generations. "Oh ye generations of men, I count you as zero," proclaims the chorus in Sophocles' *Oedipus Rex* just as Oedipus has discovered the dreadful truth of his past (1186–88). Clearly the sort of family relationships portrayed in the great tragic dramas could easily discourage reproduction and the orderly passage of generations. If parents are killing children, if children have no love for parents, if husbands and wives, brothers and sisters, betray each other and thereby destroy the children, why have families? At the same time, within these plays there is the assumption—indeed the ideal—that the house and line should be continued, that families exist to propagate and to bind the generations together. The tension between "why continue?" and "continue!" is an intricate one, for the acts of betrayal, the crimes, including the murder of children, are somehow committed in the name of continuing and enhancing the line, or at least enhancing one line over another. Should Agamemnon sacrifice his daughter, Iphigenia, a part of his house, in order to fight the Trojan War and thus preserve his house? Should Agamemnon kill the children of Troy and many of the children of Greece, "the flower of Greece," in order to propagate his house and perpetuate his rule?

Underlying such cruel dilemmas is the ever-present awareness of death and, even worse, the dread of extinction that comes from having no progeny, leaving no one behind who can listen to and retell the tales of greatness and epic heroism. The hero of *Macbeth* is obsessed with the dynastic consequences of his childlessness—there are no descendants to whom he can leave the fruits of his labors (and crimes). That all is lost, that all is extinguished, "out, out, brief candle," that the house of Macbeth is at an end, is signified by the image of a meaningless story: "a tale told by an idiot, full of sound and fury, signifying nothing."

The thesis of this work, then, is that great tragic drama is fueled by the problematic of the birth and death of the family. The begetting of children within a family is the only sure way open to mortals to gain immortality. At the same time, the passions, rivalries, conflicts, and consequent ambivalence of relationships within the family engender a destructiveness that threatens extinction as much as does the "natural" fact of death. Epic heroic tales are centered around cheating death, achieving immortality by performing great deeds, and begetting children who will remember and retell such deeds. Tragic drama is centered around the dilemma arising from the painful realization that striving for immortality by the creation of a union, a family, by bearing and rearing children, is fraught with enormous and ineluctable difficulties.

As an integral part of the propensity in tragic drama to curse birth and generation, there appears to be an attack on woman. Female sexuality, including female reproductive powers, is repeatedly damned or wished away. Characters in several Greek tragedies voice the wish that babies could be born without women, perhaps bestowed as gifts from the gods or born from men. In fact, the resolution of Aeschylus' *Oresteia* depends upon Apollo's assertion that the father is the true parent and the mother only the vessel, the ground that holds the seed. The "hole" into which the penis enters and from which babies emerge is recurrently cursed and reviled, as in Lear's "Down from the waist they are Centaurs. . . . There's hell, there's darkness, there is the sulphurous pit." The denouement of *Macbeth*, of course, depends on a man who is not "of woman born," whose existence is not dependent on passing through the birth canal. "Astride of a grave and a difficult birth. Down in the hole, lingeringly, the grave-digger puts on the forceps," muses Vladimir in Beckett's *Waiting for Godot*, not bitterly denouncing the "hole" but simply equating it with the grave.

The major tragedies not only rage at and dread female sexuality, they also search for alternate ways of achieving the immortality that comes through begetting progeny. These "solutions" include fantasies of having been begotten by the earth, of not having been born to mortal parents, of getting different parents, of being made out of clouds and air (Euripides' *Bacchae*), or of being concocted in a pot (*Macbeth*). The quest to bypass the ordinary ways of reproducing and thereby avoid terrible dangers is incessant in tragedy. In fact, the effort of characters in tragedy to bypass, to short-circuit, to avoid the formidable but inevitable difficulties of kinship can be viewed as the generator of tragedy. Many of the great tragedies include a character or agency that says, "Stop—accept what is—don't make this into a Greek tragedy!"

A related problem around generation and procreation also found in tragedy is an anxiety and concern about generating and propagating stories. Early in Greek tragedy, one begins to detect an uneasiness about storytelling, related to the kinds of stories being told. How can one tell children stories about the murder of children? Is not the telling of such tales a way of traumatizing children, a repetition in telling of the deeds within the story? This concern finds its culmination and "perfection" in certain modern dramas, particularly Beckett's *Endgame*. There, progeny, hope, caring, connecting, and the *telling of tales* are together condemned to death by attrition and starvation.

At this point the reader only slightly acquainted with the history of criticism involving tragic drama may well ask, "But where is the tragic hero? Where the tragic flaw? Where purgation through, or of, pity and terror?" The reader with a deeper knowledge of the unresolved questions in the study of tragic drama will have a more elaborate set of questions, inquiring (tactfully, one hopes) why still another book on tragedy, why still another attempt to define tragedy? Where does this book belong among the hundreds of other works on these questions? Readers who have thought at all about tragic drama, whether or not they are learned in the critical disciplines, may have legitimate expectations about what an author should address in a book on tragedy. What makes these great plays and not just stories about terrible doings within families? What is the difference between Euripides' *Medea* and a newspaper account of a mother who killed her child by baking him or her in the kitchen oven? What about the aesthetics and the impact of these plays? What about the differences between ancient and modern plays—have Aeschylus and Pinter indeed both written tragedies?

My psychoanalytic colleagues, as well as readers interested in psychoanalytic contributions to the study of tragedy, may well ask what is psychoanalytic in this work. How do my approaches to drama fit in with the large body of literature by psychoanalysts, starting with Freud's early works, on the relationship between tragic drama and psychoanalysis?

Definitions of tragic drama, beginning with Aristotle's in *The Poetics*, have inevitably addressed questions about both form and content. The best definitions have attempted to specify:

What are tragic contents or themes: what stories are tragic?
What are tragic qualities?
What constitutes the form of tragedy: what features of language, plot, and presentation are necessary and sufficient for tragic drama?

Such attempts have been only partially successful, but they do provide a matrix, a scaffolding or foil for subsequent attempts at definition. They are by necessity empirical and somewhat circular—they abstract characteristics from existing works already labeled tragedies by popular agreement. Definitions of tragedy are also never free of presuppositions, which means that in defending them, their authors select the plays that best illustrate or support them and ignore or even suppress those that are not so apt. This selection process begins with Aristotle. "Recognition," *anagnorisis*, and "reversal," *peripateia*, were crucial formal elements in his view, and he selected for special praise two "model plays" containing these elements. He picked Sophocles' *Oedipus Rex*, which modern sensibilities also find quintessentially tragic (though whether moderns can ever understand it as the Greeks did is debatable), but he also chose Euripides' *Iphigenia in Tauris*, which now is considered to verge on melodrama. He did not discuss Euripides' *The Bacchae* or his great antiwar play, *The Trojan Women*. Definitions of, and tastes in, great tragic drama have varied considerably over the centuries, as has the importance of the tragic as a genre or as an ideal. Particular plays become popular and influence the definition, and the definition in turn influences what is written and becomes popular.

Some definitions or characterizations emphasize formal features, and some emphasize content (Nevo 1972; Simon 1984). Both sorts of definition require some sense, implicit or explicit, about what constitutes "the tragic"—that is, the quality apart from the literary genre, or the quality that is found in both life and literature. Statements of this "quality," especially in the nineteenth and twentieth centuries, employ such terms as *compulsion* and *irreversibility*. A comic paraphrase of the sense of tragic compulsion in Sophocles' *Antigone* puts it thus: "the Gods who drive the hearse, seldom shove it in reverse" (Sagoff 1980).

There is entrapment, combined with protest or heroic rebellion against such entrapment; catastrophe avoided only to yield a worse catastrophe; clashes of values; inevitable clashes and contradictions among basic and unavoidable human desires and needs. Irony and paradox are two of the qualities associated with entrapment and the attempt to escape. These statements, in turn, require "retranslation" into the particular terms of storyline, imagery, structure, and character.

Among the definitions of tragic qualities, or of how such qualities find formal expression, are a number of characterizations of *tragic rhythm* or *tragic progression*. One definition of tragedy that emphasizes both "tragic qualities" and tragic structure specifies a sequence of four elements (Krook 1969). First there is an act of shame or horror and/or the revelation of such an act. This produces a profound social and familial disequilibrium, which acts as the "spring" that impels the action of the play. Second, there is suffering, which is tragic only if it generates the third element: knowledge about fundamental human problems and dilemmas. The fourth element is affirmation, or reaffirmation, of values or worth.

The language and imagery of tragedy have also been discussed repeatedly since Aristotle. Elevated language, dialogue, not narrative, poetry—these are among the elements emphasized. In the twentieth century, discussions of tragic dialogue have tended to focus on irony, multiple perspective, the ambiguous and polysemous nature of communication, and the relation of tragic dialogue to other forms of human dialogue including psychotherapy and psychoanalysis.

Definitions of the essential content of tragic drama emphasized stories of royal or significant personages in which not only the welfare of the royalty but that of the commonweal as a whole is at stake. But as great tragic dramas began to be written that were set in the kitchen or living room rather than the throne room, tragic significance came to be defined as some universal struggle intrinsic to the human condition, not necessarily involving the social station of the characters. There is still room for dispute about whether ancient and modern dramas can be properly considered species of the same genus, tragedy. Witness contemporary discussions that assert "the death of tragedy" (a consequence, in part, of "the death of God"). Such terms as *anti-tragic* and *post-tragic* are part of today's critical vocabulary.

Some definitions of tragedy take the form of, "tragic drama is really a transformed version of *X*," where *X* is some important timeless myth, ritual, or recurrent human dilemma. A recent work of great interest talks of tragic drama as really about death and funerary rites de passage (Cole 1985). At the turn of the century, a group of classicists at Cambridge with keen anthropological interests, such as Jane Harrison and Gilbert Murray, saw Greek tragedy as representing the dying and resurrected vegetation god. A modern classicist, Walter Burkert, speaks of tragic drama as an elaboration of the ritual of sacrifice (1966). Sigmund Freud, in *Totem and Taboo*, calls tragic drama the re-presentation of the overthrow of the father by the primal horde, and some psychoanalysts after Freud have argued that each tragic drama is a repetition of the drama of the Oedipus complex. Each of these views, limited as it is, touches upon something important and fundamental in the nature of tragic drama, thus contributing to the dialogue on "what is tragedy."

Where then do my formulations fit in with these various approaches to understanding tragic drama? First, my claim that tragic drama is about destructive conflict within the family, that the deeds triggering the conflict are often done in the name of preserving the house and yet may ruin the house, belongs to the group of theories that says "tragedy is about a particular theme." As such, my theory claims that plays dealing with the death of children contain the essence of tragic conflict. Further, my formulations emphasize a continuity from ancient to Renaissance to modern tragedy. On the face of it, my theory scarcely touches on questions of the formal structure of the plays; and only in a very general way—since stories about families can have a strong emotional appeal—does it address the question of impact and effect upon the audience. As for tragic hero and tragic catharsis, in the course of this book I present my views on the perspective afforded these terms by viewing tragedy as a study of warfare within the family.

Needless to say, I do not rule out other theories of tragic content and context, such as those about the "political" nature of tragic drama, beginning with Greek tragedy's examination of man and woman in the polis. All tragedies presume a particular social and historical context, often a composite of the society portrayed on stage and the society of the audience viewing the play. Tragedy can certainly be viewed as a powerful exploration of the painful relationship between individual and society or the contradictions inherent in any political and social world. I urge the reader to allow my formulations to become "figure" with others as "ground" for long enough to apprehend the full implications of my analysis of tragedy and the family. My hope is that figure and ground can then be reversed with a richer appreciation of both.

I further believe that viewing these plays as dramas of conflict that threaten the continuity of the family, facilitates a discussion of tragic form and tragic effect. Tragedy, in *content*, deals with breakdowns in meaningful relationships within the family and the threat of discontinuity in the generational links—ancestors, present family, and progeny. Tragic *form*—plot, dialogue, modes of narration, use of language, and stagecraft—convey these conflicts and these threats. Twisted and interrupted narration, including silences, signifies and is consonant with twisted and interrupted generational relationships. Turns and sudden reversals in plot reflect stumbling and distortion in the transmission of values and in caring among the characters and generations. Breakdown in the use of language reflects and conveys breakdown in the fundamental communicative relationships among family members. *King Lear*, with its iteration of monosyllabic words, indeed of mere syllables—its howls, its nonsense sounds—dramatizes the message of the plot: the degradation of meaningful family relationships into cannibalism, anarchy, and senseless slaughter.

Tragedy, then, in form and content confronts us with an awesome dialectic between the meaningful and the meaningless, between the linking and connecting of persons, ideals, and values to each other and the breakdown, the dissolution of these links and connections. Tragedy deals with a tension or dialectic between the interpretable and the uninterpretable. This way of looking at the unity of content and form allows a closer examination of some of the debates on modern tragedy. Tragic drama, from its ancient inception, especially in the work of Euripides, has contained and represented tensions that threaten to burst the bounds of the genre. Modern tragic drama and the attendant critical literature have represented these tensions more explicitly, at times providing elaborate "metacommentary" within the plays on the nature of plays. Pirandello, Genet, Ionesco, Stoppard, and others have written plays that "play" with the idea of what is a tragic play.

The artistic presentation, within a play, of conflicts between "it makes no sense" and "it is meaningful," between "generation" and "degeneration," is itself "generative" of audience response. There ensues an enlargement, for the audience, of understanding and responsiveness to core human dilemmas. I suggest that the multiplicity of often contradictory interpretations that can legitimately arise among audiences and critics is made possible, indeed inevitable, by the way tragic drama "plays off" the contrast between meaningful and meaningless.

What is psychoanalytic in this approach? A careful reading of Freud's writings on tragic drama reveals that there are several "psychoanalytic approaches" to questions about tragic drama. Freud made proposals, however sketchy, for a psychoanalytic understanding of how tragic dramas are constructed, the reasons for their power over the spectators, the relationship between tragic process and psychoanalytic process, the creativity of the playwright in relation to his inner conflicts and personal history, and the origins of tragic drama. He also demonstrated the didactic use of tragic drama in explicating and illustrating crucial aspects of psychoanalytic theory. Psychoanalysts writing during Freud's lifetime and since 1939 have expanded upon these topics, and there is now a formidable body of psychoanalytically informed literature about tragic drama. Not surprisingly, the single most frequently discussed play is *Oedipus Rex,* and the playwright who has received the most attention is Shakespeare. My own approach is influenced and informed by my predecessors and by some important work of my contemporaries. I attempt here briefly to locate myself within this vital and ongoing tradition.

Psychoanalysis from its beginnings, especially with Freud's discovery of the Oedipus complex, has been concerned with intergenerational issues, with the process by which each generation in turn can supplant the preceding one while still maintaining some continuity. The monumental importance of the Oedipus complex to intrapsychic conflict and fantasy life, and its implications for psychoanalysis as a treatment, tended to overshadow the importance of these theories as a framework for viewing family life, especially its intergenerational aspects. Freud's more speculative works, such as *Totem and Taboo,* were the locus of this "psychocultural" perspective, although it is also implied in his discussions of development and especially of the formation of the superego. By focusing on the family, on destructive family conflict, and on the transmission of trauma from one generation to the next, I inevitably highlight this one facet of psychoanalytic thinking and move intrapsychic issues into the background. In this process, I lean heavily on object-relations models of psychoanalysis, often skillfully exploited in clinical psychoanalytic studies of family life and family pathology.

By focusing on the efforts of the characters in the plays to short-circuit or bypass inevitable conflicts between the generations and the genders, by attending to the symbolism and imagery of "perverse" attempts to evade birth and reproduction, I tend to rely on intrapsychic models of conflict. By attending to tragic dialogue's relationship to family and psychoanalytic dialogue, in effect I construct a jerry-rigged theory, using pieces and spare parts from both intrapsychic and interpersonal models.

I disagree with the position that tragic drama is necessarily based on Oedipal conflicts; or at the least I take issue with a simplistic use of that notion. The history of psychoanalytic study of tragedy demonstrates how the search for the Oedipus complex in each play has been only a first stage in a progressively deeper and richer exploration of the variety of developmental conflicts and issues represented in tragic drama.

For better or for worse, I am shameless in borrowing and appropriating bits and pieces from whomever seems to provide them. I have learned much from Klein, Bion, Fairbairn, Winnicott, Kohut, and Erikson—even though they have said relatively little, let alone anything systematic, about psychoanalysis and tragedy. Numerous others—psychoanalysts and psychoanalytically informed literary critics—are cited in the discussions of particular plays. Overall, I apply psychoanalytic findings and formulations to the understanding of tragic drama, but both tragic drama and the best of psychoanalytic thinking are so rich that there is a mutual enhancement, a two-way dialogue. Thus, this book also represents a part of my more strictly professional psychoanalytic task of making sense of the diversity of theories and methods currently utilized by practicing analysts.

The ancient, Shakespearean, and modern plays discussed in this book were selected because:

They are acknowledged to be great plays.

They involve adults killing children; in some, parents literally or symbolically kill their own offspring.

They are plays that I have found compelling, indeed devastating, yet I have been able to master my own distress and perplexity by explicating them to others.

Though not representative of all countries and ages in which there has been tragic drama, these plays represent three major epochs: the birth of tragedy in ancient Greece, its incredible flowering in late Renaissance Europe, and its appearance in the modern era.

All these plays are problematic, having generated much conflicting interpretation. Hence, they afford an opportunity to see if my formulations help elucidate these conflicts of interpretation.

I have omitted important plays, such as Sophocles' Oedipus dramas and *Hamlet*. I ignore Roman, French, and Spanish classical tragedies as well as German and Scandinavian tragedy. I hope readers will extrapolate my findings to works and epochs I have not discussed.

Chapter 1 deals with, to borrow Nietzsche's phrase, "the birth of tragedy." Tragedy is presented as *psychologically* emanating from epic poetry—debates about the historical progenitors of tragic drama are only briefly considered. The ethos of heroic epic is not only part of the background of tragedy but a foil for other value systems within tragic drama. Heroic epic attempts to circumvent the problem of death; tragic drama attempts to circumvent the problem of living among one's own kin—the problem of birth. The notion of sacrifice and scapegoating, especially sacrificing one member of the family in order to preserve the others, is also introduced in chapter 1, both as an aspect of theories of the origin of tragedy and, more important, as a crucial and recurrent theme in tragedy.

Chapter 2 takes up Aeschylus' *Oresteia*, focusing on the history of child-murder in the house of Atreus and the attendant confusions of marriage and sacrifice, marriage as war, nursing as cannibalism, and intercourse as murder. I discuss the "solution" proposed in the *Eumenides* to the problems of conception through heterosexual intercourse and reliance on women to nurse male children.

Chapter 3 deals with Euripides' *Medea*, the most famous play about a parent murdering or, in terms of the imagery of the play, sacrificing her children. I trace out indications of anxiety around the telling of heroic stories when the hero finds that the enemy is his or her own family and that warfare is directed against his or her own progeny.

Chapter 4, on *King Lear*, brings us to the heart of the most profound and wrenching assault on procreation and parent–child relationships. I take up in some detail the narcissistic rage that infuses the play, rage at one's dependency on another for birth and for rearing.

Chapter 5 focuses on *Macbeth*, the play par excellence about the consequences of childlessness, the murder of children, and the futility of story-telling. The counterpoint between the successes and failures of the epic-heroic, the martial and masculine ethos, is vividly heard there, and the contradictions in the wish to have heroic sons are laid bare. I take seriously the critic's mocking question, "how many children had Lady Macbeth?" and argue for the existence of (monstrous) offspring of Macbeth and Lady Macbeth.

In chapter 6 I turn to the greatest American tragic drama, O'Neill's, *Long Day's Journey into Night*. In his autobiographical portrayal of the tortured and torturing Tyrone family, O'Neill intertwines the themes of the death of the good child and the wish of the surviving child never to have been born. I argue that the very nature of the dialogue replicates the tragic storyline: the dialogue kills. Feelings, intentions, passions, and yearnings to love come into existence, live briefly, and then are killed by ridicule or attrition. I consider whether the play succeeded in exorcising the demons of the playwright and halting the transmission of trauma from one generation to the next.

In chapter 7, I take up the archetypal modern tragedy, Beckett's *Endgame*: an assault on all procreation, on all generative feeling, on emotions that connect one person to another, on storytelling as a link between people and generations. This play recapitulates and condenses the major themes of the tragic genre. Here too, the life of the playwright, the lives of the characters in the plays, and the post–World War II world are viewed in concert. I offer some observations about concerns common to modern tragic drama and contemporary psychoanalysis.

In chapter 8, I conclude by examining what Freud, Erikson, and Kohut had to say on the nature of tragedy. I argue that the three psychoanalytic models they present reflect different aspects of the creation of tragedies or the audience's experience of the plays. These three perspectives are expressions of the power of psychoanalytic theory to address generative works of art.

This work, then, is an effort to share with the reader my own experience of the affirmative values of tragic drama. My studies have allowed me to examine in detail some of the greatest poetry ever written and some of the most profound efforts to understand what it is to be human. I have come to realize that the power of these dramas to instruct and move us resides in their capacity to generate and regenerate an array of interpretations and responses. These responses continually shift as we experience ourselves differently within our own life cycle and within history. For the opportunity to study these experiences of the dramas, both in critics and in myself, I am indeed grateful.

REFERENCES

Aristotle. 1981. *Aristotle's Poetics: A Translation and Commentary for Students of Literature*. Trans. Leon Golden. Tallahassee: University Presses of Florida.

Burkert, Walter. 1966. Greek Tragedy and Sacrificial Ritual. *Greek, Roman and Byzantine Studies* 7:83–121.

Cole, Susan L. 1985. *The Absent One: Mourning Ritual, Tragedy, and the Performance of Ambivalence*. University Park: Pennsylvania State University Press.

Krook, Dorothea. 1969. *Elements of Tragedy*. New Haven: Yale University Press.

Nevo, Ruth. 1972. *Tragic Form in Shakespeare*. Princeton: Princeton University Press.

Sagoff, Maurice. 1980. *Shrinklets*. New York: Workman Press.

Simon, Bennett. 1984. "With Cunning Delays and Ever-Mounting Excitement" or, What Thickens the Plot in Tragedy and in Psychoanalysis. In *Psychoanalysis: The Vital Issues*, ed. George H. Pollock and John E. Gedo, vol. 2, pp. 387–436. New York: International Universities Press.

CHAPTER 1

From Epic to Tragedy:
The Birth of Tragedy

The birth of tragedy has been the subject of inquiry since well before Nietzsche's extraordinary essay in 1871. There is astonishingly little solid historical information about tragedy's origins; it appears as if out of nowhere in the early part of the fifth century B.C. Aristotle gave us his version of the various choral, epic, musical, and perhaps even satyric roots of tragedy, and scholars over the centuries have provided a host of additional speculative theories, some expanding upon Aristotle's but others taking off in completely different directions.[1] In this chapter I attempt another version of that story, one that is psychological, not historical in intent, though I believe it does not contradict what history we have. It describes the transition from epic to tragedy in terms of two interrelated themes: the portrayal of family relations, and the appearance of the motifs of sacrifice and scapegoating.

A distinguished critic, struggling with the definition of tragedy, outlined the two tragic conditions of our existence, death and kinship. Oscar Mandel wrote, "The act of birth is tragic not only because it is simultaneously the condemnation to death (so that as we watch our newborn child, we may fancy that we have brought another death into the world), but also because it fastens on the child the inevitability of suffering among his own species."[2] I use this laconic and depressing epigram as a framework for elab-

---

1. See Else (1972), for a biased but clear discussion of the controversies on how to read Aristotle's account of the origins of tragedy and his own view, which focuses heavily on Thespis as the great synthesizer. Lesky (1983, pp. 1–36) is impartial and more detailed.

2. Mandel (1961), p. 163. Nevo (1972, p. 3) uses Mandel's summary to highlight the difference between tragic facts and tragic drama, the latter requiring artistic elaboration of the former.

orating the transition between epic and tragedy, a shift that illuminates for us the nature and role of the family in tragic drama. When I speak of the epic, I refer to the Homeric background of Greek tragedy. There is no doubt of the tragic quality of the Homeric epics, especially *The Iliad*. Aristotle too clearly held this opinion.[3]

In somewhat simplified terms, let us consider the possibility that of these two tragic limitations, death and kinship, epic poetry derives more of its power from the former and tragic drama from the latter. Awareness of death and its inevitability, the deep injury and outrage to one's powers and strivings—these are among the most insistent feelings that shape and move Homer's *Iliad* and *Odyssey*. The characters live with the ever-present realization that immortality is for the gods; men must seek consolation for the pain of their own mortality, principally epic-heroic glory and heroic children.

The figure of Achilles dominates *The Iliad*, and critical to the poem is his forced choice between a long life at home, without heroic glory, and a short but "epic" life, full of glory and leading to immortalization in memory and song. Another facet of Achilles' conflict is seen in *The Odyssey*, namely, the desire and need for heroic children.

Odysseus, in his trip to the underworld, encounters the shade of Achilles. Achilles, in lamenting voice, asks him how he can endure to come down to Hades, where "the senseless dead men dwell, mere imitations of perished mortals."[4] Odysseus answers him:

> "Achilleus, no man before has been more blessed than you, nor ever will be. Before, when you were alive, we Argives honored you as we did the gods, and now in this place you have great authority over the dead. Do not grieve, even in death, Achilleus." So I spoke and he in turn said to me in answer:
> "O shining Odysseus, never try to console me for dying. I would rather follow the plow as thrall to another man, one with no land allotted him and not much to live on, than be a king over all the perished dead. But come now, tell me anything you have heard of my proud son, whether or not he went along to war to fight as a champion." (11.482–93)

Note the bitterness and renunciation of epic glory, but note too how swiftly follows Achilles' question about his son, Neoptolemus. Odysseus gives a full account of the epic heroism of Neoptolemus in the capture of

3. Throughout the *Poetics* but especially in the later chapters, Aristotle takes this for granted. For a recent exposition of the tragic within the epic, see Redfield (1975)—his thesis is that *The Iliad* is "the tragedy of Hector." Also see Goldhill (1986), esp. pp. 138–67 and refs.

4. 9.475–76, Richmond Lattimore's 1965 translation. Subsequent quotations are from this translation. "Achilleus" is Lattimore's spelling.

Troy and also tells Achilles that he is alive, unscathed in battle. Achilles rejoices and with giant strides, his psyche goes off to the Asphodel Meadows (11.538–40). Thus, knowing that his heroic son is still alive to beget sons finally consoles Achilles and releases him from his brooding melancholy.

Odysseus himself has been given a choice between literal immortality and the figurative immortality that comes with heroic deeds and progeny. In *The Odyssey*, Calypso tries to make Odysseus immortal: "and I gave him my love and cherished him, and I had hopes also that I could make him immortal and all his days to be endless" (5.135–37).[5]

Typically, Homer offers a two-tiered account of Odysseus' decision to go home instead of remaining forever with Calypso. It is not only that the gods begrudge such immortality; also, Odysseus spends all his days pining for his home, parents, wife, and child. Implied, then, is that human fulfillment comes only from attaining the human forms of immortality—that Odysseus' life with Calypso is only a variant of the life of a shade in the underworld.

In Homeric epic poetry, as well as in biblical and Babylonian writings, we find the assumption that death is terrible, that it cannot be undone, and that the afterlife is grim, shadowy, and unfulfilling. We see this in portrayals of Hades and the underworld of the Babylonians, and in the hints about the biblical Sheol.[6] Heroic progeny—sons to do battle and daughters to bear heroic sons—and heroic tales told to and by such progeny are the forms of immortality for men.[7]

There is, however, another form of immortality implicit in epic: the sense of time that is conveyed. Homeric epic begins at a particular point in what is clearly an endless story—we might even say a continuously recycling story. The "tale" may begin with an incident in the tenth year of the Trojan war, but it is implicit that heroic tales and deeds have always existed and always will exist. There is no sense of urgency, of a finitude of time.

5. See also 7.255–60; 9.27–36; 23.333–37. Odysseus spurns this offer, as well as Circe's offer of immortality and the quasi-immortality of the Phaiakians.

6. See, e.g., Psalm 115, "The dead do not praise god, nor those who descend into the silence." See also the portrait of Sheol in Job 3. The *Epic of Gilgamesh* is concerned explicitly with the literal quest for immortality, which is defeated. The background assumption is there is only a bleak afterlife. For a discussion of the tragic dimensions of this epic, see Humphries (1985), pp. 9–22.

7. The observation that epic immortality rests upon a combination of heroic deeds, songs that celebrate such deeds (perhaps even songs that create such deeds), and progeny to hear the songs and to themselves be heroic has been made by many critics of epic tales. Two important modern works that present this view are Nagy (1979), and Zeitlin (1982), esp. pp. 38–40. The latter work has proved especially valuable for my discussion of the problem in Greek tragedy of how the house divided against itself can propagate.

Various literary devices project this sense of time as an unlimited commodity. Although everyone in the story must die sooner or later, there is an ever-present assumption of continuity, including a continuous audience, articulated in such lines as "the generations of heroes are as the leaves of the trees" (*Illiad* 6.146) and "a song for men in times to come" (*Odyssey* 7.580). When we turn to tragedy, however, we see an intense sense of limit or urgency—time is not infinitely expansible (de Romilly 1968). The Renaissance readers of Aristotle's *Poetics*, who insisted on the unities of time, place, and action, were correctly intuiting something about the sense of limitation and finitude in tragedy.

Buttressing this sense of a never-ending chain of generations is the epic device of never-ending narrative. Interruptions in the flow of narration are rare; the bard occasionally needs a refueling from the Muse (as in the Catalogue of Ships in *The Iliad*), or the narrator suggests that the hour is late and perhaps all should repair to sleep. Narratives within narratives are similarly important in conveying the intensity of the narrative urge. Odysseus narrates large chunks of *The Odyssey*, at the feast of the Phaiakians and in the scene of his reunion in bed with Penelope. Tragedy, as we shall see, introduces what might be called a note of anxiety about narration—there are many more pauses than in epic and expressions of apprehension in speaking. "But as for the rest, I shall remain silent. A large ox has stepped on my tongue," says the watchman in the famous opening speech of Aeschylus' *Agamemnon*.[8] "What followed I saw not, neither do I tell" announces the chorus as it comes to the point of describing the actual slaughter of Iphigenia. Silence, refusals to speak—the exception in epic—become an important part of the dialogue in tragedy. My thesis, exemplified in later chapters, is that the silences and narrative interruptions in tragedy are the implementations in *form* of the problem in the *content* of the play. That problem can be stated in two complementary ways: how do we speak of unspeakable deeds done by one family member to another? And will there be a terrible interruption in the chain of generation?[9]

We should also note—for this is an important contrast to the tragic genre—that much of the pathos in heroic epic centers around the loss of the companion or companions. Gilgamesh and Enkidu, Achilleus and Pa-

8. 2.35–36. The subject of stopping and starting again in epic narrative deserves treatment in its own right. The motives for stopping or offering to stop (as Aeneas does to Dido at the opening of bk. 2 of *The Aeneid*—"horresco referens") are complex. Aeneas' speech, for example, includes the unspoken warning that the story he tells of betrayal by the Trojan horse foretells that he himself will betray Dido.

9. This thesis has become common in contemporary literary criticism—e.g., see Tobin's *Time and the Novel* (1978).

troklos, Odysseus and his comrades (all of whom perish, even if some die by their own foolishness)—these pairs or bands constitute a major source both of strength and of painful loss. These comrades together fight an external enemy, external in the sense that it is not part of the immediate family, although the enemy may be a member or members of the same army or an adjacent clan. In tragedy, this kind of bonding is not absent, but it recedes from centrality.

When we move to tragic drama, there is a crucial dramatic shift of the action and tension to conflicts among members of the same family— husband and wife, or parents and children.[10] Stories of intrafamilial conflict exist in epic, but they are at the periphery of the main action. Certain characters, such as Phoenix, who is cursed by his father for seducing his concubine (*Iliad* 9), or Aiolos in *The Odyssey*, whose children all live incestuously with each other, flit in and out of the main story line. Other accounts of intrafamilial betrayal or terrible behavior are told or alluded to: the story of Meleager and Althea, the story of Oedipus (Odysseus sees Jocasta in Hades), the murder of Agamemnon by his wife and her lover, Aegisthus. In tragedy, as contrasted to epic, such stories move to center stage. Often we see in tragedy different versions of stories that are told in epic, and the tragic versions are likely to include terrible things done by parents to children, or vice versa. Thus in Homer we hear of Iphigenia as a daughter of Agamemnon and Clytemnestra, but there is no tale of her sacrifice.[11] Early in *The Agamemnon* we find that the story of Iphigenia's sacrifice is central to the plot, and it remains an important mover throughout.

Even in *The Odyssey*, which is manifestly concerned with wifely fidelity and filial reliability, the audience knows that Penelope has been faithful and Telemachus loyal. The bulk of the action concerns Odysseus' adventures against powerful outside enemies before his arrival at Ithaca and the plotting of and battle against Penelope's suitors after his homecoming. From a psychoanalytic perspective, one can discern themes of Oedipal rivalry and perhaps even Penelope's wish that Odysseus not return home, but these have to be inferred; they form part of the unconscious resonances of the story. From the same perspective, one has to say that the theme of murderous father–son rivalry is represented by *displacement* to the suitors— Telemachus and Odysseus are not at odds with each other. If one examines

10. See *Eumenides* 858–67. Athena appeals to the Furies not to encourage war at home (*Arē emphulon*); rather, she claims, the war should be outside (*thuraios estō polemos*).

11. It seems that the opening of *The Iliad*—the story of Agamemnon's demand that Achilles give up Briseis, as Agamemnon is giving up Chryseis, in order to win the Trojan war—is the epic equivalent of the tragic tale of the sacrifice of a daughter by her father.

later epics and mythic traditions involving Odysseus, one finds evidence of
more overt father–son sexual and aggressive rivalry, albeit still disguised.[12]
But even these stories tend to have folkloric "happy endings" and do not
explore the depth of tension and negative feeling between father and son.
Furthermore, *The Odyssey*, which is told with the understanding that there
are later tales of Odysseus and "supplementary" post-Homeric narratives,
can defer the terrible encounter and its accompanying pain. Tragedy obviously exploits the negative affects of intrafamilial strife far more, as in
Sophocles' two Oedipus plays, and there is no deferral or evasion of the
impact of these horrible intrafamilial deeds.

As part of the contrast between epic and tragic representations of the
locus of action and warfare—outside versus inside the family—consider
the treatment of marriage in epic, especially in *The Odyssey*. The epic
presents a more serene and lovely view of marriage and of women, the
tragic a more terrifying and destructive view. In *The Odyssey*, negative
representations of women are largely to be found in the form of monsters
(Scylla and Charybdis) or divine seductresses (Calypso, Circe, and the
Sirens), not in mortal women. The fantasy of female destructiveness is
projected and displaced. In tragedy, the sense of woman as monstrous is
concentrated, condensed—Clytemnestra herself is Scylla and Amphisbaina.[13]

In Homer, generally speaking, the images of marriage are quite positive,
affirming the happiness of the partners and their families and the continuation and prosperity of the house. From the picture of the wedding feast on
the shield of Achilles (and the related scenes of girls and boys on the
dancing-floor in Cretan Knossos) to Odysseus' praise of marriage in his
speech to Nausikaa, a glow and a loveliness is imparted to marriage.[14]
Odysseus praises both Nausikaa and harmonious marriage in general:

12. See, for example, the tale of Telegonus, son of Odysseus, who unwittingly slays his
father. "Telegonus, on learning his mistake, transports his father's body with Penelope and
Telemachus to his mother's [Circe's] island, where Circe makes them immortal, and Tele-
gonus marries Penelope and Telemachus Circe." *The Telegony*, in Hesiod, *The Homeric
Hymns and Homerica*, trans. H. G. Evelyn-White, Loeb Classical Library (Cambridge:
Harvard University Press, 1977), pp. 530–31.

13. *Agamemnon*, 1232–36. Amphisbaina is probably a two-headed mythical monster,
comparable to Scylla. Note in this passage how the idea of war against one's own children is
made explicit (cf. *Libation-Bearers*, 994–95). Another way of emphasizing the monstrosity
of woman in tragedy is to label her as masculine (a theme treated in greater detail in chaps. 2–
3 on *The Oresteia* and the plays of Euripides).

14. End of *Iliad* 18; *Odyssey* 6.180–85. The marriage between Alcinous and Arete is an
exemplary one. It is also quasiincestuous, since Arete is Alcinous' niece, the daughter of his
brother Rhexenor.

and then may the gods give you everything that your heart longs for; may they grant you a husband and a house and sweet agreement in all things, for nothing is better than this, more steadfast than when two people, a man and his wife, keep a harmonious household; a thing that brings much distress to the people who hate them and pleasure to their well-wishers, and for them the best reputation.

Note how the value of a good marriage is related to the epic valuation of "harm to enemies and good for friends." "A husband and a house" seems to mean not just a comfortable place to live but a family, progeny, stalwart sons, and daughters who in turn will raise more stalwart sons.

The Odyssey is in most respects a poem in praise of marriage. The central marriage, of course, is that between Penelope and Odysseus, and it is just the sort of marriage that is praised in the speech quoted. Penelope's and Odysseus' steadfast insistence on the primacy of their marriage is moving and allows for the incredible reunion scene around their marriage bed. Odysseus built that bed, a marriage bed made unmovable because one of its posts is a living olive tree, and Penelope holds out until Odysseus blurts out this secret—testimony to that steadfastness.

This does not mean that marriage is without anxieties, discord, or problems. Adultery seems to be an ambient anxiety in the poem (even apart from the central dramatic question of whether Penelope remains convinced that Odysseus is still alive and resists remarriage). Adultery is what triggered the Trojan war, and the treachery of Clytemnestra and her paramour Aegisthus is recounted as a cautionary tale for Odysseus.

What is striking in Homer, however, is that female adultery is not associated with misogyny or the representation of women as monstrous. The bawdy tale of Ares and Aphrodite cuckolding her husband, Hephaistos, is told for the pleasure and amusement of the assembled Phaiakians and Odysseus.[15] This tale conveys a sensuous appreciation of lustful sexuality rather than a ferocious condemnation of womanhood. More striking, however, is the poet's handling of the story of Helen and Menelaus. Helen seems to be forgiven, in part because she says that while at Troy she came to regret her elopement with Paris; she also, in good Homeric fashion, ascribes her behavior to a madness inflicted by Aphrodite and refers to herself as "shameless."[16] Helen seems to have a gift that allows people to recount and recall painful facts without being overwhelmed by the pain—she puts a

15. 8.266–369. Even though adultery is condemned and Ares must pay a penalty, clearly the pleasure of the story overrides its cautionary note.

16. 4.259–64. At 145–46 she says, "because of dog-faced me the Achaeans went to fight beneath the walls of Troy."

potion, "no pain and no bitterness," in the wine, so powerful that no loss, no matter how great, can make a man cry.[17]

The adultery and treacherous murder committed by Clytemnestra is associated with condemnation of women in *The Odyssey*, but even here the poem is not globally misogynistic.[18] The story puts more emphasis on the criminality of Aegisthus than does Aeschylus' version—the murder takes place in Aegisthus' house. Clytemnestra, however is strongly condemned:

> "[Aegisthos] killed me there
> with the help of my sluttish wife. . . .
>   . . . but the sluttish woman
> turned away from me and was so hard that her hands would not press shut my
> eyes and mouth though I was going to Hades." So there is nothing more deadly
> or more vile than a woman who stores her mind with acts that are of such sort, as
> this one did when she thought of this act of dishonor. . . .
>   . . . but she with thoughts surpassingly grisly
> splashed the shame on herself and the rest of her sex, on women still to come,
> even on the ones whose acts are virtuous.   (11.410–11, 424–34)

The assumption is not that women as a group are dangerous but that this act of one woman is so awful as to bring disgrace on even virtuous women. *The Agamemnon*, in contrast to *The Odyssey*, portrays womanhood grimly. Clytemnestra, an embittered wife and mother of a child murdered by her husband, becomes her husband's murderer. Cassandra is deranged, doomed never to be believed, and murdered. Electra is not present or even mentioned; Iphigenia, the other daughter, has been slaughtered. Some serving girls of Clytemnestra are mentioned, but they are quite incidental. The other major female presence in the play is Helen, who is repeatedly cursed and damned. A joyful, sensuous, and loving portrayal of a woman is nowhere to be found in *The Agamemnon*.

Related to the contrast between the epic and tragic representations of woman and marriage is the portrayal of pregnancy, birth, and nursing. In *The Odyssey*, for instance, these three functions are mentioned casually and naturally, without any special affective charge. These functions are also portrayed in displaced and disguised forms that are typically more terrifying and destructive: the comparison of Scylla to a newborn pup, and the

17. 4.220–32, including the story of how Helen got this drug in Egypt. *The Iliad* too conveys a sense of awe about the beauty of Helen and the power of eros; indeed, the Trojans are quite gentle in their treatment of her, even though her arrival has meant endless death and destruction for them.

18. 11.385–434. Note how the epic version includes, indeed emphasizes, the death of comrades as well as murder within the family. Aeschylus' focus is solely on Agamemnon and Cassandra as victims.

story of the cave of the Cyclops—the site both of serene birth, nursing, and milking of animals and of a terrifying cannibalistic feast—*suggest* a good deal of latent or potential anxiety about these situations.[19] However, it takes an act of interpretation to make this other side of infancy apparent, and undoubtedly they are brought together only somewhere in the depths of the audience's minds.

Even a cursory reading of *The Oresteia* suggests at once a striking contrast with epic in the portrayal of pregnancy and nursing. One of the early images in the play is that of eagles destroying a pregnant hare. The central terrifying image of *The Libation-Bearers* is Clytemnestra's dream of giving birth to a snake who nurses at her breasts and then bites the nipples, extracting clotted blood mixed with milk. The resolution of the trilogy toward the end of *The Eumenides* demands a denial of the importance of the mother in conception and gestation. The dramatic power of the trilogy derives in large measure from the admixture of violence and destruction with the supposedly tender and altruistic acts of begetting and nursing.

If war against the outside world in epic becomes war within the family in tragedy, we might well expect to find a subtle shift in the portrayal of war in tragedy. The shift is discovered both in the description of more of the pain and disaster of war, even for the victors and in the suggestion that warfare against other people's sons may be a form of warfare against one's own. The chorus of *The Agamemnon* denounces the bad trade that Ares brings: the gold of Troy does not make up for the urns of ashes that are sent home instead of young men. The play depicts the muttering resentment of the people who have lost their sons, husbands, and fathers, all for the sake of Helen and the honor of the Atreidae (e.g., 431–55). Thus, the heroism of war—which in the discussion between Odysseus and the ghost of Achilles was a consolation for mortality—is now viewed through a different lens. War destroys our offspring and robs us of the very immortality we thought we were seeking.

War in Greek tragedy, especially in Euripides, over time becomes more and more associated with the image of sacrifice. Our children become sacrificial animals upon the altar in order to achieve some goal, a goal whose ultimate worth begins to be questioned. The theme of sacrifice and the implicit theme of the scapegoat become important both in Greek tragedy and in tragedy as a whole. An examination of these notions sheds further light on the portrayal of family relationships within tragedy.

19. For references to intrauterine life, birth, and nursing in *The Odyssey*, see Simon, "The Hero as an Only Child" (1973), which demonstrates that the hero is the one who overcomes all his rivals, even fantasy ones within his mother's womb.

In recent years, especially among classical scholars, there have been a number of investigations of the relationship between ritual sacrifice and tragedy and the related topic of sacrifice within tragedy. It is striking that many years earlier, around the turn of the century, several theories of the origins of tragedy emphasized a violent sacrifice and consequent ritual worship. I refer especially to those theories associated with the names of James Frazer, Frances Cornford, Jane Harrison, and Gilbert Murray (the school of Cambridge classicists with anthropological interests) and to that of Sigmund Freud (in *Totem and Taboo*, 1913). These theories, highly speculative hypotheses at best, more likely "psychohistorical" fantasies, have generally been regarded as implausible.

They do, however, reflect an important truth about tragedy, namely, its concern with sacrifice in the family. The Cambridge theory, in its broadest form, postulated a ritual origin for tragedy: the annual death of the vegetation or corn god, an exemplar of which is found in the myths of the god Adonis. The god is killed or somehow dies, is mourned, and then is resurrected. The Cambridge theory associates Dionysus with the image of the dying and resurrected god and goes on to link Dionysus with Greek tragedy as its patron god. Tragedy, then, originates in and shows traces of the mimetic representation of the death, mourning, and restoration of a vegetation god, incarnated as Dionysus. The hero is thus a derivative of the god, and the chorus is a derivative of the worshipers who mourn his murder or death.[20]

Freud, who had read Frazer, in *Totem and Taboo* comments briefly on the origin of the chorus in Greek tragedy (1955, pp. 155–56). Earlier in the essay, he develops his theory about the origins of civilization, the Oedipus complex, and guilt. He posits a primal horde of men, women, and children ruled by an all-powerful father. The brothers unite, kill and eat the father, divide his women among them, and make a pact not to kill one another and steal the women. Out of their newly experienced guilt, they institute a worship of the slain father as the tribal totem. The father's animal incarnation is to be revered and never eaten—except once a year to commemorate the original murder. It is fanciful history indeed, with regard to various efforts to extrapolate from primate societies to the origins of human guilt and human complexes. However, one can properly call it a *tragic view* of the origin of human civilization and of sacrifice.

Freud cites Greek tragedy, with its chorus, as an instantiation of his theory. By a tendentious twist, he says, the chorus, representing the band of brothers that has killed the primal father, hypocritically begins to weep

20. See Harrison (1962) for one statement of this line of thinking, esp. pp. 30–49, 118–57.

and bemoan the fate of this slain hero (or the hero about to be slain). The tragic hero is thus sacrificed for the supposed good of the brothers, the chorus. We have, then, a tragic theory of the origins of tragedy, a view that says inevitably someone must die so that others might live. The hypocrisy of which Freud speaks lies in the way the sacrificed hero is also a scapegoat, a repository of the sins of the brothers.

While not specifically a sacrifice or murder theory, Nietzsche's view of "the birth of tragedy" posits a violent atmosphere in its begetting.[21] He speaks of the Apollonian and Dionysian duality as intermittent warfare:

> Just as procreation depends on the duality of the sexes, involving perpetual strife with only periodically intervening reconciliations . . . [the Apollonian and Dionysian are] for the most part openly at variance; and they continually incite each other to new and more powerful births, which perpetuate an antagonism . . . till eventually . . . they appear coupled with each other, and through this coupling ultimately generate an equally Dionysian and Apollonian form of art—Attic tragedy. (1967, p. 33)

Along with the imagery of violent intercourse, there is Nietzsche's tale of the death of tragedy—a murder at the hands of Euripides and Socrates. Socrates, who as a philosopher was called a "midwife," delivered the final blow. Thus, Nietzsche too has a tragic theory of the birth and death of tragedy—composed along the lines of a tragic drama.[22]

The theme of sacrifice is prominent in Greek tragedy. Medea's murder of her children is presented with the imagery of a sacrifice, and Jason is willing, figuratively, to sacrifice his children and Medea for his own peace and security. In *The Oresteia*, the sacrifice of Iphigenia, the murder of Agamemnon and Cassandra, the history of the slaughtered children of Thyestes are all accompanied by the language and imagery of ritual sacrifice. In Euripides' *Bacchae*, the ultimate sacrifice to Dionysus is the dismembered body of Pentheus, the king who opposed him.

21. The metaphors of warfare followed by some sort of unification and procreation are probably related to Hegel's ideas on tragedy, especially Greek tragedy. Hegel's treatment of Greek tragedy involves a model of clashing values, reconciliation, and the new product of that reconciliation. The notion of sacrifice is implicit in much of his theorizing on tragedy, but the term is in fact scarcely used. Issues of guilt and responsibility, however, occupy an important place in his work on tragedy. Space does not allow for a discussion of his work in relation to the thesis of this book. See the compilation of his writings on tragedy in Hegel (1962), esp. pp. 1–96, and 237–302.

22. See Holmes (1983) for an illuminating discussion of Freud and Nietzsche on the interrelated subjects of the origins of civilization and the nature of tragedy. For a full account of the relationship between Nietzsche's view of tragedy and the history of classical scholarship see Silk and Stern (1981).

Animal sacrifice was a daily part of Greek religious life, and scholars have addressed the significance and impact of such continuous slaughter at the altars of the gods. The relationship between such sacrifice and tragedy has been especially advanced in the work of René Girard. In his *Violence and the Sacred* (1977), Girard places the notion of ritual sacrifice at the very heart of Greek tragedy.[23] Walter Burkert (1966) earlier argued, in essence, that the *ambivalent attitude* of the sacrificers toward the animal—love and desire to slaughter, guilt and remorse over the killing, tenderness and anger—was what linked sacrifice and tragedy. At the core of tragic drama the characters have the same mix of attitudes toward each other, particularly toward the tragic hero.

Girard argues that violence is ineradicable from human society (and from the human family) and that sacrificing or scapegoating is always necessary to preserve the unity of society and/or family. Animal sacrifice and, when and where it is practiced, human sacrifice are attempts to control and channel such violence, particularly between clans. He emphasizes how a society can suddenly unite against one member, chosen as the scapegoat, and he brilliantly analyzes Oedipus as scapegoat in *Oedipus Rex*.

Clinically, it is an illusion that the sacrifice of one member of a family or society can preserve the group and establish a new equilibrium.[24] The act generates so much guilt, desire for revenge, and dread about who may be sacrificed next that there is a propensity to commit violent extrusion again whenever a new threat arises, from within or outside the family. The sacrifice of one member invites repetition of traumatic sacrifice.[25] This formulation could be called *the tragic view of sacrifice*. Tragic drama repeatedly shows us attempts to solve intractable intrafamilial ambivalence by sacrifice or scapegoating. But tragedy is also the art form that exposes as illusory the belief that sacrificing one person to spare the others is a satisfactory solution.

From a slightly different perspective, that of the continuity of the house,

23. See also Vellacott (1975), Griffiths (1979), and Foley (1985), for extensive review and original treatment of several "sacrifice" plays. Burkert (1983) is devoted largely to the meaning of animal sacrifice in ancient Greece; see chap. 4.

24. See Simon (1984, pp. 396–98) for a review of some theories of tragic structure that emphasize redress or restoration of equilibrium. This article focuses especially on the work of Victor Turner (1980) about "social drama" as following the patterns of Aristotelian tragic drama.

25. Freud's theory/fantasy in *Totem and Taboo* about the slaughter of the primal father by the band of brothers who then elevate the slaughtered father to the sacred status posits that the brothers must pledge not to repeat that crime against each other. Freud's theory of the Oedipus complex, in effect, posits a diluted but inevitable repetition of this sacrifice in the life of each child.

we can say that sacrifice is a two-edged sword. For the act of sacrifice, especially of one's own children, risks the extinction of the line, although it may be proposed as a way of saving the community, the family, and the house.

In this context, the tragic hero might be defined as one who is willing, in the name of some ideal or ideals, to sacrifice what is most precious in order to save and perpetuate the house. But, at the same time, his or her behavior risks destroying that house. The sacrifice may be of another (Agamemnon sacrificing Iphigenia) and/or of oneself (Sophocles' Antigone both sacrifices herself and is sacrificed by Creon). Orestes kills his mother to redeem his father and save his house, as well as to avoid punishment by Apollo. By doing so, he risks self-destruction, including loss of his sexual potency, at the hands of the Furies. The language attending him, especially in *The Eumenides*, includes sacrificial imagery.

The aggression and ambivalence toward the victim implicit in sacrifice and the ideal or ideals in whose name the sacrifice is made lead to great dramatic tension but leave an unstable equilibrium. I suggest that the sense of an unstable equilibrium within the play is reflected in the diversity of audience reactions to the sacrifice. Some members of the audience (or readers, critics, scholars) read the sacrificial solution as viable and satisfying, perhaps even as successfully cathartic. For them, tragic knowledge consists of the knowledge that someone must suffer and be sacrificed for the larger good, while the survivors forever mourn him or her. Others in the audience respond to the exposure of illusion and regard that exposure as the important part of tragic knowledge.

Great tragic dramas are distributed along a spectrum. Some make it easier to idealize and feel the sacrifice as a resolution, while others portray such complete wastage that the illusion of closure and the catharsis are impossible to experience. Also, each era has its dominant reading of these dramas. Euripides' plays about the voluntary sacrifices of young people to the cause of war have been viewed as portraying patriotic idealism, especially by German and British scholars before World War II era (Vellacott 1975, pp. 19 ff). Contemporary readings emphasize the antiwar message of these plays. *King Lear* is the epitome of wastage—the illusion of closure is all but absent—but some critics and readers respond to the idealism of Cordelia as redeeming even this play.[26] Ibsen's *Wild Duck*, in which a teenage girl, Hedvig, is sacrificed, portrays the two poles of this spectrum. Some characters, including Hedvig herself, say the sacrifice is magnificent;

26. "Upon such sacrifices, my Cordelia, / The gods themselves throw incense" (5.3.20–21).

others claim that it is fraudulent—a young girl has committed suicide in order to preserve her parents' narcissistic illusions, equivalent to being murdered by her parents. Among the plays discussed in this book, O'Neill's *Long Day's Journey into Night* presents most painfully the inadequacy of sacrificing and extruding one member of the family in order to preserve the others. Tragedy, in my reading, shows sacrifice as an inevitable but illusory solution to the problem of intrafamilial or intraclan aggression.

Thus, sacrifice initiates or perpetuates a chain of traumatic repetition, from one family member to another, from one generation to the next. Another facet of the prominence of sacrifice in tragedy is its relationship to guilt. Sacrifice imports into tragedy the dimension of guilt. In comparison to epic, guilty conscience, especially primitive and destructive guilt, is omnipresent in tragedy. In some plays guilt and retribution are literally actors on the stage—the Furies in *The Oresteia*, for example, or the various hallucinated presences in *Macbeth*. Tragic characters, tragic heroes, are often driven by a sense of guilt, which tends to lead to further destructiveness.

To summarize, in the transition from epic to tragic, the plot is thickened by two interrelated changes. The first is the shift in emphasis from warfare outside the family to warfare within the family. The second is the addition of the themes of sacrifice and guilt. With these shifts in mind, I take up a detailed study of Aeschylus' *Oresteia*.

REFERENCES

Aristotle. 1981. *Aristotle's Poetics: A Translation and Commentary for Students of Literature*. Trans. Leon Golden, Tallahassee: University Presses of Florida.

Burkert, Walter. 1966. Greek Tragedy and Sacrificial Ritual. *Greek, Roman and Byzantine Studies* 7:83–121.

———. 1983. *Homo Necans: The Anthropology of Ancient Greek Sacrifice, Ritual and Myth*. Trans. Peter Bing. Berkeley: University of California Press. Original German edition published 1972.

De Romilly, J. 1968. *Time in Greek Tragedy*. Ithaca: Cornell University Press.

Else, Gerald F. 1972. *The Origin and Early Form of Greek Tragedy*. New York: Norton. Originally published 1965.

Foley, Helene P. 1985. *Ritual Irony: Poetry and Sacrifice in Euripides*. Ithaca: Cornell University Press.

Freud, Sigmund. 1955. *Totem and Taboo*. In *Standard Edition*, trans. James Strachey, vol. 13, pp. 1–161. London: Hogarth Press. Originally published 1913.

Girard, René. 1977. *Violence and the Sacred*. Trans. P. Gregory. Baltimore: Johns Hopkins University Press. Original French edition published 1972.

Goldhill, Simon. 1986. *Reading Greek Tragedy*. Cambridge: Cambridge University Press.

Griffiths, Frederick T. 1979. Girard on the Greeks / The Greeks on Girard. *Berkshire Review* 14:20–36.

Harrison, Jane E. 1962. *Themis: A Study of Social Origins of Greek Religion*. 2d ed. Cleveland: World Publishing. Originally published 1927.

Hegel, George F. 1962. *On Tragedy*. Ed. A. Paolucci and H. Paolucci. Garden City: Doubleday, Anchor Books.

Holmes, Kim R. 1983. Freud, Evolution, and the Tragedy of Man. *Journal of the American Psychoanalytic Association*. 31:187–210.

Humphries, W. Lee. 1985. *The Tragic Vision and the Hebrew Tradition*. Philadelphia: Fortress Press.

Lattimore, Richmond. 1965. *The Odyssey of Homer: A Modern Translation*. New York: Harper and Row.

Lesky, Albin. 1983. *Greek Tragic Poetry*. Trans. M. Dillon. New Haven: Yale University Press. Original German edition published 1972.

Mandel, Oscar. 1961. *A Definition of Tragedy*. New York: New York University Press.

Nagy, Gregory. 1979. *The Best of the Achaeans: Concepts of the Hero in Archaic Greek Poetry*. Baltimore: Johns Hopkins University Press.

Nevo, Ruth. 1972. *Tragic Form in Shakespeare*. Princeton: Princeton University Press.

Nietzsche, Friedrich. 1967. *The Birth of Tragedy* and *The Case of Wagner*. Trans. Walter Kaufmann. New York: Random House, Vintage Books.

Redfield, James M. 1975. *Nature and Culture in the Iliad: The Tragedy of Hector*. Chicago: University of Chicago Press.

Silk, M. S. and J. P. Stern. 1981. *Nietzsche on Tragedy*. New York: Cambridge University Press.

Simon, Bennett. 1973. The Hero as an Only Child: An Unconscious Fantasy Structuring Homer's *Odyssey*. *International Journal of Psycho-Analysis* 55:555–562.

———. 1984. "With Cunning Delays and Ever-Mounting Excitement" or, What Thickens the Plot in Tragedy and in Psychoanalysis. In *Psychoanalysis: The Vital Issues*, ed. George H. Pollock and John E. Gedo, vol. 2, pp. 387–436. New York: International Universities Press.

Tobin, Patricia D. 1978. *Time and the Novel: The Genealogical Imperative*. Princeton: Princeton University Press.

Turner, Victor. 1980. Social Dramas and Stories About Them. *Critical Inquiry* 7:141–168.

Vellacott, Philip. 1975. *Ironic Drama: A Study of Euripides' Method and Meaning*. Cambridge: Cambridge University Press.

Zeitlin, Froma I. 1982. *Under the Sign of the Shield: Semiotics and Aeschylus' Seven Against Thebes*. Rome: Edizioni dell' Ateneo.

CHAPTER 2

Aeschylus' *Oresteia*

Aeschylus put on his great trilogy, *The Oresteia*, in 458 B.C., and won first prize in the annual dramatic competition. The only extant trilogy we have of the several hundred produced in fifth- and early fourth-century Athens, it is one of the most enduring monuments of Athenian civilization. The playwright assumes the audience's deep immersion in the Homeric tales of the Trojan War and in later tales of the return of the Greek heroes.[1] *The Agamemnon* details the return of Agamemnon from the Trojan War, the vengeance of Clytaemestra for his sacrifice of their daughter, and the story of her adulterous betrayal.[2] *The Libation-Bearers* recounts the subsequent revenge taken by Orestes on his mother for slaughtering his father and the beginnings of his madness, the affliction sent by the Furies. The trilogy concludes in *The Eumenides* with the struggle between Apollo and the Furies over Orestes and the resolution in the court set up at Athens and presided over by Athena. Justice is done and the contending forces are reconciled.

The Oresteia is a trilogy in which critics and audiences have found a variety of meanings, often treated as if mutually exclusive. Justice, especially the justice of Zeus, the perplexing relationships between humankind and the gods, the working out over several generations of a family curse, relations and confusions between the sexes, conflicts between political obli-

1. In antiquity, it was said that Aeschylus served "slices from the banquet of Homer" (Athenaeus 8.347e, 1930). That is, Homeric tales formed the basis of the Aeschylean material, but these tales are obviously prepared and served very differently in *The Oresteia*. The title of the trilogy denotes "the deeds of Orestes" and connotes tales of epic, heroic deeds. See Lesky's (1983) chapter on Aeschylus for detailed treatment of numerous problems in interpretation and for a more extensive bibliography.

2. The spelling *Clytaemestra* is a transcription of the form of the name in Aeschylus' trilogy and is used in Richmond Lattimore's 1959 translation. Unless otherwise indicated, translations are taken from that edition.

gations and blood loyalties—these are a few of the many "central themes" that have been proposed. What I suggest here is both simple and overarching, subsuming as derivative many if not all of these one-phrase characterizations. *The Oresteia* manifestly deals with the house of Atreus, which has been problematic from its beginnings and is on the verge of destroying itself, yet is struggling to find a way to propagate itself in the face of terrible intrafamilial destructiveness. Thus, in the middle of *The Eumenides*, Orestes exclaims, "O, Pallas Athena, having saved my house . . ." (754).[3]

The trilogy opens with the speech of the watchman, describing his anxious waiting and his fear for the house, and it ends with a great reconciliation between the avenging, bloodthirsty demons, the Erinyes, and the power of Apollo. This reconciliation, effected by Athena, will allow Orestes to live and procreate. In between are accounts of the earlier terrible deeds of the house—betrayal, cannibalism, child sacrifice, and adultery— and the bloody deeds perpetrated as part of the trilogy's dramatic action. Toward the end of *The Agamemnon*, Clytaemestra pleads that she be allowed to make a truce with the demon of the house—to let the destructive Fury go to another household (1570–73). The second and third plays can be seen as describing why the demon must stay longer in the house and how it can finally be "domesticated." The Furies (under the new name of Eumenides) will receive offerings on behalf of children and marriage and will become the protectors of interests in the house wider than those of literal blood ties (*Eumenides*, 834–36). This "domestication" is Athena's attempt to reverse and undo the effects of warfare within the house, to move the warfare "outdoors" (858–66).

The storyline basically concerns repeated violation of norms, boundaries, and hierarchies.[4] Generational boundaries are collapsed as the generations murder and/or devour each other, literally and symbolically. Marriage boundaries are violated repeatedly by adultery—Thyestes, Agamemnon, Clytaemestra, and Aegisthus. Boundaries between the divine and the human are shattered by Apollo's seduction of Cassandra. Animal and human separations collapse as humans are sacrificed instead of animals, or as if they were animals. Hubris, so central and so rampant in the trilogy, represents the wild, unpruned, untamed growth of plants in its basic metaphor; it is one name given to these violations. Justice, *dikē*, so much abused and so

3. Translation mine.
4. Girard (1977), pp. 49–51, among others, makes the violation of such distinctions central to his theory of tragedy and violence. In his view and mine, tragedy dissects and examines this issue much more extensively than myth does. See Shakespeare's *Troilus and Cressida* 1.3.83–137 for Ulysses' speech on "degree." In my schema, epic poetry becomes tragic as it represents more and more the shattering and restoration of boundary.

much the subject of the plays, especially *The Eumenides*, requires restoration of differentials and divisions. But the trilogy is far from being a morality story—it is a searing exploration of these destructions and disruptions and how they concatenate, perpetuate themselves, and resist the restoration of order.

This conception of the trilogy leads me to focus on certain aspects of the plays:

the killing of children and the vision of childhood;
marriage, intercourse, and the begetting of children;
becoming a parent, being a child;
becoming a tragic hero;
telling and not telling, silence and frozen grief.

All these are subdivisions of the themes of violation and thwarted reparation. Frozen grief represents the inability to escape from or come to terms with the past. Silence, the inability to tell a tale, is similarly tied up with a blockage, a resistance, as it were, to continuing the story, especially to making the story come out differently.

A reminder to the reader: to analyze an Aeschylean text is to attempt to describe a seamless web of many colors, intricately interwoven. One cannot neatly pick out one thread or one color without paying attention to all the others. Analyzing any one set of images at once brings out how dense, compressed, and condensed is every line, every phrase. George Devereux (1976, p. xxxvi) instructively compares the analysis of lines in Greek tragedy to the rehearsals of a symphony orchestra—the conductor deliberately isolates and exaggerates a theme, an instrument, a line of the music in order to reinsert the element into the piece as a whole and give the impression of a more harmonious performance. Hence, each bit of analysis in what follows is by definition partial and exaggerated. The test of its validity will be the quality of one's experience of the plays after having assimilated this line of interpretation.

THE DESTRUCTION OF CHILDHOOD

As soon as the opening speech of the watchman concludes, the chorus of old men of Argos enters, chanting in anapestic, marching rhythms, like soldiers, relating their version of the history of the Trojan War (40–257). The version they tell here emphasizes parents robbed of children or parents killing children. They begin by describing the majesty of the Atreidae and their expedition. It is ten years since the "twin-throned, twin-sceptered" Atreidae, Agamemnon and Menelaus, led against Priam the thousand ships driven by Zeus, the great protector of the rights of guest and host—to avenge Paris' seduction of Helen:

> Their cry of war went shrill from the heart,
> as eagles stricken in agony
> for young perished, high from the nest
> eddy and circle
> to bend and sweep of the wing's stroke,
> lost far below
> the fledgelings, the nest, and the tendance.   (48–54)[5]

Thus, Menelaus' reaction to Paris' seduction is first compared to that of eagles being robbed of their young—as if Helen were a baby, not a wife. Only after this metaphor is there mention of Paris' having violated the Zeus-given laws of hospitality (60–66). The marriage bed is merged with the nest, the cradle; and the two royal brothers, Agamemnon and Menelaus, are bereaved parents. As a consequence of this violation, continues the chorus, many young men have died for the sake of Helen, "a woman manned by many" (62). As the chorus makes explicit later, the fact that the Atreidae were bereft of their "child" will lead to many other parents' being robbed of their children (e.g., 429–74). Trojans, Argives, and Clytaemestra and Agamemnon will all lose their children on account of this one "kidnapping." Also compressed in this choral entrance is the implication that infidelity in marriage and in the guest–host relationship leads to increasing destruction of progeny and family.

The widening circle of child-destruction is vividly conveyed in the chorus' second image of birds—the omen of the two eagles who attack and destroy the pregnant hare and what follows from that omen (105–59):

> Kings of birds to the kings of the ships,
> one black, one blazed with silver,
> clear seen by the royal house
> on the right, the spear hand,
> they lighted, watched by all
> tore a hare, ripe, bursting with young unborn yet,
> stayed from her last fleet running.
> Sing sorrow, sorrow: but good win out in the end.   (114–21)

The prophet Calchas interprets the eagles' killing the hare and her unborn babies as an image of the attack of Agamemnon and Menelaus,

---

5. See Fraenkel ad loc. for commentary on the unusual use of *paides* (human children) to signify animal children. The word translated as "nest" is *lexeon* (pl.), which means both nest and bed. One commentary that—rightfully, I believe—emphasizes the theme of children in the chorus' entrance is Lebeck (1971), pp. 7–16.

leading the Greek host, on the city of Troy: as the eagles kill the hare, so
will the Greeks kill many cattle beneath the walls of Troy.[6] By implication,
the city pregnant with people, with children—including the unborn progeny of Troy—will be devoured. But he also hints at a graver danger:

> Artemis the undefiled
> is angered with pity
> at the flying hounds of her father
> eating the unborn young in the hare and the shivering mother . . .
> She is sick at the eagles' feasting.
> Sing sorrow, sorrow: but good win out in the end.
>
> Lovely you are [Artemis] and kind
> to the tender young of ravening lions.
> For sucklings of all the savage
> beasts that lurk in the lonely places you have sympathy.
> Grant meaning to these appearances
> good, yet not without evil.
> Healer Apollo, I pray you
> let her not with cross winds
> bind the ships of the Danaans
> to time-long anchorage
> forcing a second sacrifice unholy, untasted,
> working bitterness in the blood
> and faith lost. For the terror returns like sickness to lurk in the house;
> the secret anger remembers the child that shall be avenged.   (133–55).

The implications of this omen become progressively clearer as the trilogy
proceeds. For the Greeks to devour Troy, it will be necessary that Greek
children also be devoured—first Iphigenia will be sacrificed, then the flower
of the Greek youth will be destroyed in battle. By retrospective allusion, the
"second sacrifice" connects up with the history of the house of Atreus—
Atreus slew and served to his brother Thyestes a feast of Thyestes' own
children.

The spirals grow wider, for these "sacrifices" lead in turn to the murders
of Agamemnon and Cassandra, and to Orestes' slaughter of his own mother
and her paramour, Aegisthus. These murders threaten to bring about the
destruction of all future children of the house of Atreus, all the unborn and
unconceived children, by leaving Electra unmarried and childless and
Orestes mad, persecuted by the Furies. The Furies attack the marrow and
testicles of young men, sucking out and crushing the procreative and life-

---

6. Nussbaum (1986), p. 33, argues that Calchas' interpretation emphasizes the bestiality
of the Greeks' behavior, especially as regards the sacrifice of Iphigenia.

giving substances;[7] thus Orestes loses his desire to father children. Justifying to the chorus his having murdered his mother, he proclaims, "may no wife such as this one share my house. Rather would I perish childless [apais] at the hands of the gods."[8] Thus, this omen and its implications set up the "problem" that *The Oresteia* must solve—how to end this spiraling so that the murder or abduction of one person's child does not inexorably lead to the murder of all the family's subsequent children.[9]

This connection between the omens at the beginning of the trilogy and the questions of fertility and sterility in *The Eumenides* is apparent to any careful reader of *The Oresteia* in virtually any translation. Study of the Greek text, building upon centuries of scholarship, reveals many more allusions and cross-references connecting the various parts of the trilogy in terms of birth and childrearing. Some examples:

The pregnant hare is "stayed from her last fleet running" (120). The word translated as "stayed," *blabenta*, is the same verb used later by Apollo to describe the fragility of the fetus inside the uterus of the mother. Apollo asserts that the male's role in reproduction is primary and the mother's secondary. "The parent is the one who mounts. A stranger, she preserves a stranger's seed, if no god interfere [*blapse*]"—that is, if there is no miscarriage or stillbirth (*Eumenides*, 660–61). Similarly, Artemis is kind to the "sucklings" (literally, "breast-lovers," *philo-mastois*). Helen, compared to a lion cub, is also described as *philomastos* and untimely torn from the breast (717–19). In *The Libation-Bearers* there are two pivotal scenes about the breast (*mastos*): Clytaemestra's dream of the snake she begets biting her breast and drawing blood, and the scene where she pleads with Orestes to contemplate the breast that had nursed him and to spare her life. These myriad cross-threads that the Greek text provides must have spun a powerful poetic web for ancient audiences.

Following its description of the omen, the chorus proceeds with the famous "Hymn to Zeus" (160–84), alluding among other things to Zeus' victory over his father, Kronos, and perhaps to the associated stories of Kronos' swallowing his children.[10] Behind the generational struggle of

---

7. E.g, *Eumenides* 179–97, the speech of Apollo commanding the Furies to stop torturing Orestes.

8. *Libation-Bearers* 1005–06. Translation mine.

9. Lebeck's (1971) is the best study I know of these intricate cross-connections. See her comments on "proleptic introduction and gradual development" in *The Oresteia*, pp. 1–2, as well as the rest of her introduction.

10. 2.166–75, Zeus as victorious wrestler. Fraenkel doubts that the playwright intended an allusion to a particular myth of a wrestling match between Zeus and Kronis—he assumes,

Zeus and Kronos is the earlier one of Kronos, who castrated his father, Ouranos. Zeus, who is invoked as an explanation for the horrors past and those yet to come, is himself heir to terrible intrafamilial, specifically intergenerational, destruction.

The larger significance of these verses has been much disputed, but my own reading assumes that the chorus' anxiety about beginning to narrate the story of Iphigenia leads it to search for a larger, protective power, especially male. From Zeus alone can they hope to gain clear knowledge about the conflicted and terrible course of retribution for some one person's wrongdoing, retribution that somehow keeps perpetuating the original violation. "Through suffering comes knowledge," and the knowledge that is spelled out over the course of *The Oresteia* is that there is divine retribution for crimes, including the crime of destroying anyone's children. A related lesson is that the payment often comes in the form of "like for like"; the perpetrator suffers the acts he or she inflicted on others, principally the destruction of children, but also the associated acts of betrayal in marriage and in guest–host relationships.[11] The trilogy as a whole spells out such knowledge as it is learned by characters within the play and by the audience. It is also taught by characters within *The Oresteia*, as in the mantic lyrics of Cassandra. But the chorus brings in Zeus and his powers to

---

with most scholars, that the verses refer to the myths recorded in Hesiod of the generational struggles of the gods. He does not suggest an allusion to the stories of Kronos and his children, especially the swallowing of children. Cf. Clay (1969) for the argument that the history of the "house of Zeus" is background for the house of Atreus. Zeus knows whereof he speaks regarding destructiveness among family members, including parents devouring their children.

11. The literature on "knowledge through suffering" (*pathei mathos*; 176–77) is immense; much of it is summarized in Fraenkel's commentary (1950) and in Gargarin's (1976) appendix on the "Hymn to Zeus." Lebeck (1971) also has an excellent discussion that demonstrates the superimposition of multiple *tragic* meanings upon a proverb (pp. 25–36). I am a bit puzzled by Rosenmeyer's (1982) caveat about the danger of overinterpreting the psychological appropriateness of maxims in Aeschylean choruses and am unsure whether he accepts Lebeck's reading (pp. 182–83). The most interesting and impressive reading of these passages I have encountered is Smith's (1980). His connection of the "Hymn" to the surrounding passages about Iphigenia considerably clarifies the significance of the passages about Zeus. His entire discussion strengthens my reading of the play, including the parados, that anxiety about the implications and meaning of intrafamilial betrayal and murder is central. His understanding of *pathei mathos* is that "fools finely learn their folly through having to endure terrible punishment for their crimes—they can't learn in advance": he argues that the phrase does not refer to "tragic knowledge." My reading is that Aeschylus does not bind the phrase so much to its literal meaning that it cannot reverberate with larger meanings of "tragic knowledge" as well—e.g., that crime and vengeance inevitably seem to perpetrate and perpetuate suffering, including the suffering of innocent children.

prevail, to know, and to teach, as a bridge between the destruction of children in the Trojan War and the specific destruction of Iphigenia by her father in order that he might proceed to destroy both Trojan and Greek children.

In 2.184–257, the chorus unfolds the dreadful tale of the sacrifice of Iphigenia. Agamemnon is torn between his apprehension about letting the army and the expedition waste away in the harbor of Chalcis, forever awaiting a favorable wind, and the dread of sacrificing his own daughter to Artemis. In effect, he is torn between indirectly destroying the flower (*anthos*) of the Greek youth, one kind of offspring, and destroying a literal child. Either someone else's flower must be destroyed or the flower of his own household must be slaughtered and deflowered.[12] The horror of having to squelch one's pity and slaughter one's own child is elaborated. But as some commentators have pointed out, once Agamemnon feels compelled by necessity to kill Iphigenia, he all too eagerly proceeds with the terrible deed.[13]

> Her supplications and her cries of father
> were nothing, not the child's lamentation
> to kings passioned for battle.
> The father prayed, called to his men to lift her
> with strength of hand swept in her robes aloft
> and prone above the altar, as you might lift
> a goat for sacrifice, with guards
> against the lips' sweet edge, to check
> the curse cried on the house of Atreus
> by force of bit and speech drowned in strength.
>
> Pouring then to the ground her saffron mantle
> she struck the sacrificers with
> the eyes' arrows of pity,
> lovely as in a painted scene, and striving
> to speak—as many times

12. The Greek text does not play on *flower* and *deflower* but does convey a vivid sense of the underlying connections between the sacrifice of the maiden's life and her deflowering, whether by rape or marriage. Stanford's (1983) commentary on this passage makes the strongest case I have seen for such a reading (pp. 126–31). Euripides' *Iphigenia in Aulis* elaborates even more the confounding of marriage and sacrifice. *Anthos* (flower) or the associated verb "to be in flower" are found in *The Agamemnon* at 658, where the sea is flowered with corpses of Greeks, and at 955, where Cassandra is described as the flower of the Greek spoils, as such granted to Agamemnon.

13. See Nussbaum (1986), pp. 23–50, for detailed discussion and review of the literature on Agamemnon's dilemmas.

at the kind festive table of her father
she had sung, and in the clear voice of a stainless maiden
with love had graced the song
of worship when the third cup was poured.
What happened next I saw not, neither speak it.   (227–48).

The interweaving of the Trojan War, fought on account of the despicable
woman Helen, with the killing of children is vividly taken up again in the
first stasimon of the chorus, the longest choral ode in the surviving Greek
tragedies. Here, the theme of unresolvable grief leading to rage and murder
is gradually articulated. Starting at 404, the chorus sings of Helen, who left
behind her "the clamor of shields and spearheads. . . . She took to Ilium
her dowry, death." Menelaus is left behind, a shell or a phantom, vainly
reaching after phantom images of Helen. Menelaus, "the agony of [whose]
loss is clear before us," initiates actions that lead to the death of beautiful
and noble young men and multiple agonies for the people.

Such have the sorrows been in the house by the hearthside;
such have there been, and yet there are worse than these.
In all Hellas, for those who swarmed to the host
the heartbreaking misery shows in the house of each.
Many are they who are touched at the heart by these things.
Those they sent forth they knew;
now, in place of the young men
urns and ashes are carried home
to the houses of the fighters.

The god of war, money changer of dead bodies,
held the balance of his spear in the fighting,
and from the corpse-fires at Ilium
sent to their dearest the dust
heavy and bitter with tears shed
packing smooth the urns with
ashes that once were men.
They praise them through their tears, how this man
knew well the craft of battle, how another
went down splendid in the slaughter:
all for some strange woman.

Thus they [the citizens] mutter in secrecy,
and the slow anger creeps below their grief
at Atreus' sons and their quarrels.
There by the walls of Ilium
the young men in their beauty keep
graves deep in the alien soil
they hated and they conquered.

The citizens speak: their voice is dull with hatred.
The curse of the people must be paid for.   (427–57).

Thus many a family loses a son or a husband, children lose their fathers, and parents lose their children on account of Menelaus (and, by implication, Agamemnon), who has been robbed of his child-wife, Helen. Also, by implication, among the grieving and muttering citizens is Clytaemestra, robbed of her child; soon she will exact her revenge.

Part of the working out of the scheme of justice and talion-punishment in this trilogy is that children are not only victims but also murderers. An ambivalence toward children, with their potential to grow into murderers in their own right, is hinted at in a later chorus about Helen, describing her allure and her destructiveness, explicitly to the house of Priam, but implicitly to the house of Atreus as well. She is likened by metaphor to a lion cub:

Once a man fostered in his house
a lion cub, from the mother's milk
torn, craving the breast given.
In the first steps of its young life
mild, it played with children
and delighted the old.
Caught in the arm's cradle
they pampered it like a newborn child,
shining eyed and broken to the hand
to stay the stress of its hunger.

But it grew with time, and the lion
in the blood strain came out; it paid
grace to those who had fostered it
in blood and death for the sheep flocks,
a grim feast forbidden.
The house reeked with blood run
nor could its people beat down the bane,
the giant murderer's onslaught.
This thing they raised in their house was blessed
by God to be priest of destruction.   (717–36)

This metaphor, among other functions, continues the theme of nursing and nurturing that informs *The Oresteia*. Artemis, who protects all nursing young, is angry because the eagles have killed the pregnant hare. But the metaphor of the lion cub also anticipates the pivot of the plot of *The Libation-Bearers*, Clytaemestra's dream of the snake that sucks milk and blood from her breast. Literal blood—blood that can be shed—and blood as kinship, connection, and family are inextricably mixed with milk, the stuff of nourishment, the withholding of which becomes an incitement to rage at one's own "blood." Nursing children can become snakes or lions; the darling can become a monster, destructive especially of parents.[14] Who makes whom into monsters is never definitively settled; instead that question becomes the subject of self-justifying murderous debate between parents and child, husband and wife. In brief, it can be said that in *The Agamemnon* and *The Libation-Bearers* confused admixture and the blurring of boundaries are dramatically and thematically important. The confusions between victim and victimizer, child and parent, just revenge and savagery, sexuality and destructiveness, blood and milk, are central to the impact of the dramas. In *The Eumenides*, the dramatic task is to sort and separate these distinctions and to establish a new order based on clear distinctions and then, harmonious blendings.

The scene between Cassandra and the chorus (1069–1330), important from many viewpoints, is also replete with the theme and images of the murder of children. Early in the interchange, Cassandra asks what house it is that Apollo has brought her to, and the chorus answers her literally, the house of the Atreidae. She responds, "No, it is one that hates god, bearing witness to many evil deeds of murder of kin and of beheadings, a slaughterhouse of men, where the ground is sprinkled with blood" (1090–94).[15] The chorus proclaims Cassandra a keen-scented hound, and she begins to specify what she means: "For these are testimonies that persuade me: babies bewailing their own slaughter and their roasted flesh devoured by their father" (1095–97).

The chorus acknowledges its painful awareness of the house's history of child-slaughter and cannibalism. Atreus, revenging his brother Thyestes' adultery with his wife, has Thyestes' children killed and served up to him at a banquet of "reconciliation." The chorus characteristically does not know, or does not want to know, the other possible implications of Cassandra's words—especially the impending murder of Agamemnon. A few lines later, the chorus compares Cassandra to the nightingale, who cries, "Itys, Itys":

Chorus: Maddened in your heart and transported by a god, you sing a tuneless song of your own fate, like a tawny one, the nightingale, insatiate in her

---

14. In the stasima following this account of Helen as a lion cub (750–80), the language is about the begetting of deeds, good and bad, what it is that truly begets evil and retributive deeds, and which child resembles its parents, "a black *Ate* [fury] for the house, just like her parents."

15. The translations of the Cassandra scene are mine, drawing upon the commentary and translation of Fraenkel.

weeping, alas, with pitiable heart, bemoans "Itys, Itys," her life beset with
sorrow on both sides.

Cassandra: Oh, the fate of the sweet-voiced nightingale: for the gods draped
around her a feathered shape and a sweet life, without wailings. But what
remains for me is being split in two by a two-edged weapon.   (1140–49)

Condensed in these lines is the poignant myth of Philomela and her sister
Procne, a "myth within the myth" of the house of Atreus. Procne and
Philomela were daughters of Pandion, king of Thrace. Tereus, the husband
of Procne, raped Philomela and then cut out her tongue to prevent her from
telling. She managed to convey what had happened by weaving the story
into a tapestry, and she and her sister plotted revenge by killing Itys, the
infant son of Tereus and Procne. In some versions, the infant Itys was
served up as a dish to the unwitting father. The gods thereafter changed
Procne into a nightingale, who eternally mourns the son she slew for
revenge. Her sister becomes a swallow. In *The Agamemnon*, Cassandra is
likened to both the nightingale and the swallow, thus she can be seen as
embodying both sisters. But what is important at the moment is that the
poet introduces a tale of child-murder in revenge for marital infidelity and
intrafamilial rape. Clearly this tale is woven from the same fabric as the tale
of the house of Atreus.[16]

The theme of the slaughter of children is counterpointed briefly by
Cassandra's reply to the chorus about her "marriage" to Apollo. She
indicates that she somehow betrayed Apollo and refused to have children
(1205), for which he seems to have punished her by making it so that no one
believes (or understands) her prophecies. Cassandra is then further caught
up in the violent swirls of true prophecy as she describes her vision: "Do
you see the young ones sitting here, at this house, in the form of dream-
images? Children dead at the hands of their own kin, their hands full of the
meat that is their own flesh; I clearly distinguish them holding their intes-

---

16. Countless marvelous details integrate these allusions to the Philomela story with other
parts of the trilogy. The mutilative muting of Philomela, for example, paralleling the gagging
of Iphigenia at the sacrificial altar, and the word *philoiktois* (pitiable; 1143) is applied to
Procne as the nightingale, reverberating with the *philoikto belei ommatos* (pitiable missile of
the eye) that Iphigenia casts at the men about to kill her after she has been silenced. These
verses also point to the difference between epic and tragedy. The tale of Philomela is told in
The Odyssey (19.518–23) by way of describing Penelope's sorrows and her fitful sleep. The
characters in the epic poem have been transformed into birds and have gained a certain epic
immortality thereby. But Cassandra's fate is tragic, for she is not even granted the possibility
of transformation but is simply slaughtered. This is a commentary within the play on the
difference between the epic view and the painful sense of limitation and the end of familial
continuity that is part of the tragic view.

tines and entrails, a most pitiable burden, of which their father did taste"
(1217–22).

Cassandra not only sees what has happened—how Atreus avenged Thyestes' adultery with his wife—she also predicts the murder of Agamemnon
and herself by Clytaemestra, a monster, a Scylla among the rocks, who
grabs and devours those who sail by. Murder, betrayal, and cannibalism are
all interwoven here.

A pivotal episode in the trilogy, Clytaemestra's dream in *The Libation-
Bearers* (523–53) also involves biting and devouring. Here it is the child
who bites and begins to devour the parent. The terror of this dream, related
by the chorus of women to Orestes, awoke Clytaemestra and prompted her
to relate it:

> Orestes: Do you know the dream, too? Can you tell it to me right?
> Chorus: She told me herself. She dreamed she gave birth to a snake.
> Orestes: What is the end of the story then? What is the point?
> Chorus: She laid it swathed for sleep as if it were a child.
> Orestes: A little monster. Did it want some kind of food?
> Chorus: She herself, in the dream, gave it her breast to suck.
> Orestes: How was her nipple not torn by such a beastly thing?
> Chorus: It was. The creature drew in blood along with the milk.
> Orestes: No void dream this. It is the vision of a man.   (526–34)

The chorus tells him that Clytaemestra has sent libations to the tomb of
Agamemnon in an attempt to cure her own disease, as it were. Orestes
proceeds with his interpretation:

> If this snake came out of the same place whence I came,
> if she wrapped it in robes, as she wrapped me, and if
> its jaws gaped wide around the breast that suckled me,
> and if it stained the intimate milk with an outburst
> of blood, so that for fright and pain she cried aloud,
> it follows then, that as she nursed this hideous thing
> of prophecy, she must be cruelly murdered. I
> turn snake to kill her. This is what the dream portends.   (543–50)[17]

---

17. See Devereux (1976), pp. 182–218. These pages are full of important insights and
suggestions, many of them controversial, but all thought-provoking and important. Especially important is his observation that the chorus of women in effect enacts the content of
Clytaemestra's dream: "They too *bare* their breasts . . . and then *traumatize* them with
blows. Even the libation they offer recalls the mixture of *liquids* Orestes draws in dream from
Klytaimestra's breasts" (p. 186). Both the dream and the libation are unsuccessful in enabling
Clytaemestra to allay her anxieties and guilt about the import of her murder for her status as

This dream acts dramatically as a pivot or switch-point, after which each actor and every element of the dream turns out to be reversible and is transformed into its opposite. Orestes and Clytaemestra are both snakes; nursing portends (and retrospectively refers to) the devouring of children; victor and victim will be interchanged. Affectively, the dream conveys a terrible vision of infancy and maternal tendance, a vision in large measure shared by Orestes and Clytaemestra. Nursing is a form of sadistic oral attack and murderous revenge. This most natural and loving act converts infant into snake and mother into murdered victim. Blood and milk are inseparable, not only in the fundamental sense that each is a liquid that implies ties of love and obligations of tendance, but in the sense that each entails a murderous dependence. What should be a natural, loving union of mother and child that eventually leads to a proper differentiation of each from the other is converted into a sadistic and brutal fusion and confusion.

Another aspect of the vision of children within the play concerns their utilitarian value. From one perspective, children are an "investment in the future"; in fact they *are* the future of the house and as such should be cherished. But in *The Oresteia* this view is in conflict with the sense that children are a threat to parents or are pawns to be used and manipulated in deadly games among adults. Children preserve the very values over which the adults are willing to kill each other and their own children—this is the cruel paradox of the trilogy. Glory, ambition, power, and dominance are "commodities"; accordingly there are the attendant needs for battle and revenge against those who threaten one's ownership. In *The Oresteia* children are part of such commodities, and alternatively can be prized for their survival or as means of revenge on adversaries within the family. All of this must somehow be resolved so that the curse will not be transmitted and reenacted by each generation in turn trying to destroy its own children.

One contravening view of childhood, especially of infancy, is held up in the trilogy, expressed in the speech of the old nurse, Cilissa, when she hears of the death of Orestes and genuinely weeps for him:

> But never yet did I have to bear a hurt like this.
> I took the other troubles bravely as they came:
> but now, darling Orestes! I wore out my life

---

a mother. It is important for the dramatic action that dreams and oracles in Greek tragedy (and in Shakespeare) be either misinterpreted or interpreted only partially. What Orestes does not include in his interpretation is that, in retaliation for his becoming a snake who attacks his mother (who herself is called a snake at 994 and 1047), he is persecuted by the snakelike goddesses, the Furies (1050).

for him. I took him from his mother, brought him up.[18]
There were times when he screamed at night and woke me from
my rest; I had to do many hard tasks, and now
useless; a baby is like a beast, it does not think
but you have to nurse it, do you not, the way it wants.
For the child still in swaddling clothes can not tell us
if he is hungry or thirsty, if he needs to make
water. Children's young insides are a law to themselves.
I needed second sight for this, and many a time
I think I missed, and had to wash the baby's clothes.
the nurse and laundrywoman had a combined duty
and that was I. I was skilled in both handicrafts,
and so Orestes' father gave him to my charge.   (*Libation-Bearers*, 747–62)

This scene is virtually comic relief by comparison with the grimness of
the bulk of the trilogy. But it evinces not only a more benign view of the
difficulties children can cause (and a less benign view of the labors of the
nursemaid), but also a certain pathway of resolution that is blocked to the
other characters in the trilogy. That is, it presents a more benign picture of
the horrific phenomena that occur before and after this speech. Terrors in
the night and frightening dreams, such as Clytaemestra's, are replaced by a
baby's awakening a parent or nurse. The lawlessness of infanticide, adultery, and murder are replaced by the lawlessness of the infant's bowels and
bladder. Cassandra's grim prophesies are represented by the nurse's procla-
mation that you have to be a prophet to catch the child in time. The
shedding of blood is replaced by the shedding of urine and feces, and
atonement through sacrifice or further crimes is represented by the wash-
ing up of soiled clothing.

MARRIAGE, INTERCOURSE, AND
THE BEGETTING OF CHILDREN

The vision of marriage conveyed by *The Oresteia* is epitomized by the
choral account of the wedding of Helen in Troy (681–715). There a pun is

---

18. *Exethrepsa* (I brought him up) might also mean "I nursed him." If so, there is a
problem to be resolved: Clytaemestra, baring her breast to Orestes, says that she nursed him.
Devereux (1976) claims that Clytaemestra is lying, that she never nursed Orestes, and
adduces this as evidence that she is a "schizophrenogenic mother." Knox (1975) ridicules
Devereux, and the debate over whether Clytaemestra nursed Orestes becomes silly rather
than productive. See Simon (1980) for the argument that Aeschylus left the question unclear
with *dramatic purpose*, for the important question in the play is: what is it that establishes
Clytaemestra as Orestes' mother? See also Mejer (1979), presumably an admirer of Knox,
who argues that the poet meant to say the nursemaid actually nursed Orestes, although he
does not draw the same extreme conclusions as Devereux.

made on the name Helen, "death of ships, death of men and cities," as if it derived from the root √ele- (to kill). Helen, that "bride of spears, about whom is strife," is married, in the choral imagination, with the bloody armies of Greece and Troy as the wedding guests. Sensuous luxuriance is converted into battle, and the whole ceremony is, as in Lorca's play, a "blood wedding." The text (699) uses the double entendre of *kēdos*, signifying "mourning" and also used to denote "relatives by marriage," to convey this confusion of war and marriage:

> And on Ilium in truth
> in the likeness of the name
> the sure purpose of the Wrath drove
> marriage with death: for the guest board
> shamed, and Zeus kindly to strangers,
> the vengeance wrought on those men
> who graced in too loud voice the bride-song
> fallen to their lot to sing,
> the kinsmen and the brothers.
> And changing its song's measure
> the ancient city of Priam
> chants in high strain of lamentation,
> calling Paris him of the fatal marriage;
> for it endured its life's end
> in desolation and tears
> and the piteous blood of its people.   (699–715)

The chorus continues with the account discussed above, of the lovely lion cub reared in the house. The cub, at first mild and playful, in time grew up and showed its lion's nature, wreaking havoc and bloodshed among those who have raised it. The chorus then returns to the sensuality of Helen:

> And that which first came to the city of Ilium,
> call it a dream of calm
> and the wind dying,
> the loveliness and luxury of much gold,
> the melting shafts of the eye's glances,
> the blossom that breaks the heart with longing.
> But she turned in mid-step of her course to make
> bitter the consummation . . .   (737–45)

The marriage of Helen and Menelaus, ruptured by her elopement with Paris, leads to the vision of Menelaus, numbed, grasping for phantoms and in a mood of sullen despair, a mood lifted only by the destruction of the Trojan War (404–27). Other marriages mentioned or alluded to are those in the myth of Philomela (1140–49)—marked by adultery, betrayal, mutilation, child murder, and perhaps child-cannibalism—and the "marriage" of Cassandra and Apollo (1199–1212).[19] Apollo was the one who brought her to this terrible house, or at least he allowed her to be led away captive. He mated with her ("wrestled . . . and breathed sensuality"; 1206) and then punished her for refusing to bear his child. Her prophetic and mantic experience is a fusion of sexual ecstasy and sexual torture, all at the hands of the god who took her. The sacrifice of Iphigenia too has overtones of the confusion of mating and slaughter. What should have been wedding rites became the scene of a father slaughtering his daughter.

The theme is redundantly represented in the trilogy: marriage is grim, bloody, and destructive. But the most powerful evocation of this union of sexual lust and blood lust is found in Clytaemestra's song of triumph over her slaughter of Agamemnon and Cassandra:

> Thus he went down, and the life struggled out of him;
> and as he died he spattered me with the dark red
> and violent driven rain of bitter savored blood
> to make me glad, as gardens stand among the showers
> of God in glory at the birthtime of the buds.   (1388–92)

> [speaking of Agamemnon and Cassandra] while he,
> this other, is fallen, stained with woman you behold,
> plaything of all the golden girls at Ilium:
> and here lies she, the captive of his spear, who saw
> wonders, who shared his bed, the wise in revelations
> and loving mistress, who yet knew the feel as well of the men's
> rowing benches. Their reward is not
> unworthy. He lies there; and she who swanlike cried
> aloud her lyric mortal lamentation out
> is laid against his fond heart, and to me has given
> a delicate excitement to my bed's delight.   (1437–47)[20]

Clytaemestra exults, then, in the sexually arousing and fertilizing effects of the murder of her doubly betraying husband, the murderer of Iphigenia and the womanizer. This is the vision of intercourse, impregnation, and childbirth that underlies the play. Scholars have often pointed to the contrast between this speech and a fragment surviving from Aeschylus' lost play *The Danaids*. There, Aphrodite makes a speech about the power of love, probably delivered as part of a defense of the one daughter, Hyper-

---

19. Cf ll. 1178–82 for an image of Cassandra as a young bride.

20. "Golden girls of Ilium" renders *Chryseises*. Chryseis is well known from *The Iliad* as the captive mistress of Agamemnon, whom he much preferred to his wife, Clytemnestra. *Paropsonema*, a spicy banquet dish, is translated "delicate excitement." The oral imagery persists as slaughter and lust are mixed with cannibalistic images.

mestra, who disobeyed her father and did *not* murder her husband on the wedding night: "The holy heaven yearns to wound the earth, and yearning layeth hold on the earth to join in wedlock; the rain, fallen from the amorous heaven, impregnates the earth, and it bringeth forth for mankind the food of flocks and herds and Demeter's gifts; and from that moist marriage-rite the woods put on their bloom. Of all these things I am the cause."[21]

Not surprisingly, the allusions to and metaphors about pregnancy and gestation throughout *The Oresteia* tend to be grim and bloody. The omen of the eagles devouring the pregnant hare and her fetuses is one example. Clytaemestra's self-justifying account of the demon of the House of Atreus who repeatedly murders children is, "the demon, three times fattened . . . from him there is gestated in the belly a blood-licking passion [*eros*]" (1475–79; my translation).

In this trilogy, one does not readily find in contrast an underlying sense of love or tenderness being nourished and growing deep inside. When such images are suggested, they are quickly associated with violence.

Interspersed with these representations of marriage and begetting are numerous linguistic expressions, typically proverbial and moral ones like "this begets that." These seemingly incidental instances are quite relevant to the plays' central concerns of continuity, procreation, and responsibility for who brings about whom and what. Causality is typically cast in the language of something begetting something. A few examples: "A man's prosperity, when it has reached maturity, begets and does not die child-less. . . . there grows insatiable distress . . . wicked deeds beget like deeds . . . the fate of a house of justice and rectitude is always a fair child" (750–62).[22] Thus, the storyline informing the play, the transgenerational transmission of evil and of trauma, is paralleled by the incidental imagery of bad qualities begetting bad qualities.

Along with these destructive representations of marriage, intercourse, and pregnancy, the theme of the dangerous and vicious nature of women is repeatedly brought forth.[23] Helen and Clytaemestra are killers and mon-

21. Frag. 25 (44) in Smyth, *Aeschylus* (1926). See introduction to Fagles' translation of *The Oresteia* (Aeschylus 1982), pp. 34–35. Even this passage betrays a problem in male–female relations in its use of *trosai* (to wound).

22. My translation. See esp. 764–71, and also, 265, 528, 959, and 1628 for other examples. See *Libation-Bearers* 585 ff. for an image of the earth breeding numerous monsters, the most horrible of which is female passion.

23. The most interesting account of this theme is in Zeitlin (1978), pp. 149–84, including a discussion of the dramatic sequencing of the motif of the dangerous woman. See esp. pp. 163–65, on woman as monster. See also Devereux (1976), pp. 177–78, on the female viper who is killed by her children eating their way out of her belly, and chaps. 6, 9.

sters. Clytaemestra, among other accusations, is analogized to a Scylla among the rocks, an Amphisbaina (a two-headed monster) and an echidna (a female viper who bites off the head of the male during intercourse). She is "a sacrificing hellish mother and a curse-Fiend blasting trucelessly against her near and dear ones" (1235–36).[24] Clytaemestra's crime is compared to the worst crime in the history of mankind, that of the Lemnian women, who as a group slaughtered their husbands. The chorus in *The Libation-Bearers* (585–651) recounts this tale as the climax of its recital of hideous deeds perpetrated by women. Finally, the Furies or Erinyes are the archetypical dangerous and destructive female, especially maternal, element. All in all, in Aeschylus' trilogy woman is potentially and often actually extraordinarily vicious and dangerous.

Thus far I have discussed the themes of marriage, mating, and begetting children as they appear throughout the trilogy, without paying attention to the dramatic sequencing of these themes. I now must give some account of how these issues are resolved, at least resolved enough for *The Oresteia* to come to an end. The theme of woman as monster, for example, is introduced in *The Agamemnon*, but is controverted and not monolithic in that play. She is portrayed, both in others' reproaches and in her own self-praise, as having masculine traits. Clytaemestra is enraged and embittered by Agamemnon's sacrifice of their daughter Iphigenia. There is some balance in her taking a lover, given Agamemnon's involvements with various captive women. There is also room in this play for debate about the intrinsic evil of women, as exemplified by the interchange between Clytaemestra and the chorus after she has killed Agamemnon and Cassandra (1448–80). The chorus condemns "mad Helen," cause of the death of multitudes, "bedecked with blood that can never be washed out." The language of passage reverses the opening of *The Iliad*, where it is the "wrath of Achilles" that has sent down to Hades countless psyches of the Achaeans; here Helen is the destroyer. Clytaemestra protests that they should not lay all that blame at the feet of a woman, Helen. The chorus then alludes to the terrible history of the house of Tantalus, the house of Atreus, and Clytaemestra says, "Yes, now you have named it right"—the child-destroying demon of the house is the cause of all these troubles (1475–80). The chorus then ascribes all this horror to Zeus, "cause of all, doer of all." A debate continues throughout the play, with arguments justifying and condemning Clytaemestra's murder of her husband.

Consonant with this fluctuation in assigning blame to the woman is the fact that in *The Agamemnon*, in contrast to the other two plays, the Erinys

24. Trans. Zeitlin (1966), cited by Hogan (1984) in his comments on 1.1235. See also Zeitlin (1965) and Burkert (1966).

or Fury may be male as well as female.[25] By the middle of *The Libation-Bearers*, however, the gender of the Furies is unequivocally female—they are the avengers of maternal blood. In *The Eumenides* the Furies are the vilest of creatures, embodying the worst male fears of the ravenous, relentless, castrating, foul-smelling, dysmenorrheic, and childbearing woman. But at the end of the trilogy the Furies are transformed into kindly spirits, beautiful, sweet-smelling, interested in marriage and fertility, guards of marriage ties as well as blood ties, in short, good protective citizens of Athens.

Many critics, including some psychoanalytically oriented ones, have discussed these transformations in detail.[26] It is clear that the transformations and the resolution of murderous intrafamilial conflict within the play depend upon the fixing of clear and unequivocal boundaries between the sexes. These boundaries are established or, better, redrawn in the wake of their terrible confusion in the action of *The Oresteia*. This "clarification," offered by Apollo, which entails downgrading the procreative and reproductive role of the female, is in some sense accepted by at least half the citizens and, finally, by Athena herself. The chorus of Furies argues at Orestes' trial that he has spilled his mother's blood upon the ground and cannot be acquitted, can never be admitted to any altar. Apollo replies, in effect, that although Orestes *has* killed his mother, he has not really killed a parent (*tokeus* = begetter)—because the mother is not a parent!

> The mother is no parent of that which is called
> her child, but only nurse of the new-planted seed
> that grows. The parent is he who mounts. A stranger she
> preserves a stranger's seed, if no god interfere.
> I will show you proof of what I have explained. There can
> be a father without any mother. There she stands,
> the living witness, daughter of Olympian Zeus,
> she who was never fostered in the dark of the womb
> yet such a child as no goddess could bring to birth.   (658–66)

The artistic success of this ending depends in part on the psychological success of the resolution. The dangerous androgyny of Clytaemestra is "sublimated" into the androgyny of Athena, true daughter of her father, bound by a devotional and asexual bond, bypassing the inconvenience of a mother. So this unsavory compromise is accepted by the Furies (and the rest of the citizens) because it makes it possible to bypass messy and

25. Observed by Winnington-Ingram, 1983.

26. See Zeitlin (1978) and Green (1979), pp. 35–87. For a major study done from a post-structuralist set of perspectives (Derrida, Kristeva, Barthes), see Goldhill (1984).

dangerous sexuality and mother–father–daughter triangles. Additional wish-fulfilling elements in the successful compromise are those that denigrate and thereby detoxify the primary role of the mother in gestation and birth. Both in broader psychodynamic terms and more specifically in terms of the issues of this trilogy, the woman is a dangerous creature because of the power of her generative and nurturant faculties—she has been given by nature and biology the power of life and death over the child, including, of course, the precious male child.

Part and parcel of this dread of the reproductive powers of the woman is a vision of woman's anatomy, especially her sexual anatomy, as dangerous and ensnaring. The imagery of the net, the snare, the robe, the trap, evoked in relation to the murder of Agamemnon bespeaks such a view of the dangers of sexual involvement with a woman who will also be a mother and wife.

The solution, however, is a perverse one, both in its reversal of common sense and in the psychoanalytic sense. The psychoanalytic term *perversion* implies a form of the attempt (almost always a male's) to solve the interwoven conflicts engendered by dependence on the female and fear of castration either by the father or by an androgynous version of the mother (the so-called phallic mother). Perversions entail a kind of game: "I am separated from her, I am not separated; she has a penis (stolen from my father or from me), she doesn't have a penis." The dressing up, ritual beating, fetishes, exhibitionism, and peeping involved in sexual perversion all seem to have some such "theater of the absurd" as their basis. Analysis of some instances of fetish, such as a whip or a corset string, reveals how the object represents in fantasy both the umbilical cord and the "on-again, off-again" mother's penis.[27]

One variant of the perverse game in this trilogy is, "She can give or take life; she cannot give or take life," or "She is more powerful than the father; she is less powerful than the father." Another is, "She is sexual and a mother at the same time; no, she is not a mother," or "No, she is not sexual; yes, she is sexual." An even more extreme attempt to wish away the dangers of femininity can be seen in the delusion of a young paranoid schizophrenic man, whose life was dominated by his dread of women. He

27. There is a large and controversial literature on the perversions. Some articles representing the viewpoint presented here are Bak (1968) and Greenacre (1968, 1969). A colleague reported on the analysis of a man who needed the sight of a man on a crutch to get sexually aroused. The crutch represented both an anchor to the mother and her fantasied penis. See also Chasseguet-Smirgel (1985) for a discussion of patients who fantasize that there is no such thing as a vagina.

had finally figured out, and now rested secure in the knowledge, that there were no women in the world, only men—but many men dressed up to look like women!

In *The Oresteia*, the resolution involves a new form of reallocation of power within the family and within the extended kinship system of gods and man. That new form is the city and its laws. The city or polis, at least as Aeschylus portrays it, is a new form of reconciliation between the genders and between the generations, as well as between warring clan groups within the city. Many scholars have pointed out that the resolution of *The Oresteia* reflects the changes in Athenian law from the sixth to the fifth century, changes that gave more power to the city and to new political units within the city and diminished the power of the clan and the family. Among the changes were restrictions on the power of the father to put children to death for disobedient or disgraceful acts. The death penalty was given over to the state.

Thus, to an important degree, the Athenian audiences watching *The Oresteia* may have experienced a more intense, immediate, and gratifying satisfaction at the ending than is possible for us. The physiology of conception and gestation espoused by Apollo was more consonant with the beliefs of the ancient audience than modern. We are more troubled by the sleight of hand performed by Apollo and Athena in relation to gender roles and the power of the female and we find the ending more troublesome, or at least less artistically gratifying. But Apollo's statement devaluing the reproductive role of women is separated from the end of the play by several hundred lines, and this separation, I believe, helps both ancient and modern audiences "scotomatize" the biological distortion in the service of a much-wished-for resolution of the conflict.

In terms of my thesis, that tragedy is centrally concerned with the problem of procreation within the family at war with itself, it is important that the resolution in *The Oresteia* involves a new statement about *generation*. In order to allow for the orderly flow of generations and the transmission of value and authority from one generation to the next, a new definition of the act of generation is constituted in which no females, only males, are progenitors.

BECOMING A PARENT AND BECOMING A CHILD

The Oresteia abundantly demonstrates the interferences in the orderly progression and succession of generations. The mantle and the crown are not easily passed on, only the bloodshed, guilt, and intergenerational hatred. Along with dramatizing the interferences, the trilogy also demonstrates, mainly by implication, what is necessary to permit such a resolution of intergenerational and intersexual rivalries.

First, in terms of the theology or religious assumptions of the play, it is necessary that there be some reconciliation and resolution between the warring forces among the gods. The rivalries between Artemis and Apollo, Apollo and the Furies, and the earlier generations of the family of Zeus, even the "justice of Zeus"—how his will affects the events of the trilogy—bring considerable conflict. The fights among these divine "parents" and "grandparents" of the human agents do not allow much hope for resolution or warfare among the latter. While Aeschylus does not represent humans as mere victims of the gods, they are certainly heavily under their power and sway. Like other great Greek poets and philosophers, Aeschylus portrays a rather complex interaction between divine power and human choice. The intervention of Athena at the end of *The Oresteia* is absolutely necessary to mediate among the divine forces contending whether to save or kill Orestes. She interacts with a human jury—their vote is evenly divided and Athena casts the deciding vote in favor of Orestes' life—and facilitates a resolution among all the warring factions.

For modern readers, whether psychoanalytically inclined or not, it is easy to see the divine agents as representations or projections of forces and tensions within the human family. We are accustomed to equating "fate" with the terrible burden of a family history, and our modern tragedians, such as Eugene O'Neill, have set the stage for this way of looking at religious entities such as fate and the gods.[28] From the perspective of characters in the Greek tragedies, and to a great degree from the perspective of the contemporary audiences, one might talk of a certain sense of childlike helplessness and dependence upon the whims and will of the gods. While this discrepancy between the power of man and the power of the gods is absolute and given, it is not necessarily paralyzing. But in the classical Greek framework, the humans are certainly unable to make the divine agencies relinquish their own feuds and vendettas.

Also necessary for a resolution is the ability of the human parents, the husband and wife, to operate in enough of a harmony to beget and rear children and to preserve the house. In essence, the marriage partners must be able to recognize themselves as progenitors and parents, not as warriors pitted against each other. In most tragedy, and in *The Oresteia* in particular, nonrecognition of kin is one of the characteristics of family relations.

---

28. See Chabrowe (1976) for detailed discussion of O'Neill's ideas on the equivalence of fate, gods, and unconscious forces.

Clytaemestra and Agamemnon scarcely look at or address each other—or at least there is quite a delay in recognition in the scene of Agamemnon's entrance. Nonrecognition of children by parents and uncertainty of one's own parenthood are the earmarks of parent–child relations. *The Libation-Bearers* contains several important scenes of efforts, failed and successful, to recognize kin and role.[29] The message is conveyed that biology is necessary but not sufficient for parenthood; one must act like a parent in order to make a claim on the debt the child owes the parent, to claim the recognition due a parent from a child.

The most famous recognition scene in the trilogy is Electra's gradual realization that her lost brother, Orestes, is nearby (163–245). The recognition involves several signs or tokens—a lock of Orestes' hair, which resembles her own; his footprint (presumably Orestes approached the tomb unshod); and finally, when Orestes appears before her, a weaving that Electra had made for him years before. Electra resists recognizing Orestes because of her fear of false hopes, her fear of being trapped in a net or a "weaving" of deception.[30] The matching of the lock of hair to Orestes' head, of his foot to the footprint, and finally the scenes on the weaving—blade strokes and wild beasts, the work of Electra—clinch the recognition. Important in the scene on the weaving is the acknowledgment of a bestial and murderous aspect to their kinship. Full recognition involves an acceptance of the caring and tendance that are part of the sister–brother relationship and also acceptance of the shared violent wishes.

In stark contrast to this is the nonrecognition scene between Orestes and his mother, Clytaemestra (668–718). Orestes poses as a stranger, "a Daulian among the Phokians," bringing news from "Strophius the Phokian" (who was keeping Orestes) that Orestes is dead. There is not even a hint that Clytaemestra recognizes (but represses the recognition of) her own son. The contrast with *The Odyssey* is instructive—Penelope does not recognize Odysseus, but from their first encounter, the poet begins to hint that somewhere in her mind she knows who this beggar bearing tales of

29. Needless to say, the parental role, what defines maternal and paternal behavior, is not the same in every society and culture. The father in *The Oresteia* is expected to set a good model of aristocratic excellence and heroism, to protect the house both literally and figuratively, and to protect the lives of the children, but not to change diapers or play with the children. The child's role in classical Greece carried with it what might seem in our society extremely onerous demands with regard to caring for parents.

30. At 220, Electra fears a deceit that Orestes might be weaving or contriving (*plekeis*), and at 231, he offers a weaving (*huphasma*). See Hogan (1984) on this passage. Exactly what that weaving is, is unclear. Sense seems to call for a belt or bandolier, rather than a full costume, but the word *huphasma* denotes a robe. The word *spathē* seems to mean both the weaver's blade in putting threads through and "blade" as weapon.

Odysseus is. Further, Clytaemestra's reaction is hardly one of deeply personal grief—it is the hope of the household that is dead, not the babe she nursed and reared (contrary to what she later asserts when Orestes is about to murder her).

The reaction of Orestes' nurse to the false news that he is dead (731–65) is also comparable with the story of Eurykleia, Odysseus' nurse in *The Odyssey*. Odysseus' nurse is the first to see through the disguise, and she must suppress public show of her deep love for the man lest she betray him. Here, the nurse does not see "the stranger," but her reaction clearly involves a feeling for Orestes as a creature with whom she had an intimate physical relationship. She describes her pain and her labors at caring for the infant Orestes.

Clytaemestra finally does realize what is happening when a servant pounds on her door and shouts, "The dead are killing the living." She recognizes Orestes when he appears to murder her and then stakes her claim for mercy in large part on the ground that she is his mother who nursed him. In whatever gesture the conventions of the Greek stage allowed the costumed male actor playing Clytaemestra, she "shows" him her breast, and he is startled. Even this scene makes it clear that Clytaemestra had not previously "recognized" Orestes in her terror dream of nursing the snake to whom she gave birth. Orestes, in his interpretation of that dream, recognizes himself as the nursing babe and the killer of his mother. It is striking that what finally affirms Clytaemestra as a mother, as the mother of Orestes (in *The Libation-Bearers*, at least), is the threat of being killed by her own son.

> Clytaemestra: Ah woe, that I bore and reared this serpent!
> Orestes: In truth the fear your dream inspired was prophetic!   (928–29)[31]

This picture of Clytaemestra's ambivalent maternity is also consonant with her portrayal in *The Agamemnon* as the mother of Iphigenia. It is Iphigenia slain who arouses her maternal assertion, not an evocation of Iphigenia as a babe or young girl whom she tended and raised. The chorus evokes more of Iphigenia as daughter than does Clytaemestra. Electra in *The Oresteia* has, by her own account, no recognition of being a daughter of Clytaemestra, and Clytaemestra shows no evidence of proudly owning her.[32] The "blood" that constitutes the bond between mother and son thus

31. Trans. Lloyd-Jones (1979), as are lines from the lament and invocation scene.

32. See 444–50 for Electra's lament and her account of how she has been shut away like a dog. In an unpublished paper, Rachel Parens argues that Electra is here expressing a primal scene fantasy of being locked up and forced to witness the sexual behavior of her parents, presumably Clytaemestra and Aegisthus.

appears more as bloodshed than as the nurturant, bonding substance shared by the two.[33]

What about Agamemnon as a parent, as a father? How firmly is his identity established? In *The Libation-Bearers* he is "a ghost of a father." The extended *kommos* (lament) and the long scene (306–509) in which Orestes and Electra evoke the literal spirit of their father is a conjuration of the dead Agamemnon to aid them in their murderous revenge. At a psychological level, it is an attempt to get him to be a substantial and supportive father, a significant presence. Clearly the children, especially Orestes, attempt to heroize the father, who has fallen in esteem because of the way he was slain.

> Would that beneath Ilium
> pierced by the spear of one of the Lycians,
> father, you had been slain!
> You would have left glory in your halls,
> and for your children a life
> that would have made men turn to view them
> in their walks abroad.   (345–50)

Orestes, Electra, and the chorus in turn try to arouse, promise, bribe, persuade, and even shame the dead king into helping his children. They also appeal to other deities, such as Earth or Persephone and Zeus, to release or empower their father. Electra promises rich libations, including wedding libations—she needs the help of her father if she is ever to marry and beget children (486–88). Orestes urges Earth to send up his father that he may survey the battle to come, and his sister prays that Agamemnon, as warrior (a commander-in-chief from the grave), be granted victory. Orestes and Electra then remind him of his ignominious death in the bath, caught in fetters and in the snares of shameful deceit.

> Orestes: Do these shameful words not rouse you, father?
> Electra: Do you not raise erect your beloved head?
> Orestes: Either send Justice to fight by your dear one's side,
>   or grant that we in turn get a like grip on them,
>   if it is your will to atone for your defeat by victory.
> Electra: Hear also this last cry, father!
>   Look upon your nestlings here at your tomb,
>   and pity alike my woman's and his man's cry!

---

33. The tragic counterpart of Clytaemestra's failures in acknowledging her children is the resolution of the fight between Apollo and the Furies in *The Eumenides*, whereby the mother is declared to be not the true parent of the child but merely the vessel or soil that contains the child (658–66).

Orestes: Do not wipe out this race [*sperma*] of the Pelopidae!
For if we live you are not dead, even in death.
For children preserve a man's fame
after his death; like corks they hold up the net,
retaining the cord of flax that reaches up from the deep.   (495–507)

The final appeal to the ghost is a reminder that unless he responds to the children he risks extinguishing the house and losing whatever immortality he might gain from progeny. The children need him to be a parent, and he, they remind him, needs them lest he lie dead and forgotten. Important too is the clear appeal to him to be a man, a warrior, to lift up his head; the whole picture is of stirring up the dead to become a powerful, phallic father.[34] The children in this sense try to create, to resurrect the father they need to have. What is so amazing is that the father never responds in any way, shape, or form![35] That a presence or a sign, might appear from the grave was not an unusual belief in ancient Greek culture, and ghostlike presences are represented in other Greek tragedy. Thus Agamemnon's lack of response is the epitome of nonrecognition by the father of his own children.

At the end of this conjuration scene, Orestes hears of Clytaemestra's dream and at once identifies or recognizes himself in the serpent baby that draws blood from the mother. That Orestes, receiving no response from his father, then turns to identifying himself as the one drawing fluids from the mother suggests the fantasy structure of his appeal. What is enacted here is a fantasy of infusion of vital substances from the father: courage, hot blood for revenge, and semen to prove manhood and to perpetuate the house. The dynamic between Orestes and his parents is such that his rage at and dread of his mother is organically intertwined with his father's failure to provide what is necessary for his full development as a male. It is a fantasy found in many patients, both heterosexual and homosexual, about what is needed to become a potent male, and in recent years anthropologists have brought to our attention whole cultures with grim rituals elaborating this fantasy. A group in New Guinea believes that men are contaminated by the blood of their mothers and must be purged of that blood (by bleeding) and insemi-

---

34. I cannot prove it but I believe that "raise erect your beloved head" has phallic overtones. There is much in Greek culture pointing to the equivalence of "head held high" and erect penis. For example, the traditional Athenian *herm*, common in private courtyards and public places, consists of a block with a bearded head of Hermes and a large erect penis below.

35. I thank Froma Zeitlin (pers. comm., 1985) for this observation.

nated through fellatio by the semen of older men in order to make new, all-male blood (Herdt, 1981).[36]

Thus, Orestes' evocation of the stalwart father is an attempt to enhance his identification as the father's avenger and son and as killer of the mother, but it does not solve for him the problem of dread, rage, and dependence upon his mother. Though the process of identifying himself as such begins at the outset of the play (see 269ff.), it is clear that Orestes' full self-realization as father-avenger and matricide requires a number of steps, of which the conjuration of the father is one.

In the scheme that unfolds in *The Oresteia*, children and parents are not automatically acknowledged as such by each other. It is in acts of violence and retaliation that the clearest affirmations of identity are to be found. At best, there are only hints of tenderness and caring as grounds for recognition of kinship and its obligations.

Clearly, the process of growth and maturation of the child involves the ability to form stable and judicious identifications with his or her parents. Clinical data, especially from child psychiatry and criminology, make it abundantly clear that excessive parental aggression toward children, or sexual exploitation and overstimulation, or neglect and understimulation (which often drives the child to provoke the parent into some extreme response) affect the child's ability to identify with the parents as role models for parenting. It is not just that the child has defective models—parentally administered trauma can make all the child's identifications brittle, totalistic, and unselective. In short, there may be major interferences with the normal processes of identification, not just with the formation of good identifications.

The Oresteia not only provides us with a picture of children who cannot emulate their parents easily or without extreme conflict, it is also replete with the imagery of failed or inadequate processes of identifying. I refer particularly to the powerful, disturbing, and ubiquitous oral-cannibalistic imagery of the trilogy. I now review and examine the redundant imagery of the slaughter and devouring of offspring. The pregnant hare and her fetuses, the sacrifice of Iphigenia (analogized to a banquet and to the sacrifice of a goat), the cannibalism contrived by Atreus, and the dream of Clytaemestra giving birth to and nursing a snake—all these and more

36. The same fantasy, I believe, underlies the sequence early in *The Agamemnon* where the chorus (at 72–82) describes its lack of male prowess and potency (no juices left), and at 104 says, "I do have the power to proclaim"—these are men looking for infusion of victorious male potency, and they turn to Zeus in their anxiety. It is also this same "stuff" that the Furies drain from young men.

emphasize some sort of oral destruction.[37] In addition, the Furies suck blood and then vomit up clotted blood (*Eumenides*, 183).

There are numerous ways of looking at this plenitude of oral imagery. One useful perspective is to see these various kinds of eating as the *violation of boundaries* and interferences with the orderly progression of identification, which requires the development of a boundary between parent and child. Failure in identification arrests the processes of growth, differentiation, and succession. The laws of marriage, guest–host relationships, ritual sacrifice, and the mutual debt of parents and children all involve regulation of greed. Hubris in this play (as elsewhere in Greek culture) represents a certain kind of greed, taking more than one's share. The devouring of children is an expression of such unbridled greed, whether for revenge or for one's share of honor (*timē*). Cause and effect are not clearly differentiated in the poetic presentation—child-sacrifice and child-eating are both the precipitants and the results of violations of rules and of the sense of measure.

The devouring of children becomes a powerful image and fantasy representing non-differentiation between the generations, refusal to let the next generation grow and replace the older one in a lawful manner.[38] Eating one's own is a way of denying separateness, denying one's mortality, and denying the sense of limit and boundary that is implied in laws of incest, inheritance, and marital rights. The cannibalistic imagery also expresses, it seems, a certain rage at not having gotten enough, having been cheated, and is therefore a determination to "have one's cake and eat it too."[39]

The resolution in *The Eumenides* of the fight between Apollo and the Furies includes Athena's promise to give the Furies their proper due. This includes proper food for them to eat—instead of blighting birth and devouring the vital substance of young men, they will now enjoy "first fruits in offerings for children and the marriage rite for always" (833–36).

37. See, for example, Clytaemestra's speech about the murder of Cassandra—she is a spicy dish who enhances Clytaemestra's main course, the bed of luxury with Aegisthus, and presumably adds to her delight in the murder of Agamemnon (1447).

38. A jocular illustration of identification by oral incorporation made the rounds in the 1960s when researchers discovered that planaria worms could become "smart" by eating other planaria who had been trained by the experimenters. The moral: if you eat your professors, you will become smart.

39. For an overview of psychoanalytic approaches to *The Oresteia*, including classical approaches to the oral themes, see the references to the trilogy in R. Caldwell's bibliography (1974), including his own articles on Aeschylus. For "Kleinian" readings of *The Oresteia* see Klein (1975). See also Tolpin (1969). Green's (1979) work on *The Oresteia* is extremely important and has been helpful in my own thinking. His emphases are more on Oedipal conflicts, positive and negative.

The Eumenides gradually sets the scene for a larger variety of routes toward identification, not merely an incorporative or cannibalistic fantasy. "Stepping into someone's shoes," empathizing with the position of the other person, begins to be encouraged by the civic resolution of the play. More mature, more durable identifications, especially the healthier identifications of children with parents, take place more silently; in them, devouring is replaced by the milder *taking on*. Such processes allow suspension of the continuous chain of vendetta and murder and continuation of generation and reproduction.

BECOMING A TRAGIC HERO

In contrast to such Greek tragedies as *Prometheus Bound*, *Oedipus Rex*, *Ajax*, and *Medea*, there is no central hero in *The Oresteia*. If anything, Clytaemestra is the heroine of *The Agamemnon* and Orestes the hero of *The Libation-Bearers*. If there is a hero in *The Eumenides*, it would have to be the chorus of Furies. But I would like to propose a sense in which Agamemnon, Clytaemestra, Orestes, and even the Furies can be considered tragic heroes, or at the least tragic figures.

My definition of the tragic hero is as follows. First, he or she (or they) undertakes, more or less willingly (even though "compelled") and independently of the consequences, to fulfill an ideal or virtue that is necessary for the preservation and propagation of the family. In the course of following through on the action deemed necessary, he or she risks consequences that might destroy the family's ability to propagate and continue. Taking the risk entails a willingness to chance and/or actually to endure tremendous suffering. The tragic figure is at once the perpetrator of the necessary action and its victim; caught between two millstones, doer and sufferer—in short, he or she is willing to be or ends up being a sacrificial offering. The central and novel part of this definition is that the actions are undertaken for the sake of preserving the family, both implementing an ideal deemed absolutely necessary for its survival and simultaneously coming close to destroying the family.

Orestes, from his own perspective, is carrying out the task of restoring the correct—male—line of authority to the house of Atreus. From this perspective (his own, that he is being robbed of his inheritance, plus the perspective urged on him by Apollo), bloody revenge on his mother and her paramour is necessary to preserve the line. That his actions might lead to his own destruction and thereby the destruction of the house is hinted at early in *The Libation-Bearers* and made abundantly clear by the end of that play and throughout much of *The Eumenides*. With his apparent destruction all hopes for the house come to an end. His suffering is most extreme, or at least most extended, and he is portrayed as a potential sacrificial victim or hunted quarry of the Furies.

In what sense is Orestes (or any other tragic hero) a "responsible" agent? Action and choice in Aeschylean drama is typically shown as driven and motivated by a number of sources, human and divine, so that responsibility is not a simple matter and, in fact, is arguable and argued, as in *The Oresteia*. Some sense of "being responsible," that is, being held to account, comes from a character's *willingness* to participate in what may be an inescapable, divinely ordained action. Thus, Agamemnon was compelled by divine necessity either to sacrifice his daughter or to give up the expedition, but once he opted for the sacrifice, he did it a bit too willingly, too ruthlessly, and was therefore complicit (*Agamemnon* 219–27). Orestes is seemingly trapped just as his father was—forced either to kill his mother and suffer persecution by the Furies, or not to uphold the male line and be punished by Apollo. Part of his suffering comes from seeing the dilemma clearly and agreeing, after some hesitation, to do what he has to do. His subsequent madness is in part an expression of this unbearable conflict, which makes him into a sort of sacrificial animal. His responsibility lies also in his clear vision, his ideal, that unless male authority is restored and constituted in the house—no matter what the reasons for its having been undermined in the first place—there cannot be a house.

Clytaemestra has a contrasting vision of what is needed to preserve the house. For her, revenge on her husband is necessary to assert and affirm that child-killing is not to be forgiven, because it is part and parcel of the family history of her husband and is incompatible with sustaining a house that can reproduce and endure. She is tragic also in that her sensuality, her sexuality, drives her to take on a lover, Aegisthus, who helps give her the male authority and power to gain her revenge. At the same time, it is the exercise, especially the immoderate exercise, of male authority that has threatened and can once again threaten the existence of the house and the commonwealth.[40] In her efforts to punish Agamemnon for, and to stop, child-slaughter, she ends up sacrificing or bartering (though not murdering) her remaining children.[41] In her efforts to be a mother and defend her children—to fulfill one crucial function of the house—she too risks the destruction of the house.

Agamemnon similarly starts to destroy his own household and actually destroys countless others—Greeks and Trojans—to implement an ideal of

---

40. See *Agamemnon* 1567–76 for her plea that the demon of the house go reside in another house; 1654–62 for her urging Aegisthus to help end the cycle of violence.

41. In the eyes of Orestes, she has sold him for her lust (*Libation-Bearers* 913–17).

honor that is part of his essential definition of his house. To refuse to go to war is shameful; it places at risk his proper rulership and manhood, his worthiness to sire progeny and continue the house.[42] His tragic situation is only briefly in focus in *The Oresteia*, primarily in the early choral odes about the sacrifice of Iphigenia. Iphigenia herself becomes a tragic heroine in another play, Euripides' *Iphigenia in Aulis*, where she agrees to accede to her father's wishes and die unmarried and childless in order to preserve his status and male stature, which, fragile as it is, she deems necessary to preserve his house. Most tragic heroes and heroines are both sacrificed and sacrificers. Iphigenia, sacrificed in one set of tales, becomes a professional sacrificer in Euripides' *Iphigenia in Tauris*.

I also suggest that tragic heroes do not appear full-blown upon the stage but rather that protagonists, as part of the dramatic action, become heroes. The development of the tragic hero involves an increasing awareness of the often nightmarish complexity of the situation and of the necessity to make choices and to act. It also involves the knowledge that there is no choice free of dire consequences and no choice free of guilt or fear of retaliation. Part of the process of making a tragic hero takes place via the audience (or their surrogate in the play, the chorus).[43] As we, the audience, are gradually brought into the worldview, including the inexorable dilemmas, of the protagonists, our responses include gradually surrendering simple, comfortable, or "bourgeois" solutions. We move with the burgeoning tragic hero, although not always exactly in synchrony, gradually toward seeing and comprehending something crucial about his situation. As such, we have a certain complicity in the inexorable march of events, in the headlong course chosen by the hero. Of course, we interact with the protagonists and heroes in many individual ways. There are always differences in the sympathy or antagonism we feel toward a particular character, and accordingly we differ on whether we can designate that character a hero. To sum up, the state of being a protagonist is a relatively fixed feature of the play; the state of being or becoming a hero involves complex processes of interaction with the audience.

SILENCE, NOT TELLING, AND UNSPEAKABLE GRIEF

Epic poetry, *epos*, the "winged words" of Homeric heroes—all these terms evoke and demand talking and telling. Within the poems the poet and the

42. See Keuls (1985), esp. chap. 1, "Military Expeditions."

43. I have found Nussbaum (1986, pp. 49–50 and n. 65) very instructive, including her comments about the chorus' respecting the gravity of the situation. Choruses, however, are not uniform in this regard; they are not all or always respectful. They too partake in the *process* of heroization.

characters continually tell; even when a main character is asleep, there is narration and often action in the form of a dream. Implied in the epic frame too is that these tales are being told for, and to, one's children. The chain of telling is the chain of generational continuity. Tragedy, by contrast, deals in thwarted communication, in the frustration and inhibition of telling.[44] Silence—something almost unknown in epic dialogue—is an important hallmark of tragic dialogue. The misunderstood oracle, prophecy, or dream, the lie and disguise—peripheral features of epic plot—become central in Greek tragedy. *Oedipus Rex* is the most famous of the tragedies built upon failure to understand, failure to read, framed by an insistence on knowing, searching out, and reading the true meaning. But numerous other tragedies, such as Euripides' *Iphigenia in Tauris*, also devolve upon misunderstood or incompletely understood dreams or oracles. *Macbeth*, among Shakespeare's great tragedies, is built on misunderstood prophesies; his other tragedies also hinge dramatically on misunderstanding and partial understanding. Punning and ambiguous banter in *Hamlet* and the meaningful nonsense of the fool and madmen in *King Lear* are of a piece with misunderstood dreams and oracles.

Patterned misunderstanding is to me one of the essential features of tragic dialogue, not only in Greek tragedy, but in the tragic drama of Shakespearean and modern times (Simon 1984). Using a variety of contemporary critical and philosophical frameworks, scholars in recent years have reexamined tragedy, including Greek tragedy, as expressions of semiotic and metacommunicational issues (Goldhill 1984; Vernant 1972; Zeitlin 1982). Incomplete telling, ambiguities in telling, what is told by not telling, the layerings and interweavings of different societal and semiotic codes— these are now important topics in the study of tragedy, reflecting the long-standing awareness that great tragic drama is marked by frustrated and failed understanding. Such studies on meaning and codes, however, risk neglecting the *affective* core of tragedy, the deep enmeshment of meaning and of feeling.

I believe that one approach to understanding the emotional impact of problems of meaning and narrative in tragedy can be made by focusing on the relation between the generation of narrative, the generation of meaning, and the generation of children. If tragic content involves the problem of how the family at war with itself can propagate, then tragic form involves

44. Havelock (1985, 1986) and Segal (1986) have argued that an important aspect of the power of Athenian tragedy has to do with the unique mixture of oral and literate habits in fifth-century Athens. This argument about modes of transmitting knowledge from one generation to the next has important ramifications for my own thesis about generational continuity as a problem of tragedy.

the problem of how to tell and whom to tell—or, one could say, how to propagate the story.

Silence in Aeschylean drama has been a topic of great interest from antiquity.[45] Aristophanes admiringly makes fun of Aeschylus' prominent use of the silent character. In *The Frogs*, the comedy involving a contest between Aeschylus and Euripides in Hades, Aristophanes has Euripides attack Aeschylus as a pretentious quack who beguiles an audience of silly fools:

> Euripides: He gypped and cheated them with ease, and here's one thing he used to do.
> He'd start with one veiled bundled muffled character plunked down in place,
> Achilleus, like, or Niobe, but nobody could see its face.
> It looked like drama, sure, but not one syllable would it mutter.
> Dionysos: By Jove, they didn't, and that's a fact.
> Euripides: The chorus then would utter
> four huge concatenations of verse. The characters just sat there mum.
> Dionysos: You know, I liked them quiet like that. I'd rather have them deaf and dumb
> than yak yak yak the way they do.
> Euripides: That's because you're an idiot too.
> Dionysos: Oh, by all means, and to be sure, and what was Aeschylus trying to do?
> Euripides: Phony effects. The audience sat and watched the panorama breathlessly. *"When will Niobe speak?"* And that was half the drama.   (910–20)[46]

Aeschylus, in a lost drama, had Achilles sitting silent and grieving after the loss of Patroclos. In contrast, Achilles is not portrayed as silent in *The Iliad*, though he deeply grieves. From the first news of Patroclos' death at the hands of Hector to the end of the poem, Achilles speaks and when not speaking, acts—as when he drags Hector's corpse behind his chariot. In his sleep he dreams and speaks to Patroclos; even his horses talk to him and he to them! The silent Achilles is a plausible conception, but it is not the traditional one. The allusion to Niobe also refers to a lost play. She is dumb with sorrow after Apollo and Artemis have slain her twelve children in revenge for Niobe's boast that her children were superior to those of Leto, the mother of these two deities.[47] We do not know if Niobe's silence was

45. See Taplin (1972, 1979), esp. chap. 7; Rosenmeyer (1982), chap. 7; and Goldhill (1984), chap. 1. Several critics have spoken of Beckett-like silences in Aeschylus, a comparison that, though made in an off-hand manner, is a most important one.

46. Trans. R. Lattimore, in W. Arrowsmith, ed., *Aristophanes: Four Comedies* (Ann Arbor, 1969).

47. See Keuls (1985, pp. 344–48) for a fine discussion of the play and its implications for the portrayal of the plight of women on the Athenian stage.

only one of several mythological variants available to Aeschylus, but we see that he clearly exploited it for his dramatic purposes. She sits silent while various other characters talk to her, or around her; her only vocalization seems to be wailing toward the end of the play. It is noteworthy that here total muteness is tied up with the loss of all progeny: not only is there nothing more to say, but there is virtually no one left to whom to say it! Perhaps this is the most "dramatic" illustration (though not a proof) of the thesis that in the transition from epic to tragic, interruptions in the chain of generations are entailed by interruptions in the flow of speech and narrative.

In *The Oresteia* there are several prominent instances of silences, principally that of Cassandra when Clytaemestra urges her to speak and the possible silence of Clytaemestra during the choral entrance (it is much debated whether she is on stage). I direct my attention, however, primarily to several instances of *interruptions* in tellings, points at which a speaker stops with, "I will say no more." Second, I point out contrasts in the language of the play between the epic insistence on telling and the tragic reworking of that imperative.

The very beginning of *The Agamemnon*, the speech of the watchman, is marked by the tension between telling and not telling. First he details how fear, instead of sleep, has become his companion on his long watch. He can no longer comfort himself with "singing" or "humming" (16). Condensed in that line are the connotations arising from the verb *aeidein* (to sing), which implies *epic* singing, not merely the singing of a tune to oneself. It is as if the watchman is saying that the epic scheme of things—the heroic king gone off to glorious battle to avenge an insult—is no longer working out so well. Epic tales no longer serve as comfort or consolation. Instead of singing, the watchman bewails the fate of the house (18). The sight of the beacon light suddenly arouses him to great excitement. He will communicate, he will signal the news to the queen, and there will be great shouting for joy. He will also make his own choral prelude to rejoice in the homecoming of his lord, Agamemnon. But then anxiety intrudes, an anxiety about the state of the house and the state of relations between the king and queen: "The rest I leave to silence; for a large ox stands upon my tongue. The house itself, if it could take voice, would speak most eloquently. Thus willingly I speak to those who understand, but as for those who do not understand, I have forgotten [whatever I know]" (36–39; my trans.).

First, it is the tale of the house, the house divided against itself, that he cannot tell and that instead he bemoans (silently). The house itself would speak if it could, he asserts—and the story it would tell is of betrayal and rage. The theme that the story *will* be told by someone or something—here the stones of the house—is an important one in tragedy. We encounter it most prominently in *Macbeth*, where (e.g., 2.4.123–28) after Banquo's (silent!) ghost has appeared, Macbeth affirms to his wife that his secret will be out, somehow. "Blood will have blood / Stones have been known to move and trees to speak." Enforced silences will necessitate some other speaker or some other way to tell.

Second, let us consider the "large ox" (*mega bous*) that has stepped on the watchman's tongue. This is not only a proverbial phrase[48] but, I believe, also an anticipatory allusion to the slaughter of Agamemnon as "the cow" (*boos*), while Clytaemestra is the bull (*tauros*; 1125–26), in Cassandra's unheeded cry, "Keep the cow away from the bull." The Homeric formula for the slaughter of Agamemnon is "as one cuts down an ox in his manger" (*Odyssey* 9.410). Thus, the ox on the tongue of the watchman represents the story he cannot tell about how his king, who should be a bull (*tauros*), will be slaughtered like a cow—not even like the castrated ox in Homer. The confusion of masculine and feminine, already sounded in the watchman's description of Clytaemestra (10), is thus also encoded in his words "ox on my tongue." Things have not been and will not be well with the house, and the house is at risk and almost as if in pain—if only the stones could speak.

The watchman's "I have forgotten" is another allusion and counterpoint to the epic values of telling—forgetting is the worst fate that can befall a bard. Thus, he is a frightened bard manqué, and his telling is not smooth, because he dreads what he must tell and to whom he must tell it.

The second instance of silence is also one in which telling is interrupted because what must be told is too terrible, portending the destruction of the house and of children. This is the chorus' account of the sacrifice of Iphigenia. They sing a song that begins with an account of the Trojan War—"it is ten years since . . . " (40) and continues with the tale of the eagles and the pregnant hare, the anger of Artemis and the absence of winds keeping the fleet at Aulis. The sacrifice of Iphigenia is demanded, and the chorus describes several forms of the conflict between speech and silence, between telling and not telling. The father, like the other princes, ignores her pleas—they were as naught (229–30). The father speaks—that is, he prays—and calls upon the men to lift her up onto the altar like a goat.[49] She is not allowed to speak—the guards gag her lest she curse. Gagged, she tries

---

48. See the sources collected in Fraenkel's note ad loc. George Thomson (1966) has argued for overtones of Eleusinian mystery rites in this speech and in the "large ox." I am not sure that this is correct, and if so, exactly what it contributes to this passage, except the possibility of adding overtones of secret things that can be known but never revealed, especially to "those who do not understand."

49. If we follow Burkert's (1966) argument that the word *tragedy* means "a song sung at the sacrifice of a goat," then the sacrifice of Iphigenia is the quintessential *tragic* scene.

to speak with her eyes, looking lovely as in a painting—her forced silence in contrast to all the times she had sung at her father's festive table. The chorus then announces, "From thence on, I neither saw, nor do I speak it" (248; my trans.).

The verb form *out' ennepo* (I do not speak), also alludes to epic values: it implies, "I cannot sing as a bard." *The Odyssey* opens with "andra moi ennepe, Mousa" (Of the man to me sing, o Muse). Thus the chorus cannot perform the proper bardic function of telling the full story, because what they have to tell is that one member of the family, the father, slaughtered another, the daughter.[50]

There are numerous other allusions throughout *The Agamemnon* to epic telling and the grim contrast afforded by the tragic narration. At 979, fear is personified as a song (*aoida*), a chorus unbidden and unhired; at 1186–93, the song of the Erinyes is that of a choir drunk on blood and betrayal within the household.

These instances could be augmented by detailed study of how Cassandra is both understood and misunderstood. Two details are worth mentioning. The first is the Philomela story within Cassandra's lament—Philomela had her tongue cut out, and could tell her story only indirectly or, in one sense, by action (killing her own child). The second is the interchange between the chorus and Clytaemestra about why Cassandra does not speak. Clytaemestra commands her to enter the house and provides her with an example from mythology—even Heracles was cast into bondage and had to serve as a slave. Cassandra, standing frozen, does not seem to comprehend. Clytaemestra, impatient, says perhaps Cassandra uses wild, incomprehensible speech like an animal or a barbarian. The chorus says she needs an interpreter—she is like a frightened captive animal (1062–1063). Clytaemestra, now furious at being disobeyed, says Cassandra does not understand because she is caught up in the passion of her captured city. She is untrained to be bridled and curbed "and will not understand until her rage and strength have foamed away in blood" (1066–67).

Cassandra's silence surrounds a story that cannot be told, of past slaughter and impending slaughter, including the slaughters within the house and within the trilogy. Clytaemestra correctly but unempathetically surmises that grief makes Cassandra dumb and that the solution is to be found only in bloodshed.

50. Iphigenia's "striving to speak" = *thelousa prosennepein* (241–42). *Prosennepein*— translated by Liddell, Scott, and Jones (1940) as "calling out the name of" (her father)— reverberates with the epic *ennepein*, a verb of epic singing, which appears in 248, as the chorus says "I cannot speak it" (*out' ennepo*). *Prosennepo* appears again at 1291, where Cassandra, looking at the gates of the palace, says, "I call these gates the gates of Hell."

Images of frozen or inexpressible grief are recurrent in the trilogy. Unexpressed outrage, shame, humiliation, and feelings of betrayal and loss are the concomitants of such mourning. They bespeak an inability to come to terms with the past, an inability to find any solution other than repetition and propagation of bloodshed. The most striking of these images is the portrait of Menelaus drawn by the chorus after Helen has run off with Paris.[51] The prophets of the house wept aloud and spoke:

Alas, alas for the house and for the champions,
alas for the bed signed with their love together.
Here now is silence, scorned, unreproachful.
The agony of his loss is clear before us.   (410–13)

Her images in their beauty
are bitterness to her lord now
where in the emptiness of eyes
all passion has faded.

Shining in dreams the sorrowful
memories pass; they bring him
vain delight only.
It is vain, to dream and to see splendors,
and the image slipping from the arms' embrace
escapes, not to return again,
on wings drifting down the ways of sleep.   (416–26)

As the chorus goes on to detail, the "treatment" for Menelaus' frozen and numbed grief was to launch the Trojan War, thus bringing similar grief to his countrymen! The silence in the house of Menelaus betokens a tale that cannot be recounted, a suppressed and numbing rage that speaks only through countless slaughters.

The other striking image of grief that cannot be discharged or worked through comes at the beginning of *The Libation-Bearers*, where the chorus of captive (Trojan?) women are bringing the libations ordered by Clytaemestra in a vain attempt to assuage her terrors in the night. The dream-diviners of the house interpret her dreams to mean that "under earth / dead men held a grudge still / and smoldered at their murders" (39–41). They go on to sing of blood once spilled that cannot be washed away from the hearth of the house.

Through too much glut of blood drunk by our fostering ground
the vengeful gore is caked and hard, will not drain through.

51. See Devereux's (1976) detailed and evocative discussion of what he calls "Menelaos' Reactive Depression and Dream," pp. 59–145.

>The deep-run ruin carries away
>the man of guilt. Swarming infection boils within.   (66–70)[52]

They conclude their ode by extending the image of the blood/sorrow that cannot be washed away. They weep under their veils "and freeze with sorrow in the secret heart" (84). Grief is frozen, caked, congealed, and, as blood clots cannot percolate through the earth, it cannot disappear. Again, only violence—heralded by the arrival of Electra, praying for her brother to appear as an avenger—can wash away the blood. Words, telling, narrating, do not suffice, for the story is not one fit for the ears of the children.

Epic tales are designed to be sung about great deeds of heroes to save and preserve wives and children, not to destroy them. With tales of the murder of children, the storyteller is, like Iphigenia, gagged, able to plead for pity and communicate terror through the silence, but no longer freely able to tell. Narration and child are gagged and killed, and silence and absence communicate the essence of tragedy.

REFERENCES

Aeschylus. 1926. *Aeschylus.* Vol. 2. Trans. H. W. Smyth. Loeb Classical Library. Cambridge: Harvard University Press.

———. 1982. *The Oresteia.* Trans. Robert Fagles. Ed. W. B. Stanford. New York: Bantam.

Athenaeus. 1930. *The Deipnosophists.* Vol. 4. Trans. Charles B. Gulick. London: Heineman.

Bak, Robert C. 1968. The Phallic Woman: The Ubiquitous Fantasy in Perversions. *Psychoanalytic Study of the Child* 23:15–36.

Burkert, Walter. 1966. Greek Tragedy and Sacrificial Ritual. *Greek Roman and Byzantine Studies* 7:83–121.

Caldwell, Richard. 1974. Selected Bibliography on Psychoanalysis and Classical Studies. *Arethusa* 7:115–134.

Chabrowe, Leonard. 1976. *Ritual and Pathos: The Theater of O'Neill.* Lewisburg: Bucknell University Press.

Chasseguet-Smirgel, Janine. 1985. *The Ego Ideal.* Trans. Paul Barrows. New York: Norton. Original French edition published 1975.

Clay, Diskin. 1969. Aeschylus' Trigeron Mythos. *Hermes* 97:1–9.

Devereux, George. 1976. *Dreams in Greek Tragedy: An Ethno-Psycho-Analytical Study.* Berkeley: University of California Press.

52. This verse is followed by a remarkable image of the blood shed at the defloration of a bride as a stain and a pollution, irreversible, comparable to blood guilt from a murder. The confusion of sex with murder here is so striking that it is easy to read right through the condensed poetic image and miss it. The theme of endless repetition of bloodshed is also brilliantly presented.

Fraenkel, Eduard, ed. 1950. *Aeschylus: Agamemnon*. 3 vols. Oxford: Oxford University Press.

Gargarin, Michael. 1976. *Aeschylean Drama*. Berkeley: University of California Press.

Girard, René. 1977. *Violence and the Sacred*. Trans. P. Gregory. Baltimore: Johns Hopkins University Press. Original French edition published 1972.

Goldhill, Simon. 1984. *Language, Sexuality, Narrative: The Oresteia*. Cambridge: Cambridge University Press.

Green, André. 1979. *The Tragic Effect: The Oedipus Complex in Tragedy*. Trans. A. Sheridan. Cambridge: Cambridge University Press. Original French edition published 1969.

Greenacre, Phyllis. 1968. Perversions: General Considerations Regarding Their Genetic and Dynamic Background. *Psychoanalytic Study of the Child* 23:47–62.

———. 1969. The Fetish and the Transitional Object. *Psychoanalytic Study of the Child* 24:144–164.

Havelock, Eric A. 1985. Oral Composition in the *Oedipus Tyrannus* of Sophocles. *New Literary History* 16:175–197.

———. 1986. *The Muse Learns to Write: Reflections on Orality and Literacy from Antiquity to the Present*. New Haven: Yale University Press.

Herdt, Gilbert H. 1981. *Guardians of the Flutes: Idioms of Masculinity: A Study of Ritualized Homosexual Behavior*. New York: McGraw-Hill.

Hogan, J. C. 1984. *A Commentary on the Complete Greek Tragedies: Aeschylus*. Chicago: University of Chicago Press.

Keuls, Eva C. 1985. *The Reign of the Phallus: Sexual Politics in Ancient Athens*. New York: Harper and Row.

Klein, Melanie. 1975. Some Reflections on *The Oresteia*. In *Envy and Gratitude and Other Works, 1946–1963*. Glencoe: Free Press. Essay originally published 1963.

Knox, Bernard. 1975. Review of George Devereux, *Dreams in Greek Tragedy*. *Times Literary Supplement*, Dec. 10. Pp. 1534–35.

Lattimore, Richmond. 1959. *The Oresteia*. In *The Complete Greek Tragedies*, ed. David Grene and Richmond Lattimore. Chicago: University of Chicago Press.

———. trans. 1969. *The Frogs*. In *Aristophanes: Four Comedies*, ed. William Arrowsmith. Ann Arbor: University of Michigan Press.

Lebeck, Ann. 1971. *The Oresteia: A Study in Language and Structure*. Cambridge: Harvard University Press.

Lesky, Albin. 1983. *Greek Tragic Poetry*. Trans. M. Dillon. New Haven: Yale University Press. Original German edition published 1972.

Liddell, Henry G., R. Scott, and Henry S. Jones. 1940. *A Greek-English Lexicon*. 9th ed. Oxford: Clarendon Press.

Lloyd-Jones, Hugh, ed. 1979. *The Libation-Bearers*. London: Duckworth.

Mejer, J. 1979. Recognizing What, When and Why? The Recognition Scene in Aeschylus' *Choephoroi*. In *Arktouros: Essays in Honor of Bernard Knox*, ed. G. Bowersock, W. Burkert and M. C. J. Putnam. Berlin: de Gruyter.

Nussbaum, Martha C. 1986. *The Fragility of Goodness: Luck and Ethics in Greek Tragedy and Philosophy*. Cambridge: Cambridge University Press.

Parens, Rachel. Unpubl. MS. The Electra and Oedipus Complexes: A Psychoanalytic Study of Five Tragedies.

Rosenmeyer, Thomas. 1982. *The Art of Aeschylus*. Berkeley: University of California Press.

Segal, Charles. 1986. Tragedy, Orality, Literacy. In *Oralita: Cultura, letterature, discorso: Atti del Convegno Internazionale a cura di Bruno Gentili e Giuseppe Paioni*. Rome: Edizione dell' Ateno.

Simon, Bennett. 1980. Review of G. Devereux, *Dreams in Greek Tragedy. Psychoanalytic Quarterly* 49:150–155.

———. 1984. "With Cunning Delays and Ever-Mounting Excitement" or, What Thickens the Plot in Tragedy and in Psychoanalysis. In *Psychoanalysis: The Vital Issues*, ed. George H. Pollock and John E. Gedo, vol. 2, pp. 387–436. New York: International Universities Press.

Smith, P. M. 1980. *On the Hymn to Zeus in Aeschylus' Agamemnon*. Missoula: Scholars Press.

Stanford, W. B. 1983. *Greek Tragedy and the Emotions: An Introductory Study*. Routledge and Kegan Paul: London.

Taplin, Oliver. 1972. Aeschylean Silences and Silences in Aeschylus. *Harvard Studies in Classical Philology* 76:57–97.

———. 1979. *Greek Tragedy in Action*. Berkeley: University of California Press.

Thomson, G. 1966. *The Oresteia of Aeschylus*. 2 vols. Prague: Czechoslovak Academy.

Tolpin, Marian. 1969. Aeschylus, *The Oresteia*: A Cure in Fifth Century Athens. *Journal of the American Psychoanalytic Association* 17:511–527.

Vernant, J.-P. 1972. Tensions et ambiguités dans la tragédie grecque. In J. P. Vernant and P. Vidal-Naquet, *Mythe et tragédie en grèce ancienne*. Paris: F. Maspero.

Winnington-Ingram, Reginald P. 1983. *Studies in Aeschylus*. Cambridge: Cambridge University Press.

Zeitlin, Froma I. 1965. The Motif of the Corrupted Sacrifice in Aeschylus' *Oresteia*. *Transactions American Philological Association* 96:463–505.

———. 1966. Postscript to Sacrificial Imagery in the *Oresteia* (*Ag.* 1235–37). *Transactions American Philological Association* 97:645–653.

———. 1978. The Dynamics of Misogyny: Myth and Mythmaking in the Oresteia. *Arethusa* 11: 115–134.

———. 1982. *Under the Sign of the Shield: Semiotics and Aeschylus' Seven Against Thebes*. Rome: A.E.P.

CHAPTER 3

Euripides' *Medea*

In Aeschylus' *Agamemnon*, the chorus balks at describing the sacrificial slaughter of Iphigenia; the act of Thyestes eating the cooked pieces of his own slaughtered children is represented in a nightmare vision of a character who was not there. Euripides moves the portrayal of the slaughter of children distressingly closer, virtually from the wings to center stage. In his *Bacchae* we see the head and tattered fragments of the body of Pentheus, killed by a band of Bacchic women led by his mother, Agave. In *Medea* we hear and almost see the actual murder. Child-murder comes closer and closer and threatens to overwhelm the audience or the reader. But somehow Euripides "manages" to depict the horror so as to allow his audience, including ourselves, to watch the play, to be open to its impact, and even to assimilate and think about the play. Consider, briefly, some aspects of the differences between Aeschylus and Euripides in their manner and style of regulating the audience's experience of such terrible deeds.

Both Aeschylus' *Oresteia* and Euripides' *Medea* open with the speech of a servant anxious about both the present and the future condition of the house. As the plays unfold, the reasons for apprehension become abundantly clear—the servants were right in their fears. The ending of *The Oresteia*, however, is one in which order, authority, and even predictability have been restored. The rhythms are now regular, peace descends, and the Furies, "children of the Night, yet childless" (1034), are reconciled to a new civic order.[1] By whatever "tricks" this state has been achieved, the ending of the play succeeds in affectively binding, healing, and restoring. The ending of *Medea*, in contrast, is one in which a hideous pseudo order,

---

1. *Nuktos paides apaides* is usually translated as "children, but aged, of the night," but here I think it is critical to read *apaides* with a double entendre to include "childless." The Furies are sterile and involved in causing sterility in others; the Eumenides have come to terms with their sterility and can become generative and promoting of the fertility of others.

including the establishment of a ritual around the slaughtered sons of Medea and Jason, has been precariously and momentarily established. As in a number of Euripides' plays, "the unexpected" (*aelptōs*) concludes the play—a rhythm of predictable unpredictability. The choreography of *The Oresteia* is one of passion and at times near horror, but with smooth crescendos and decrescendos. That of *Medea* is jerky, contorted, erratic. The music, as it were, of Aeschylus, is classical, while that of Euripides is atonal.[2]

Corresponding to these differences in tone, movement, and equilibrium are differences in treatment of the themes of children and the killing of children. *The Oresteia* concludes with a joyful renewal of fertility and continuity, while *Medea* concludes with Jason wailing over the slaughter of his children and proclaiming, "I wish I had never begot them" (1413).[3] We see in Euripides' work evidence of the same concern over perpetuation of the family, of the house, that is found in the plays of Aeschylus and Sophocles. But in Euripides there is a much greater consciousness about children. The value of children, affection and love for children, dread of what can and does happen to children, and murderous rage toward children are all much more explicit and central than in the work of the other two playwrights. Surveying the extant plays of Euripides and reviewing what can be reconstructed of the lost plays, we find an extraordinary preoccupation with children and the killing of children. *Medea, Heracleidae, Hippolytus, Andromache, Hecuba, The Suppliant Women, Heracles, The Trojan Women, Iphigenia in Tauris, Electra, Ion, The Phoenician Women, Orestes, Iphigenia in Aulis,* and *The Bacchae*—fifteen of about nineteen extant plays—are quite explicitly involved with stories about the death, murder, or sacrifice of children.[4] *Alcestis* (438 B.C.) also entails a parent who allows a child to die, hence one could argue that it also belongs on the list. That murder or abuse of children (or murder of a parent by a child) is an aspect of that play is suggested by the (lost) three other plays presented

2. In antiquity, Euripides was noted for adapting the most "modern" musical styles to his metrical and musical needs. See Gould (1985), p. 281.

3. Translation, unless otherwise indicated, by Rex Warner (Euripides 1944) in the University of Chicago Press volumes edited by Grene and Lattimore. The Greek text is taken from the edition of Allan Elliot (Euripides 1969).

4. Lost plays that involve cruelty of father to daughter include *Protesilaus* and *Danae.* Other lost plays whose (reconstructed) plots are here relevant include *Thyestes, Ino* (before 425 B.C.), *Polyidos, Meleager, Melampe Sophe, Melampe Desmotis* (late works), possibly *Alexandros* (which may have included a scene of Hecuba almost killing her son, Paris), and *Phaethon* (between 415 and 409). The tentative conclusion is that child-death was a major recurrent theme throughout Euripides' career, sometimes appearing as the main plot element and sometimes as a peripheral element. See Collard (1981), Lesky (1983).

with *Alcestis*: *The Cretai*, in which a father intends his daughter to be drowned for her unchastity; *Alcmaeon in Psophis*, whose protagonist killed his own mother; and *Telephos*, in which the young Orestes is abducted, held hostage, and threatened with murder while being held over the altar.

My hypothesis about Euripides' work in general and about *Medea* in particular is that the problem of form and the problem of content go hand in glove: discordant rhythm, dissonances, erratic and jerky movements of plot express the message of the dangers of discontinuity and interruption, and the even greater danger of destruction of the lineage. Similarly, Euripides calls attention much more than do the other two playwrights to problems of form and artistic tradition; concomitantly, he calls attention much more to the intensities and complexities of parents' relations with children. The hypothesis can be extended, then, to include some propositions about Euripides' relationship to the artistic tradition. His concern was to declare himself autonomous, independent, private, and autochthonous (sprung from the earth with no parents—the adjective used by the Athenians to describe themselves)—while at the same time trying to assert his connection to the tradition. If he were completely unconnected, then there would also be no possibility of artistic progeny. The abundance of fantasies and wishes in Euripides' work concerning false pregnancies and alternative methods of begetting children—especially methods that involve only one gender (typically, male wishes to reproduce without women)—reflects a concern about whether he can propagate if he eschews traditional methods of creating and begetting. Euripides' artistic ancestry goes back to Homer and epic tales seemingly earlier. To illustrate these hypotheses, I begin with an examination of the way epic traditions and epic narration are portrayed or alluded to in Euripides' *Medea*.

THE EPIC BACKGROUND OF *MEDEA*

Medea, first performed in 431 B.C., draws upon a body of legend well known to Euripides' audience, though it is only partially clear what modifications he made to this tradition. As Euripides tells it, Medea is the story of a foreign woman in exile in Corinth with her Greek hero-husband, Jason, and their two sons. Jason, to advance himself and presumably to get rid of Medea, who has become tiresome or burdensome to him, agrees to marry Glauke, the daughter of Creon, king of Corinth. Creon, fearing Medea's destructiveness, exiles her, but yielding to her plea, allows her one day to prepare for the journey. During this day, she successively sends poisoned gifts to Glauke, which hideously destroy her and her father; fortuitously meets Aegeus, the king of Athens, and tricks him into swearing to give her sanctuary; kills her own children; and then becomes transformed into a quasi-divine creature. Finally, she is provided by her grandfather, Helios (the Sun), with a chariot in which she will escape to Athens and from which she mocks Jason and exacts further revenge on him.

The background and antecedents to the actions of the play were well known. However, that Medea kills her own children deliberately may not have been known to the first audience who saw the play (and awarded it third prize in the annual competition). There were ancient cult legends about Medea *accidentally* killing her children as she was attempting to make them immortal in the temple of Hera. In the legend she makes the graves of the children in the temple the basis for a cultic celebration. Euripides alludes to this at the end of *Medea*. Medea herself was known as a magician and a sorceress. Such stories as the Golden Fleece, Medea's offer to the daughters of Pelias to rejuvenate him by "first" cutting him up into pieces and boiling him in a pot, and her cutting up and scattering the pieces of her own brother to help the Argo escape were undoubtedly common knowledge to the audience. Indeed, Euripides' first trilogy (455 B.C.) included a play about Medea and the daughters of Pelias. The story of Jason and the Argonauts' adventures in the Black Sea was, according to Circe's account in *The Odyssey*, already famous in her day. She describes to Odysseus the dread clashing rocks through which he must sail: "That way the only seagoing ship to get through was the Argo, known to all in song [*pasimelousa*] sailing away from Aeetes. And even she would have been quickly driven onto the great rocks that time, but Hera escorted her through because Jason was dear to her" (12:69–72).[5]

Thus, an epic within an epic, an epic older than the story of Odysseus, an "Argonautica" within *The Odyssey*, was known to the poet Homer and his audience. The clear association of Jason's tale with the epic-heroic is exploited skillfully by Euripides. As we have seen in Aeschylus' *Oresteia*, the tragedian explores the domestic implications of the male hero's epic adventures and makes the tale much more of a revenge story—revenge of the betrayed woman for her husband's infidelity—than do the epic versions.[6] An aura of epic frames *Medea*; epic is bemoaned at the beginning of the play and almost ridiculed at the end. The nurse of the children of Jason and Medea begins her lament thus:

How I wish the Argo never had reached the land
Of Colchis, skimming through the blue Symplegades,

5. Translation mine. *Pasimelousa* is usually rendered as "known to all," "world famous," but I believe there is also an overtone of *melos* as a sung story.

6. Even the later epic, *The Argonautica* of Apollonius (3d c. B.C.), does not take up the storyline of Medea and Jason in Corinth but is restricted to events prior to the breakdown of their relationship.

Nor ever had fallen in the glades of Pelion
The smitten fir-tree to furnish oars for the hands
Of heroes who in Pelias' name attempted
The Golden Fleece! For then my mistress Medea
Would not have sailed for the towers of the land of Iolcus,
Her heart on fire with passionate love for Jason;
Nor would she have persuaded the daughters of Pelias
To kill their father, and now be living here
In Corinth with her husband and children.   (1–11)

Would that the whole epic adventure had never taken place—it was not worth it. The imagery of these lines reinforces the phallic male, content of the heroic adventures—mighty trees felled to make oars, and the "towers of Iolcus" (a city in Thessaly). There is an ambiguity in the image of the felling of the mighty fir trees—such an effort is itself both heroic and a prelude to the heroic, but the image also alludes to fallen phallic prowess. The ending of the play reinforces the deflated and defeated side of the ambiguity in Medea's vengeful prediction to Jason about his death. The murdered children shall be buried in the temple of Hera (who in legend had helped Jason!) and will become the center of an annual cultic ritual; Medea shall go to live freely in Athens. As for Jason, he "will die without distinction, / Struck on the head by a piece of the Argo's timber" (1386–87).[7]

Thus, the epic expedition of Greek legend second in fame only to the Trojan war is condemned as the source of all the trouble. In between, we find Jason asserting the value of being famous among men—hypocritically, in the speech where he defends himself to Medea. He argues that he has brought her to Greece from a land of complete obscurity:

And all the Greeks considered you a clever woman.
You were honored for it; while, if you were living at
The ends of the earth, nobody would have heard of you.
For my part, rather than stores of gold in my house
Or power to sing even sweeter songs than Orpheus,
I'd choose the fate that made me a distinguished man.   (539–44)

Ironically, it is Medea who ends up with epic fame and epic gloating over her victory, while Jason is hoisted on his own petard.[8]

7. *Leipsanō*, translated "timber," means "leftover" or "remnant," not specifically a beam or prow, though apparently the scholiast's version implies this meaning. But it also means, especially in the plural, the traces or even the *memory* of something. Fine irony— Jason killed by the memory-traces of the *Argo*. He will die as a *kakos*, a base man, not an *aristos*, one of the best, a hero.

8. There is the additional irony of Jason's placing fame over the ability to sing like Orpheus, who, in fact, was one of the heroes on the *Argo*. Jason is reaching for one aspect of epic virtue—fame—and disparaging the singer, the very instrument of the fame.

Medea undermines and assails epic poetry and epic values principally through the odes of the female chorus and the speeches of the nurse. Here Euripides most clearly assaults traditional ways and values. As the nurse increasingly gives vent to her dread about what Medea might do, she explains that it will probably be of no avail for her to try to mollify Medea, who is like a lioness guarding her cubs. She bemoans not explicitly the futility of epic, but the futility of music, song, and tale to heal human griefs and grievances:

> It is right, I think, to consider
> Both stupid and lacking in foresight
> Those poets of old who wrote songs
> For revels and dinners and banquets,
> Pleasant sounds for men living at ease;
> But none of them all has discovered
> How to put to an end with their singing
> Or musical instruments grief,
> Bitter grief, from which death and disaster
> Cheat the hopes of a house. Yet how good
> If music could cure men of this!   (190–200)

The moans, curses, and shrieks of Medea that bracket this speech highlight the inadequacy of traditional song and music to deal with the real pain and real danger the chorus and nurse are just beginning to confront.[9]

After Medea has explained her position to the chorus, after they have heard Creon banish her but then grant her one day's respite, they are privy to the fact that she is scheming a hideous revenge. The chorus now sings that there is something fundamentally wrong with epic singing and epic tales—the deeds of Medea are exposing a gap, an omission, an error in these tales:

> Flow backward to your sources, sacred rivers,
> And let the world's great order be reversed.
> It is the thoughts of *men* that are deceitful,
> *Their* pledges that are loose.
> Story shall now turn my condition to a fair one,
> Women are paid their due.
> No more shall evil-sounding fame be theirs.
>
> Cease now, you muses of the ancient singers,
> To tell the tale of my unfaithfulness;
> For not on us did Phoebus, lord of music,

---

9. Cf. Aeschylus' *Agamemnon*, where Iphigenia is envisioned by the chorus singing at her father's banquets; the chorus contrasts that with her gagged shrieks and curses as she is brought to sacrifice.

bestow the lyre's divine
Power, for otherwise I should have sung an answer
To the other sex. Long time
Has much to tell of us, and much of them.   (410–30)

In effect, the chorus is proclaiming that when male–female relationships
are examined closely, when women are allowed a voice, things will indeed
be topsy-turvy, the rivers of the world will run backward.[10] Traditional
storytelling is based, so the chorus and before it the nurse proclaim, on
certain assumptions about stable relationships between men and women, in
which women are supposed to breed sons for epic heroism, sons who will
hear the heroic tales of their fathers and produce new tales in turn. Women,
as muses, are the sources of inspiration for the tales and the deeds entwined
with them, but they are not themselves the heroes. They are breeders of
sons and of tales, and when they are the subject of tales (according to the
chorus), it is on account of their infidelity. But as the action of the play
unfolds, as the chorus gradually realizes that Medea is plotting the murder
of her own children, it sings a famous ode about all the reasons not to have
children. The ode includes the assertion that women too have a muse
("goddess" in the translation here cited), and the song, the wisdom that
their muse teaches, is that it is better not to have children at all:

Often before
I have gone through more subtle reasons,
And have come upon questionings greater
Than a woman should strive to search out.
But we too have a goddess [mousa] to help us
And accompany us into wisdom.
Not all of us. Still you will find
Among many women a few,
And our sex is not without learning [ouk apomouson = not museless].
This I say, that those who have never
Had children, who know nothing of it,
In happiness have the advantage
Over those who are parents.   (1081–93).

Thus, we move from the inadequacy of poetry and song (in the nurse's
speech), to the falsity of epic poetry in omitting the woman's view, to the
statement that it is better not to have children at all. In a very important
sense, this assertion is Euripides' most powerful assault on the epic-heroic
worldview. Later in this chapter, I return to this ode as we examine
attitudes toward and assumptions about children in Medea.

Immediately after it hears the screams of the children being murdered,

10. See Knox (1983, esp. pp. 291–92) for discussion of this point.

the chorus, horrified by the deed, denounces Medea and turns to the mythic tradition to find some context, some way of comprehending this terrible act:

> O your heart must have been made of rock or steel,
> You who can kill
> With your own hand the fruit of your own womb.
> Of one alone I have heard, one woman alone
> Of those of old who laid her hands on her children,
> Ino, sent mad by heaven when the wife of Zeus
> Drove her out from her home and made her wander;
> And because of the wicked shedding of blood
> Of her own children she threw
> Herself, poor wretch, into the sea and stepped away
> Over the sea-cliff to die with her two children.
> What horror more can be? O women's love [*lexos* = bed],
> So full of trouble,
> How many evils have you caused already!   (1279–92)

The chorus implies that the tale of a mother killing her children is rare, indeed peripheral, in the body of received myth and epic. It is incredible to the chorus that such an action appears "today," virtually in its presence; what is peripheral in epic becomes central in tragedy. Indirectly, the implication of the chorus' statement is that child-murder by the mother is not the stuff of which traditional epic can be composed.[11]

Various scholars and critics of this play have pointed to the way Euripides, by means of linguistic usage, narrative style, and plot construction, in effect undermines the epic tales. The most articulate of these critics, Pietro Pucci (1980), refers to Euripides' " 'deconstruction' of the epic 'truth' " (p. 48) and analyzes in detail how this deconstructive process goes far beyond ridiculing or minimizing some mythological and epic themes. Among the points of Pucci's analysis most relevant here is the way Euripides' style, as in the nurse's description of Medea's complaints and in Medea's own wailing, does not aim at psychological veracity or coherent narrative. Rather, it aims at chaotic and incongruous juxtapositions— Medea, as described by the nurse, is both a rock and a wave of the sea— piling up stock rhetorical themes (*topoi*), and aiming at what Pucci calls a *coup de théâtre*. Another important observation is of the "blanks" in Euripides' style—frequent interruptions, omissions, and bold elisions in narrative. These discontinuities are also very "unepic," for the traditional epic style emphasizes smooth and continuous narrations. Epic eschews

---

11. Either Euripides alludes to a version of the Ino story we do not know or he changes the tale. In the standard version, a man kills one child of Ino, who in her attempt to escape drowns herself and the other child (See Euripides 1969, p. 98).

silences. The silence of Medea's children is not noticed until it is broken by their terrified screams and pleadings as their mother is about to kill them—a scene in which Medea is completely silent. The mental twists and turns, "second thoughts" and more, especially around Medea's struggles over killing her children (1018–80) are "unepic" in the sense that epic portrays even indecision much more smoothly than Euripides does.[12]

The rendering of stock epic speeches with a tendentious twist in both content and form is another of Euripides' methods of attacking epic language and values. Pucci points out, however, that Euripides' attacks also call attention to the power of epic—he attacks the epic tradition but invokes it simultaneously or alternately. He thereby calls attention to contradictions within the epic system and strains among epic values.

The attacks on the value of epic and on epic values, insofar as they are articulated by characters in the play, are expressed by women—the nurse and the chorus. A more detailed examination of the complex and tortured relationship between men and women in the play is needed to further our understanding of the role of epic-heroic poetry therein.

THE WAR BETWEEN THE SEXES

Male–female relationships are not merely deeply problematic and troubled in *Medea*. There is an intense physicality to the portrayal of the problems between the sexes, but it is a negative physicality—there is hardly any touching.[13] Early on, the nurse refers to the *former* closeness between Medea and Jason, their former clasping of hands in exchange of vows (21; 496). Bemoaning how much Medea has done to help Jason, she proclaims that a wife "not standing apart" [*me dixostatei*] from her husband is the greatest good—indeed, the greatest salvation (15). But Medea and Jason *are* standing apart, and the Greek word used describes, for instance, the separation of oil and vinegar.[14] Jason and Medea never touch—even in the faked reconciliation scene, where Medea summons her children to witness

12. Cf. Odysseus' indecision in the opening scene of *Odyssey* 20. Though he cannot sleep, tosses and turns, and is compared to a sputtering sausage being cooked, the net effect of the narrative is to sooth, compose, and to allow a transition from wakefulness to sleep. See Pucci (1980, pp. 92–93) for the contrast between heroic moments of choosing and Medea's. See also Segal (1986, esp. pp. 212–15) for a complementary view of the nature of epic and tragic narrative from the perspective of the creative tension between oral and literary habits.

13. See Segal, 1985, for general comments on corporeality in Greek tragedy, as well as particular observations about *Medea*.

14. That example of nonmiscibility is also used in Aeschylus' *Agamemnon* by Clytemnestra to describe how the vanquished and vanquishers do not mix—literally, their cries do not mix (322–23). There is no notion here of the complementarity of oil and vinegar, how together they enhance and augment each other.

that she and Jason are friendly once again, she urges the children to take their father's hand, but she herself does not do so. In the closing tableau of the play, they are enormously far apart, she above him in her chariot, untouchable and unreachable. Medea clings to Creon's hand, imploring him to let her stay another day in Corinth (339). Creon calls her clinging violent, and later she tells the chorus that she would never have touched him if she hadn't needed him for her murderous plan (370). Medea clasps, kisses, and embraces her sons. She speaks of the "sweet embrace" and of their lovely skin and breath, but this is prior to murdering them (1074–75). Medea implores Aegeus by his beard and grasps his knees as a suppliant (709–10), but though he grants her request for an oath of sanctuary, he does not appear to touch her and, in political terms, takes some pains to distance himself from her. The nurse and the tutor do not touch each other, nor do Jason and his bride-to-be, Glauke. Creon and Glauke, father and daughter, touch each other only in the hideous scene in which both are burned and flayed alive by the poisonous garments sent by Medea. The only other physical contact in the play is that of servants reaching out to touch the children after it seems that Glauke has received their gifts and accepted them. In the end, of course, Jason pleads to be allowed to embrace or kiss his slain sons, and Medea taunts him with her refusal.

Scattered throughout is the language of skin and skin contact—not just in the scene where Glauke and Creon are burned. At 158 the chorus advises Medea, "Don't scratch"—that is, she ought not to get so exercised about her husband's infidelity. Medea's curse on Jason a few lines later includes the image of his house and his bride being "scraped away". Jason reproaches Medea for letting a matter of infidelity to the marital bed "chafe" her so much (568); the same verb appears at 555. Medea describes her toils with her children as now in vain, since they will be killed. I toiled and I was "carded" with pains, she says: metaphorically tortured and literally carded as wool is carded with a sharp comb (l. 1030, Euripides 1938, ad loc.). In short, the words of touching and of skin contact describe discomfort, pain, even torture.

The main form of contact between men and women in this play is verbal, in both the extended interchanges and especially in the alternating-line interchanges (stichomythia) between Medea and Creon, Medea and Jason, and Medea and Aegeus. I return later to detailed examination of these passages, in particular the encounter between Aegeus and Medea, the longest of these stichomythia. But the quality of the contact that is primarily conveyed in these exchanges is "don't touch me," "you can't reach me"—there is a sense almost of physical revulsion (e.g., 1393 uses *mus-aros*, abominable).

More than any other play surviving from antiquity, *Medea* details the battle between men and women and argues the rotten lot of women in the world. Medea's famous speech to the "women of Corinth" conveys what a woman faces in a world ruled by men:[15]

Of all things which are living and can form a judgment
We women are the most unfortunate creatures.
Firstly, with an excess of wealth it is required
For us to buy a husband and take for our bodies
A master; for not to take one is even worse.
And now the question is serious whether we take
A good or bad one; for there is no easy escape
For a woman, nor can she say no to her marriage.
She arrives among new modes of behavior and manners,
And needs prophetic power, unless she has learned at home,
How best to manage him who shares the bed with her.
And if we work out all this well and carefully,
And the husband lives with us and lightly bears his yoke,
Then life is enviable. If not, I'd rather die.
A man, when he's tired of the company in his home,
Goes out of the house and puts an end to his boredom
And turns to a friend or companion of his own age.
But we are forced to keep our eyes on one alone.
What they say of us is that we have a peaceful time
Living at home, while they do the fighting in war.
How wrong they are! I would very much rather stand
Three times in the front of battle than bear one child.   (230–51)

Domination by husband and husband's family, the need to be an object of purchase and sale, the lopsidedness of the relationship with the husband, the dangers of birth—all this is vividly and cogently portrayed. The tenor of the speech is deliberately (speaking from the perspective of the character, Medea) rational. It is carefully crafted with well-wrought rhetoric and presented in iambic trimeter, the meter of speech, rather than in one of the more emotional choral meters. Medea's speeches until this point have been wracked with emotion. Thus the form of this speech is designed to refute one of the calumnies of men (and women) against women: namely, that women are too emotional, not rational enough. Medea characterizes women (to use a literal translation): "of all creatures who are endowed with psyche and have intellect, we women are the most wretched genus." She

15. See Knox (1977) for a discussion of male–female relationships in this play and for comments on a lost play of Sophocles, *Tereus*, which contained a similar speech, also made by a woman who kills her own son.

alludes to biology—women as living beings—but also invokes a mental term, *gnomē*, judgment or intellect. She further comments on the uses to which woman must put her intelligence, her skills—she must become a kind of practical prophet who can read the omens and foretell the moods of her masters.[16] Overall in the play woman is portrayed as passionate, irrational, and not easily subject to rules of reason and logic, and this speech gives some hints about why women may not appear so logical: their intelligence is needed for sheer survival.

Woman is portrayed, in Medea's speeches and in the words of the chorus (and in Jason's speeches as well), as inordinately sensitive or as placing too high a value on the marriage bed. Women, in one of the few things that men and women agree upon in this play, take betrayal of that bed very seriously, indeed, grimly. Further, it is assumed, especially in Medea's speeches, that woman's vengefulness is extreme. Arguing with herself whether to proceed with her evil plans, she says, "And besides, I was born a woman, and women while most unmechanical at doing noble [aristocratic] deeds are the most skilled craftsmen of every evil [base-born] deed" (407–09).

My translation of these lines is skewed to emphasize the contrast between male and female in terms both of noble versus base-born and skilled versus inept. It is as if the retort of the injured woman to the assumption of her inferiority and ineptness is to become diabolically and excellently skilled at revenge. At the same time, we see women objecting to men's projecting onto them what are actually undesirable *male* traits, especially unfaithfulness (422).

While *Medea* conveys a richly textured sense of the difficult situation of women, of a kind of enslavement and oppression, Medea the woman actualizes men's fears that women may be quite dangerous and annihilative. The play, in contrast to a political tract whether for or against the rights of women, depicts the mutual entrapment of men and women and the limited and unsatisfactory escape routes available. What makes the play a tragedy is that none of the solutions really allows men and women to live together in harmony and to beget and cherish children. There are two main lines of resolution. First is identification with the aggressor—that is, the woman becomes more like the oppressing male hero. Second is that of separation or segregation of the sexes, each being removed from its dependency on the other.

The section of Medea's "Women of Corinth" speech detailing the posi-

16. See the speech of the nurse in Aeschylus' *Libation-Bearers*, who uses similar language in describing the need to be a prophet to predict when the baby will poop (758).

tion of woman as subservient in spirit and body—indeed, as selling and risking her body—ends with an ironic anticipation of Medea's resolution of the male–female emnity. She argues here that the woman in labor is a braver warrior than the man with shield and spear (248–51), an image that anticipates her becoming, in her own language and imagery, the female equivalent of an epic hero. She not only argues here that childbirth is more dangerous and takes more courage than battle, she will show that child-murder is the most daring of all. To murder her own sons, she commands her heart to "armour yourself" (*hoplizou* = be like a hoplite; 1242). She takes up the sword and exhorts herself, as a warrior-athlete, to proceed to the starting rope of the race course (1245).

She will do heroic deeds such as might make a father proud of a child, especially a daughter who acts with manlike courage. She is of the lineage of Helios and will act to exemplify the dignity and nobility of her lineage. (She bypasses mentioning her father, whom she had betrayed for Jason, and focuses on her grandfather, Helios.) Her behavior is glossed by the boast of another woman warrior, Agave, in the last of Euripides' plays, *The Bacchae*. After having dismembered her own son, whom she delusionally mistakes for a lion, she calls to her father and to her son (whose head she now carries) to praise her for her hunting skills. She taunts the men of Thebes, who with their arms and armor could not do what she, a woman, has done with her bare hands (1165–1258). Medea, like Agave, does terrible things to her own children, though unlike Agave she is not portrayed as insane or deluded. Both women perform their hideous deeds in a setting of protest against male domination.

The sense of Medea's becoming a warrior comes primarily from Medea herself. As Pucci (1980) points out, she imitates, she mimics, epic heroic speeches; she articulates in various forms the epic value of not letting your enemies gloat over their victories, of not being mocked by an adversary. Jason, on the other hand, does not "masculinize" her (in Aeschylus' *Agamemnon*, by contrast, the men ascribe male attributes to Clytemnestra) but rather "monstrifies" her, calling her lioness and Scylla (1342–43). Jason does not grant her the heroic status of a man even in insult.

The transformation of Medea from the aggrieved and victimized one to the murderous avenger is quite skillfully done, because the audience, as well as the chorus, know her history of deceit and bloody deeds. We know that she will murder Creon and his daughter and her own children, but we can watch the unfolding of her decisions about revenge in such a way as to understand why she does what she does. In this sense Medea is an example of Euripides' propensity to show that victims may in turn become victimizers. In contemporary psychoanalytic terms, Euripides demonstrates how the traumatized person moves from this passive position to the active one of traumatizing others. Identification with the aggressor is a perverted form of golden rule—do unto others as others have done unto you.

Psychoanalytic studies of both adults and children suggest that the victim undergoes a process of internalizing the persecutor, and that the pain of experiencing an inner persecutor is part of what turns the former victim into a victimizer.[17] I believe something of this sort is portrayed in Medea's inner debates, particularly the long speech in which she several times wavers about killing her children (1018–80).[18] She addresses her *thumos*— a word difficult to translate, but denoting anger, an angry urge, and also the seat or agency of anger and zeal within the person. Medea pleads with her thumos, which has enormous control over her: "Oh no, don't, o my thumos, do not do these things!" (1056). And, at the end of the debate, she yields:

> I know the evils I am about to do,
> And *thumos* is now master over my better counsels,
> *Thumos*, which is the cause of the greatest evils for men.
>   (1078–80; trans. Pucci 1980)

Elsewhere in the speech, Medea apostrophizes her heart (*kardia*), urging it not to be too soft, to arm itself. In sum, we can observe in this debate internalized representations of the experiences of submission and domination, of dominant male or yielding female, and the resolution of the inner struggle by means of an external enactment of it. She will simultaneously yield to one master, her thumos, and conquer and humiliate her former master, Jason. Her conscience is composed, as it were, of warring parties; she oscillates between victim and victimizer, and the outcome here is a decision to be the victimizer. The only alternative allowed within her scheme, within the scope of her internal regulations, her conscience, is to repeat humiliating submission.

Related to the solution of Medea's becoming a victorious hero, imitating and turning the tables on Jason, is the "solution" at the very end of the play, where a *deus* provides a *machina* in which Medea can escape to Athens. As many critics and readers have pointed out, Medea here becomes immortal or like an immortal.[19] As such she is beyond the reach of ordinary

---

17. See especially Fraiberg, Adelson, and Shapiro (1980); also, Beckett, Robinson, and David (1956).

18. See Pucci (1980, pp. 138–41), who alerted me to the master–slave language of this inner debate, as well as to the nuances of the shifting nature of Medea's inner splits.

19. See Schlesinger (1983) for insights into the significance of Medea's transformation. He points out that the modern playwright Jean Anouilh has Medea commit suicide. Another modern *Medea* story is Puccini's *Madame Butterfly*, whose variation on the theme of

mortals and the ordinary rules of mortals. She has done what the warrior-heroes strive for but cannot accomplish—she has become like a god, immortal. From metaphorically inhuman she has become (in the eyes of the chorus and of Jason), literally nonhuman. Her transformation to quasi-divine status is the ratification of her suicide as a human and as a mother. This is the final paradox of the simultaneous fulfillment and destruction of the epic-heroic ideal—Medea is heroicized, she and her sons worshiped, while Jason is devastated; Medea is no longer human, her sons are dead and the house and the lineage are destroyed.

The second unsatisfactory resolution in *Medea* is that of the wished-for separation of the sexes, an undoing of the natural interdependency of male and female. The most blatant example of this wish is Jason's expression of how much better it would be if men could beget children without women (a typical Euripidean wish):

There should have been another way for mortals
To beget children, and not have to have the female race.
Then there would have been no such evil for mankind.   (573–75)[20]

The sentiment is as blunt as the motive—we men could really have it all, wealth, power, and children too, if we didn't need women. Behind this is the more subtle fear of male dependency on women, the dependency of the boy on the mother, and the need of the adult man to prop up his own masculine vulnerabilities by having a wife who will bear sons.[21] Incidentally, Jason

---

seduction and abandonment also has the woman commit suicide, in effect, to avoid murdering the child. In Goethe's *Faust*, Marguerite kills her infant and goes insane. In actual clinical and legal practice, there are many combinations and permutations of mothers' enactment of murderous rage toward children—infanticide and filicide, child abuse, maternal psychosis or extreme depression, maternal suicide, and occasionally murder of the betraying husband. Many cases of severe postpartum depressions and other psychoses involve massive emergency defenses against killing the child. The dynamics between the new mother and her own mother are also critical—note that Medea is like a woman without a mother. From one perspective, the play could be seen as a dream or a fantasy of a woman struggling with murderous impulses toward her husband and children and feeling utterly deprived of any mothering herself.

20. Translation mine. Jason not only envisions the deletion of women but uses the generic term *anthropos* (humankind) to designate this world of only men (Euripides 1969, ad loc.) Cf. Euripides' *Hippolytus* 616–23 for a similar wish, couched much more blatantly in commercial terms than is the antiwoman sentiment in *Medea*. The word for "beget" in this passage allows for some ambiguity in that it can be used in the active voice to mean male begetting or in the middle voice for either female begetting or (as here) to mean "being born to" or being furnished with children (Liddell, Scott, and Jones, *Greek-English Lexicon*). The words in *Hippolytus* more clearly designate male begetting (*speirai, sperma*).

21. Slater's *The Glory of Hera* (1963) is still the best presentation of this male dread of women and its relation to the theme of mothers killing their sons.

previously hinted at this wish by asserting to Medea that she shouldn't mind if he keeps the boys, since she has no need of children! (565). If mothers don't need their sons, then perhaps sons don't need their mothers.

Women's wishes for separation from men are more subtly represented in the play. I believe, following Pucci's (1980) analysis and translation, that the choral ode praising Athens encodes such a wish (824–50). Medea has just extracted an oath from Aegeus to give her sanctuary in Athens, and she is clearly planning to kill her sons. The chorus asks how Medea can expect to be welcomed in such a lovely and holy land with kindred blood on her hands:

> The Erechtheans [Athenians], happy from the olden time and children of the blessed gods from the holy and unravaged land, are fed by the most famous Sophia and walk always through shining air, elegantly here where once the nine chaste Pierian Muses—they say—produced blonde Harmonia. On the Kephisos' fair streams—they tell—Cypris draws water and blows upon the country smooth breezes, sweet-scented, a perfumed wreath of roses on her hair: Erotes escort Sophia, the helpers of all sorts of excellence.   (824–45; trans. Pucci 1980)

Pucci's interpretation leads to a literal translation with a tone and import different from other standard translations. Rex Warner's translation subtly introduces male words—"sons of the blessed gods" where the Greek has "children"; or "helpers of men" (845) where "men" does not appear in the Greek at all. Interpreters have generally also emphasized that the hymn alludes to Athens as the seat of philosophy and the home of the Sophists when it speaks of "the most famous Sophia." I believe the tone is quite different, even opposed to that view. The clue is that two "peculiar" births are alluded to in this ode. The first is the Athenians' being called the children of Erechtheus, the mythical founding king of Athens (here perhaps deliberately confused with Erichthonius, the earth-born child of Athene and Mephaestus, who was earth-born, as are the Athenians. The second is unambiguously female—the nine (female) Muses begot the woman Harmonia. (The text, however, is ambiguous on whether the Muses begot Harmonia or Harmonia the Muses.) Athens is here the place of unusual births that give more prominence to the role of women and less to men. The ode conveys virginity—the Muses are chaste and the land is unravaged, never sacked. Further, the atmosphere of the ode is very much like that of Sappho's poems—a female ambience, perfumed, airy; Cypris is the goddess more of flowers and fragrance than of maddening, conquering lust. Compare the figure of Cypris here with that of Aphrodite, whom Jason invokes as the cause of Medea's betraying her family and running away with him (527). Whatever is meant by Sophia here and elsewhere in Euripides—it is an important term for him—it does not evoke the picture of Protagoras or Anaxagoras or Parmenides, let alone Socrates. It is rather a blurred, coenesthetic atmosphere—touch, fragrance, graceful movement, visual beauty—of parthenogenesis.[22] The chorus, expressing horrified astonishment that the child-killer Medea could arrive at such a holy and beautiful place, indirectly appeal to her to allow them to maintain the fantasy that such an unsullied and harmonious female world of grace, pleasure, and unisexual begetting can exist.

Another "fantasy" attempt to resolve intractable hatred between the genders occurs in the scene of cooperation between Aegeus and Medea (662–763). At the literal level, there is a coming together; the man understands the woman; the woman appreciates the man's need for offspring; and there is agreement between the two. Aegeus offers sanctuary—if Medea can provide transportation and pay her own carfare—and Medea offers to help him and his wife have an heir. Both the form and the content of this exchange are significant. Recall that Aegeus is on his way back from Delphi, where he has consulted the oracle about his childlessness and has received a cryptic reply. He has gone "searching out how the *sperma* of children might be born to me" (669). Medea establishes that he has a wife, and, as I read the text, that they have had intercourse.[23] The oracle given to Aegeus, which has elicited much commentary from antiquity on, is, "I should not loosen the hanging foot of the wineskin. . . . before I again reach the hearth of my fatherland." The oracle was understood by the audience, and presumably Medea, but only dimly by Aegeus, to mean that he was to refrain from intercourse until he had returned to his wife in Athens. In the context of the play, there is a paradoxical effect. On the one hand, the oracle enjoins the man to be faithful to his wife—a striking

22. Compare this with a wish-fulfilling "escape ode" in Euripides' *Hippolytus* (staged only a few years after *Medea*)—the second stasimon, especially 732–51. It comes at a point when there is a need to escape from the terrible effects of male–female relationships. There the blissful imagery is also heavily female—the garden of the Hesperides, of maidens—but male elements and marriage intrude more. The "escape" is less successful, because anxiety, mourning, and conflict remain on the surface of the ode.

23. She asks the first and basic question in an evaluation of an infertile couple. Medea asks if he, singular, is childless (670). He replies that *we* are childless (671)—a bit equivocal, since it could be a "royal we," but it still conveys that he has a woman, probably a wife. She then asks, "Is there a wife, or are you untried in the marriage bed?" (672)—not a naive question in the world of Greek myth when it comes to problems of begetting. In the Oedipus legends, Laius and Jocasta refrained from intercourse lest the oracle of begetting a patricide and mother-marrier be fulfilled. Aegeus, in his complementary inquiry about Medea's relations with Jason, tactfully asks if she and Jason are still sleeping together—or so I read the innuendo of 697.

contrast with Jason—but on the other, it alludes to a myth of husbandly infidelity. The drift of the myth is that Aegeus in fact did sleep with another woman on his way home, and the offspring of that intercourse was Theseus, the prototypical Athenian king and hero (as well as a notorious womanizer). Thus, the oracular saying conveys faithfulness and duplicity at the same time, which is consonant with what Medea is doing, making a faithful bond with Aegeus and deceiving him at the same time.

Medea first persuades him to share the oracle, and Aegeus grabs the bait because he knows of Medea's cleverness. Medea at first does not promise him anything, but after she has told him her story of Jason's infidelity and has seen Aegeus' outrage, she strikes the deal for sanctuary, saying, "Receive me in your land at your own hearth. Thus your *eros*, with the help of the gods, will be one of fulfillment, of the begetting of children, and you shall die a happy man. You don't know what a find you have here. I shall put an end to your childlessness, and I shall make you able to sow the seeds of children. Such are the drugs I know" (713–18; translation mine).

After Medea has extracted a sacred oath from Aegeus to receive her as a refugee, he departs and the chorus wishes him well and hopes that his wishes will be fulfilled, for he is a *gennaios* man. This word, formed from *gen*, has been translated here variously as noble (well-born), high-minded, and generous. The chorus is clearly praising him for qualities that are a mix of these various shades of meaning, but the root of "born" and "generative" words here also points to a prediction that he is a man who can generate. This is another ambiguous point, for he is in fact childless; Medea's offer is a dupe; and yet in myth, as the audience knows, he will have a child.

Another way of looking at this scene is from the perspective of the unconscious fantasy meaning of "to rescue," particularly a man's rescuing a woman in distress. As Freud (1910) pointed out, to rescue a woman can mean to give her a baby. Thus, at another unconscious level, Aegeus' rescuing Medea (as she promises to rescue him) is equivalent to their having a baby together. In some later mythic versions, Medea and Aegeus have a baby together, named Medeus.

What can be concluded from the content of this scene, then, is that Medea and Aegeus will cooperate to make a baby. But, as in certain modern plays, such as *Who's Afraid of Virginia Woolf?*, there is doubt and ambiguity about whether there really is or will be a baby. The baby they make together is a promise of a baby—a false promise—but somehow there will also ensue a real baby—a baby that has nothing to do with the pact between Medea and Aegeus.

The form of the scene confirms this view and shows Medea and Aegeus on stage having a kind of intercourse that does not take place elsewhere in the play. The contact between them is marked by the longest stichomythia in the play, and it is an exchange in which they cooperate and come to understand each other's needs. The other scenes of stichomythia—between Medea and Creon (324–39) and between Medea and Jason (605–09 and 1361–77)—involve much more anger and hatred. The last is the polar opposite of the interchange between Medea and Aegeus, for it concerns the killing of their children and the bitter exchange of recrimination. Yet Medea deceives Aegeus, thus the one piece of cooperative fructifying interchange in the play is in part a sham. Thus for the main portrayal of "successful" male–female relations within the play.

There is one other kind of attempt to deal with otherwise intractable problems in male–female relationships: the paranoid solution, projecting the evil onto an outsider. The "outsider" is, of course, Medea, the foreigner, the barbarian. The chorus, as noted above, is horrified by Medea's filicide and claims that Greek women hardly ever commit this kind of crime.[24]

Several critics have noted that the chorus ignores numerous such instances in Greek mythology, a number of them, such as Procne and Agave, the subject of subsequent plays by Euripides.[25] The thrust of this defensive denial is that Medea is a barbarian, not a Greek woman, a point made throughout the play, but mostly in Jason's final denunciation:

> For the sake of pleasure in the bed you killed them.
> There is no Greek woman who would have dared such deeds,
> Out of all those whom I passed over and chose you
> To marry instead, a bitter destructive match,
> A monster, not a woman, having a nature
> Wilder than that of Scylla in the Tuscan sea.   (1338–43)

Here is a partial return to the epic solution to hostility within the family, whether between the sexes or between the generations. That solution is

24. See Zeitlin (1985), esp. p. 71 and n. 24. Zeitlin argues cogently that Greek tragedy typically uses woman as "the other" or the "outsider," suitable for representing impulses and behaviors unacceptable to men.

25. E.g., Page (Euripides 1938), ad loc. It is hard to know how to read Page's comments (p. xxi) on the significance of Medea's being an Oriental woman—does he *approve* of the view that only a barbarian would do such deeds? That is, does Page reveal his own class-bound, colonial view of male–female and imperial–colonial relationships? See Vellacott (1975, pp. 19–20), who discusses the scotomata of generations of classical scholars living in almost monastic settings, beneficiaries of class and imperial privilege. Page clearly does not believe that the Medea story has any connection with life as we know it. In his world, it also hardly ever happens. One classical scholar, Easterling (1977), took the trouble to consult criminal statistics and document that murder of children by parents is, tragically, not a rare event.

joining to fight the outsider, the foreigner, or the member of another clan. Thus woman as woman is not here denounced as evil and destructive—it is rather a *foreign* woman who is the enemy. The defensive maneuver within the play can be tracked by looking at the word *miaiphone* (bloody-murderer, 1346).[26] "Go to hell, you who have done such shameless deeds, bloody-murderer of your own children," shouts Jason at Medea the barbarian. The same word, in the comparative, is used earlier by Medea to describe women in general. She says that woman is "full of fears and cowardly when she sees battle and steel. But when it happens that she is wronged in regard to the marriage bed, there is no other sentient creature who is more murderous" (263–66). The contrast between Medea's global characterization of women sexually wronged and Jason's characterization as relevant mainly to a foreign woman not only shows up the differences in temperament and position of the two protagonists but suggests the instability of the solution of projection. It also points to a fundamental technique of Euripides. Medea is dangerous both because she is a woman wronged in love and because she is a barbarian woman who overvalues love and sex. Both positions are "true"—that is, both are represented within the play, and the audience can simultaneously experience both. The more general view of woman wronged teaches us something about the human predicament, while the defense "only barbarian women do this" allows us to tolerate what might otherwise be too much to bear—a mother murdering her own children.

CHILDREN AND CHECKERS IN *MEDEA*

A famous painting of the story of Medea and her children, found at Pompeii, shows the two boys playing a game, tossing knuckle-bones or "draughts," a well-known game of antiquity. Their tutor stands at the left and behind them, watching them, while their mother stands to the right, dagger drawn, the largest figure in the painting.[27] In *Medea* it is "at the place where the old men who play draughts gather" that the old slave in charge of the boys hears the terrible news that Creon intends to send Medea and her children into exile (67–72). These two associations of the children with game counters or checkers help articulate a sense in the play that the

26. Page (Euripides 1938, ad loc.) points out that this line verged on offending ancient sensibilities about what is proper and improper stage language. Euripides was often accused, both in his own day and after his death, of going beyond the bounds of acceptable sentiment and language.

27. Reproduced on the front cover of Elliot's edition of *Medea* (Euripides 1969).

children are being used as pieces in a power game. They are valuable pieces, not to be sacrificed lightly, but nevertheless, at the right moment, for the right amount of gain, they are available to be sacrificed.

At the same time, *Medea* as well as Euripides' other plays show us much about the emotional importance of children and the powerful bonds between children and parents. By highlighting the use of children as counters in deadly adult games, the playwright brings home the depth and the risks of such attachments. Euripides accomplishes this not only by providing a tale of how a mother can come to kill her children, but also by showing how parents can come to feel "better they should not have been born." Children are killed twice in the play, once offstage by Medea and once before they were born or even conceived. The counterpart of the fantasies of one gender bearing children without the other is that each expresses the wish never to have had children. Jason, denouncing Medea as a disgusting, leonine monster and child-killer, says, "I wish I had never begot them to see them / Afterward slaughtered by you" (1413–14).[28] As for the women, the chorus sings its plaintive ode that the childless are most fortunate:

> This I say, that those who have never
> Had children, who know nothing of it,
> In happiness have the advantage
> Over those who are parents.   (1090–93)

This is an astonishing declaration from women, whose lives are so dedicated to and entwined with the bearing and rearing of children. It is both an abdication of a major source of power in the struggle between men and women and at the same time a crystallization of another possibility in the struggle—to refuse children. It is the acknowledgment that having children, which is a major factor in how women can justify and accept their position vis-à-vis men, is just not worth it. At the same time, as Vellacott points out (1975, p. 107), the task of women from the point of view of the polis is to bear children who will bear the shield—Medea's equation of childbirth and battle. This function can be carried out only if there is some love and fidelity between husband and wife; if those virtues disappear, women might come to the conclusion that it is not worth bearing children. This is the death of the city, a more certain death than enemy conquest.

---

28. The lioness (*leainēs*) as monster image (1407) is prefigured by the use of the same word at 187 to describe how Medea is as ferocious as a lioness guarding her new-born cubs. Euripides uses the same word to show the psychological transformation between woman's ferocity as guardian (a female perception) and her ferocity as killer of the offspring (the male perception).

But other parts of the ode, as well as some of Medea's speeches, indicate more specifically what children mean emotionally to women and name the anxieties that go along with the deep attachment:

> The childless, who never discover
> Whether children turn out as a good thing
> Or as something to cause pain, are spared
> Many troubles in lacking this knowledge.
> And those who have in their homes
> The sweet presence of children, I see that their lives
> Are all wasted away by their worries.
> First they must think how to bring them up well and
> How to leave them something to live on.
> And then after this whether all their toil
> Is for those who will turn out good or bad,
> Is still an unanswered question.
> And of one more trouble, the last of all,
> That is common to mortals I tell.
> For suppose you have found them enough for their living,
> Suppose that the children have grown into youth
> And have turned out good, still, if God so wills it,
> Death will away with your children's bodies,
> And carry them off into Hades.
> What is our profit, then, that for the sake of
> Children the gods should pile upon mortals
> After all else
> The most terrible grief of all?   (1094–1115)

Disappointment after having invested so much, cared so much, toiled so much—this is the nub of the plaintive rejection of childbearing.

Medea's feelings about children, about her children, are scattered throughout the play, but the most affirmative, and therefore most painful, view comes in her address to her children just after the deceptive truce between her and Jason has been arranged and the children have returned from bringing the poisonous gifts to Glauke, their father's bride. She has thus used them in the most callous way as instruments of her own revenge, not as human beings in their own right. She prepares them for her exile and mourns losing them, though she has already decided to murder them. She has just hinted to the children's tutor that she will kill them, but only the audience understands. The tutor fails to grasp her intent, and we are left uncertain whether the children apprehend the threat.

In this long speech (1022–80), while addressing the children, Medea continues to argue with herself about whether to kill them. It is important that this speech, which expresses most tenderly what children can mean to parents, ends with Medea's announcement that she knows what she is doing but that her *thumos*, her rage, prevails, and she will kill them. She addresses them:

O children, O my children, you have a city,
You have a home, and you can leave me behind you,
And without your mother you may live there forever.
But I am going in exile to another land
Before I have seen you happy and taken pleasure in you,
Before I have dressed your brides and made your marriage beds
And held up the torch at the ceremony of wedding.
Oh, what a wretch I am in this my self-willed thought!
What was the purpose, children, for which I reared you?
For all my travail and wearing myself away?
They were sterile, those pains I had in the bearing of you.
Oh surely once the hopes in you I had, poor me,
Were high ones: you would look after me in old age,
And when I died would deck me well with your own hands;
A thing which all would have done. Oh, but now it is gone,
The lovely thought. For, once I am left without you,
Sad will be the life I'll lead and sorrowful for me.
And you will never see your mother again with
Your dear eyes, gone to another mode of living.
Why, children, do you look upon me with your eyes?
Why do you smile so sweetly that last smile of all?   (1022–39)

This passage can be and has been read to signify something of the tenderness that Medea feels, even with all her ambivalence toward her children, and/or the extent to which she views the children as creatures existing for her gratification. My own reading of this passage is that it conveys both—in fact, it conveys the easy slippage between the two. Taken by themselves, Medea's wishes to be at her sons' weddings and to be buried with proper love and respect by them are appropriate parental expectations. At a particular life stage, adolescence, all of us can easily view such wishes as selfishness, spoken from the perspective of parental needs and not address-ing the autonomy of the child. But overall, what is striking in this speech is how the tenderness she feels so easily slides into an intention to use the children for revenge and for protection of her own self-esteem. I believe that her statement that she will kill the children rather than "suffer my children / To be the prey of my enemies' insolence" (1060–61) is not only a rationalization of using them for revenge but is also sincere. The sincerity, however, rests upon a confusion of boundaries between her and the children—it is her pride and her children, and her children as her pride, that shall not suffer insolence at the hands of others.[29]

Medea has no doubt about the importance and value of children, and she responds angrily to Jason's cynical description of them as almost purely instrumental (which matches his view of intimate relationships). Jason explains his motives for marrying the king's daughter, disclaiming that he merely grew tired of Medea:

> Nor with any wish to outdo your number of children.
> We have enough already. I am quite content.
> But—this was the main reason—that we might live well,
> And not be short of anything. I know that all
> A man's friends leave him stone-cold if he becomes poor.
> Also that I might bring my children up worthily
> Of my position, and, by producing more of them
> To be brothers of yours, we would draw the families
> Together and be happy. *You need no children.*
> And it pays me to do good to those I have now
> By having others. Do you think this is a bad plan?
> You wouldn't if the love question hadn't upset you. [literally: if the bed didn't
>   chafe you so much]   (556–75; emphasis mine)

The speech concludes with Jason's cry of how much better it would be if men could have children without women!

The differences in what children mean to women and what they mean to men is an important issue in *Medea*, but part of its dramatic unfolding is the gradual exposition of what those differences are. For example, it is not clear early in the play that Jason wants his sons to remain with him; the option seems open for Medea to take them with her into exile. By the end of the play, he desperately wants them, even dead. Schlesinger (1966) points out how Medea's decision to kill her sons for revenge develops alongside her realization of how important an asset (as it were) children are to fathers. The more valuable, the greater the revenge. The scene with Aegeus, in Schlesinger's argument, is pivotal for crystallizing in Medea's mind how much a man is willing to give for children. Her plan for revenge is better than killing Jason himself—it is killing his chance for the immortality that comes through children. Jason wails at the end of the play that, with his bride-to-be and his sons dead, he is utterly desolate and, worse, seething with rage he cannot discharge. The punishment fits the crime with diabolical specificity—if you, Jason, view the people in your life as pawns,

---

29. Most mothers who have lost a child, including mothers who may have killed their children, harbor fantasies of a reunion with the dead child.

checkers, and commercial assets, the punishment is to deprive you of your pieces and of the possibility of getting new pieces. Only when you have lost all do you realize how much they meant to you.

At the end, what do the children mean to Jason? He yearns to kiss them and touch them, but there is nothing in his speeches of a lament for the lives not lived, for the hopes not fulfilled, for the now-unattainable moments of tenderness and exchange at their marriage and at his death. Medea's anticipatory mourning for the children she is about to kill reveals a more intimate and affectionate bond than does Jason's final pleading to be allowed to touch them. But worst of all, of course, is the competition between husband and wife about who cares more for the children, the lethal competition expressed in the interchange between them:

> Jason: Oh, I hate you, murderess of children.
> Medea: Go to your house and bury your bride.
> Jason: I go, without my share of two children.
> Medea: You don't know yet what it is to grieve. Wait till you are old. [i.e., and lonely without children]
> Jason: Oh my most beloved children!
> Medea: Most beloved to their mother, not to you.
> Jason: And still you killed them?
> Medea: To hurt you.   (1393–98)[30]

The form of the dialogue, even more clearly in the Greek, is one of entwining and interweaving, not just an exchange of lines.[31] It is as if the two are entwined in some murderous wrestling match, not entwined as husband and wife in procreative sex or in complementary efforts on behalf of children.

And what about the children, what do they have to say in all this? While in general Greek tragedy does not give children much of a voice—the onstage lines spoken by Alcestis' son (*Alcestis,* 393–415) are exceptional—the silence of the children in *Medea* is all the more striking because of the few off-stage lines they are given. The boys say nothing in the several scenes where they appear, not to Jason, their tutor, or the nurse; nor are they quoted as saying anything to Glauke when they deliver the poisonous gifts. (Medea charges them to plead with Glauke as she gives them the gifts.) But they are heard from offstage, pleading with the gods in terror, trying to

30. Translation mine. At 1394, *oikous* = house, palace, but also the metaphorical house of Jason, which is now in ruins.

31. In the Greek text, 1398, Medea's last word is elided to the first word of Jason's next line—*pemainous'. / omoi*—as if to be spoken by one person.

escape Medea's murdering sword (1271–78). Their silence in the rest of the play is thus ended by their screams. Moreover, they do not directly address or plead with their mother. Thus, they are given no voice with their parents and act as if they can in no way address or influence them. They are parentless children even before they are murdered.

What is it that Medea kills in murdering her children? What does the play *Medea* teach us about the value of children? Clearly Medea is murdering whatever it was in her that fell in love with Jason and that wanted to bear his children. She is murdering herself as a caring woman and as a caring mother. Her transformation into some kind of deity or "hero" and the transformation of her children, now dead, into an aspect of ritual worship constitute the destruction of the basic human relationships between mother and child and between man and woman.

The playwright depicts for us the intensity, but also the fragility, of Medea's maternal attachments and yearnings. An important detail about her, a significant absence, is the lack of any mention of her own mother. Nor are the wife of Creon or the mother of Glauke mentioned, let alone named. The two principal women are motherless. In fact, even in antecedent and subsequent versions of the tale of Medea, her mother is scarcely mentioned.[32] It as if the woman who can finally murder her own children must be depicted as motherless—a detail tragically in keeping with clinical experience in many cases of child abuse and murder.

Why is there a need to murder these feelings, to destroy love and caring? Euripidean drama in general speaks to the deep anxieties, indeed the dangers, that attend upon too close an involvement of the self with the other.[33] In *Medea* that danger is expressed in the choral ode about the pain of bearing and rearing children (1090–1115)—what profit is there in it if there is so much worry at every stage, and then, worst of all, the danger that one might lose these precious children? This sentiment is generalized and amplified in Euripides' *Hippolytus*, an early version of which may have been contemporaneous with *Medea*. (The version we have was staged a few years after *Medea*.) The nurse, seeing Phaedra's sickness but only dimly understanding that it is love-sickness, proclaims:

> It is necessary that the mixture of affections that we mortals have in our common mixing bowl be kept in modest proportion and not let these affections reach the deepest parts of our marrow; but rather the ties of love must be loosable bonds that can be slackened or tightened. And that one soul must bear the labor pains

32. Idyaia, or Eidyia; the former is in Hesiod, *Theogony*, 961–62, and the latter in *Argonautica*, 3.243, 269. Her name means "knowing" or "skilled" and is related to one possible etymology of *Medea* as meaning "cunning."

33. See in particular Pucci (1980, pp. 146, 224–25 and n. 21) for discussion of this theme in Euripides.

for two is a difficult burden, as witnessed by the way I suffer so much on behalf of her [Phaedra]. (253–60; my translation)

Strong love—the word *philtata* from the root *phil-* connotes blood ties and obligations as well as the affectionate feelings that may accompany them—is like undiluted wine in the bowl. We must always add enough water to prevent intoxication. Deep involvement leads to deep disappointment, anger, and frustration when the beloved one cannot or will not fulfill one's expectations, and from there it leads to the problems of conflict, jealousy, and the attendant desires for revenge. In a later play, the theme is again expressed in relation to childbearing—*The Suppliant Women* repeats the lament about how painful it is to have and to lose children—perhaps those without are after all much better off.[34]

Another index of the extent to which Euripides conveys the importance of love and deep affiliation, even while showing us the destruction of love bonds, is the frequency of *phil-* words in his work—they appear significantly more frequently than in Aeschylus and Sophocles. In *Medea*, which is so full of hatred of kin, the great frequency of words with this root—about 60 in 1,400 lines—along with the fact that words for children are the most frequent substantives in the text, conveys how crucial and dear are the bonds implied by these terms.

The ambivalence of both Jason and Medea toward their children can also be viewed from the perspective of the theme of sacrifice. In order to enhance his own position and to build a more secure house Jason will marry the king's daughter, hoping to beget more sons to perpetuate his house. Jason is willing to sacrifice Medea and to some degree their children in order to achieve this purpose. Here the term *sacrifice* is metaphorical, as is the term *scapegoat* to describe his view of Medea.[35] If she is driven out, all will be well. Medea's own solution also involves sacrifice in order to restore equilibrium, an equilibrium satisfying to her but devastating to Jason. But throughout Greek antiquity, Medea's slaying of her own children was viewed more literally as an act of ritual sacrifice, as evidenced, for example,

34. The mothers of the slain heroes, the seven who had attacked Thebes, lament the death of their sons and plead for their burial. At 778–837 is the third stasimon, the mothers' lament and wish that they had never been wedded and had never had children—would that their father, father time, had never given them in wedlock. The chorus, late in the play, catalogues the woes of having children. The mothers lament further at 918–24 and 955–88, followed by the scene in which Evadne, the wife of Capaneus, immolates herself on the pyre with her slain husband. Her father, Iphis, helpless to stop her, describes how much he had wanted children and how he is now bereft (1080–1113). He wishes that he had not come to yearn for children so much that he envies other people's children.

35. The Greek word for scapegoat is *pharmakon*, not used in this play, but the plural *pharmaka*, which means drugs, often poisonous drugs, is of course quite important in *Medea*. It is as if the poisonous drugs are Medea's antidote to being made a scapegoat.

by vase-paintings of Medea sacrificing her children at an altar. Indeed, within the play, Medea speaks of her bloody deed as a sacrifice; those for whom it is not religiously proper to stand at her sacrifice must be sure to leave the scene (1053–55). At the closing, she announces that the children will be buried in Hera's temple at Corinth and that she will establish a sacred annual feast and sacrifice to atone for her blood guilt (1378–83).

From the perspective of the continuity of the house, sacrifice is a two-edged sword. For the act of sacrifice, especially of one's own children, risks the extinction of the line, and at the same time it is proposed as a way of saving the community, the family, and the house. Medea and Jason are each determined to preserve or build a family, even if Medea's solution may appear bizarre and Jason's self-serving. Medea spares her children by killing them, and she bestows upon them a symbolic immortality or at least renewal in the form of the ritual she establishes. Jason envisions not only a new family with the king's daughter but also an extended family that includes his sons with Medea and even Medea herself as some sort of retainer. But the readiness to sacrifice, whether Jason's well-rationalized sacrifice or Medea's painful and tormented decision to kill the children, undoes the house and the propagation of the house.

EURIPIDES' [PRO]CREATIVITY AND AUDIENCE RESPONSE

What can be said, however speculatively, about Euripides' inner creative experience and his relationship to *Medea?* In terms of the images of pro-creation and destruction of children that so pervade the play, what can we say about how Euripides conceived, gestated, labored, and gave birth to the play, and about his relationship to this child?

The modern idea that the creative and procreative processes of the artist might be reflected or discernible within the work itself probably originated in the Romantic era.[36] The rhetoric of the fusion of opposites, copulation, birth, and engendering in relation to Greek tragedy was of course introduced by Nietzsche in *The Birth of Tragedy* (1967). Nietzsche had mixed feelings about Euripides and blamed him, ironically, for the death of tragedy, that creature which had only so recently been born. Currently, in part as a response to work in contemporary literary criticism and in the philosophy of literature—such works as Harold Bloom's *The Anxiety of Influence* (1973) and the writings of Derrida—the problem of the artist's psychic involvement with "parents" and "descendants" has received more atten-

36. See Abrams (1958, pp. 272–85), "Poet as Heterocosm"; and Feinstein (1968).

tion.[37] From a psychoanalytic perspective, the work of Lacan has also called attention to issues of and fantasies about origins, the processes of engendering creative works, and the fantasies about begetting poetic children. Such approaches are difficult enough to substantiate convincingly with regard to modern or living authors, and they are understandably extremely tentative in relation to ancient writers. But the basic working method, common to psychoanalysis and to more current modes of analysis, is to look at fantasy representations of *origins* within the work as evidence of the psychology of the author in relation to his or her own origins and fate.[38]

Let us begin with an image that combines a statement about a playwright's inner life with a statement about audience reaction to his plays. Ibsen is said to have described the writing of his plays by an analogy to a poisonous spider: the plays, like poison in the poison sac of the spider, accumulate inside of him, and if he does not inject them into others, he will die of the poison. I speculate that something of this sort was at work in the construction of *Medea*, and that something similar is at work in audience reaction to the play.[39] Poisoned gifts, and the *pharmaka*, the drugs, that Medea has at her disposal, whether for harm or as promised for fertility to Aegeus, are of great importance within the play. One cannot help but ask whether we, the audience, have been given a play that is like a beautiful gown dipped in lethal drugs.[40] For this is a play that makes us writhe, twitch, and feel uncomfortable. As with many of his plays, Euripides does not let us off the hook easily—and we know we have been put on the hook. The deus ex machina that ends several of his plays (or, as in *Medea*, the "machina ex deo," machine from a god) gets the actors off the stage and sends the audience home but does not clean the irritants out of our system. If Aristotle had known only plays by Euripides, I think he could have made

37. Pucci (1980), in his theories about Euripides and his vision of his poetry, is obviously very much indebted to the work of Derrida. See Derrida (1978) for an example of his approach to paternity and continuity.

38. Ancient biographies of the poets (and this is especially true of Euripides) are short on objective detail and long on invented facts, typically culled from the sorts of things characters said or did in the plays. The result is a series of fantasy biographies—but the method, more judiciously applied, has continued in various forms as we attempt to reconstruct authors' psychology and personal outlook from their works. See Lefkowitz (1981) on the ancient *Vitae*. The little material we do have on Euripides' life and career is found in Collard (1981) and Lesky (1983), with their references.

39. See Pucci (1980) for the most elaborate discussion of this possibility, esp. his chapter "Euripides' Writing as Remedy." My discussion owes a great deal to his and does not supplant it but takes off in a somewhat different direction.

40. See Orgel and Shengold (1968) for an elegant discussion of the narcissistic context of "fatal gifts" with reference both to *Medea* and to several clinical cases.

the notion of irritation as much a part of his definition of tragedy as
catharsis. I have pointed out above the many terms in the play based on
metaphors of skin distress—chafing, itching, scraping. The rhythms of
contact and distance suggested by the text are either disjunctive or lethally
entrapping. The movements conveyed by the messenger's description of
Creon trying to save his tormented daughter are a hideous combination of
excessive closeness and excessive separation:

> And when he had made an end of his wailing and crying,
> Then the old man wished to raise himself to his feet;
> But, as the ivy clings to the twigs of the laurel,
> So he stuck to the fine dress, and he struggled fearfully [literally: terrible was the
>   wrestling].
> For he was trying to lift himself to his knee,
> And she was pulling him down, and when he tugged hard
> He would be ripping his aged flesh from his bones.
> At last his life was quenched, and the unhappy man
> Gave up the ghost, no longer could hold up his head.
> There they lie close, the daughter and the old father,
> The dead bodies, an event he prayed for in his tears.   (1211–21)

These are not comforting rhythms, allowing for closure. Even this narrative description ends with a slightly better sense of closure than does the
play itself, with its emphasis on lack of contact and total disjunction between husband and wife and father and children.[41] The portrayal of character similarly leaves us with no one to admire, no one with whom we can
make a comfortable and sustained identification, let alone a heroic identification.

I conjecture that encoded in this scene is an account of Euripides' inner
state during the creation of the play, or an account of the inner state that
generated the impulse to write the play. Was writing or presenting the play
unconsciously perceived as an act of wrestling or a tearing of the flesh from
the bones? In short, as Euripides "conceived" his play, he saw no way to tell
a story of a mother killing her children, of a father dying a horrible death
struggling to embrace his daughter—no way to tell such a story without
traumatizing the audience and probably himself. *Medea*, in this construction, is a tale caught between the need and desire to tell and the
reticence, indeed horror, of the telling. If its construction is unsatisfactory
from some viewpoints, if plot elements are jerky, intruded without clear
explanation (Aristotle criticized the play in these terms), at least it conveys

---

41. The disjunctive rhythms are also conveyed by the extreme frequency of *my* and *mine*
in the play and the rarity of *us* and *our*. See McDonald (1978).

something of the uneasy compromise that allowed it to see the light of day. I submit that the conception, gestation, labor, and delivery of this play may have been difficult, and that the possibility of killing his own artistic child was always present for Euripides. As Pucci (1980) in particular has argued, the play veers between construction and deconstruction, between rescue (*soteria*) and annihilation—while Medea herself swerves between killing the children and sparing them. As Freud has suggested, and as clinical experience often confirms, to rescue—as Aegeus promises to rescue Medea and as the god Helios provides magical means of rescue—is to give someone a baby.

For the audience and readers, Euripides' gift, the "baby" he has delivered and left on our doorstep, stirs up mixed feelings of gratitude for the experience and irritation at its disturbing content and form. To modify the metaphor a bit further, let me say that the *experience of the play* is generated in the interaction between Euripides' play and the audience. The baby in question, then, is not only what Euripides begot but what is engendered in the intercourse between play and audience. A more elaborate statement of this analogy would, of course, have to speak of interplay among the author, his created characters, his inner world, his artistic traditions and ancestors, the performers, and the audience.

Clearly Euripides struggled with the problem of originality. Contemporary ancient evidence as well as traditions from later antiquity point out that he was considered both creatively and outrageously original, untraditional. Discussions of Euripides' art in modern times have often centered around the problem of his uneasy balance between innovation and tradition. Scholars have demonstrated how he transforms his mythic sources, his relationship to his tragic "predecessors" (who were also his contemporaries—Sophocles, older than Euripides, outlived him and led his funeral procession), and his relationship to rhetoric, the sophistic movement, and the early stirrings of philosophy. I have pointed out ways in which *Medea* uses the epic tradition as a foil, if not as a whipping-boy. To be original implies a unique birth and a unique relationship to one's parents and ancestors and often raises the question of subsequent reproduction—creatures too unique may not be able to replicate themselves.

To follow through on the symbolic equivalence of children and plays, let us recall that in the extant Euripides plays there is a striking number of references and allusions to peculiar births, false births, and to doubles and false duplicates of the real person (a related theme). *The Bacchae* (Dionysus born from his father's thigh; Dionysus made from the ether), *Electra* (Clytemnestra brought to see Electra by a deception about Electra being pregnant and at term), *Helen* (her double went to Troy and the real Helen stayed in Egypt), *Alcestis* (a double), and *Hippolytus* (the wish that men could get babies by bringing gifts to gods and allusions to doubles) represent this concern with fantasies about birth and reproduction. Euripides, in *Medea*, expresses visions of birth that involve separation of the genders. He also gives voice to the unspeakable—the wish never to have engendered children; wishes about and actual abuse and murder of one's own children. This is in striking contrast to the "polyphiloprogenitive" values of the epic world (e.g., Priam's hundred children). There is also the ode in praise of Athens, the city whose people are autochthonous, born from the earth not begotten by the usual means. Athens is the garden of the Muses and of Harmonia, a parthenogenetic, female place where Sophia—in part poetic wisdom and poetic craft—lives, rules, and flourishes.

What kind of creature, then, is the play *Medea*? I have drawn an analogy between the play and the poisoned gifts (as well as one between the play and Medea's fertility drugs). The offspring in the play, the children of Jason and Medea, are the fruits of a union between a powerful, dangerous, barbarian woman and a good Greek epic hero. I venture to say that Euripides might well have experienced his own creation as engendered in this kind of union between the "wild" and the "civilized." Following through with this metaphor, the play, the children, are hybrids that cannot survive youth, or sterile hybrids. Or we might invoke the possibility that the wishes for unisexual reproduction in *Medea* (and in other Euripidean plays) represent his fantasy, his wish, his perception of himself as thoroughly unique in conception and birth.

The detailed presentation in this and many other of his plays of the plight of women, of the underdog, of the precarious position of children, suggests that Euripides was suspicious of the "traditional" relationships he criticizes in his plays. In his own fantasy life, he might well have needed to envision alternative modes of begetting, especially his own poetic begetting.

As for propagating his work, according to ancient traditions he frequently had to revise and modify his plays, to revise plot and rewrite individual lines, in order not to outrage Athenian audiences. His offspring were not fully accepted as they were. He won few first prizes, though he was obviously considered great enough to have competed for many years in the tragedy contests. He was close enough to tradition to succeed in a very traditional society, but original enough to have to struggle for that success.

But his children, as it were, not only survived but flourished. Starting in the fourth century B.C. and continuing throughout Graeco-Roman antiquity, Euripides was the most popular and probably the most influential of the three great ancient tragedians. Perhaps his maverick modes, a hybrid of old and new, home-grown and exotic, portraits of worlds turned topsy-turvy, were highly flexible and better adapted for survival in the more complex, confused, and cosmopolitan atmosphere of later antiquity. His most famous "descendant" in antiquity was undoubtedly Seneca, who himself wrote a *Medea*. That play, as well as his others, became extremely influential in the pre-Elizabethan and Elizabethan eras. Shakespeare, among others, owed an important debt to Euripides, principally through Seneca. In particular, as we shall see in chapter 5, the atmosphere of Shakespeare's *Macbeth* is suffused with Senecan elaborations of Euripides' disturbing portrayal of parents' murdering little children.

REFERENCES

Abrams, Morris H. 1958. *The Mirror and the Lamp*. New York: Norton. Originally published 1953.

Beckett, Peter G. S., David B. Robinson, et al. 1956. The Significance of Exogenous Traumata in the Genesis of Schizophrenia. *Psychiatry* 19:137–42.

Bloom, Harold. 1973. *The Anxiety of Influence*. Oxford: Oxford University Press.

Burkert, Walter. 1966. Greek Tragedy and Sacrificial Ritual. *Greek, Roman and Byzantine Studies* 7:87–121.

———. 1983. *Homo Necans: The Anthropology of Ancient Greek Sacrificial Ritual and Myth*. Trans. Peter Bing. Berkeley: University of California Press. Original German edition published 1972.

Collard, C. 1981. *Euripides*. No. 14 in Greece & Rome: New Surveys in the Classics. Oxford: Clarendon.

Derrida, Jacques. 1978. Coming into One's Own. In *Psychoanalysis and the Question of Text*. Ed. Geoffrey Hartman, pp. 114–48. Baltimore: Johns Hopkins University Press.

Easterling, P. E. 1977. The Infanticide in Euripides' *Medea*. *Yale Classical Studies* 25:177–192. Cambridge: Cambridge University Press.

Euripides. 1840. *The Medea of Euripides*. Trans. T. W. C. Edwards. London.

———. 1938. Ed. Denys L. Page. Oxford: Clarendon Press.

———. 1955. *The Medea*. Trans. Rex Warner. In *Euripides I*. Vol. 3 of *The Complete Greek Tragedies*. Ed. David Grene and Richmond Lattimore. Chicago: University of Chicago Press.

———. 1969. *Medea*. Ed. Allan Elliott. Oxford: Oxford University Press.

Feinstein, Blossom G. 1968. *The Faerie Queene* and Cosmogonies of Near East. *Journal of the History of Ideas* 29:531–550.

Foley, Helene P. 1985. *Ritual Irony: Poetry and Sacrifice in Euripides*. Ithaca: Cornell University Press.

Fraiberg, Selma, Edna Adelson, and Vivian Shapiro. 1980. Ghosts in the Nursery: A Psychoanalytic Approach to the Problems of Impaired Infant–Mother Relationships. In *Clinical Studies in Infant Mental Health: The First Year of Life*, ed. Selma Fraiberg, pp. 164–196. New York: Basic.

Freud, Sigmund. 1955. A Special Type of Choice of Object made by Men. In *Standard Edition*, trans. James Strachey, vol. 11, pp. 163–175. London: Hogarth Press. Essay originally published 1910.

Gould, John. 1985. Tragedy in Performance. In *The Cambridge History of Greek Literature*. Vol. 1, *Greek Literature*, ed. P. E. Easterling and B. M. W. Knox, pp. 263–281. Cambridge: Cambridge University Press.

Griffiths, Frederick T. 1979. Girard on the Greeks / The Greeks on Girard. *Berkshire Review* 14:20–36.

Knox, Bernard M. W. 1983. The *Medea* of Euripides. In *Greek Tragedy: Modern Essays in Criticism*, ed. Eric Segal, pp. 273–293. New York: Harper and Row. Essay originally published 1977.

Lefkowitz, Mary R. 1981. *The Lives of the Greek Poets*. Baltimore: Johns Hopkins University Press.

Lesky, Albin. 1983. *Greek Tragic Poetry*. Trans. Matthew Dillon. New Haven: Yale University Press. Original German edition published 1972.

McDonald, Marianne. 1978. *A Semilemmatized Concordance to Euripides' Medea*. Irvine, Calif.: TLG.

Nietzsche, Friedrich. 1967. *The Birth of Tragedy* and *The Case of Wagner*. Trans. Walter Kaufmann. New York: Random House, Vintage Books.

Orgel, Shelley and Leonard L. Shengold. 1968. The Fatal Gifts of Medea. *International Journal of Psycho-Analysis* 49:379–383.

Pucci, Pietro. 1980. *The Violence of Pity in Euripides'* Medea. Ithaca: Cornell University Press.

Rascovsky, Arnaldo and Matilde Rascovsky. 1968. On the Genesis of Acting Out and Psychopathic Behaviour in Sophocles' *Oedipus*: Notes on Filicide. *International Journal of Psycho-Analysis* 49:391–394.

Schlesinger, Eilhard. 1983. On Euripides' *Medea*. In *Greek Tragedy: Modern Essays in Criticism*, ed. Eric Segal, pp. 294–310. New York: Harper and Row. Essay originally published 1966.

Segal, Charles. 1985. Tragedy, Corporeality, and the Texture of Language: Matricide in the Three Electra Plays. *Classical World*. 79:7–23.

———. 1986. Tragedy, Orality, Literacy. In *Oralita: Cultura, Letteratura, Discorso*, ed. B. Gentili and G. Paoni, pp. 199–231. Urbino: Edizioni Dell'Ateneo.

Segal, Eric, ed. 1983. *Greek Tragedy: Modern Essays in Criticism*. New York: Harper and Row.

Simon, Bennett. 1984. "With Cunning Delays and Ever-Mounting Excitement" or, What Thickens the Plot in Psychoanalysis and Tragedy. In *Psychoanalysis: The Vital Issues*, ed. G. H. Pollock and J. E. Gedo, vol. 2, pp. 387–436. New York: International Universities Press.

Slater, Philip E. 1968. *The Glory of Hera*. Boston: Beacon Press.

Vellacott, Philip. 1975. *Ironic Drama: A Study of Euripides' Method and Meaning*. Cambridge: Cambridge University Press.

Zeitlin, Froma I. 1985. Playing the Other: Theater, Theatricality and the Feminine in Greek Drama. *Representations* 11:63–94.

CHAPTER 4

All Germains Spill at Once: Shakespeare's *King Lear*

King Lear is an unbearable play. Witness its theater history.[1] Written in 1605, it was performed more or less as Shakespeare wrote it (and exactly what Shakespeare wrote is as much a subject of controversy as any Shakespearean text)[2] until 1681, when Nahum Tate, the poet laureate, rewrote the plot. In Tate's version, which became theatrical canon for about a century and a half, there was no Fool, Edgar and Cordelia were lovers, and there was a happy ending with Lear and Cordelia reconciled and living happily ever after. Tate not only reworked the plot but excised much of the original poetry. His intolerance of ambiguity, a characteristic dear to the modern sensibility, is demonstrated by his reducing the frequency of the word *if*, one of the most commonly used words in the play. In the 1830s, when something like the original plot was restored in performance, how much of the poetry to cut was still being debated.

Even after much of Shakespeare's play had been restored, *Lear* was not often performed in anything like an uncut version. There were some great actors and noteworthy stage performances, but until the 1920s the play was not performed with great frequency. In New York in the first decades of the twentieth century, a Yiddish version, with Jewish setting and Jewish characters, heavily bowdlerized and "Tated," was performed far more often

1. For *Lear's* theater history, see Furness (1880), Rosenberg (1972), and Trewin (1981). For critical history, see also Champion (1980), and Snyder (1979, esp. pp. 168–69).

2. See Champion (1980), Urkowitz (1980), Reid (1982). An important current controversy is around the widely accepted practice (since the eighteenth century) of producing an edition by conflating the Quarto and the later Folio texts. Urkowitz (a minority view) argues that each of these is a viable dramatic version of what Shakespeare wrote and that the Folio represents Shakespeare's own revision of the earlier version found in the Quarto. The text of *King Lear* used here is the Signet Edition, ed. Fraser (Shakespeare 1963).

than *King Lear* in English.[3] Clearly something in the story and in the power and ambiguity of the poetry has been difficult for audiences to bear. It seems that only in the modern age can we "men of stones" (5.3.259) tolerate such a play. In fact, in recent decades, both in performance and in the critical literature, there has been a push to make the play *less* bearable: Jan Kott (1974, pp. 127–68) compares it to Beckett's *Endgame*, and Peter Brook stages it so that several acts of pity and compassion are eliminated from the script.

Critical history, especially the early criticism, similarly reveals difficulty in tolerating the intense emotionality and horror of the play. Samuel Johnson related that, watching a performance, "I was so shocked by Cordelia's death, that I know not whether I ever endured to read again the last scenes of the play till I undertook to revise them as an editor."[4] Charles Lamb, in 1836, while not endorsing Tate's version, thought the play could be read but not staged, because it would come across as ridiculous or pitiable. Modern criticism too is torn over whether to opt for meliorative readings and, accordingly, less searing performances of the play. Critics (e.g., Goldman 1972) have pointed out that there is a rhythm in the play: when things appear to be their absolute worst, they get a bit better, only to get yet worse again. Part of the play's terror is that hopes for improvement or justice are intermittently raised and frustrated.

Another way of looking at the difficulties in encompassing *King Lear* is more cognitive—the play doesn't always make sense. It not only presents us with the ravings of a madman or a pseudo-madman and the prattlings of a Fool; also, important motivations are not always clear—for example, exactly why Lear divides up his kingdom; why Cordelia says "nothing"; and why Lear's character isn't always consistent.

I believe that *Lear*, more than any other of Shakespeare's great tragedies, presents us with a creation that is always threatening to fall apart, to become unviable, not just unbearable. The title of a recent study, "Creative Uncreation in *King Lear*" (Calderwood 1986), suggests a point of entry into the way the play handles both form and content: there is a tension between creation, procreation, and generation, on the one hand, and destruction, sterility, and degeneration, on the other. This tension always threatens to break through the limits of the aesthetically feasible and the psychologically bearable.

The contents of the play deal first and foremost with the violation of the

3. The Yiddish version is Jacob Gordin's *Der Yudisher Kenig Lear* (microfilm in NY Public Library), Warsaw, 1907.

4. Obviously Tate's version, while the most popular, was not the only one performed in Johnson's day. See Holland (1978).

sacred bonds between parents and children, violation by characters who "Like rats, oft bite the holy cords atwain / Which are too intrince t'unloose" (2.2.76–77). The action of the plot leads to the destruction of present and future progeny, to a curse on all generation, and to the vertiginous madness of Lear, with its challenge to all creation. The form of the play, especially its imagery of savage animals, its punning, reversals, monosyllabic screams, nonsense, and psychotic ravings, is similarly strained by the problem of finding the right artistic means for a creative portrayal of "uncreation," the dissolution of all engendering of meaning, kinship, and justice.

In this play, as in other great tragedies, the "normal" or the ideal is defined and realized by the abnormal. Breakdown within the play, the uncreation implicit in the plot, reveals to us the nature of the structures and bonds that we take for granted.

For example, the theme of nonrecognition of kin in *King Lear* powerfully illuminates what it means to recognize. Recognition of the other implies acknowledgment of a balance between autonomy and dependency; acknowledgment of the power, but also the limits, of the bond between father and daughter (e.g., Cordelia's "I love your Majesty / According to my bond; no more nor less"; 1.1.94–95). Pathological grief, unresolved mourning over separation and loss, reveals what is entailed in ordinary acceptance of such losses. Lear refuses to weep, but he can rage. When he does cry, his tears are as scalding lead. His rage at his inability to control the progression of life from womb to tomb and to mold his own children teaches us what we must, albeit with great difficulty, accept as beyond our power, though not as beyond our wishes. Attempts to impose order and control over the messy processes of creation and procreation, especially the interpersonal processes, are doomed to failure, but again they reveal the nature of our yearnings and of our limited powers.

In my analysis of this play, I argue that Lear's narcissistic character structure entails defects in empathy, rage at his inability to control natural and familial processes, and delusional attempts to reconstruct and control his shattered world. The themes of uncreation and destruction of meaning and meaningful connection typical of the play *King Lear* emanate from and are entwined with the traits of the character Lear.

First, I examine Lear's need to command and control and his inability to acknowledge separation, loss, and division. Then, I take up the representation of sexuality and begetting and the attacks on begetting that become so central in Lear's madness. Finally, I show that the questions of empathy and its lack among the characters in the play are closely entwined with issues of establishing and destroying meaning and meaningful connection among the characters. Issues of empathy arise in the diverse audience and reader reactions to the characters. "What does the play mean?" is a question that needs to be approached in relation to what the characters in the play mean to each other.

Lear demands, Lear commands; he does not listen. Only as his suffering and his learning proceed do we sense a gradual shift from the imperative to the interrogative, from the imperious to the attentive.[5] His ability to relinquish his illusions, partial at best, allows him to accept some passivity and limitation. His plaint late in the play, "they told me I was everything; 'tis a lie, I am not ague-proof" (4.6.106–07), reflects both his grandiosity and the glimmers of what he has so painfully learned. Clearly Lear's madness involves a megalomaniac contest with the forces of nature, a delusion about his ability to control and command everything. For many viewers and readers, his behavior before his florid madness similarly involves an assumption, characterological rather than psychotic, that he can forestall some of life's inevitabilities.[6] These include not only the consequences of growing old and having to relinquish power, but the belief that one can control the separations, divisions, and differentiations that are entailed in parent–child and sibling relationships and in political matters.[7] His demand of Cordelia that she "love her father all" is as grandiose as the wrenching final scene of the play in which Lear recognizes that Cordelia is dead and still insists that she might breathe and live.

> I know when one is dead and when one lives;
> She's dead as earth. Lend me a looking glass.   (5.3.262–63)

Heinz Kohut once defined narcissism, the narcissistic conception of the people in one's life, as the belief that the other should obey you as does your right arm (1971, p. 33). Lear's definition of the outrage inflicted on him by Goneril and Regan is:

5. Levenson (1972), p. 225, and sources cited there.

6. See Furness (1880, pp. 412–17), "Insanity," for some interesting prepsychoanalytic views on Lear's character and its relation to his insanity. For some contemporary views on the relationship of narcissistic character, cosmic rage, and psychosis, see Bach and Schwartz (1972) and Kohut (1972).

7. The play opens with discussions of preference, power, and privilege; the differentiation between lawful and bastard sons; which son-in-law is preferred—all this in the thirty or so lines prior to Lear's entrance. "Differences" and distinctions are critical throughout the play. Kent, berating Oswald, whom Lear has struck and Kent tripped, says to him, "I'll teach you differences" (1.4.91–92); or, Fool to Lear, "Dost thou know the difference, my boy, between a bitter Fool and a sweet one?" (1.4.141–42). On the role of collapse of "differences" and "degree" in tragedy see Girard (1977), esp. pp. 49–52.

> Filial ingratitude,
> Is it not as this mouth should tear this hand
> For lifting foot to 't?   (3.4.14–16)

Lear cannot let go. His attempt to relinquish temporal responsibility is not combined with a realistic appraisal of the necessary loss of privilege. Goneril and Regan torture him by quite specifically understanding his vulnerability and finding every way to strip him of power and remind him of his helpless dependency upon them. The Fool taunts Lear, torturing him in his own way, with reminders that Lear does not know the difference between commonsense holding and commonsense giving away. Lear's childish expectations lead to the dramatic and tragic reversals of the play, in which children become mothers and fathers to their parents. Edgar's "He childed as I fathered "(3.6.109) epitomizes these unnatural reversals, as do the Fool's taunts, "thou mad'st thy daughters thy mothers . . . thou gav'st them the rod, and put'st down thine own breeches" (1.4.176–78).

Lear does not understand that authority and affection rest on a complex and subtle matrix of obligation, power, loyalty, reciprocal need, and love. None of these is absolute. Cordelia in vain tries to explain:

> Good my lord,
> You have begot me, bred me, loved me. I
> Return those duties back as are right fit,
> Obey you, love you, and most honor you.
> Why have my sisters husbands, if they say
> They love you all? Haply, when I shall wed,
> That lord whose hand must take my plight shall carry
> Half my love with him, half my care and duty.
> Sure I shall never marry like my sisters,
> To love my father all.   (1.1.98–106)

Lear's response to this speech is to proclaim, simultaneously, infinite distance between parent and child and no distance at all. He disowns and banishes Cordelia and then collapses generational distances and distinctions by means of a cannibalistic image of merger:

> The barbarous Scythian,
> Or he that makes his generation messes
> To gorge his appetite, shall to my bosom
> Be as well neighbored, pitied, and relieved,
> As thou my sometime daughter.   (1.1.118–23)

His disappointment in Cordelia is in proportion to how much he had counted on her to be, in return for his love for her, the nurse of his old age.

"I loved her most, and thought to set my rest / On her kind nursery"
(1.1.125–26).

Indeed, images of cannibalism, of parent and child devouring each other,
are scattered throughout the play and typically convey an ambiguity
around whether closeness, union, or all-devouring rage is at work. " 'Twas
this flesh begot / Those pelican daughters" (3.4.74–75) is the most famous
instance of such a confusion—the pelican daughters devour their father,
who begot them. In Elizabethan symbolism, the pelican is a bird that
"loveth too much her children" and allows them to smite the parents in the
face. In anger, the mother pelican then slays the children and "on the third
day"—Christ-like—sheds her own blood onto her children, who are then
quickened by the blood of the dying mother (Furness 1880, ad loc.).[8]

In Lear's rage at his other two daughters, we encounter other forms of
degradation of parent–child closeness. We see the transforming power of
narcissistic rage: the child is now an internal persecutor or poisoner. Lear
shouts at Goneril:

> We'll no more meet, no more see one another.
> But yet thou are my flesh, my blood, my daughter,
> Or rather a disease that's in my flesh,
> Which must needs call mine. Thou are a boil,
> A plague-sore, or embossèd carbuncle
> In my corrupted blood.   (2.4.219–23)

Lear, when all is said and done in the play, has achieved only a limited
awareness of the need for differentiation and relinquishing control over
one's children. One of the tenderest scenes, yet one marking Lear's tragic
inability to let go, is, "No, no, no, no! let's away to prison: / We two alone
will sing like birds i' th' cage" (5.3.8–9). "He that parts us shall bring a
brand from heaven / And fire us hence like foxes" (22–23). He ignores the
fact that Cordelia is married (as does Cordelia!), just as he refuses in act 1,
scene 1, to acknowledge any division of loyalty on Cordelia's part.

But inadequate separation and differentiation, the unwillingness to relinquish, is not only Lear's hallmark, it is a characteristic of the play. Cordelia,
especially in the last act and, according to some readings, in the first act as
well, similarly has difficulty acknowledging separation. Edmund in the final

8. Other references to children's devouring parents or sucking them dry are found at
1.4.212 (the hedge-sparrow has its head bit off by the young of the cuckoo) and 3.1.12 ("the
cub-drawn bear"). The comparison of *King Lear* with its sources is instructive in this regard.
In *King Leir*—first produced in the 1590s and of unknown authorship—the one statement
about cannibalism is in a completely different mode. Perillus, the "Kent" of that play, offers
his arm and blood from his vein to the starving Leir, who declines the offer, asserting that he
is not a cannibal. See excerpt in Shakespeare (1963), p. 205, and appendix in Furness (1880)
on *King Leir*.

act reveals that he is promised, adulterously, to both Goneril and Regan. When he learns of their deaths, as he is dying, he puns: "all three now marry in an instant" (5.3.230).

The term *pathological grief* has come to signify a refusal to acknowledge death, loss, or separation, an insistence on maintaining by denial, in fantasy or in deed, that a death (for example) has not taken place or is not final. A narcissistic relation to another person, an insistence on the other's serving primarily as an extension of the self, can also be viewed from the perspective of pathological grief as a refusal to mourn, a refusal to acknowledge separation and growth. Refusal to mourn is an important part of the play, particularly in Lear himself. Lear does not cry. If he begins to cry, he must stifle the tears; he is ashamed of his tears, curses his eyes, and threatens to pluck them out if ever they cry again (1.4.308–11). He can allude, ambiguously, to crying oneself to sleep, but this is manifestly framed as railing against Regan and her husband, Cornwall (2.4.115). He will not cry, for it is unmanly and, even worse, would involve full acknowledgment of the loss of affection and respect from Goneril and Regan.

> [You gods] . . . touch me with noble anger,
> And let not women's weapons, water drops,
> Stain my man's cheeks. No, you unnatural hags!
> I will have such revenges on you both
> That all the world shall—I will do such things—
> What they are, yet I know not; but they shall be
> The terrors of the earth. You think I'll weep.
> No, I'll not weep.
> > *Storm and tempest.*
> I have full cause of weeping, but this heart
> Shall break into a hundred thousand flaws
> Or ere I'll weep. O Fool, I shall go mad!   (2.4.275–85)

Lear, in his madness, still refuses to weep, but the flood of rain in the storm actualizes in the world of nature the torrent of tears he is keeping back. In act 4, he struggles with tears several times, primarily in his encounter with Gloucester, and then in his reunion with Cordelia. In the recognition scene, when the still mad but slightly calmer Lear meets the blind Gloucester, Lear refers repeatedly to tears, but they are literally given over to Gloucester or ascribed to the generality of mankind.[9] Lear addresses the blind Gloucester, who is crying:

9. That there is ambivalence about Lear's crying even among editors is suggested by the debate about the correct text at 4.6.83. When Edgar and Gloucester first encounter Lear, wandering and covered with flowers and thistles, Lear is muttering: "No, they cannot touch me for coining; I am the King himself." ("Coining" is interpreted as the king's right to mint coins.) The Quarto has "for crying," but most critics follow the Folio reading. See Rosenberg, (1972, 267–68), who defends "crying" as allowing for a smoother transition to the next line.

Lear: If thou wilt weep my fortunes, take my eyes.
  I know thee well enough; thy name is Gloucester:
  Thou must be patient; we came crying hither:
  Thou know'st, the first time that we smell the air
  We wawl and cry. I will preach to thee: mark.
Gloucester: Alack, alack the day!
Lear: When we are born, we cry that we are come
  To this great stage of fools.   (4.6.178–85)

Lear's struggle with weeping and his need to distance himself from his own tears is seen in the conditional tense of the verb:

Why, this would make a man a man of salt,
To use his eyes for garden water-pots,
Ay, and laying autumn's dust.   (4.6.197–98)

In the scene of his awakening and reunion with Cordelia, as he is slowly coming to recognize and acknowledge her, his tears are not salt water but a dangerous and destructive liquid.

You do me wrong to take me out o' th' grave:
Thou art a soul in bliss; but I am bound
Upon a wheel of fire, that mine own tears
Do scald like molten lead.   (4.7.45–48).

He associates tears, especially his own, to poison as he explicitly names Cordelia:

Lear: For, as I am a man, I think this lady
  To be my child Cordelia.
Cordelia: And so I am, I am.
Lear: Be your tears wet? Yes, faith. I pray, weep not.
  If you have poison for me, I will drink it.   (4.7.68–72)

Tears, then, signify for Lear everything unacceptable to his fragile yet inflated sense of self: vulnerability, need for another, feminine weakness, childish attachment, caring, and, at the bottom, mortality.

Lear's inability to recognize the realities of aging, mortality, and separation and the necessary distinctions between parent and child are thus made tangible and visible around the scenes of weeping, especially thwarted weeping. Another important image of this inability is that of childish games—especially in the Fool's songs, which for Lear are a mixture of taunting and therapy. Early in the play, as Lear is beginning to see the consequences of his foolish divestments and his rejection of Cordelia, he is irritated but intrigued by the Fool:[10]

> Lear: When were you wont to be so full of songs, sirrah?
> Fool: I have used it, Nuncle, e'er since thou mad'st thy daughters thy mothers; for when thou gav'st them the rod, and put'st down thine own breeches,
> Then they for sudden joy did weep,
> And I for sorrow sung,
> That such a king should play bo-peep,
> And go the fools among.   (1.4.176–82)

Lear has made himself into a bad child and has offered himself to be beaten by his mother. The image of the king's pulling down his pants and exposing his buttocks to be beaten has sexual reverberations as well as overtones of parental discipline. For the moment, I want to focus on the phrase "play bo-peep." Insofar as this is an allusion to the well-known nursery rhyme, "Little Bo-Peep has lost her sheep," there are several meanings condensed therein. Who is the sheep and who the shepherd is ambiguous: Lear is at once and alternately both shepherd and lost sheep. His daughters were originally his sheep, and he is lost as a leader. As a (female) shepherd, he is weak and impotent. Shall he meekly await the sheep's return home, hoping that they will be both penitent and joyful to be reconciled with him? He is also a shepherd who does not know how many sheep he has or wants. Is Cordelia one of them, or only Goneril and Regan? Is he a father or a mother—especially apt in a play where there is scarcely a mention of "Queen Lear"? Who is looking for nurturance from whom? Many other constructions and construals can arise from this line of comparison to the nursery rhyme, and I believe it is a valid and useful exegesis of what the poetic genius packed into a few words. As it happens, one cannot, strictly speaking, use "Little Bo-Peep" as a gloss on this passage, because its appearance cannot be documented before 1810, although it is probably older and may well have been Elizabethan. Though the nursery rhyme is a "modern" association to the play, the lines of meaning that emanate from using it as a gloss do correspond with features of the play as a whole.

In Elizabethan times, the meaning of "play bo-peep" corresponded more to the phrase "play peek-a-boo." This reverberates with a childhood game

10. The discussion of this passage is modified from my earlier discussion in Simon (1984). See the sources cited there on "play bo-peep," especially Seng (1967), as well as discussion of the role of the Fool as "therapist manqué" for Lear. Other nursery rhymes or children's stories alluded to in the play include "Fie, foh, and fum, / I smell the blood of a British man" (3.4.185–88) and "Little boy blue . . . come blow your horn" in an Elizabethan variant at 3.4.41–45.

that has a number of different implications. In this passage, who is the nursemaid or mother, and who the baby? Lear, again, alternately takes both roles, mother and baby, playing a game of appearance and disappearance; is it permanent or is it not? It is also a game of pretending, making believe that something is not there that really is, and vice-versa. The game can generate considerable excitement, as well as anxiety, in a baby. The Fool's interpretation to Lear, then, of Lear's giving away his kingdom and disavowing a daughter is that via the excitement of a "gone-but-not-gone" game, he was seeking to "play peek-a-boo" with aging, death, loss, and necessary separation from his children (Freud 1913). In his demand for love from them, he was also playing the game of "she loves me—she loves me not," hoping to stave off any true test of love. Other connotations of "bo-peep" in Elizabethan times are of coyness, shyness, and also lascivious looking, peeping, and peeking. The game he is playing with his daughters is thus also a sexualized one.

"Play bo-peep" enacts several kinds of childhood fantasies and fears: early mother–child separation, sexual excitement in games with mother, seduction and refusal, perpetual suspense—no ending, no culmination. In effect, the Fool's taunt is that Lear, either as a mother or as child, cannot face up to the inevitable and thereby makes things absolutely topsy-turvy.

If Lear has difficulty with processes out of his control, it is not surprising that sexuality is so problematic in the play. Loving sexuality, tenderness combined with passion, loving procreation ensuing from sexual intercourse—none of these is even alluded to except by implicit contrast with sexuality as presented in the play.[11] References to intercourse as dark, dirty, and dangerous are prominent in the play. The vagina and uterus are denounced and cursed; penises and phallic symbols tend to be ridiculed. Whoring and adultery are the primary sexual activities mentioned, but by pun, joke, and symbol; characters (principally the Fool, Edgar as Tom, and Lear) allude to sexualized beating, sadistic penetration, menstruation, and cloacal theories of birth.[12] As in so many Shakespearean tragedies, male

11. In contrast, *Macbeth* alludes to loving and procreative sexuality (the birds at Macbeth's castle and the relationship between Macduff and Lady Macduff) as counterpoint to the sadistic and murderous sexuality that is conveyed by most of the plot and imagery. *Hamlet* too, with all its denunciations of women and their perfidy, evokes in places a lively or lovely view of sexuality. In *King Lear* France lovingly accepts Cordelia, but the sexual imagery is slight, and we never again see Cordelia and France together.

12. For menstruation, see 3.6.25–28 (and Seng 1967), where the Fool sings a dirty ditty, probably about a menstruating whore—a context that would fit the mad trial scene in which Goneril and Regan are being arraigned.

and female are set up as stark contrasts; the woman who becomes masculine is dangerous and unnatural; the man who becomes feminine is a subject for taunting and ridicule. The attacks on female lust in the play are part of an assault on conception, gestation, and all of generation. Again, by indirection, we learn of the value of fecundity, of procreation, of loving to generate and of loving generations. The curses in the play highlight the blessings of the life that is excluded and portrayed as impossible.

The play's first allusions to sexuality are at the very opening, when Gloucester introduces his bastard son Edmund to Kent. In the presence of his son, Gloucester jokes about his conception and birth. Kent cannot "conceive" that Gloucester would have had a bastard, and Gloucester puns:

> Sir, this young fellow's mother could; whereupon she grew round-wombed, and had indeed, sire, a son for her cradle ere she had a husband for her bed. Do you smell a fault? . . .
>
> . . . Though this knave came something saucily to the world before he was sent for, yet was his mother fair, there was good sport at his making, and the whoreson must be acknowledged.   (1.1.13–25)

This is the first and last playful and sensual mention of intercourse and birth in the play. Quickly that spirit is undone and countermanded. In the same scene, Lear rages at Cordelia, disowns her, and pronounces it better had she never been born. In the next scene, Edmund's bitterness over his illegitimacy and his plan for revenge on his brother and father become manifest. His grimmer view of his begetting emerges as he angrily ridicules Gloucester's invocation of the eclipses and stars as explanations for evil things happening of late.

> An admirable evasion of whoremaster man, to lay his goatish disposition on the charge of a star. My father compounded with my mother under the Dragon's Tail, and my nativity was under Ursa Major, so that it follows I am rough and lecherous. Fut! I should have been that I am, had the maidenliest star in the firmament twinkled on my bastardizing.   (1.2.137–44)

Sexuality has thus been made animal—goat, dragon, bear—and compounded with choler and bile. Out of that compound is born a vindictive man, Edmund, who in fact uses his sexuality later in the play for his own power needs, playing off one sister against the other.

The interplay of sexuality and of equity—that is, the acceptance of division and difference—is important in these two first scenes and crucial to the structure of the play as a whole. Lear and Edmund, each in his own way, cannot tolerate division and preference. For Lear, Cordelia's division of affection between husband (to-be) and father is intolerable, as is for Edmund his father's preference for the legitimate over the bastard son. Neither can accept the inevitability of some hierarchy, some division, some differences, and some sharing. Lear ends up denouncing intercourse and cursing reproduction, while Edmund makes a mockery of the possibility of combining sexuality with affection.[13]

Lear's own attitudes toward sex, reproduction, and fathering come in for considerable scorn from the Fool, especially in 1.4. The Fool comes on stage sporting a coxcomb and a codpiece—phallic humor is sure to ensue. Fool offers Lear his coxcomb, not only to say that Lear is more of a fool than Fool, but also to say that Lear has given away his cock. He has, in effect, cut off his penis, and he is now empty in the middle of his crotch (or, alternatively, he has given away his testicles, who are now his two wicked daughters): "thou hast pared thy wit o' both sides and left nothing i' th' middle. Here comes one o' the parings" (Enter Goneril) (1.4.191–93).

Images of castration and of self-deception about one's phallic powers continue. Lear is a "shealed peascod," a peapod with nothing in it, no seeds, no offspring, nothing (1.4.205). Even the snail has the sense to have a house that he keeps and does not "give . . . away to his daughters, and leave his horns without a case" (1.5.31–32). Lear does not know how to conserve; the image that follows is of a penis (codpiece) that spends without thought to the future, without using its "head," and that thoughtless penis will be attacked and have its blood sucked by lice:

> The codpiece that will house
>   Before the head has any,
> The head and he shall louse: (3.2.27–29)

The counterpart of Lear's dread of being cuckolded and castrated is his ambivalence toward a feminine, maternal part of himself. In act 2, he realizes more clearly his rejection by both Goneril and Regan and addresses his insides as if he has a uterus, one that can wander out of its proper place, causing a hysterical affliction, presumably one that chokes him up or causes feelings in his heart.

> O, how this mother swells up toward my heart!
> Hysterica passio, down, thou climbing sorrow,
> Thy element's below. Where is this daughter?   (2.4.55–57)

Lear, having destroyed hierarchy, including the hierarchy ordering relations between male and female, is now desperate to restore each organ to its

---

13. In Goneril's letter to Edmund, intercepted by Edgar, she offers him what is apparently deep affection combined with sexual passion, and something fructifying—"time and place will be fruitfully offered." But this combination of affection and passion is conditional upon Edmund killing her husband, Albany, and it entails her expressing sexual loathing for that husband (4.6.266–75).

proper place. Responding to the Fool's ridicule of his head and penis and his failure to know the proper order of persons and organs, Lear's rage at his daughters escalates. At first it is Goneril who is the object of his wrath, but soon Regan is added. Lear's attack begins with a wish that Goneril be sterile or, "if she must teem," that she beget splenetic children who will in turn attack her, with the serpent's tooth that is filial ingratitude.

> Into her womb convey sterility,
> Dry up in her the organs of increase,
> And from her derogate body never spring
> A babe to honor her. If she must teem,
> Create her child of spleen, that it may live
> And be a thwart disnatured torment to her.   (1.4.285–90)

The very form of the curse is a representation of a sexual act—"sterility" is conveyed into her vagina and uterus. Lear continues to rail, and a few lines later his fears of his feminization through tears, of his faltering manhood, lead to imagery of penetration and piercing, a wound in the woman. He curses Goneril,

> That thou hast power to shake my manhood thus!
> That these hot tears, which break from me perforce,
> Should make thee worth them. Blasts and fogs upon thee!
> Th' untented woundings of a father's curse
> Pierce every sense about thee!   (1.4.304–08)

Lear portrays his curse as an instrument that causes penetrating wounds so deep they cannot be surgically probed or packed. Fructifying sexuality is attacked because it produces ungrateful children, children one cannot control. Concomitantly, Lear's organs are attacked, and he counterattacks his daughter's organs. Sexual intercourse is not possible with such blighted organs and it is replaced by a mutually sadistic, penetrating, and wounding series of encounters. Each in turn pierces and is pierced, Lear as instrument of attack and Goneril, serpentlike, with her bite.

The attack continues with allusions to the mother of the children as an adulteress (2.4.130–31), Goneril as a serpent, a curse that her as yet unborn children should be crippled (160–63), and then Goneril as a diseased part of Lear (220–25). In act 3, the storm scene, Lear generalizes his attack on his daughters to include all of nature, a curse on all reproduction. Again, the imagery suggests a violent sexual act, a cruel and perverse form of sexuality that replaces the sexuality that leads to reproduction:

> Blow, winds, and crack your cheeks. Rage, blow!
> You cataracts and hurricanoes, spout
> Till you have drenched our steeples, drowned the cocks.

You sulphr'ous and thought-executing fires,
Vaunt-couriers of oak-cleaving thunderbolts,
Singe my white head. And thou, all-shaking thunder,
Strike flat the thick rotundity o' th' world,
Crack Nature's molds, all germains spill at once,
That makes ingrateful man.   (3.2.1–9).

The speech confounds battle, disaster, sexual assault, abortion, sul-phurous-smelling violent orgasm, and the destruction of all the apparatus and seeds for reproduction, now and forevermore.[14] It is an act of cosmic onanism, a great refusal to take on the obligations of marriage and repro-duction, whose results are simply too awful to contemplate.

The "sulphr'ous" fires of this speech connect with Lear's later attack on female sexuality, an attack that includes the sulphur of hell-fires and the explicit sense of female sexual organs as foul-smelling, needing a de-odorant, as it were (4.6.109–33). That attack is clearly associated with Lear's own sense of impotence, his painful attempts to assert himself as king. He is impotent to control, here impotent to control adultery and female lust, which he implicitly blames as the cause of adultery. At the same time, "adultery" represents a wish-fulfilling explanation of Goneril's and Regan's bad treatment of him—they are the children of another man.

Gloucester recognizes him as the king, and Lear asserts, "Ay, every inch a king. / When I do stare, see how the subject quakes" (4.6.109–10).

Let copulation thrive: for Gloucester's bastard son
Was kinder to his father than my daughters
Got 'tween the lawful sheets.
To 't, luxury, pell-mell! for I lack soldiers.   (4.6.116–19)

The last phrase expresses Lear's lack of resources, lack of warriors, lack of manly equipment, and his yearning for military sons to be begotten by lawful intercourse, instead of vicious daughters. This triple emphasis on his male lack introduces the most concerted assault I know of in tragic literature on woman as a sexual and reproducing creature:[15]

14. I arrived at these formulations of the fusion of violence and sterile sexuality on my own, but I found that a nineteenth-century German critic, Delius (Furness 1880), identified "rotundity" with pregnancy, and Rosenberg (1972, pp. 191–93) also assumed the sexual overtones of the speech. The oak tree, cleft by lightning, also suggests a family tree (R. Apfel, pers. comm.). See also Kanzer (1965), who argues, exaggeratedly, that *King Lear* has a primal scene as its core fantasy.

15. Other references to the vagina include: "The dark and vicious place where thee he got / Cost him his eyes" (5.3.173–74) and "But have you never found my brother's way / To the forfended place?" (5.1.10–11), preceded a few lines before by an allusion to miscarriage. I believe also that "O indistinguished space of woman's will" (4.7.276) is an amalgam of woman's destructive lust with the male perception of a huge vaginal-uterine space without differentiation and without limit.

Lear: Down from the waist they are Centaurs,
  Though women all above:
  But to the girdle do the gods inherit,
  Beneath is all the fiend's.
  There's hell, there's darkness, there is the sulphurous pit,
  Burning, scalding, stench, consumption; fie, fie, fie!
  pah, pah! Give me an ounce of civet: good apothecary, sweeten my imagina-
  tion: there's money for thee.
Gloucester: O, let me kiss that hand!
Lear: Let me wipe it first; it smells of mortality.   (4.6.126–35)

This passage clearly splits woman into a divine "above"—that is, woman as breast, as "kind nursery"—and the diabolical "below." The motives for the splitting are several, but they cluster around a dread of male dependence on women for processes of birth and reproduction and of being reared and cared for by women. The dangerous stench of woman enlarges into the even more lethal smell of mortality. To be of woman born is to admit a dependency that is both the equivalent of death and a reminder of its reality. Edgar later glosses these lines, in effect, in his speech to his father, Gloucester, urging him not to give up and die but to move on and escape the danger of battle. "Men must endure / Their going hence, even as their coming hither" (5.2.9–10). Death, birth, and the copulation entailed are what characters in the play continually try to evade.

King Lear is an obliterative play. It is not only that characters are killed off by one another; they are also decomposed, wished into nonexistence; their births are disavowed; they must disguise their true identities; and they are not recognized by their own kin or household (Cavell 1977). Lear not only disowns Cordelia but proclaims, "Better thou / Hadst not been born than not t' have pleased me better" (1.1.235–36). Gloucester, enraged and incredulous that Edgar should plot to take his life (as Edmund falsely informs him), exclaims, "I never got him" (2.1.80). Lear partially disavows the birth and existence of Regan—that is, he disavows his role in her conception—when he tells her that if she treats him as badly as Goneril has, she too is not his child: "I would divorce me from thy mother's tomb, / Sepulchring an adultress" (2.4.130–31). And Lear, in his first speech in the storm (3.2.), places a curse on all conception and begetting—an obliterative solution to the problem of ungrateful children.

Kent, disguised as Caius, a servant to Lear, assaults Goneril's servant Oswald with both words and sword. His insults include the accusation that Oswald has been made badly, that he is ill-fitting, as if by a bad tailor.[16] He

16. The image of the botched job by an inept tailor shows up again in Beckett's *Endgame*, as a joke about how bad all creation is.

is a "whoreson zed," an insignificant, illegitimate, and unnecessary last letter of the alphabet, and, Kent threatens, "I will tread this unbolted villain into mortar and daub the wall of a jakes [privy] with him" (2.2.66–69). That is, Kent will reduce him to primal slime and shit.

Kent, like Cordelia, is banished by Lear for disobeying and disagreeing. Lear cannot acknowledge his existence as Kent, but he can acknowledge the goodness and loyalty of Kent in disguise. But even at the end, when Lear does recognize Kent, he cannot fully acknowledge his existence. His ambivalence toward Kent comes through in his acknowledgment of "Caius":

> Lear: This a dull sight. Are you not Kent?
> Kent: The same,
>   Your servant Kent. Where is your servant Caius?
> Lear: He's a good fellow, I can tell you that;
>   He'll strike and quickly too: he's dead and rotten.
> Kent: No, my good lord; I am the very man.   (5.3.283–88)

Though Kent has been unswervingly loyal to Lear, Lear's inability to admit his own shortcomings and his own error does not allow him to fully acknowledge Kent's existence.

Lear's recognition of Gloucester is similarly incomplete, especially when it comes to acknowledging directly Gloucester's blindness and pain: "I remember thine eyes well enough. Dost thou squiny at me? No, do thy worst, blind Cupid; I'll not love" (4.6.138–41). He can let himself "see" the blindness of the other only by taunting him. Clearly the playwright depicts in Lear a man so caught up in the humiliation of his own failures— to love and to see—that he is limited in his capacity to acknowledge Gloucester's plight.

The acknowledgment of Cordelia is also problematic, marked by pained stages of recognition. Lear expects that either he or Cordelia or both are in fact dead. "You do me wrong to take me out o' th' grave," he complains, and his response to her "Sir, do you know me?" is "You are a spirit, I know. Where did you die?" (4.7.46, 48–49). Even when her identity and existence are fully acknowledged, Lear's relating to Cordelia as a separate person remains problematic. When captured by enemy forces, Lear reverts to a fantasy of a world in which there are just the two of them together, "We two alone will sing like birds i' th' cage" (5.3.9). In the last scene of the play, for Lear the question of whether Cordelia is alive or dead is still unsettled. I believe that even in this poignant scene there are echoes of his fundamental doubt about whether a loved one who separates should have existed at all.

Of course, Lear's disintegration and madness present us with the most powerful form of obliteration, the virtual death of much of the personality. At the realization that his powers are being curtailed by Goneril, he is shaken in his conception of himself as a king. "Does any here know me? This is not Lear," he says (1.4.232). "Who is it that can tell me who I am?" The Fool replies, "Lear's shadow" (236–37).

Edgar, whose father disavows ever having begotten him, assumes what is by far the most elaborated, tortured, and torturing disguise in the play. He changes into the Bedlam beggar "Poor Turlygod, Poor Tom" and hopes for survival on the assumption that "Edgar I nothing am" (2.3.20–21). He is determined to avoid recognition until he is certain that his father truly acknowledges him as his own again and admits to his error in believing Edmund over Edgar. Even then Edgar refuses to reveal himself until shortly before his father's death, and his revelation seems to be instrumental in precipitating that death. Edgar has three other disguises: as the fisherman who has "witnessed" Gloucester's suicidal leap and survival; as some rustic from another area, in order to thwart and challenge Oswald, Goneril's messenger; and lastly as the masked knight who challenges Edmund. Edgar's complete change of fortune from legitimate son to less than bastard (while the bastard rises in the father's eyes to become the true son) requires an incredibly elaborate sequence of disguise and revelation in order to return to his previous identity. Regaining his identity also involves inner change and painful learning. When reestablished as Edgar, the legitimate son, he is also designated the legitimate king. But his double legitimation as son and king are purchased at the price of much pain and slaughter. Thus, the one major character who survives being "unborn" and "reborn" lives to rule over a decimated and blighted kingdom.

In this obliterative play, is there any begetting that is not aborted, accursed, blighted, and blighting?[17] It is difficult to find, and I believe that this contributes to the grimness and desolation of the play, to its being so difficult to bear. There is, for example, much less of an implied sense of continuity at the end of *King Lear* than in *Hamlet* or *Macbeth*. Hope for a succession of generations is much enfeebled. The young, in the last line of the play, shall never see so much suffering as their elders, "nor live so long." There is abdication at the end—Albany and Kent, each in his own way, abdicates ruling. It is as if Lear's curse on all generation had been fulfilled—one can easily understand the view of modern viewers and critics who compare the play to Beckett's *Endgame* and *Waiting for Godot*. Yet I believe that there is enough begetting, enough good things generated, that

---

17. See Kanzer (1965) for a discussion of birth and pregnancy imagery in the play, and his argument that there is a fantasy of male pregnancy and of a violent primal scene at its core.

the experience for the surviving characters and for the viewers is not one only of devastation and degeneration.

What is begotten is begotten slowly, at great cost, and, in an important sense, silently. The word *pregnant* is used twice in the play, once by Edgar himself (4.6.226) and once in a speech maliciously and falsely attributed to Edgar by Edmund (2.1.78). The two uses afford an important contrast. The more famous passage, in act 4, is set at a point where Edgar is still not revealing himself to his father, Gloucester, after he has staged the mock suicide-and-redemption scene—Gloucester imagining that he has jumped off a Dover cliff to die. Gloucester prays never again to be tempted to take his own life, and Edgar speaks approvingly. Gloucester then asks Edgar, "Now, good sir, what are you?" and Edgar replies:

> A most poor man, made tame to fortune's blows;
> Who, by the art of known and feeling sorrows,
> Am pregnant to good pity. Give me your hand,
> I'll lead you to some biding.   (4.6.224–27)

How has Edgar become pregnant? "By the art of known and feeling sorrows"—by direct experience of sorrow, not merely by having heard of sorrows, he has been impregnated with "good pity." His experiences as an outcast, seeing his father blinded and cast out and Lear rejected and gone mad, have taught him pity for those even worse off than himself. "Pregnant to good pity" is virtually the only instance in the play of a growth, a germination, that, first, is of a good thing, and second, is slow, gradual, and not a horde, a brood, or a teeming—terms that convey the kind of hatching and begetting of evils characteristic of Goneril and Regan (e.g., 1.3.25; 1.4.287; 3.6.76). Further, the suggestion of a feminine identification is, in effect, an instantiation of Edgar's having learned pity—he has subtly accepted a feminine side to masculine power and the masculine role. Note that in his feigned madness, Edgar focuses obsessively and excessively on the evils of female sexuality and whoring, expressions that some critics have rightly taken as, among other things, indices of rage at his father for begetting Edmund and associated rage at female lust—but not rage at his father for believing Edmund. A subtle sense of Edgar's greater acceptance of what it is to be weak, to be downcast, to be a woman, is evidenced in this scene.

Details of how Edgar has been impregnated can be seen in his attitude toward the still mad Lear at the end of their time together in the isolated farm house. Lear is to be taken to Dover, and Gloucester is soon to be captured and blinded. Throughout the scene, Edgar's pose as Tom O'Bedlam is weakening. Aside, he says, "My tears begin to take his part so much / They mar my counterfeiting" (3.6.59–60). He proceeds to one more piece of Bedlam talk, to which Lear replies, "Then let them anatomize Regan. See what breeds about her heart. Is there any cause in nature that makes these hard hearts?" (75–77).

Lear asks what begets, what breeds, what could make such evil hearts. He then tries to enlist Edgar as one of his knights. A few lines later, Gloucester warns them of imminent danger, and they arrange to carry Lear out at once to the safety of Dover. As Edgar stands alone at the end of the scene, he soliloquizes that witnessing the suffering of others, especially one's betters, makes one more humble about one's own suffering. Thus, one ingredient in the growth of Edgar's pity is the knowledge gained by realizing that others may suffer more. A second ingredient is the sharing of the burdens of pain and suffering:

> Who alone suffers suffers most i' th' mind,
> Leaving free things and happy shows behind;
> But then the mind much sufferance doth o'erskip
> When grief hath mates, and bearing fellowship.
> How light and portable my pain seems now,
> When that which makes me bend makes the King bow.
> He childed as I fathered.   (3.6.103–09)

Thus, the sharing, having "mates" and "fellowship" in the bearing of pain, helps engender the "good pity" with which Edgar has become pregnant. This passage, more specifically, describes the growth of Edgar as a parent, as a father. It is, then, not just a step in his learning pity but a step in his knowing what it is to be a father; as such, in terms of the plot, it prepares the way for him to understand better his own rejecting father. What we are witnessing, then, are steps in the process of developing empathy.

The other passage in which *pregnant* appears is Edmund's successful attempt to deceive Gloucester into believing that Edgar is plotting against his father's life. Edmund invents a speech that he claims Edgar made to him, in which Edgar threatens that no one would believe Edmund if he told a tale in which the legitimate son was evil and the bastard son the worthy one. "Edgar," as quoted by Edmund, says:

> I'd turn it all
> To shy suggestion, plot and damnèd practice.
> And thou must make a dullard of the world,
> If they not thought the profits of my death
> Were very pregnant and potential spirits
> To make thee seek it.   (2.1.74–79)

At the literal level, the lines mean that the world would have to be stupid not to realize that Edmund stood to gain tremendously by discrediting Edgar. The "profits of my death" would be "very pregnant"—that is, *teeming*—with incentives and incitement to seek that end (Furness 1880; Shakespeare 1963, ad loc.). This is, first of all, a "false pregnancy," since the whole tale is a fabrication, but it is also a "true pregnancy" in the sense that Edmund really is "teeming" with motives and means to get rid of Edgar, including the motive to avenge himself on Gloucester for the way he was conceived, his mother's becoming pregnant out of wedlock.[18] But the use of the word *pregnant* here does connote something of the sense of gestation and pregnancy in most of the rest of the play—namely, gestating and producing teeming evils and awful offspring.

These two ascriptions of pregnancy to Edgar delineate the two senses of gestation in the play: the majority, indeed the overwhelming sense, of pregnancy as producing evil, and the minority sense of being pregnant with something good. Even the best of pregnancy, however—"good pity"—is conceived with great suffering and violence and is never completely delivered by the character—for Edgar, in effect, helps kill his own father by delaying too long the revelation of his true identity to him.

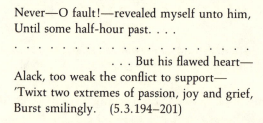

> Never—O fault!—revealed myself unto him,
> Until some half-hour past. . . .
> . . . .
>   . . . But his flawed heart—
> Alack, too weak the conflict to support—
> 'Twixt two extremes of passion, joy and grief,
> Burst smilingly.   (5.3.194–201)

His ambivalence toward his father thus interferes with his *timely* deliverance of recognition. He has helped his father psychically to survive blindness and the suicidal despair that ensued from realizing that he had misjudged his sons and condemned Edgar. But he is unable to work through his own rage and disappointment in time to keep the father alive longer.[19]

Earlier in this speech, Edgar explains to Albany that he knows of his father's miseries "by nursing them, my lord." He asks those around him to

18. A few lines later (80) Gloucester denies that he ever begot Edgar, thus amplifying the "birth" sense of the word *pregnant*. Philip Edwards (Shakespeare, 1985, p. 141) argues that *pregnant* in Shakespeare does not mean "to be with child" and cites the Oxford English Dictionary. My scrutiny of his citation and of other commentaries supports my contention that *pregnant* here means "to be with child" along with its other meanings of being ready, ripe, full.

19. Another perspective on Edgar's delaying is that he is unconsciously a patricide, as Edmund falsely accused him, and his delay in revealing himself is the enactment of this wish.

hear his tale, and then he wishes that his heart would burst. Here, like Gloucester's heart, he is swollen to bursting, pregnant with terrible pains, with trauma and guilt he cannot assimilate or master, like an engorged fetus that will kill the mother with its delivery.

Another sense in which the play suggests a more loving and caring kind of pregnancy and begetting is implied in Cordelia's behavior with Lear, both in the opening scene and in the scene of their reunion and recognition. The imagery of pregnancy, birth, and offspring seems natural enough in a scene devoted to issues of filial devotion and obligation, but still such imagery is prominent and surrounds the interchange between Cordelia and Lear around "nothing." The entrance of Lear and the "love trial" is preceded by the discussion between Gloucester and Kent about illegitimate and legitimate conception. It seems to me that Cordelia's inability to speak, her "nothing," her silence, are all "pregnant." Lear claims that "nothing will come of nothing," but Cordelia in effect argues for a space, time, and occasion to gestate and deliver the tokens of true filial love and devotion. Kent argues on Cordelia's behalf:

Thy youngest daughter does not love thee least,
Nor are those empty-hearted whose low sounds
Reverb no hollowness.   (1.1.154–56)

Cordelia's inner space is of a different sort from the other daughters' and is different from Lear's conception of an inner space that *instantly* produces.

The reunion between Lear and Cordelia, a scene that involves the slow and careful awakening of Lear, has overtones of birth, or rather of rebirth, resurrection. "You do me wrong to take me out o' th' grave," exclaims Lear as he is awakened to recognize himself and his daughter (4.7.45). What is important here is that recognition is a slow, gradual process, where all concerned urge tendance and patience for the restoration to grow and prove viable.[20]

The contrast between precipitous and violent conception, gestation, and delivery and slow, gradual, natural development opens up larger questions about the form of the play and its impact on the audience. These questions can be subsumed first under the rubric of space—that is, "room," "latitude," "play space"—and second under the rubric of meaning, connection, and continuity.

Lear in relation to his daughters demands extreme closeness, almost

20. Cf. also Edgar (still in disguise) gently admonishing his father after Gloucester's failed suicide attempt, "Bear free and patient thoughts," with a double entendre for "bear" (4.7.78). Contrast Edmund's speedy production: "Whereupon she grew round-wombed, and had indeed, sire, a son for her cradle era she had a husband for her bed" (1.1.14–15).

union and identity, and when that demand is thwarted, he angrily creates a huge distance, an unbridgeable gap (which includes sending Cordelia into exile). When enraged, he collapses the distance, creating an image of intergenerational cannibalism and devouring. His view of children as extensions of himself contrasts with Cordelia's expressed view—close relationships involving an intricate mixture of love, authority, respect, and obligation. We might look at this imbalance, lack of proportion in space and distance, from several perspectives, but one of the most useful is suggested by Murray Schwartz (1980), who draws upon the work of the psychoanalyst D. W. Winnicott. Winnicott, discussing the developing child in relation to the mother, speaks of a potential space, a free space, a play space, between mother and child, between child and family, and between child and world. Such a space, for the child, implies a trust in closeness and in the availability of nurturance, yet a sense that these others, mother, family, and world, do not violently or arbitrarily intrude upon him or her. Schwartz quotes Winnicott:

> The potential space between baby and mother, between child and family, between individual and society or the world, depends on the experience which leads to trust. It can be looked upon as sacred to the individual in that it is here that the individual experiences creative living.
>
> By contrast, exploitation of this area leads to a pathological condition in which the individual is cluttered up with persecutory elements of which he has no means of ridding himself. (1980, p. 24)

While the psychoanalytic principles behind this statement have a long and interesting history, involving the work of such analysts as Melanie Klein, Ronald Fairbairn, and Wilfred Bion, teachers and colleagues of Winnicott, the description is evocative enough to convey to the general reader something of the feeling of much tragedy, and of *King Lear* in particular. The room for play, for noninvasive development, becomes progressively more constricted as the plot proceeds. Most tragedies provide "breathing space," often through the beauty of the poetry, where, however terrible the events, there is a little room for the audience and often the characters as well to escape momentarily from a claustrophobic environment. *King Lear* seems to me, as it has to many readers and critics, the most confining of Shakespeare's major tragedies, the play that leaves the least room for "play." In *Hamlet*, the expansiveness of the language, the erotic byplay, the players' scenes, the extensive foreign travel of Hamlet, Laertes, Horatio, and Fortinbras all point to a wider world of infinite expansiveness beyond Elsinore. Even *Macbeth* portrays fecund and loving family relationships, whether in the descriptions of the birds around Macbeth's castle or in the glimpses of Macduff and Lady Macduff. *Antony and Cleopatra* similarly opens up new vistas and expanses, largely through the expansiveness of its poetry and its view of woman—who is not only the alluring and demanding destructive force she is in the other tragedies but is also a creature of infinite variety. As suggested by Schwartz (1980, esp. pp. 26–32), the sense of openness seems to go along with the enlarged vision of woman; perhaps they are even causally related.

In *King Lear*, open space is bleak, barren, treeless, unsheltering. Corresponding is the vision of the destructiveness of woman and her space, epitomized in Edgar's "O indistinguished space of woman's will" (4.6.276). The womb is destruction, and the hollow of the woman belongs to the fiend, to hell. The hovel on the heath in the storm is worse than bedlam, for the madness is concentrated in a small space. The palaces are too small to contain Lear's knights and, ultimately, Lear himself.

There is vanishingly little playfulness in this play—only a bit in the opening lines between Kent and Gloucester about Edmund's conception and birth. The Fool, verging on the grotesque, affords little or no comic relief—indeed, one can understand why the audiences who did not want their *King Lear* to be too grim preferred versions that omitted the Fool. The escape to and promise of Dover convey something of room, space, and hope opening up. The one scene where a small space is expanded to a huge one is, of course, Gloucester's invented leap off the Dover cliff onto the beach. There, imagination as well as space seems to expand. It is as if, once in the play, space that is usually as constricted as womb and vagina opens up and allows for a sort of new birth. In Winnicott's terms, the space is not only enlarged but no longer filled with persecutory creatures; indeed, Edgar, disguised as a fisherman on the beach, describes to the blind and stunned Gloucester the departure of a demon from the top of the "cliff" (4.6.67–74).

In all, the sense of this play as the grimmest and most devastating of Shakespeare's tragedies is conveyed by its rhythm of constriction and limited expansion. The rhythm is enacted in terms of space, play, hope, and, as I argued above, in terms of modes of conceiving and begetting. In every register (and I have delineated only a few of the possible ones) there is very little room and possibility within the play, among the characters. I believe these considerations are relevant to the audience's reaction to the play as an experience of wastage. Yet this characterization does not capture enough of what is elevating, ennobling in the play, or, rather, what it is that makes it so worth seeing, reading, and studying.

One source of room and space in *Lear* is in the realm of interpretation of motive and character. A brief survey of its history of character criticism reveals an enormous diversity of opinion regarding who is good and who is evil, exactly what is the mixture of motive for each of the main characters.

Generational differences in intepretation are often striking: in teaching the play to undergraduates I am struck by the tendency of many students to focus on the mischief created by Lear, how Lear makes his daughters into evil creatures. Anger at Cordelia for being snooty, uppity, and unwilling to play "by the rules" is also found occasionally in the critical literature and more often in undergraduate papers. Older readers readily identify with the misery of Lear and the bite of the serpent's tooth of filial ingratitude. In the recent psychoanalytic literature, two articles, written independently of each other, epitomize the differences in interpretation. One argues that most critics have an empathic block against appreciating Lear's difficulties and cites Coleridge as one of the few who fully grasped Lear's situation (Muslin 1984). Another analyst indicts Coleridge as blind to the role of parental narcissism in the creation of monstrous and ungrateful children (Hanly 1986). I believe that here—in our response to character and interaction, in exploration of the motives and significances of actions—the audience has its greatest degree of freedom and of play. What is uplifting and bearable about the play is precisely those values that are dramatized by their negation. What is unbearable for the characters is bearable for the audience because the members of the audience have some room and space to reverberate with both the negating and the affirming aspects of the play.

In brief, the space I ascribe to the audience is one in which empathy can grow. The growth—or constriction—of empathy within the audience mirrors processes taking place within the play and among the characters. I use the terms *empathy* and *empathic*, as well as *sympathy*, rather loosely here, in large part because the terms themselves, particularly empathy, have acquired such a range of connotations that it would take a book-length work to begin to order them. *Empathy* is the English version of a nineteenth-century German term, *Einfühling*, referring to the aesthetic act of "feeling one's way into" a work of art. The terms *pity*, *sorry for*, *weep for* within *King Lear* cover some of the semantic range of *empathy*.[21] It is worth recalling that even in antiquity, in Aristotle's *Poetics* (14), questions of how tragedy elicits pity and "sympathy" (*philanthrōpon*) were being raised. Aristotle addressed the question primarily in terms of how plot structure and the character of the hero elicit these emotions.

The question "what does the play mean?" has been a vexed and much contested one for *Lear*. Let us, for the moment, change the frame of this

---

21. For such a treatise see the two-volume work edited by Lichtenberg, Bornstein, and Silver (1984), especially the article by Reed, vol. 1, pp. 7–24, "The Antithetical Meaning of the Term Empathy in Psychoanalytic Discourse." In the eighteenth century the term *sympathy* was specifically invoked to describe Shakespeare's genius at portraying an enormous range of characters and situations. See Abrams (1958, pp. 244–49), "The Paradox of Shakespeare."

question, to ask from within the play itself, "how do the characters feel for each other and with each other?" and "what do the characters mean to each other?" What kinds of connections exist among the characters, and how are these connections broken, rearranged, and, in a few instances, restored?

I approach this thesis via a detour to consider the growth of empathy from the perspective of Shakespeare's portrayal of the family. In particular, it is important to consider the role of empathy in the relationships among the generations. It is in the context of the family that the capacity to connect, to feel with and for another, is bred.

The distinguished Shakespearean critic C. L. Barber (1980) left a posthumously published essay, "The Family in Shakespeare's Development: Tragedy and Sacredness," which condenses an enormous amount of scholarship and wisdom about Shakespearean poetry and drama. It provides us with a framework for considering familial values, familial connection, and the bases for familial closeness within the tragedies, especially within *King Lear*. Barber begins by noting that Shakespeare's art is marked by an intense investment in the human family, including its vertical continuity across generations and its horizontal continuity to the extended family or clan and then to the commonwealth. Barber goes to the heart of Shakespeare's durability and universal appeal by reminding us that "if I were writing this essay in 1876 instead of 1976, it would be called 'Shakespeare: Poet of the Family.'" Shakespeare's treatment of family relationships, in all the genres of his drama, is most extraordinary. He has the capacity to capture, often in a few lines or a phrase, the complexity, the richness, and the inevitable pain of being human and of living in a family. Shakespeare also manages, especially in the tragedies, to portray the most extraordinary families and yet to show us the most crucial features of ordinary family life.

Barber points out that in his earlier works, there is a sense of strong identification with the cherishing role of the parents in early infancy. While Barber takes into account the dark side of the way Shakespeare deals with family conflict in the romances and the *Sonnets*, he emphasizes the poet's commitment to portraying the accepting, nourishing, generative role of parents, the virtues of parenting. In his analysis of the *Sonnets* and the major tragedies, Barber distinguishes between two forms of identification or deep inner connection between generations and among family members, both of which might be called "mirroring."[22] The form in the *Sonnets*

22. "Mirroring" bridges a gap between the imagery of Shakespeare, especially in the sonnets, and the terminology of self-psychology, principally as defined by Heinz Kohut (e.g., 1971, 1977). Patients with narcissistic character disorders, according to Kohut, experienced deficiencies in the ordinary, healthy, mirroring that a child needs from parents. They have been subjected either to extreme parental withdrawal or to the kinds of pathological mirroring portrayed in *King Lear*. As such, they require large amounts of mirroring from the analyst to help understand and repair the deficit.

allows for continuity and generation, while the form in the tragedies, especially in *King Lear*, pathologically merges child with parent, collapsing differences and distinctions. One of the examples of generative mirroring cited by Barber is:

> Look in thy glass and tell the face thou viewest
> Now is the time that face should form another.
>
> . . . .
>
> Thou art thy mother's glass, and she in thee
> Calls back the lovely April of her prime;
> So thou through windows of thine age shalt see,
> Despite of wrinkles, this thy golden time.   (Sonnet 3)

The comedies and romances show that pleasurable reciprocal mirrorings between parent and child are achieved with a measure of toil and require skillful resolution of conflict combined with good luck. Many of the history plays show that these intergenerational issues can involve considerable pain and bloodshed, though there it mostly takes place in war between families or between nations rather than within the father–son relationship. With the "dark period" in Shakespeare's creativity—the first decade or so of the seventeenth century, the period of the great tragedies—there is a shift in emphasis in the portrayal of intergenerational relationships. They become grimmer, more problematic, more charged with destructive ambivalence. Contrast, for example, the father's disappointment with his son in *Henry the Fourth, Part 1*, with some examples from *Macbeth* or *King Lear*. King Henry is jealous that his enemy's son, Henry Percy, Hotspur, is so noble and heroic while his own Henry seems so irresponsible. He praises Henry Percy as a son, "the theme of honour's tongue," and sees "riot and disorder stain the brow" of his own son.

> O! that it could be prov'd
> That some night-tripping fairy had exchanged
> In cradle-clothes our children where they lay,
> And call'd mine Percy, his Plantagenet.
> Then would I have his Harry, and he mine.   (1.1.85–89)

Both the poetry and the sentiment are a lovely way to express dissatisfaction, so different from the obliterative mode of "Better thou / Hadst not been born than not t' have pleased me better" (*King Lear* 1.1.235–36).

The tragedies, according to Barber, introduce the need to confront the "self-asserting male egotism of the father" in a way that makes it impossible to resolve parent–child relationships, especially so as to allow for generational continuity. I would expand Barber's characterization of the disruptive forces in tragedy to include not only the intransigent male ego but the *intransigence of egos.* From the perspective I have developed on *King Lear*, intransigence includes refusal to acknowledge the other as separate though connected, or though connected, still separate. The kinds of mirroring in the love relationship or parent–child relationship that Barber finds in the *Sonnets* allows room for the play of connectedness and separation. The wish to have a child who is "a chip off the old block" can be seen in King Henry's speech, but he can acknowledge, however painfully, his disappointment and his *wish*, not his *intention*, to have a substitute child who would be more to his liking and more like himself. By contrast, the form of mirroring or replication of the self in the major tragedies, especially *King Lear*, does not allow for alteration, difference, deviation.

It is as if the very biological advantage of heterosexual reproduction—the ability to produce offspring who are both the same as and different from the parents—is negated. Also negated is another, almost biological imperative—a reciprocate relationship and connection between parent and child, or in any of the hierarchical relationships represented in the play. In *Lear*, characters use and exploit each other without a sense of interplay, fair play, give-and-take. Hence, the major model of familial relationship is one in which separation and difference are not tolerated, or if they are (as in male–female differences), the differences are seen to exist for the purpose of gratifying the needs and wants of the one by exploiting the other.

The model suggested in Cordelia's speeches to Lear, of a bond involving a meaningful connection but not total absorption, corresponds to the model of parent–child mirroring seen in the *Sonnets*. Cordelia's descriptions are less idealizing than those in the *Sonnets* but nevertheless indicate a proper regard for what each in the pair needs to find and can legitimately expect to find in the other. The mirror literally mentioned in the play is the "glass" Lear requests as he holds the body of Cordelia and wants to see if she breathes. It is in effect a mirror in which he asks to be able to see what he wants to see, not a mirror that gives a useful and valid reflection. Kent's relationship to Lear, and Lear's to Kent, in the opening of the play also suggest two different models of connection and mirroring. Lear expects Kent to agree absolutely with him and support him, merely to affirm and confirm Lear's rash moves. Kent views their relation as involving a complex of affection and obligation, including the obligation to disagree strenuously when necessary, to differentiate himself from Lear. Lear can see such differentiation only as betrayal, abandonment, and he must banish Kent, wish him away, and do away with him.

Hence, within the terms of the play, and among the characters, there is disagreement on what connection means, what constitutes a meaningful connection, and what kinds of obligation and reciprocity a connection signifies. One important message that gradually emerges from the play (rather than from any one character) is that unless meaningful human connections are honored, there is no meaning to the universe. The network of meaningful connections also includes the gods or the forces of nature—they too have their obligations. The interweaving of "divine" obligation and connection with human is seen in Albany's denunciation of Goneril, Regan, and Regan's husband, Cornwall:

> Tigers, not daughters, what have you performed?
> A father, and a gracious agèd man,
> Whose reverence even the head-lugged [chained and baited] bear would lick,
> Most barbarous, most degenerate, have you madded.
> Could my good brother suffer you to do it:
> A man, a prince, by him so benefited!
> If that the heavens do not their visible spirits
> Send quickly down to tame these vile offenses,
> It will come,
> Humanity must perforce prey on itself,
> Like monsters of the deep.(4.2.40–49)

Caught deep within the web of suffering and horror, one or another character proclaims the danger of chaos, of all order and all meaning falling apart. As Kent, Albany, and Edgar witness Lear entering with the dead Cordelia in his arms, Kent exclaims, "Is this the promised end? (i.e., Doomsday, the end of the world prophesied in the Bible) "Or image of that horror?" Edgar continues, and Albany proclaims, "Fall and cease" (i.e., let the heavens fall down, all things come to an end; 5.3.265–67). In this awful scene, though the most elemental forms of decency, obligation, and fairness have been violated by gods and men, the characters can relate these terrible happenings to something else—a biblical story or prophecy. Some sense and some connection remain even amidst the most horrible, wanton cruelty and slaughter. Thus, the struggle to make sense, to forge and maintain a meaningful connection, is intimately tied up with the struggle to maintain human ties, "the holy cords." The play, especially as it moves into the mad scenes of act 3, becomes replete with nonsense, which reverberates with nonconnection and nonrecognition. The sense of the words, of the sounds, gradually becomes reestablished as the human connections, so ferociously shattered, are gradually renewed and reaffirmed. Edgar's ravings subside as he and Gloucester are slowly reconnected; it becomes harder for him to feign madness and keep back tears when he hears his father declare his love for his "lost" son Edgar, and as he sees Lear so painfully struggling for justice with his daughters. Lear's madness lessens in ferocity when, in the trial scene (3.6), he establishes a new order and a new justice. The presence of Edgar, now a bit softened, Kent, and the arrival of Gloucester allows the king to fall asleep and to be held in Kent's arms. His reconciliation and renewal with Cordelia allow his own words to make more ordinary sense, let him establish more ordinary communication.

Thus, the movement in the play reflects the linkage of meaningful human connection with meaningful communication. The rhythm of this movement is not progressive, culminating in complete achievement of deep empathy, but rather involves climaxing and then slipping back, accomplishing and then partially undoing. On the whole, it is during Lear's madness—both the acute phase in the storm and the more stable but still delusional phase that continues to the end of the play—that new empathic connections are forged, and these are incomplete or unstable. Lear briefly regains his senses, enough to note that he may be losing his mind (3.2), seems to respond to the tendance of Kent (in disguise), and begins to pity the Fool. In these lines, one begins to see Lear's belated, but nevertheless genuine, recognition of the kinship of king and Fool:

> My wits begin to turn.
> Come on, my boy. How dost, my boy? Art cold?
> I am cold myself. Where is this straw, my fellow?
> The art of our necessities is strange,
> That can make vile things precious. Come, your hovel.
> Poor Fool and knave, I have one part in my heart
> That's sorry yet for thee.   (3.2.67–73)

The Fool's reply, and Lear's further acknowledgment of the need to enter the hovel, both suggest that the Fool is saying, "It's not enough to *feel* sorry for me; you actually have to do something: go into this hovel, which is the very opposite of the royal palace, and at least let us take a bit of shelter from the awful storm."

Lear does move to a more universal recognition of the plight of others, especially of the poor, in the famous speech that acknowledges his previous indifference to the sufferings of the poor and the homeless:

> O, I have ta'en
> Too little care of this! Take physic, pomp;
> Expose thyself to feel what wretches feel,
> That thou mayst shake the superflux to them,
> And show the heavens more just.   (3.4.32–36)

A dose of personal suffering is the proper medicine for pompous indifference to the plight of the poor and downtrodden.[23] The next step in Lear's

---

23. In Shakespeare's time there was an enormous increase in poverty, and consequently in landless, roving beggars, largely attributable to drastic changes in owner–tenant relationships that emphasized exploitation of land for profit. See Kernan (1981, esp. pp. 10–11 and n. 2) for detailed historical reference.

increasing appreciation of the human plight and of the fragility and impotence of all human beings comes when he encounters Edgar disguised as a madman, presumably almost completely naked. Lear starts to tear off his own clothes in a misguided kind of empathy:

> Is man no more than this? Consider him well. Thou ow'st the worm no silk, the beast no hide, the sheep no wool, the cat no perfume. Ha! here's three on's are sophisticated [three who are artifical, adulterated]. Thou art the thing itself; unaccommodated man is no more but such a poor, bare, forked animal as thou art. Off, off, you lendings! Come, unbutton here.   (3.4.105–11)

His feeling connection with Edgar-Tom is still tenuous, as it is with the others, for his appreciation of the plight of the naked and the cold is not sufficient. He therefore cannot allow himself to recognize Tom as a poor madman; rather, he needs to aggrandize him into "this philosopher," and while all are cold and hungry, he dallies in pseudo-philosophical conversation about the causes of thunder.

Consider the earlier discussion of mirroring in relation to *King Lear*. Different levels of empathic connection are represented in the play, ranging from transient to more durable, from connection in feeling but not necessarily in deed to more total acts of sympathy and pity. These different grades can also be spoken of as different ways that one person identifies with another. In considering different forms and degrees of empathy, one can envision different forms of one person using another as a mirror. A kind of mirroring in which one person demands of the other only reflected glory, or praise, or obedience will not be associated with a compassionate vision of the plight of that other. A kind of mutual mirroring, in which each person's situation is better seen and perception is made sharper, is likely to generate increased empathy and new perspectives, new imaginative possibilities. In brief, at one end of the range of varieties of mirroring is a kind of clonal replication of the aggrandized self or the degraded self, and at the other is a generative and regenerative interactional mirroring that begets deeper and more varied kinds of sympathy. Edgar's self-description as "a poor man pregnant with good pity" captures this sense of generative and reproductive empathy, an empathy associated with the variety of ways Edgar learned about and saw himself in the "mirror" of the other. It can also be argued that a necessary condition for a generative and helpful empathy is a balance between according a certain autonomy and separateness to the other and insisting on a measure of similarity and closeness. Such empathy also requires a combination of role skills, as it were. We reflexively (especially in the psychoanalytic climate of this decade) tend to connect empathy with a mother's way of knowing and connecting to her baby, but a wide variety of human situations require and elicit empathic connection. This is conveyed by Schafer's characterization (1959, quoted in Reed 1984) of what is entailed in one person's acknowledging another: "the recognition and protection of the object's [i.e., the other person] separateness involve some combination of motherly care, fatherly workmanship and command, fraternal allegiance, filial reparation, and sensuous intimacy of an intrusive and receptive nature" (p. 19). What I here call *generative empathy* or *generative mirroring* is both the result of these qualities and one of the factors that allows these different gender and role-related qualities to come into play.

Ruth Nevo (1972), a Shakespeare scholar whose special interest is in the relationship between the structure and the affective message of each of the tragedies, has pointed to the role of the subplot in *King Lear*. For her, "it constitutes Shakespeare's most sustained and complex system of mirrors; and because it is both complex and systematic, it is the matrix of unlimited interrelated relationships and cross-relationships" (p. 269). Thus, the brilliant use of the subplot of Edgar, Edmund, and Gloucester is a structural device for implementing the variety of identifications and mirrorings achieved by the play. The mirroring effect of the subplot is important for the characters within the play and probably even more effective for the audience. As Nevo suggests, it also functions as a kind of generative matrix for producing new combinations, new realizations, and new feeling-connections for characters and audience. The interweaving of plot and subplot is crucial for understanding the powerful and often contradictory reactions to the play.

My argument, then, is that while *King Lear* portrays the worst in human relations, somehow, to a limited degree for the characters and to a larger degree for the audience, it generates new depths of understanding and compassion for the other. I have suggested that the play also seems to elicit certain responses that suggest *limited empathy* for the plight of some others. I believe both assertions to be true. My own experience of the play over time and my reading of a range of critical responses have taught me that one's reactions and sympathies may be very specific upon one viewing or reading of the play but may change considerably in different life stages and situations.

There is one bit of empirical evidence about *Lear's* capacity to elicit a greater degree of mutual identification and empathy with the other. In a study done in 1970, a Shakespeare scholar and a psychologist studied actors in a production of the play that required some six weeks of rehearsal (Barron and Rosenberg 1970, in Rosenberg 1972, pp. 349–56). They interviewed the actors and administered personality inventory scales at the beginning and the end of the rehearsal period. By the end, the personality profiles of the actors playing Lear and the Fool resembled each other much more than they had at the beginning.

> As the rehearsal went on, the relationship between King and Fool became steadily more reciprocal, interdependent; the two often huddled together against the hostility of men and weather, until the troubled Lear began to take on some of the riddling, erratic—and erotic—imagery of the Fool; whereupon the Fool gave way and was seen no more. He "went to bed at noon"; and Lear in his madness, played Fool.

How does this play make many viewers "pregnant to good pity" while we know, historically, that for other viewers the play has been simply too much to bear? As Edgar tells us, the play accomplishes this by forcing us to experience directly and not merely to hear by report. We must see Lear mad, witness the cruelty of Cornwall gouging out the eyes of Gloucester, and see the depths of alienation and deprivation to which Edgar must descend in order to survive. We are confronted on stage with more suffering and cruelty than in any other Shakespearean tragedy with the exception of *Titus Andronicus*. As I suggested above, there is less "play room" in *King Lear*, a more claustrophobic atmosphere than in the other tragedies. We are put much more in the position of "unaccommodated man," huddled together in the hovel in the midst of storm and insanity. We can choose to move closer, for warmth and some consolation, and thus identify with, find reflections of ourselves in those characters. Or we can stand outside, perhaps even in the warmth of the palace where Regan, Edmund, and Cornwall stay during the storm, locking out Lear and distancing ourselves from the experience. I suggest that the plot and poetry of the play elicit, alternately, some of each kind of experience. Our empathy or enlarged sympathies come not from any simple identification with one or another of the characters but with the experience of both participating and refusing to participate in their pain.[24]

The experience of being both "within" and "without" intense emotional involvement brings us back full circle to another point in Barber's essay: namely, the role of the family in *King Lear* and in other works of Shakespeare. The family is the setting par excellence where mental life and experience are shaped on the dual template of participant and observer.

---

24. The most elaborated discussion of how the audience and the characters are engaged and distanced from various aspects of loving and acknowledging in this play is in the oft-cited essay of Cavell, "The Avoidance of Love: A Reading of *King Lear*" (1976). My discussion has been informed by and modeled on Cavell's richly textured treatment of the theme of avoidance.

How we negotiate those two activities (or two passivities), how we blend or refuse to blend them, is crucial in the issue of how we come to understand, feel empathy with, and identify with another person. Much of what is spoken of under various psychoanalytic topics such as resolution of the Oedipus complex, formation of the superego, and formation of personal ideals can also be considered in terms of the processes of participation and observation. In the family "plot" and "subplot" are constantly interwoven, providing the possibilities for different forms of empathic participation and identification among family members.

Barber suggests that we can understand Shakespeare's portrayal of the family better if we place it in the context of the decline of Catholicism and public celebration of the Holy Family. He speculates that the weakening of the cult of the Virgin Mary, consequent to Henry VIII's break with Rome, is associated with the vicious attacks on women in Shakespeare's great tragedies.[25] In brief, he hypothesizes that certain family tensions were better held in balance while there was a model of "the Holy Family" that the mortal family could aspire to emulate. While one can hardly speak of Elizabethan England as a society in which religion was weak, nevertheless the clash of religions must have weakened a sense of absolute authority. Amplifying Barber's hypothesis, one could point to a number of political and economic factors that combined to weaken the sense of some higher power enforcing right and justice. The family and family bonds become subject to greater pressures to generate and maintain a sense of stability and a reliable set of values.

The tragedies, Barber adds, reflect in their portrayal of failed families the anxieties (and, I would add, perhaps the wishes) stirred up by decline in the belief in absolute authority. *King Lear* is set in a pagan background, and characters repeatedly point to the threat of reversion to savagery and barbarism. Thus the family in the crucible, under great pressure, experiencing fundamental dissolution, reveals to us both the destructive aspect of humankind and how basic caring and cherishing form the ground substance, the matrix, of human life.

I extend Barber's speculations about the implication for the family of profound shifts in authority to a more global hypothesis about the conditions necessary for the flowering of great tragic drama. My suggestion is that periods in which there is a substantial real and perceived dislocation of authority, and therefore in which the family is subject to unusual strains

25. See now Greenblatt (1985) for a brilliant discussion of the relationships among the persecution of the Catholics, the practices of exorcism, madness, and theatricality in *Lear*. He provides a concrete link between the general statements made by Barber and details of the play.

but also to unusual opportunities, provide a necessary condition for the flowering of great tragic drama. Fifth-century Athens was one such time: there were profound shifts in the political organization, including a down-grading of the legal power of the clan and the creation of new, artificial "wards" as units of civic power. Intellectual currents that questioned and threatened certain traditional and religious beliefs, subjecting the bases of authority and belief to dialectic scrutiny, also played a role in increasing pressure on the family.[26]

Barber contends that part of what is appealing about Shakespeare to modern audiences is that he "present[s] the modern situation where religious need, or need cognate to what has been dealt with by worship of the Holy Family, has no resource except the human family and its extensions in society, including the problematic ideal of kingship" (p. 199). Whenever authoritative belief in the ideal family is shaken profoundly, but not totally destroyed, there is the possibility that great family drama, specifically tragedy, will arise. The "ideal families" have also always been problem-atic—the family life of the Greek gods is in fact the very stuff of the human families portrayed in Greek tragedy: adultery, betrayal, mutilation, castra-tion, attempts to kill offspring, and the entire catalogue of tragic disasters. And the Christian Holy Family includes a central image of a father who is willing to have his son killed, albeit for the cause of redeeming humankind.

As these belief systems are threatened or become less sustaining, the core values that have held, or failed to hold, the family together may be reex-amined. Meanings and meaningful relationships are questioned but can emerge from the chaos clarified and purified. Derangements, disturbances in equilibrium on earth, as it were, make the metastable equilibrium of the idealized family (e.g., the family of the gods) less viable and less sustaining. It is on this ground, shaken by earthquake but not destroyed, that the stage for tragic drama is built.

REFERENCES

Note: For psychoanalytic articles and books on *King Lear* and *Macbeth*, see Holland (1976, with commentary) and Willbern (1980, surveying work up to 1978).

Abrams, Morris H. 1958. *The Mirror and the Lamp*. New York: Norton. Orig-inally published 1953.
Bach, Sheldon, and Lester Schwartz. 1972. A Dream of the Marquis de Sade: Psychoanalytic Reflections on Narcissistic Trauma, Decompensation, and the

---

26. The most interesting account of the pressures on the family in fifth century Athens is still E. R. Dodds' superb work, *The Greeks and the Irrational* (1951).

Reconstitution of a Delusional Self. *Journal of the American Psychoanalytic Association* 20:451–475.

Barber, C. L. 1980. The Family in Shakespeare's Development: Tragedy and Sacredness. In *Representing Shakespeare: New Psychoanalytic Essays,* ed. Murray M. Schwartz and Coppélia Kahn, pp. 188–202. Baltimore: Johns Hopkins University Press.

Calderwood, J. L. 1986. Creative Uncreation in *King Lear. Shakespeare Quarterly* 37:5–19.

Cavell, Stanley. 1976. The Avoidance of Love: A Reading of *King Lear.* In *Must We Mean What We Say?,* pp. 267–356. Cambridge: Cambridge University Press.

Champion, Larry S. 1980. *King Lear: An Annotated Bibliography.* 2 vols. New York: Garland.

Dodds, Eric R. 1951. *The Greeks and the Irrational.* Berkeley: University of California Press.

Freud, Sigmund. 1958. The Theme of the Three Caskets. In *Standard Edition,* trans. James Strachey, vol. 12, pp. 289–301. Originally published 1913.

Furness, H. H., ed. 1880. *A New Variorum Edition of Shakespeare: King Lear.* Philadelphia: Lippincott.

Girard, René. 1977. *Violence and the Sacred.* Trans. P. Gregory. Baltimore: Johns Hopkins University Press.

Goldman, Martin. 1972. *Shakespeare and the Energies of Drama.* Princeton: Princeton University Press.

Greenblatt, Stephen. 1985. Shakespeare and the Exorcist. In *Shakespeare and the Question of Theory,* ed. Patricia Parker and Geoffrey Hartman, pp. 163–187. London: Methuen.

Hanly, Charles. 1986. Lear and His Daughters. *International Review of Psycho-Analysis* 13:211–220.

Holland, Norman H. 1976. *Psychoanalysis and Shakespeare.* New York: Octagon Books.

———. 1978. How Can Dr. Johnson's Remarks on Cordelia's Death Add to My Own Response? In *Psychoanalysis and the Question of Text,* ed. Geoffrey Hartman, pp. 18–44. Baltimore: Johns Hopkins University Press.

Kanzer, Mark. 1965. Imagery in *King Lear. American Imago* 22:3–13.

Kernan, Alvin B. 1981. *King Lear* and the Shakespearean Pageant of History. In *On King Lear,* ed. Lawrence Danson, pp. 7–24. Princeton: Princeton University Press.

Kohut, Heinz. 1971. *The Analysis of the Self: A Systematic Approach to the Psychoanalytic Treatment of Narcissistic Character Disorders.* New York: International Universities Press.

———. 1977. *The Restoration of the Self.* New York: International Universities Press.

———. 1978. Thoughts on Narcissism and Narcissistic Rage. In *The Search for the Self: Selected Writings of Heinz Kohut, 1950–1978,* 2 vols., ed. Paul Ornstein. New York: International Universities Press. Essay originally published 1972.

Kott, Jan. 1974. *Shakespeare Our Contemporary*. Trans. B. Taborski. Garden City, N.Y.: Doubleday.

Levenson, J. 1972. What the Silence Said: Still Points in *King Lear*. *Shakespeare 1971: Proceedings of the World Shakespeare Congress*, ed. C. Leech and J. D. M. D. R. Margeson, pp. 215–229. Toronto: University of Toronto Press.

Lichtenberg, Joseph, Melvin Bornstein, and Donald Silver. 1984. *Empathy I* and *Empathy II*. Hillsdale, N.J.: Analytic Press.

McManaway, J. G. and J. A. Roberts. 1975. *A Selective Bibliography of Shakespeare: Editions, Textual Studies, Commentary*. Washington: Folger Shakespeare Library.

Muir, Kenneth. 1960. Madness in *King Lear*. *Shakespeare Survey* 13:30–40.

———. 1978. *The Sources of Shakespeare's Plays*. New Haven: Yale University Press.

Muslin, Hyman L. 1984. On Empathic Reading. In *Empathy I*, ed. Joseph Lichtenberg, Melvin Bornstein, and Donald Silver, pp. 301–316. Hillsdale, N.J.: Analytic Press.

Nevo, Ruth. 1972. *Tragic Form in Shakespeare*. Princeton: Princeton University Press.

Perrett, W. 1904. The Story of King Lear from Geoffrey of Monmouth to Shakespeare. *Palaestra* 3.

Pierce, R. B. 1971. *Shakespeare's History Plays: The Family and the State*. Columbus: Ohio State University Press.

Reed, Gail. S. 1984. The Antithetical Meaning of the Term "Empathy" in Psychoanalytic Discourse. In *Empathy I*, ed. Joseph Lichtenberg, Melvin Bornstein, and Donald Silver, pp. 7–24. Hillsdale, N.J.: Analytic Press.

Reid, S. W. 1982. The Texts of *King Lear*: A Review Essay. *Shakespeare Studies* 15:327–342.

Rosenberg, Marvin. 1972. *The Masks of King Lear*. Berkeley: University of California Press.

Schwartz, Murray M. 1980. Shakespeare through Contemporary Psychoanalysis. In *Representing Shakespeare: New Psychoanalytic Essays*, ed. Murray M. Schwartz and Coppélia Kahn, pp. 21–32. Baltimore: Johns Hopkins University Press. Essay originally published 1977.

Seng, P. J. 1967. *The Vocal Songs in the Plays of Shakespeare*. Cambridge: Harvard University Press.

Shakespeare, William. 1963. *The Tragedy of King Lear*. Ed. R. Fraser. Signet Classic ed. New York: Signet.

Simon, Bennett. 1984. "With Cunning Delays and Ever-Mounting Excitement" or, What Thickens the Plot in Tragedy and Psychoanalysis. In *Psychoanalysis: The Vital Issues*, ed. George H. Pollock and John E. Gedo, vol. 2, pp. 387–436. New York: International Universities Press.

Snyder, Susan. 1979. *The Comic Matrix of Shakespeare's Tragedies: Romeo and Juliet, Hamlet, Othello and King Lear*. Princeton: Princeton University Press.

Trewin, J. C. 1981. *The Simon and Schuster Pocket Companion to Shakespeare's Plays.* New York: Simon and Schuster.

Urkowitz, Steven. 1980. *Shakespeare's Revision of King Lear.* Princeton: Princeton University Press.

Willbern, David. 1980. A Bibliography of Psychoanalytic and Psychological Writings on Shakespeare: 1964–1978. In *Representing Shakespeare: New Psychoanalytic Essays*, eds. Murray M. Schwartz and Coppélia Kahn, pp. 264–286, 288. Baltimore: Johns Hopkins University Press.

CHAPTER 5

A Tale Told by an Idiot: Shakespeare's *Macbeth*

*K*ing *Lear* is replete with the most awful reverberations of cruelty between children and parents; namely, a curse on all generation: "all germains spill at once, / That makes ingrateful man" (3.2.8–9). The seeds of reproduction should be spilled upon the ground, Onan-like, and not allowed to make human beings, "ingrateful" or otherwise. In *Macbeth* we enter a different atmosphere, in which the problem is not explicitly within the several generations of a family—it is not parents and children against each other. Rather, there are no children, and the action manifestly devolves around the consequences of this lack. But the lack is continually "present" and somehow keeps generating substitutes, replacements, or equivalents of children. As one considers the array of efforts to fill the absence, one can come to some understanding of why and how Macbeth and Lady Macbeth could not or would not procreate.

Among the effects, as it were, of the "lack" within the play is a tendency among readers and audiences to respond by "supplying" either children, explanations, or a fuller account of the lives of these fictive personalities. "How many children had Lady Macbeth?" asked a noted Shakespearean critic by way of mocking the construction of offstage or predrama lives of stage characters.[1] Yet the playwright does not make it easy to dismiss the question, for the presences and absences he provides leave the reader

---

1. Knights, *How Many Children Had Lady Macbeth? An Essay in the Theory and Practice of Shakespeare Criticism* (1933). Ironically, after posing the question in the title, Knights never returns to an examination of the foolishness of the question. He thus also falls into the pattern of "Is it there or isn't it there?" For a more literal answer see Mary Cowden Clarke's (1893) version: Lady Macbeth had an infant son who was killed by her ruthlessly exposing him to danger in battle.

"knowing" two contradictory things—there are or were children and there are no children. While we may be uncertain, neither Macbeth nor Lady Macbeth express any conscious doubt about the existence or nonexistence of children. It is our problem, not theirs. But what *is* theirs is the repeated question whether something really is or isn't present. "Is this a dagger I see before me?" Is Banquo at the banquet, there to be seen? Will Birnam Wood come to Dunsinane? Is there a man not of woman born? These are several forms of a question that I believe is related to the problem of whether or not there are children.[2]

That children exist for other people is a fact that clearly enrages Macbeth. He blames Duncan's sons for the murder of their father, plotting successfully to "kill off" Malcolm as heir apparent. He slays Macduff's children, and he attempts unsuccessfully to kill Banquo's son, in order to thereby extinguish a line of kings that extends to the crack of doom. When his outrage is almost entirely spent and numbness and despair seem regnant, Macbeth realizes that he has committed all these murders to gain a crown he cannot pass on to a son. He then declares that the whole story is "a tale told by an idiot, full of sound and fury, signifying nothing."[3] No progeny, no one to whom to pass on the royal state, no immortality, no living copies of Macbeth—all this also adds up to the conclusion that there is no story worth telling. Yet Shakespeare, while showing us the withering and final death of Macbeth, makes *Macbeth* immortal, a story repeatedly told by actors great and ordinary to multitudinous audiences.

Along with storytelling, it is clear that within the play issues of talking versus not talking, who is allowed to talk and who must keep silent, and who or what finally talks and tells despite all efforts to prevent talking and hearing are of major import. Donalbain, Duncan's younger son, says to his brother after their father has been murdered, "Why do we hold our tongues, / That most may claim this argument for ours?" (2.3.122). The answer is that, in fact, it is neither safe nor wise to speak.[4]

When is it time to speak? Macbeth several times proposes to Banquo that they set a time to speak about the import of the three weird sisters. Banquo

2. A mock uncertainty, but a grim one, is seen in the "riddling scene" 4.2 (Knights, 1933, p. 47) in the interchanges among Ross, Lady Macduff, and the son. The riddle posed by Lady Macduff about their son is "Fathered he is, and yet he's fatherless." Another riddling scene, specifically teasing and invoking equivocation, is the porter's scene.

3. "Nothing" in Shakespearean tragedy is frequently found in association to childbearing, pregnancy, or the wish that a child had never been born; see Willbern (1980), "Shakespeare's Nothing," to which I think this idea is an important addendum.

4. Citations from *Macbeth* are from the Signet Classic Edition, ed. Sylvan Barnet (Shakespeare 1963).

agrees in principle, but the time never arrives, for Macbeth has decided it is the time to kill, not to talk. Overall, time is a most peculiar commodity in this drama, considered and treated differently by different characters. The contrast between the way Macbeth and Lady Macbeth deal with time and the way Banquo does is most striking. The distinctions among past, present, and future, the linear flow and sequence of time, are confounded, wished away, and virtually trashed by Macbeth. "Beguile the time," Lady Macbeth urges her husband early in the play; by the end, time merely "creeps in this petty pace" because it has been so twisted and abused. Twisted time, blocked speech, thwarted reproduction all converge in the image of the tale told by an idiot. The thwarted tale in *Macbeth* also points to the role of guilty conscience as a form of interruption in narrative continuity, another aspect of telling and not telling.

BIRTH, PROGENY, AND DYNASTY

Macbeth is a tragedy that depends upon the tension between ambition to gain a throne—in the course of which families, including children, must be destroyed—and the escalating aggression and despair that come with the realization that these murders are meaningless because the hero will have no progeny to whom to pass on the throne. The extreme guilt felt by Macbeth and Lady Macbeth, and its consequences, must be seen in the setting of this conflict—they kill to head a royal house, to be king and queen, but as a result of both their childlessness and their murdering, there will be no house to rule or to found.

Comparison of Shakespeare's play with the mythohistorical source in Holinshed's *Chronicles* suggests that the problem of Macbeth's lack of male progeny to take the crown was introduced by Shakespeare.[5] The account in the *Chronicles* seems to emphasize that Duncan had a good deal of latitude in whom he chose to be his successor: the laws of Scotland did not demand a strictly father–son transmission. And Holinshed conveys virtually none of the "dramatic" dread of female power that Shakespeare so powerfully exploits.

5. Cf. Freud's (1916) comments on psychoanalytic aspects and psychoanalytic limitations of explaining *Macbeth* and Macbeth. He points out that Shakespeare highlights the problem of succession. Two articles on *Macbeth* by Ludwig Jekels (1952), whose work Freud mentions, are quite important; in particular, they argue for the centrality of father–son conflicts in regard to the dynastic problem. "A bad son not only sacrifices his son, but, in so doing, also forfeits the blessing of continuous descent." See discussion of these papers in Holland, (1966), pp. 221–23, and also see Baudry (1984) on psychoanalytic methodology in understanding *Macbeth*.

Early in the story and in the script. Macbeth is hailed by the witches as
"King hereafter!" Banquo, distressed that they do not speak to him, asks,

> If you can look into the seeds of time
> And say which grain will grow and which will not,
> Speak then to me, who neither beg nor fear
> Your favors nor your hate.   (1.3.58–61)

This is the first mention of issue or seed in the play, seeds of events or seeds
of children. The third witch announces to Banquo, "Thou shall get kings,
though thou be none. So all hail, Macbeth and Banquo!" (67–68). This
contrast between Macbeth and Banquo becomes more pointed as the drama
unfolds and it becomes more explicit that Macbeth has no children and/or
will not have any children. The absence of progeny becomes a critical factor
of increasing importance.

The ending of the play, or rather the last major action in the plot,
devolves around birth and progeny in the form of the prophecy provided to
Macbeth by the apparition from the witches' cauldon, which announces:
"Laugh to scorn / The pow'r of man, for none of woman born / Shall harm
Macbeth" (4.1.79–81). Macduff, who was "from his mother's womb /
Untimely ripped" (5.8.15–16), turns out to be such a man. Thus, the play
moves from a contrast between birth and no birth, progeny or no progeny,
to a birth that is both birth and nonbirth—a cesarean section.[6] Thus what is
at issue is not just having progeny, but how and with whom. The riddling
prophecy of a man not of woman born points to an unconscious dread that
being given birth by a woman involves too much dependence and interdependence upon the mother. It is akin to Apollo's fantasy-theory in *The
Oresteia* that the mother is not the true parent of the child but only a vessel
or seed-bed. This "misapprehended oracle," like many of the famous
oracles referred to in classical literature (most notably those reported in
Sophocles' *Oedipus Rex*), concerns issues of birth and progeny (Fenichel
1954, pp. 228–36). In the course of acting upon what he understands of the
witches' prophecies, Macbeth, unlike Laius, tries to kill not his own children

6. See Eccles (1982) for material on and fantasies about cesarean birth and on abnormal
presentations in Elizabethan and Tudor times. The weight of medical authority was against
attempting cesarean birth, which seemed to be almost always lethal to the mother. One
authority, however, recommended cesarean section: "Rousset had argued that the operation
might be permissible for pressing political reasons, as did Pechey, 'when a Family is like to be
extinguished; or some Kingdom or Principality is like to be lost'" (p. 115). See also Young
(1944). Also apropos of the three witches, see Forbes, *The Midwife and the Witch* (1966).
From the psychological side, see the comments of Jekels (1952, pp. 128–30) on the myth of
Dionysus, ripped from his mother's womb and then implanted in his father's thigh, therefore
not born of woman.

but the children of others—Banquo's son, Macduff's and Duncan's children, and the "downfall'n birthdom" that is Scotland (4.3.4). The atmosphere of *Macbeth*, then, is suffused with concern about children, their existence, their value, and whether they will be killed or will survive. Interwoven with these concerns are others about the power of women over men, the constancy and reliability of female figures and their expendability (see 4.3.57–76), and the definition of male potency as both military and procreative.

In the second scene of the play—the first contains no human figures—we have an account of Macbeth's heroism, military prowess, and loyalty to the king. But the language already hints at a need for ultra-powerful phallic and violent activity in order to establish the hero as a man. This need is tied up with a deprecation of women and the language of teeming reproduction. The captain reports that Macdonwald is

> Worthy to be a rebel for to that
> The multiplying villainies of nature
> Do swarm upon him. . . .
>
> .   .   .   .
>
> And Fortune, on his damnèd quarrel smiling,
> Showed like a rebel's whore: (1.2.10–15)

And Macbeth, disdaining the whore, went forward with his steel, "which smoked with bloody execution," and "carved out his passage" (18–19). Further, Macbeth did not just kill the rebel-traitor, but persisted "Till he unseamed him from the nave to th' chop [jaws] / And fixed his head upon our battlements" (22–23).

There is an amazing symmetry between this first battle scene (related in narrative) and the last, the encounter between Macbeth and Macduff. In the first, the reference to birth is muted ("multiplying villainies of nature") but there is a variant of the "cesarean section" in the wound Macbeth inflicts on his enemy. Both scenes end with the beheading of the vanquished.

Macbeth and Banquo, fearless and undaunted, quickly face the next battle:

> As cannons overcharged with double cracks;
> So they doubly redoubled strokes upon the foe.
> Except they meant to bathe in reeking wounds,
> Or memorize another Golgotha—   (1.2.37–40)

Here too the imagery suggests some violent quasi-sexualized assault, an impression buttressed by Ross's picture of Macbeth (or perhaps of some other heroes) as "Bellona's bridegroom"—Ares, the bridegroom of the goddess of war.

What is the "issue" or the consequences of these battles and of the military prowess of the two heroes, Macbeth and Banquo? The first issue is the encounter with the three witches and the prophecy encoded in their greeting Macbeth as Thane of Glamis (which he is by virtue of his father's demise), Thane of Cawdor, and King hereafter. The next consequence is a "seed" planted in Macbeth's heart around the knowledge that Banquo's seed will grow into a line of kings. (In the later apparition in 4.1 of a child crowned and holding a tree in his hand, the metaphor of seeds has grown into a family tree.) As the three witches leave and we reenter the ordinary human realm, Ross and Angus announce the execution of the traitor Cawdor and Macbeth's appointment to that title. What is begotten now is a *hope* in both Macbeth and Banquo (1.3.118–20). Banquo suggests that hope might kindle desire and warns that the instruments of darkness may bring us to harm by telling us small truths that will lead to disaster by betraying us "in deepest consequence," in the most important consequence or offshoot of their schemes. Within a few lines, however, barely assimilated knowledge leads to hope, to a kindling of desire, then to an almost fully conceived plan that literally possesses Macbeth.[7] He momentarily fends off "the horrid image" of murder and tells himself that perhaps he should leave the future to chance, without overt action on his part. "Come what come may, / Time and the hour runs through the roughest day" (1.3.150–51). This is Macbeth's first reference to time, and it is one of his last to allow for the ordinary flow of time, for the patience of accepting what time brings.

In the next scene (1.4), the king welcomes Macbeth and Banquo, and the imagery of procreation and fertility continues:

King: Welcome hither,
  I have begun to plant thee, and will labor
  To make thee full of growing. Noble Banquo,
  That hast no less deserved . . .

. . . .
                  . . . let me enfold thee
  And hold thee to my heart.
Banquo: There if I grow,
  The harvest is your own.
King [announcing Malcolm as his heir]: My plenteous joys
  Wanton in fullness, seek to hide themselves
  In drops of sorrow. Sons, kinsmen, thanes,

7. The sense of *sterile* and *fertile* is conveyed in this scene, not just by the reference; to seeds and children, but also by the "blasted heath" and Macbeth's metaphor of "Two truths are / As happy prologues to the swelling act / Of the imperial theme" (1.3.127–29).

And you whose places are the nearest, know,
We will establish our estate upon
Our eldest, Malcolm, whom we name hereafter
The Prince of Cumberland;   (1.4.28–39)

What is fullness and harvest for the king—generosity and rewards to his
loyal Thanes and naming his son as his successor—is for Macbeth a stumbling block. The fact that Banquo was told he would father kings begins to
loom larger in his mind, as evidenced by a curious omission, unnoticed by
most critics—Macbeth does not tell Lady Macbeth about that part of the
witches' prophecies. Lady Macbeth is never once in the text distressed about
not having progeny. Her ambition is to be queen; Macbeth's ambition is to
be king, progenitor, and immortal. In my reading of the play, it is around
this (literally) unspoken issue that the two begin to drift apart.[8]

The interweaving of the theme of the woman's power to make the man be
a man, or more than man, with the theme of procreation continues in the
last three scenes of act 1. In scene 5, Lady Macbeth reads the letter from
Macbeth and clearly articulates her intentions and her fear of Macbeth's
queasiness—he is too full of the milk of human kindness, and she is willing
to have an "exchange transfusion" of gall to replace her milk. By implication, she will have to infuse Macbeth with some of that gall and remove
some of his milk. "Come, you spirits / That tend on mortal thoughts, unsex
me here" (1.5.41–42)—make me into a man. However, the man to whom
she aspires to be transformed is only an ambitious killer, not a man who
seeks immortality in progeny as well.

In scene 6, Duncan comes to Macbeth's castle, first as a guest and then as
a murder victim. The scene is set by the justly famous passage about the
birds in the castle, a description of the loving and lovely aspects of sexuality,
nesting, and procreation. It is summer—Duncan is coming to the castle;
Banquo comments on the air, the beauty, and the birds—

Banquo: This guest of summer,
    The temple-haunting martlet, does approve
    By his loved mansionry that the heavens' breath
    Smells wooingly here. No jutty, frieze,
    Buttress, nor coign of vantage, but this bird

8. See 3.2, esp. 36–39; Macbeth is tortured ("full of scorpions is my mind") because
Banquo and Fleance live, while Lady Macbeth responds that they are not immortal: "in them
nature's copy not eterne." Macbeth is in fact convinced that the ability to make a "copy" does
make them "eterne." See Knights (1933, p. 45), who glosses "copy not eterne": "when
Shakespeare wrote . . . copyholders [tenants] formed . . . the largest land-holding class in
England, whose appeal was always to 'immemorial antiquity' and 'times beyond the memory
of man.'"

Hath made his pendent bed and procreant cradle.
Where they most breed and haunt, I have observed
The air is delicate.   (1.6.3–9)

Even though the castle will quickly become a "mansion" of betrayal, and falsehood, home to an orgy of confused, impotent, sexualized slaughter, the poet holds up for us in these few lines a contrasting statement about what a house and family can and should be. Recall an opposite poetic effect in Aeschylus' *Agamemnon*, where Cassandra's opening speech, after she is told to go into the house and mutely refuses, is a pained vision of the palace as a charnel house, reeking of blood and terrible murderous sexuality: "keep the cow away from the bull!" (1125–26). Here, Banquo, ultimately the procreative one, sings this ode of quiet joy. The murder of Duncan, which is shortly to take place, with false blame assigned to his own chamberlains and sons, is therefore also Macbeth's attack on family and on building a house.

The plotting of Duncan's murder, Macbeth's vacillation, the gelling of the plan, and the actual execution also invoke and evoke images of parenting and of infancy. Upon the murder of such a gentle king,

> his virtues
> Will plead like angels trumpet-tongued
>
> . . . .
>
> And pity, like a naked newborn babe,
> Striding the blast, or heaven's cherubin horsed
> Upon the sightless couriers of the air,
> Shall blow the horrid deed in every eye.   (1.7.18–24)

Lady Macbeth explains to Macbeth that she would have murdered Duncan herself had he not so resembled in his sleep her own father. Her taunting speech to Macbeth about his manhood includes the famous lines about her child or children:[9]

> I have given suck, and know
> How tender 'tis to love the babe that milks me:
> I would, while it was smiling in my face,

9. Among the taunts hurled by Lady Macbeth at her husband is that he is a pussy cat (1.7.43–44), perhaps equivalent to the modern colloquialism of a man being "pussy" or "pussy-whipped." Later Macbeth calls himself "the baby of a girl" . . . i.e., a little girl's doll, or perhaps a baby girl (3.4.108). Note too that "given suck" and the image of the breast are subtly echoed in the exchange where Ross reveals the slaughter of Macduff's wife and children. Macduff: "What concern they? / The general cause or is it a fee-grief / Due to some single breast?"—both the ones who sucked at the breast and the one who gave suck are killed, bringing pain to his breast.

Have plucked my nipple from his boneless gums,
And dashed the brains out, had I so sworn as you
Have done to this. (1.7.54–57)

Lady Macbeth immediately lays out the plan for getting the chamberlains drunk, in effect treating them as nursing babes whose brains will be dashed out. "Bring forth men-children only; / For thy undaunted mettle should compose / Nothing but males" (72–74) is Macbeth's response to her vision of courage and manhood. Again, birth, the tendance of children, and a vision of a woman as powerful, destructive, and waiting to pounce on the faltering manhood of her mate are all interwoven.[10] The message gradually unfolds: who would or could have children within such a world as that created and peopled by Macbeth and Lady Macbeth!

Thus, we begin to glimpse the peculiar ambiguity about the existence or potential existence of offspring from this union. It is not that the poet gives us an explicit answer or resolution; rather, he creates an atmosphere, a climate that (in contrast to the martlets' nest-building) is so inhumane and uncongenial to expressing the tenderness needed for the bearing and rearing of infants as to blunt the will to procreate.

In contrast to the imagery of the death of babes (and death and babies) in this scene, (2.1) opens with Banquo and his son, Fleance. Their very existence as father and son rubs salt in Macbeth's wounds. He cautiously tries Banquo: could he be enlisted in the plot? (in Holinshed's *Chronicles* he is a fellow conspirator). But Banquo, without explicitly discussing a conspiracy, declares his allegiance to Duncan. Macbeth is gradually apprehending the actuality of Banquo and his offspring in contrast to his own sterility.

But what do this husband and wife actually beget? I believe it is plausible to read the next sequence as a symbolic response to the encounter with Banquo and his son, a partial filling in of an "absence," the absence of a son. What the two produce, in a complexly choreographed mutual encitement and seduction, is a conspiracy and a murder. The equation of deeds, especially bloody deeds, and offspring is seen in Macbeth's grim resolve, "From this moment / the very firstlings of my heart shall be / The firstlings of my hand" (4.1.144–46).[11] This is the first and last time that they come to-

10. See Kahn (1981), esp. chap. 6, "The Milking Babe and the Bloody Man in *Coriolanus* and *Macbeth*," for the dynamics of the dread of woman and the fragile masculine identity that seems continually to need either milk or gall from the woman. Her approach has been enormously useful to me in my reading of this play. See also Adelman (1987), a rich and detailed study of the dread of the feminine which came to my attention after I had written this chapter.

11. Cf. "unnatural deeds / Do *breed* unnatural troubles" (5.1.75–76), a metaphor familiar from Greek tragedy, especially *The Agamemnon* (see chap. 2).

gether and jointly make something of consequence. The method by which Macbeth and Lady Macbeth interact to produce the bloody deeds is paralleled symbolically by the imagery attending the murder—namely, a sadistic, mutually destructive, grim primal scene.[12]

I have alluded to Macbeth's vacillation and to Lady Macbeth's taunting him that she, not he, is the real man. The image of her dashing out the brains of the suckling infant is also a representation of what she is doing to Macbeth right in front of our eyes. She is also dashing out her own brains, in effect, and beginning to bring disease to her brain. After this point in the play, "brains" are invoked a number of times, usually in the form of "brainsickly" or a disease of the brain, or referring to Banquo as if his brains had been dashed out.[13]

The hallucination of the dagger and the accompanying speech introduce other elements that "thicken" the meaning, add new overtones to the murder (2.1.33–64). The dagger is a bloody, sexual symbol, consonant with the image of the murder as a rape.

> witchcraft celebrates
> Pale Hecate's offerings; and withered murder,
> Alarumed by his sentinel, the wolf,
> Whose howl's his watch, thus with his stealthy pace,
> With Tarquin's ravishing strides, towards his design
> Moves like a ghost.   (2.1.52–56)[14]

Murder is withered, a phrase evoking impotence and the desperation and sadism that may accompany frenetic attempts to restore potency.[15] The Tarquin–Lucrece story, as told in Shakespeare's *The Rape of Lucrece*, evokes images of rape and betrayal, both leading to a terrible chain of

12. See Nevo (1972, pp. 235–36) for a similar view of the murder as their child.

13. "Heat-oppressed brain," 2.1.39, and "brainsickly," 2.2.45, both refer to Macbeth; "the written troubles of the brain" refers to Lady Macbeth, 5.3.42; "The times has been / That when the brains were out, the man would die, / And there was an end; but now they rise again" refers to Banquo's ghost, 3.4.78–81. "Brains" may represent a condensation of head, procreative organ, and child. In classical antiquity, in medicine and folklore, brain and semen were regarded as the same substance (Simon, 1978, pp. 263–66), and I wonder if the symbolism persisted to Elizabethan times.

14. "Pale Hecate's offerings" may echo Seneca's *Medea*: Medea bares her breasts and lets blood from her arm at Hecate's altar, in preparation for murdering her own children. See Ewbank (1966), pp. 82–94.

15. The porter scene (2.3) of course focuses on impotence in a way that replicates in content (though not in affect) much of what is said just before and just after—especially involving equivocation, impotency ("makes him stand to and not stand to"; 35), cowardice, and crime. Macbeth's potency has been challenged by Lady Macbeth, and the dagger-hallucination is at some level a restoration in fantasy of a member withered by her blasts.

destruction (Lucrece's suicide, revenge, bloody warfare). Important reversals that add to the tragic dimensions of the play are hinted at by mention of
that tale. Lady Macbeth is both treacherous and ultimately the betrayed
Lucrece, since she commits suicide. Duncan is thus also an honorable
woman being betrayed and raped. The grooms, bloodied and murdered by
Macbeth, are, I believe, analogized to the child/children Lady Macbeth
would have killed.[16]

In addition to the dagger in this scene there is Macbeth's hallucination of
a voice crying out, "Sleep no more!" These hallucinations are the creatures
of Macbeth's sick brain, but they also thicken the question in the play of
whether things are really there. This question comes to haunt Macbeth and
Lady Macbeth as they gradually realize the full reality of what they have
done and its consequences. Do deeds really beget consequences; do they
always beget just the precise consequences you wish; and can you accept
that what has been begotten is not always to your liking?

The murder itself has been read by many critics as a form of parricide,
and certainly Lady Macbeth sees it as such—she sees in Duncan asleep the
image of her father, and it stays her hand. Macbeth makes up the lie that
Duncan's sons have conspired to have their father murdered, so he promul-
gates a kind of patricide theory. Jekels (1952) emphasizes not just the
patricidal aspect of Macbeth's deed but the fact that the murder also sets the
pattern for Macbeth as a father. As the king and father of Scotland he is a
murderer. What is begotten in the murder is an endless chain of further
crimes, paralleling, with a primitive causality, Macbeth's nightmare of the
endless chain of Banquo's descendants.[17]

Macbeth and Lady Macbeth are scarcely together after Duncan's murder—Lady Macbeth complains to him, "How now, my lord! Why do you
keep alone, / Of sorriest fancies your companions making" (3.2.9–10).
After Banquo's murder and the disastrous banquet, Macbeth and his wife
are never alone, or even in the same room, again. Even the sleepwalking
scene and the scene with Macbeth and the doctor are artfully contrived so
that husband and wife never meet, let alone touch. When she dies, commit-
ting suicide, Macbeth has no time to mourn her.

16. Does the phrase "daggers / Unmannerly breeched with gore" (2.3.118–19) suggest
breeches stained with blood? Are they stained with the blood of childbirth, menstruation,
defloration?

17. Cf. 5.8.68–69, "Producing forth the cruel ministers / Of this dead butcher and his
fiendlike queen," and the echoes with "you murd'ring ministers" in Lady Macbeth's "take
my milk for gall" (1.5.49–50); murdering ministers are another expression of "offspring" of
this couple.

There is, however, one further begetting in the play, in the "life" of Macbeth. I believe that there is a symbolic conception and creation of a baby by Macbeth and the three witches. In 4.1, Macbeth returns to meet the witches, despairing after he has murdered Banquo and been terrified by Banquo's ghost. This is the famous scene in which three apparitions appear from the witches' cauldron to prophesy Macbeth's future. Let us examine this scene in some detail, for out of the mix of ingredients poured into the cauldron comes the equivalent of a baby, the closest Macbeth comes to having progeny.

When Lady Macbeth announces her plan to make drunk (and drug) the chamberlains Macbeth bursts out with:

Bring forth men-children only;
For thy undaunted mettle should compose
Nothing but males.   (1.7.72–74)

The language here is of *substances* [mettle = metal = substance], especially bodily substances and "corporeal agents" (80).[18] Given what Lady Macbeth is made of, she should produce (or be able to produce) only males. But what are males made of?—the gall she would exchange for milk? Recall the nursery rhyme, "What are little boys made of? Snips and snails and puppy dogs' tails . . . " I believe such a "concoction" fantasy underlies Macbeth's comment here, and even more so the literal concoction produced by the witches. Let us look at the setting and at the ingredients.

At the end of 3.4, Macbeth tells Lady Macbeth that on the morrow he shall go to speak to the weird sisters. Act 4 opens with the meeting of the witches, planned by them in 3.5 (if that scene was written by Shakespeare). After brewing their "stew," apparitions of a head and then people appear from the pot. Thus, the pot brews the armed head, the bloody babe, and the crowned child with a tree in his hand. Next appears the line of Banquo and his descendants. Thus, a head, children, and progeny emerge from the cauldron.

Invoking their respective familiars—a cat, a toad, and Harpier (perhaps a harpy)—the witches begin to add ingredients to the boiling cauldron: first, poisoned entrails, then a toad that for thirty-one days has sweated out poison under a rock while sleeping. These two are boiled. The next ingredients are not per se poisonous, but they come from small animals or are

18. Ingredients and qualities relevant to concoction in this scene include milk (55); wine and wassail, fume, limbeck, drenched, spongy (64–71). I detect also a fantasy of reversing the processes of gestation and rearing as evidenced by the image of plucking out the nipple and dashing out the brains. The concoction is thereby decomposed.

small parts: a slice of marsh-snake, eye, toe (of newt and frog), fur, tongue, a snake's forked tongue, the sting of a legless lizard, a leg of lizard, and wing of owlet. These are blended in. The next group consists of parts from larger animals (except for two vegetable ingredients), including humans:

> Scale of dragon, tooth of wolf,
> Witch's mummy, maw and gulf
> Of the ravined salt-sea shark,
> Root of hemlock digged i' th' dark,
> Liver of blaspheming Jew,
> Gall of goat, and slips of yew
> Slivered in the moon's eclipse,
> Nose of Turk and Tartar's lips,
> *Finger of birth-strangled babe*
> *Ditch-delivered by a drab,*
> Make the gruel thick and slab:
> Add thereto a tiger's chaudron,
> For th' ingredience of our cauldron. (4.1.22–34; emphasis mine)

And after this batch of ingredients is brewed, the whole thing is cooled with baboon's blood, and "then the charm is firm and good" (37–38). Macbeth then demands of them to tell him the future, even if the whole universe must be turned upside down and all of "nature's germens" be confused and confounded—that is, all reproduction mixed up and halted.[19] The witches then bolster the fire and turn up the heat.

> Pour in sow's blood that hath eaten
> Her nine farrow; grease that's sweaten
> From the murderer's gibbet throw
> Into the flame.   (4.1.63–66)

There are several observations to be made about this list, a list that for modern readers needs much glossing. It seems to me that however much it draws upon traditional witches' ingredients, the list is nevertheless Shakespeare's own. Such scholarship as I have been able to locate does not pin down any specific known recipe or group of recipes as Shakespeare's source, though apparently many if not all of the particular ingredients have some "traditional" precedent. The brew begins with some definite poisons: poisoned entrails (of which animal we know not) and a toad that exudes some poison, even when sleeping—a detail that seems to reverberate with the

19. *Germens* is a condensation of "seeds" and "germane," in the sense of "relevant" and "relatives," i.e., Macbeth calls for all the differentiated aspects of reproduction and all ordered relationships to be destroyed. See Furness (1873), *Variorum,* ad loc.

play's great interest in sleep, normal and disturbed. The next ingredients are small animals or parts of small animals and suggest to me a kind of "ontogeny recapitulates phylogeny" model; namely, start out the mix with infrahuman and mostly inframammalian ingredients, and let it become the anlage for the next stage. The next stage, moving up some fantasy evolutionary scale, involves more vicious and larger animals, especially man. "Witch's mummy" seems to be a mummy prepared by witches, not pieces of mummified witches; it may represent pieces of any dead body passed off as royal or Egyptian and used for healing purposes.[20] Is it also, as in many a child's fantasy, a piece of "mommy"? The mouth and gullet of a ravenous shark add to our list of available organs, imparting the idea of greedy, cannibalistic impulses let loose—like Duncan's horses that ate each other. Hemlock is a well-known poison, though its place here is not entirely clear, and yew is a poison for any bird or animal that eats it. Then comes another important organ, liver, and derived from a sinful source. Nose of Turk and Tartar's lips add additional facial features—we already have a tongue or two and a mouth—and then the first human "limb" or projection is added (we have an animal's leg and a wing)—the finger of a babe who has been strangled at birth by her prostitute (and destitute) mother, who delivered her in a ditch. (It is possible that the drab was an inept or ignorant midwife, not the mother.) Tiger's entrails now increase the proportions of the creature in question and add to the ravenous, oral-destructive quality of the stew. Baboon's blood may be used to suggest the human-but-subhuman quality of what is happening. The last set of ingredients, after Macbeth has demanded of the witches that they answer him at any cost (to the world, that is), invokes their masters (presumably those who can send apparitions): to do this they add the blood of a mother (sow) who has devoured her children and grease from a hanged murderer.

I suggest, then, that some embryological fantasy here finds expression and dramatic use. The ingredients seem to add up to a deformed and monstrous birth; the creature has viscera, including copious entrails, liver, and gall bladder; a face, including mouth and hair (or fur); it has hardly any limbs, but some protruberances. It is monstrous in the moral sense as well, compounded of forked tongue, poison, blasphemy, betrayal, cannibalism, including of one's own children, and infanticide at birth by the mother. This particular feature suggests not only that the brew may be a deformed and monstrous baby but also what kind of baby is produced by an irregular

20. "What our druggists are supplied with is the flesh of any bodies the Jews can get" (*Hill's Pharmacopeia*, cited in Furness 1873, n.).

and unholy relationship. In short, the monster that is brewed from this pot is the same as that emerging from the union of Macbeth and Lady Macbeth, or from the union of Macbeth and the witches.[21]

My argument is buttressed by the appearance of the apparitions after the mixing of the witches' brew. Macbeth has come driven by his sense of despair at having failed to kill Banquo's son. What the witches and their apparitions now assert is that children and issue will be even more important in Macbeth's life and near future than he had imagined. But what emerges is first an armed head that warns him, "Beware Macduff." If we read this sequence of apparitions as both a continuation and a *correction* of the process started in the cauldron, then we have a symbolic and imagistic representation of ordinary birth and succession, not monstrous birth. First comes the head—this is not an arsey-versey breech delivery, as is perhaps suggested in Macbeth's speech a few lines earlier about everything being confounded. Answer me, he says,

> Though castles topple on their warders' heads;
> Though palaces and pyramids do slope
> Their heads to their foundations;   (4.1.56–58)[22]

The second apparition is a bloody child, who cries out "Macbeth" three times, and Macbeth responds, "Had I three ears, I'd hear thee"—a reference that thickens the atmosphere of abnormal births. The child cries:

> Be bloody, bold and resolute!
> Laugh to scorn
> The pow'r of man, for none of woman born
> Shall harm Macbeth.   (78–81)

The image of the bloody child again condenses normality in birth and succession with violence.[23] (Ordinarily a baby is not bloody at birth.) Macbeth takes it as an injunction for him to be bloody, bypassing or misunderstanding the impact of the image of birth and focusing instead on the absurdity in "of woman born." He vows to slay Macduff as insurance

---

21. The association of witches and midwives in the Elizabethan mind has been well documented. Witches are traditionally interested in babies, especially unbaptized ones, and need parts of dead babies for their unholy rites and their brews. Grease from a dead baby seems to be a common ingredient of witches' "flying ointments." See Forbes (1966), esp. pp. 112–32, 123–24 for references to *Macbeth*.

22. Another image of blighted reproduction is found in 54: "Though bladed corn be lodged—" i.e., the kernels beaten down before the corn is ripe.

23. Throughout *Macbeth* blood signifies both violence and kinship, as in Donalbain's warning, "the near in blood, the nearer bloody" (2.3.142–43). The bloody child is a reminder of the obligations of "blood," which Macbeth remembers mainly in the violation.

against his own defeat, "That I may tell pale-hearted fear it lies, / And sleep in spite of thunder" (84–85).

The third apparition is a child crowned, with a tree in his hand. Macbeth, affrightened, first reads the apparition correctly: it is the issue of a king with a crown, representing a sovereignty and a descent, a family tree, that is not his own. But the apparition, a lying oracle, allows him to evade the pain of this message by its words:

Apparition: Macbeth shall never vanquished be until
   Great Birnam Wood to high Dunsinane Hill
   Shall come against him.
Macbeth: That will never be.
   Who can impress the forest, bid the tree
   Unfix his earth-bound root? Sweet bodements, good!
  . . . .
                     . . . Yet my heart
   Throbs to know one thing. Tell me, if your art
   Can tell so much: shall Banquo's issue ever
   Reign in this kingdom?   (91–102)

Macbeth both knows and does not know, wants to know and is terrified to know, the outcome of ordinary birth and succession, which will undo his monstrous progeny and monstrous ambitions. The witches respond by showing him in great detail Banquo and (omitting his son, Fleance) his line of descendants, who all are kings.

What, will the line stretch out to th' crack of doom?
. . . .
                . . . and some I see
That twofold balls and treble scepters carry:
Horrible sight! Now I see 'tis true;
For the blood-boltered Banquo smiles upon me,
And points at them for his.   (116–23)

Banquo has the descendants, and they have "balls," emblems of both coronation and male potency and procreativity. The entire speech conveys Macbeth's horror at *succession*, lineality, for his effort has been geared to leaping over obstacles and trying to bypass the flow of time.

In sum, the succession, the witches brewing in their cauldron, and the apparitions present both the image of monstrous birth and the gradual reassertion of ordinary and normal birth. Included in this "normalization" is an image that I believe evades Macbeth and perhaps has evaded most commentators: the crowned child carrying a branch hints at Birnam wood coming to Dunsinane—that is, men lopping off branches and carrying them for camouflage. Macbeth cannot imagine a tree unfixing its earth-bound root. What is encoded here, I believe, is that Macbeth cannot envision another possible method of succession, taking a branch from someone else's tree—that is, *adoption*. He cannot envision what is in fact implicit in much of the political background of the plot: that people other than the son of the monarch might rule, and that, had he ruled aright, he might have taken on a protégé or passed the rule to someone of his liking. He does not envisage being the kind of monarch Holinshed portrays: a Macbeth who murdered the king but who thereafter rules for ten years as a very good king, leaving behind him memorable and enduring laws and reforms. (Holinshed's Macbeth goes bad again after that.) Shakespeare presents us with a Macbeth dominated by a rigid view of masculinity and a too-literal view of procreation.

This brings us back to the fragile sense of masculinity conveyed in Macbeth's relationship with his wife. Macbeth, "of woman born" and dependent on woman, experiences himself as always on the verge of de-masculinization: he is a pussy cat, or a baby, or a girl's doll. His masculinity depends upon what he draws from the woman, her substances and her approval. What contributes to the tragic sense of this play is the consonance between such a view of masculinity and Macbeth's inability to shift goals, to modify, to accept second rank, or to accept symbolic substitutes for either progeny or monarchy.

The sense of inability to change is solidified in the seesaw relationship between Macbeth's and Lady Macbeth's determination to commit crimes and live without remorse. Macbeth starts out as the equivocator and Lady Macbeth as the more ruthless one, but by the end of the third act the roles are reversing. It is finally Lady Macbeth who disintegrates and kills herself. Macbeth becomes progressively more bloody and more willing to play out all the consequences. It as if some version of the "exchange transfusion" proposed by Lady Macbeth had actually taken place—"Come to my woman's breasts, / And take my milk for gall, you murd'ring ministers" (1.5.48–49). Macbeth, too full of "the milk of human kindness" (17), has now gotten all the gall she had prayed for from the "murd'ring ministers," and she has gotten too much of his milk. His manliness depends on getting rid of milk, and she has, metaphorically, been flooded by his milk and thereby left helpless against the onslaughts of conscience. There is no room in this marital system for fructifying exchange, exchange that leads to increase; there is only a grim and murderous inverse relationship between the success of one and the defeat of the other. The system is tragic insofar as the playwright shows us the inevitability of disaster emerging from such a relationship, but he does not attempt to prescribe any simple solution, be it adoption or marital counseling.

The end of the play picks up again on the problems of male–female relationships, the dread of woman, and the difficulty of proper procreation. Macduff, revealing that he was not of woman born but rather "was from his mother's womb / Untimely ripped," condenses both the problem and its attempted solution. Dramatically and symbolically, Macduff is needed as the slayer of Macbeth, and not only because he has such multiple causes for wanting revenge and justice. The corrective for Macbeth's hubris in trying to defy and deny the facts of birth and succession is a man who has himself defied a part of those laws. Macduff is an answer to the problem posed by Macbeth's fragile sense of masculinity; namely, there is a way not to be utterly dependent on a woman, but that way is itself unnatural, fantastic, and, in Elizabethan times, almost always entailed the death of the mother. Macduff is also a proper counterpart to, or double of, Macbeth, since he now has no wife and no children. Of course, the fact that he is a very different person from Macbeth allows us to hope for the possibility of a more loving relationship between man and woman.

But what Shakespeare provides is the consummate tragic ending, an ending that resolves the terrible situation of the play but shows us that the seeds of repetition are there; the underlying problems have not been solved. This hint of nonresolution is conveyed in an extremely moving and uplifting sequence in which old Siward, one of the stalwarts of Malcolm's forces, learns that his son has been killed in battle, that he "has paid a soldier's debt" (5.8.40). He lived only till he reached manhood and then affirmed that manhood by a heroic death in battle. Siward asks a soldier's question:

Siward: Had he his hurts before?
Ross: Ay, on the front.
Siward: Why then, God's soldier be he!
  Had I as many sons as I have hairs,
  I would not wish them to a fairer death:
  And so his knell is knolled.
Malcolm: He's worth more sorrow,
  And that I'll spend for him.
Siward: He's worth no more:
  They say he parted well and paid his score:
  And so God be with him. Here comes newer comfort.

Enter Macduff, with Macbeth's head.   (5.8.47–53)

The seeds of the next tragedy, then, lie in the reassertion of the epic-heroic ethos, the epic-heroic definition of manhood. The battles and rebellions shown at the beginning of the play here are subtly reinforced as desirable, for it is in battle that true manhood is asserted. Thus, these lines about Siward and his son must be read, together with Macduff's status as "not of woman born," as an assertion of masculine virtue that denies a frightening dependency upon woman. This, I believe, is one definition of the tragic situation and a skillful dramatization: one has learned but not learned. Though matters will be reinstated in the proper time, place, and measure, the odds are that there will be another such tragedy, albeit of a different name. In the corpus of Shakespeare's work there follows a tragedy of attempting to use heroic battle as the solution to male dependence on female power (*Coriolanus*).

TIME IN *MACBETH*

Macduff's encounter with Macbeth in the final scene of the play is bracketed by two references to time: the assertion that "Macduff was from his mother's womb / Untimely ripped" just before he and Macbeth begin their fight, and his announcement, as he enters carrying Macbeth's head on a pole, that "the time is free." Macbeth the character and *Macbeth* the play are deeply involved in questions about the nature of time, especially around Macbeth's quest to master, bend, "o'erleap," "beguile," and forget time. Macduff's victory over Macbeth redeems time from its predator and restores it to its proper order.

Macbeth as a story and as an unfolding plot is beset with certain problems and inconsistencies of time. Just as it is left ambiguous whether Lady Macbeth and Macbeth have or can have children, so it is unclear how long the story takes. The appendix of the *Variorum* edition (Furness 1873) dutifully examines the chronological sequence and comes up with a figure of nine days for the stage action. At the same time the editor acknowledges that the action presupposes a longer period of time during which the lords and people of Scotland come to realize the tyranny and evil of Macbeth as king. At a microscopic level, there is a contradiction between the chronological assumptions of 3.6 and the next scene, 4.1, leading some editors to remove the earlier scene. In terms of the experience of the characters, there is confusion of day and night (2.4) and several discussions about how time can be used, spent, and bartered (e.g., 3.1.26). One of the most famous speeches of the play, Macbeth's "Tomorrow and tomorrow and tomorrow" (5.5.17), represents a blurring and confusion of experienced time.[24]

My thesis is that the distortions and ambiguities around time that charac-

---

24. See Driver's (1960, pp. 143–67) discussion of time in *Macbeth*, which supports my own views that the play involves considerable distortion of time. See also Turner (1971), pp. 128–45. My observations and conclusions are independent of these works, but in Shakespeare studies, "discovery" is almost always rediscovery.

terize the play at every level are entailed with the questions about conception, gestation, birth, procreation, and lineage that are so central to the play. Disturbances in time go along with disturbances of progression, succession, and proper lineal sequence. The most important tension around time within the play and among its characters is between Macbeth's attitude toward time and the attitudes of the other characters. Macbeth not only tyrannizes Scotland but also tyrannizes time.

Early in the play, time and lineage are subtly linked by Banquo as he asks the witches at the first encounter:

> If you can look into the seeds of time
> And say which grain will grow and which will not,
> Speak then to me,   (1.3.57–59)

Banquo's references to time in his appearances present what we might call an ordinary view of time, a view predicating a flow, an uncertainty about what the future holds, and an assumption of the limitations posed by time. In a seemingly casual reference to how long it will take him to return to Macbeth's castle for the banquet in the evening (the evening he is to be murdered), Macbeth asks, "Is 't far you ride?" and Banquo replies:

> As far, my lord, as will fill up the time
> 'Twixt this and supper. Go not my horse the better,
> I must become a borrower of the night
> For a dark hour or twain.   (3.1.23–27)

The details of Banquo's murder are replete with references to time, especially to exact time, as if he is the exemplar of the kind of time that must be killed. Indeed, since his future is to bear a line of kings, he represents just the kind of succession that is so inimical to Macbeth.

Macbeth's attitude toward time changes gradually. In the first encounter with the witches, when Banquo asks about the "seeds of time," Macbeth later says, "Come what come may, / Time and the hour runs through the roughest day" (1.3.147–48). At this point he is still treating time as something that cannot be avoided. One must await the outcome—"If chance will have me King, why chance may crown me, / Without my stir" (143). But even at this juncture, as he has been hailed as Thane of Cawdor and King hereafter, there is an impatience.

There are two other interchanges between Macbeth and Banquo about time, in both cases fixing a time to speak with each other about their encounter with the three weird sisters. In 2.1, after Macbeth has determined to commit the murder, he meets Banquo, who says he has dreamed of the witches. Macbeth claims that he thinks not of them.

Macbeth: Yet, when we can entreat an hour to serve,
  We would spend it in some words upon that business,
  If you would grant the time.
Banquo: At your kind'st consent.   (2.1.20–24)

Macbeth here still talks of time in ordinary terms: it would be worth-while to spend the time, time must be granted. After the murder, when Banquo has grown suspicious, Macbeth again says that it would be good to take counsel with him; there's no time today, "but we'll take tomorrow" (3.1.20–22). Macbeth has decided to murder Banquo, and this speech, together with the previous exchange about making time to get together, must be taken as examples of "mocking time" and "beguiling time," activities at which Macbeth and Lady Macbeth become more and more adept.[25]

"To beguile the time, look like the time," advises Lady Macbeth to her husband. Manifestly this means "deceive the present people, the people of this time," but clearly it also has overtones of "fool time," for Lady Macbeth then urges her husband to proceed with the plans to entertain Duncan.

                                       you shall put
  This night's great business into my dispatch;
  Which shall to all our nights and days to come
  Give solely sovereign sway and masterdom.   (1.5.64–72)

In the next scene Macbeth gives vent to both his wishes and his doubts about the possibility of achieving such "masterdom."[26]

  If it were done when 'tis done, then 'twere well
  It were done quickly. If th' assassination
  Could trammel up the consequence, and catch
  With its surcease, success; that but this blow
  Might be the be-all and the end-all—here,
  But here, upon this bank and shoal of time,
  We'd jump the life to come. But in these cases
  We still have judgment here;   (1.7.1–8)

If, standing at one point and place in time, we could jump over all the other points and achieve what we so yearn for—this is the language of the denial

---

25. Macduff taunts Macbeth: "Yield thee, coward, / And live to be the show and gaze o' the time" (5.8.23–24), a fitting talion punishment for Macbeth. On Lady Macbeth's distor-tion of time, see 1.5.56–58: "Thy letters have transported me beyond / This ignorant present, and I feel now / The future in the instant."
  26. Cf. 3.1.41, "be master of his time."

of the necessity to live time moment by moment, point by point.[27] But after the interchange with Lady Macbeth, whose various rhetorical devices, persuasions, tauntings, and promises finally win him over, he concludes:

> I am settled, and bend up
> Each corporeal agent to this terrible feat.
> Away, and mock the time with fairest show:
> False face must hide what the false heart doth know.   (1.7.79–82)

Again, it is not just "deceive and mock those present"; clearly Macbeth is also expressing a piece of self-deception and self-mockery. He ultimately proceeds in "mocking time" so well that he himself retains only a muddled, vague sense that the world may live by the regular progression of time, but, to his despair, not he himself. The last act is marked by two of his speeches about time, expressing such confusion and despair.

In between, however, it is in the scene with the witches' cauldron, the apparitions, and the prophecies that Macbeth experiences the horror of time as it really is, not as he wishes it to be. That scene brings together the relentless succession of generations and the relentless progression of time. As the witches show Macbeth the line of Banquo's descendent-kings, Macbeth shouts, "What, will the line stretch out to th' crack of doom?" (4.1.116) and still the procession of kings continues. "Horrible sight"—he is impotent to stop it. The witches tease Macbeth, dance and vanish.

> Where are they? Gone? Let this pernicious hour
> Stand aye accursèd in the calendar!   (4.1.133–34)[28]

He makes one further frantic attempt to conquer or fool time, time that now "anticipat'st my dread exploits." "From this moment / The very firstlings of my heart shall be / The firstlings of my hand." No more delay! He will slay Macduff's wife and children, again hoping to destroy "His wife, his babies and all the unfortunate souls / That trace him in his line" and again leap over or bypass time (4.1.144–48).

In the last act, Lady Macbeth, albeit in her somnambulistic state, becomes less "sanguine" about their control over time: "Out, damned spot! Out, I

27. "Jump the life to come" is ambiguous: "jump" means "risk" as well as "leap over," and "the life to come" means both the next world and the rest of life on earth, which may be filled with revenge against Macbeth for the murder. There is ample warrant within the commentaries to take the phrase in all its senses, including that of the violation of time.

28. For a similar conjunction of cursing time and birth see Job, 3, "Let the day perish wherein I was born, and the night in which it was said, There is a man child conceived. . . . let it not be joined unto the days of the year. . . . Because it shut not up the doors of my mother's womb, nor hid sorrow from mine eyes." For other Biblical echoes in *Macbeth*, see Shaheen (1987), pp. 157–74.

say! One: two: why, then 'tis time to do 't" (5.1.37–39). "Come, come, come, come, give me your hand! What's done cannot be undone" (70–71). Lady Macbeth begins to acknowledge the painful reality of deeds and of time, what's done cannot be undone, despite the impressive effort in her dissociated state to reverse the flow of time and go back to the moment of the bloody deed.

As Macbeth surveys the reality of the revolt and the attack marshalled against him, he utters the penultimate speech of his despair, acknowledging slowly that he may finally be overthrown. He unfolds his vision that he will never have what is appropriate or what will be appropriate for him in old age, "honor, love, obedience, troops of friends"—only "curses not loud but deep, mouth-honor, breath" (5.3.25–27). He dons his armor, though he is told it is not yet needed, still disregarding proper time. Yet he begins, in small measure, to mourn the kind of time he has destroyed. "The time has been . . . " he says—repeating a phrase used previously in the play to designate an attempt to distort and deny time—when I might have been afraid to hear a shriek from the women within announcing the death of Lady Macbeth.[29] "The time has been" when he was closer to being a feeling, sentient, and even caring human.

Seyton informs him of his wife's death.

Macbeth: She should have died hereafter;
    There would have been a time for such a word.   (5.5.18–19)

There is no room, no time, in his scheme of things for such an event as the death of a wife, his wife. Furthermore, her death signals the end of whatever ambiguous hope there might have been for progeny. It is at this point, then, that the final admission of defeat in his struggle with time emerges:

Tomorrow, and tomorrow, and tomorrow
Creeps in this petty pace from day to day,
To the last syllable of recorded time;
And all our yesterdays have lighted fools
The way to dusty death. Out, out, brief candle!
Life's but a walking shadow, a poor player
That struts and frets his hour upon the stage
And then is heard no more. It is a tale
Told by an idiot, full of sound and fury,
Signifying nothing.   (5.5.19–28)

The meaninglessness of his life and the meaninglessness wrought by his attacks on and denial of the limits of time are reflected in the poetry, which

29. Here, 5.5.9–10. At 3.4.78–79, "the time has been" when dead men would stay dead, not come back like Banquo. See Driver (1960, pp. 151–53), citing Middleton Murray on time in *Macbeth*.

itself does not make simple or easy sense.[30] It reflects the confusion of past, present and future, a confusion about who is a fool, even who is the idiot. He who has tried to mock, beguile, and fool time is now the fool of time. At the same moment, he is also trying, almost in an anesthetized state, to make some order and sense of the senselessness he has wrought.

The final encounter with Macduff brings home to him that he is not the only one with some power to deceive and fool time—Macduff has fooled the natural order of conception, gestation, and delivery with his "untimely" exit from his mother's womb. He slays Macbeth and then brings back his head, a gesture that unites the end of the play with the beginning, that closes the circuit of time, for Macbeth had brought back the head of the traitor Macdonwald.

With the death of Macbeth, "the time is free" (5.8.55), for the people of Scotland are no longer enslaved to the man who would enslave time. But what has freed time must also be viewed in the tragic perspective. Military prowess, the praise of manhood in war articulated by Siward upon his son's death, and even Macbeth's enlisting some of our sympathies by rising to the occasion of martial valor—these restore the proper order of things by again resorting to an epic-heroic definition of masculinity and of immortality.

Malcolm's closing speech uses "time" three times, restoring the term to its more ordinary and customary usages. The last use announces the reinstatement of the proper order of things, both sacred and secular, that Macbeth had almost totally destroyed.[31]

> this, and what needful else
> that calls upon us, by the grace of Grace
> We will perform in measure, time, and place: (5.8.71–73)

WHAT IS THE IDIOT'S TALE?

I have argued that disturbances in time and narrative sequence are to be understood in relation to disturbances in the natural lineal succession of progeny and generations. It remains to amplify the problem of narration

30. See Nevo (1972, pp. 252–55) on the "perspectivist trick" in this speech. We are uncertain where we are in time, and there is a sense of "a loop in time." Nevo opts for interpreting "hereafter" as "she should have died later," after she could have seen better results from what they had done. I opt for that meaning along with "she would have died in any case," for that sentiment is consonant with Macbeth's belated acknowledgment of the power of time over his life. Note that "signifying nothing" is an incomplete poetic line—the failure of Macbeth's "line."

31. The sacred aspect of the order of things in *Macbeth*, including the sacredness of the order of time, is emphasized by Driver (1960), Turner (1971), and Knights (1933).

and telling in *Macbeth*, for it is a play replete with statements about what can and cannot be told, and it culminates in the assertion that all of life is meaningless, a tale told by an idiot. Yet the poet-playwright has told us a tale, and it is important to consider the relationship between the tale that is *Macbeth* and the denunciation of storytelling that comes from the character Macbeth.

At the outset of the play, telling and reporting are central as the king infers a story from the wounds of the captain who comes to the camp. The king's son, Malcolm, urges the captain to speak in words as well:

> Hail, brave friend!
> Say to the king the knowledge of the broil
> As thou didst leave it.   (1.2.6–8)

The first telling, then, is of the state of the battle, and the report that Macbeth and Banquo have been victorious. A good military story follows, replete with excited interactions between narrator and listeners. Macbeth and Banquo are true epic heroes, intent on establishing a lasting memorial of bravery "to memorize another Golgotha," and the captain is a fine narrator. But he must stop: "I cannot tell—but I am faint; / my gashes cry for help." The king replies that his words and wounds both bespeak his honor (40–44). Enter Ross, to tell another tale of glorious victory, complete with mythological, epic allusions (Bellona's bridegroom). Thus, the tone is established of a heroic tale told, rebellion punished, loyalty rewarded. Macbeth is to be granted the title of Thane of Cawdor. Note the language of inanimate, nonhuman objects speaking: wounds and blood narrate and cry out. At this juncture, the two forms of telling are syntonic, but as the play proceeds there will be a progressive *disjunction* between what, for example, stones, earth, or pillows tell or hear, and what narrative reveals in words. The former, the "mute" narrative, grows louder and more insistent while ordinary telling becomes difficult.

The way the inanimate world hears things that should not be told or spoken is exemplified in Macbeth's "dagger" speech:[32]

> Thou sure and firm-set earth,
> Hear not my steps, which way they walk, for fear
> Thy very stones prate of my whereabout,
> And take the present horror from the time,
> Which now suits with it. Whiles I threat, he lives:
> Words to the heat of deeds too cold breath gives.   (2.1.56–61)

Compare this prohibition of hearing and telling with the speech of the

---

32. For other examples of the inanimate world's finally speaking out, see 3.4.123–27, "Stones have been known to move and trees to speak"; 5.1.76–77; 5.6.8–10.

watchman in Aeschylus' *Agamemnon*, who says that the stones of the house could tell much, much too much, things that he will not say. Words are enfeebled—they are too cold for the hot deeds.

The theme of imperfect or defective narration is introduced in the encounter between the two heroes and the three witches. Macbeth and then Banquo urges the witches to speak as the witches stand there seeming to understand, but each holding a finger over her lips. Macbeth says, "Stay, you imperfect speakers" (1.3.70). Throughout, the witches, and later the apparitions they conjure, are the model of "imperfect speakers," speaking but silent, encouraging speech and then imposing silence, understandable but riddling. They are oracles, as Banquo labels them, the archetypes of ambiguous speech.

Exclamations of the horror or impossibility of narrative apply to virtually all the major characters, but impatience and anger with narration come mainly from Macbeth, especially in the last act.[33] There he berates and insults those who bring the bad news:

Macbeth: The devil damn thee black, thou cream-faced loon![34]
   Where got'st thou that goose look?
Servant: There is ten thousand—
Macbeth: Geese, villain?
Servant: Soldiers, sir.
Macbeth: Go prick thy face and over-red thy fear,
   Thou lily-livered boy. . . .
            . . . Those linen cheeks of thine
   Are counselors to fear. (5.3.11–17)

Macbeth attacks the pale and white colors, which tell a story he cannot bear to learn. Macbeth is also the one who, earlier in the play, is unsure whether something has been spoken, who cannot "say amen," and who hallucinates a voice (2.2). As he reports to Lady Macbeth the details of murdering Duncan:

I have done the deed. Didst thou not hear a noise? (2.2.14)

List'ning their fear, I could not say "Amen,"
When they did say, "God bless us!" (28–29)

But wherefore could not I pronounce "Amen"?
I had most need of blessing, and "Amen"
Stuck in my throat. (31–33)

33. E.g., in 2.3, Macduff cannot bear to tell of Duncan's murder, and Lady Macbeth should not hear it; at 122, Donalbain and Malcolm discourse on *not speaking*. In 4.3, Ross cannot bear to put into words the story of the murder of Macduff's wife and children.

34. See Goodfellow (1983, pp. 13–14) on loon and goose as well as other birds in *Macbeth*, including kites, owls, martins, and rooks.

And finally, Macbeth has heard a voice cry out, "Sleep no more! / Macbeth does murder sleep" (34–35).

Two crucial incidents—the scene of Banquo's ghost and the report to Macduff of the murder of his family—reveal the connections between storytelling and the themes of male–female tension, storytelling, and blood relationships.

The banquet scene (3.4), taking place just as the murder of Banquo has been completed, contains the most complicated dialogue in the play, in which the confusion around who is telling what to whom is critical to the dramatic effect. Macbeth speaks to the lords, then goes aside to speak to the murderers and learns that Banquo is dead and Fleance is fled. Lady Macbeth then talks to Macbeth and the lords as Banquo's ghost enters and Macbeth begins a dialogue with the ghost. Lady Macbeth carries on a sotto voce dialogue with Macbeth while she reassures the lords. Banquo is sublimely silent, unmoved by Macbeth's demands that he speak, flitting in and out and shaking his "gory locks." Macbeth is appalled by the ghost and Lady Macbeth is appalled by Macbeth. She reproaches him for his hallucinatory habits (e.g., the dagger):

> O, these flaws and starts,
> Imposters to true fear, would well become
> A woman's story at a winter's fire,
> Authorized by her grandam. Shame itself!   (3.4.63–66)

"A winter's tale" is one "of sprites and goblins," as the little boy Mamillius explains in the play of that name. It's fit for telling among women and children, and it's a tale passed on through the female chain of storytelling, a *bawbaw may'sah*, a grandmother's silly story, as the Yiddish phrase conveys. Lady Macbeth, then, tells her husband that he, as a man frightened by ghosts, is a fit subject for women's tales, not the heroic sagas of men. Macbeth continues to address Banquo and also turns to speak to the assembled and distressed group of lords. His reply, as it were, to Lady Macbeth's taunt about the women's tales is to evoke an image of men's tales and challenge Banquo to a fair fight:

> What man dare, I dare.
> Approach thou like the rugged Russian bear,
> The armed rhinoceros, or th' Hyrcan tiger;
> Take any shape but that, and my firm nerves
> Shall never tremble. Or be alive again,
> And dare me to the desert with thy sword.
> If trembling I inhabit then, protest me
> The baby of a girl.   (3.4.99–106)

These images of masculine martial potency allude to established legends or epics of male prowess.[35] Ironically, the phrase "authorized by her grandam" also suggests a legitimate chain of transmission of tales through the generations, and it is precisely around the issue of his inability to transmit from father to son that Macbeth is beginning to crack. He has no son to tell his heroic stories, and he has no heroic stories to tell because he has no son.

As the lords leave, Macbeth continues to address Lady Macbeth:

It will have blood, they say: blood will have blood.
Stones have been known to move and trees to speak;
Augures and understood relations have
By maggot-pies and choughs and rooks brought forth
The secret'st man of blood.   (2.3.123–27)

Secrets will be out, someone or something will reveal them. "Blood" not only denotes murder but connotes blood-relationship and exploits the double entendre, as in Donalbain's "the near in blood, the nearer bloody" (142–43). "Understood relations" is usually glossed as a legal or evidential term—the trail leading to the murderer will be discovered as these auguries and magic birds find the connections, or relations, among disparate pieces of evidence. But relations are also relatives and narrations (i.e., "relating a tale"). The tales that cannot be told are those that involve betrayal and murder of kin, and the attendant threats to progeny and to the storytelling that is associated with progeny.

This combination of narration and kinship encoded in "relation" is also seen in 4.3, where Ross bears the terrible news to Macduff of the extermination of his family. Even before the news has been broken, the characters are speaking the language of slain kin—Scotland is not our mother but our grave. No one will smile who knows anything about what is going on; alternatively, no one will smile in recognition of any kin. Shrieks and cries are so common that they have become "a modern ecstasy"—that is, only ordinary emotion.[36] Macduff, by way of affirming the truth of these

35. The note in the *Variorum* (Furness 1873) says the "Hyrcan tiger" is taken to refer to an area of the Caspian sea and is based on an account in Pliny. I believe it also echoes with Dido's outraged description of Aeneas as he is about to abandon her: "No goddess was thy mother . . . traitor, but rough Caucasus bore you on his iron crags, and Hyrcanian tigresses nursed you!" (*Aeneid*, 4.366). The allusion, if present, is especially apposite because it refers to a male's successful escape from a relationship with a furious and injured female, an escape because he must fulfill his fate as an epic hero.

36. Ironically, "a modern ecstasy" is an apt phrase, in our usage, to convey the history of murder of kin in modern tragedy—the shrieks have become blunted and moans are so commonplace as not to create any excitement. Pinter and Beckett demonstrate this blunting of affect in relation to crimes within the family.

descriptions, says, "O, relation / Too nice, and yet too true" (173–74). "Nice" means accurate, but there is also a pun on "nice relations" and on the dire condition of one's kin.

The dialogue continues the account of the debasement of intense feeling in the wake of so many awful crimes. As Malcolm asks for news of the latest grief, Ross tells him, "That of an hour's age doth hiss the speaker; / Each minute teems a new one" (175–76). An event an hour old is already stale news, and the audience hisses to hear it. But then Ross has to go on to tell the whole story to Macduff, and the narration of the murder of his kin is marked by riddling and by a plea about how impossible it is to tell the tale.

> But I have words
> That would be howled out in the desert air,
> Where hearing should not latch them.   (4.3.192–94)
>
> Let not your ears despise my tongue for ever,
> Which shall possess them with the heaviest sound
> That ever yet they heard   (201–03)
>
>   To *relate* the manner,
> Were on the quarry of these murdered deer,
> To add to the death of you.   (205–07; emphasis mine)

Malcolm, hearing all this, then urges that the story be narrated, that Ross not fear killing Macduff by telling, since *not talking* is far more dangerous.

> Give sorrow words. The grief that does not speak
> Whispers the o'er-fraught heart, and bids it break.   (4.3.209–10)

Dramatically, this insistence on the virtue and indeed necessity of telling comes as prelude to the last act of the play, where in Lady Macbeth's sleepwalking there is a crescendo of the conflict between telling and not telling, confessing and not confessing. As the whole act moves toward fuller narration, revelation, and untying the knots of the riddles, Macbeth then asserts the meaninglessness of the telling of tales.

In the sleepwalking scene (5.1), the gentlewoman describes Lady Macbeth's nightly ritual of rising, taking the paper, writing on it, reading it, sealing it, and returning to bed. What is she writing? Clearly, the story she cannot tell. The doctor presses the gentlewoman for information on what Lady Macbeth says, and she avows, "That, sir, which I will not report after her." The doctor urges her to tell him, and still she demurs. The struggle between recording, telling, and not telling continues around Lady Macbeth, as the doctor says he will write down her speech to remember it, and then, after hearing it, tells the gentlewoman to leave—she has heard what she should not have. The gentlewoman replies: "She has spoke what she should not, I am sure of that. Heaven knows what she has known" (51–52). The interchange between the two concludes with the doctor's speech, alluding again to muffled and muted telling:

Foul whisp'rings are abroad. Unnatural deeds
Do breed unnatural troubles. Infected minds
To their deaf pillows will discharge their secrets.   (5.1.75–77)

In Lady Macbeth's sleepwalking speeches, she reveals all in progressively less disguised and less riddling form. The sight and smell of the bloody hands tell all—wash them to stop them from revealing their terrible secret. But she cannot narrate and still live; soon after her telling, she must die by her own hand.

As the act continues, Macbeth becomes more impatient with telling, as discussed above. His speech on time is preceded by his seeming indifference to the news of his wife's death and is immediately followed by his screaming at the messenger, "Thou coms't to use thy tongue; thy story quickly!" (5.5.26). He hears about Birnam Wood coming to Dunsinane and tells the messenger:

            If thou speak'st false,
Upon the next tree shalt thou hang alive,
Till famine cling thee. If thy speech be sooth,
I care not if thou dost for me as much.
I pull in resolution and begin
To doubt th' equivocation of the fiend
That lies like truth.   (5.5.38–45)

He simultaneously denies and affirms that he cares about the true story. His speech and subsequent behavior, with Macduff's revelation about his own birth, suggest that Macbeth has wanted to live with the "equivocation" of the witches' oracles ("That palter with us in a double sense"; 49), that he has not wanted the whole truth or the whole story. As Macduff is about to fight and kill Macbeth, he insists that Macbeth hear the story told unequivocally:

Macduff: Despair thy charm,
   And let the angel [i.e., fallen angel] whom thou still hast served
   Tell thee, Macduff was from his mother's womb
   Untimely ripped.
Macbeth: Accursèd be the tongue that tells me so,   (5.8.12–16)

We see, then, that Macbeth has not only attacked, distorted, and tried to deny time and its power, but that he has done the same with telling. Telling, in turn, entails also revealing, making connections, and "relating." For it is when his most important "relation," his wife, dies that he utters his despair about both time and telling. It is in this context of the end of all meaningful connection with others, that Macbeth proclaims about all life:

> It is a tale
> Told by an idiot, full of sound and fury,
> Signifying nothing.   (5.5.26–28)

The lineal succession of children, of time, and of the meaningful story have all eluded him and are now reinstated without him.

THE TALE TOLD BY THE VOICE OF CONSCIENCE

The tale told by Shakespeare, the tragedy of Macbeth and the play that is *Macbeth*, is told from beginning to end and succeeds in an act of generation. It succeeds by engendering in us a vivid picture of a man, of the progress of a life, of the core of the inner being and character of the protagonists. It does this not by a literal presentation of a whole life and all of the character but by building up an incomplete gestalt via portrayal of action, word, image, and gesture. The gestalt is at times ragged or inconsistent or ambiguous. In the act of completing the gestalt we experience the creation of persons and personages beside and within us. It is in the coupling of Shakespeare's partially told stories and our need and capacity to complete the tale that progeny and succession are achieved.

From the perspective of *Macbeth* as a tale of a struggle between the urge to narrate and the wish to stop narration, we can see that Shakespeare, in effect, tells us a story of what thwarted stories are like. In the process of telling such a story, or in order to convey what such a story is like, he has to impart a number of twists and turns in the narrative structure and in presentation of the flow of time. Paralleling the contortions in form are contortions of content, and these contortions can be described, albeit a bit simplistically, as portraying intense conflict, especially inner conflict.

If we combine the language of thwarted narrative and that of inner conflict, we can see that the stifled and muffled narrative voice reappears and reasserts itself as the voice of conscience. That voice tells its own story, a story of what happens when one carries out deeds that cannot be told, particularly bloody murders of one's own kin. It is in the character of Macbeth that we see this alternate story most clearly, as it were, being told. It is told in a variety of forms, not all of them by mouth. "Macbeth does murder sleep" is one part of the tale of conscience, an alternate form of the tale that Macbeth has murdered Duncan. The hallucinated dagger is another description of what is happening, a statement that Macbeth is not as much in charge of his desires and his fear as he might imagine or wish himself to be. That speech, as we have noted, also contains references to silence and to what cannot be told—the earth should not hear him lest its stones prate about what he is doing. The presence of Banquo's ghost is another form of the narrative of conscience. If Banquo is prevented from carrying out his intentions to talk with Macbeth about the witches and the sequelae thereof, what he has to narrate will be told in another form.

Similarly, Lady Macbeth's account in the sleepwalking scene can be construed as an alternate narrative version of the story she might have told while awake (i.e., the story she wouldn't tell). It is conscience filling in a narrative gap, as it were. For both Macbeth and Lady Macbeth we would rightfully consider this a rather primitive form of conscience, hardly a mature and responsible guilty conscience. Neither of them expresses remorse for the harm done to others, only regret and fear of the consequences for themselves. These "dramatic" forms in which they experience conflicts of guilt make good stories, but not good consciences.

If we consider other characters in the play, we can see other forms of conscience at work, especially in Malcolm and Macduff.[37] Malcolm, in a scene that has bothered many critics (4.3), invents tales of his own wickedness and incapacity to be a righteous and just ruler of Scotland. Macduff hears these graded self-accusations; at first he accepts unbridled sexual lust as compatible with kingship, then, more reluctantly, unbridled avarice, but he finally balks when Malcolm "confesses" that he has none of the kingly graces and in particular would chronically create discord.

> Nay, had I the pow'r, I should
> Pour the sweet milk of concord into hell,
> Uproar the universal peace, confound
> All unity on earth. (97–100)

When Malcolm reveals his ruse, that he is indeed a righteous and abstinent man—his motive for the ruse remains unstated and obscure—Macduff can only breathe a sigh of relief, but he is a bit puzzled and says it's a bit hard to reconcile "such welcome and unwelcome things at once."

The artistic motive here, I believe, is to demonstrate another grade of conscience, less "dramatic" than Macbeth's but more mature and "conscientious." Psychologically speaking, Malcolm has been accused of being a patricide and a traitor and might well be struggling with inner doubts about

---

37. I am indebted to Heilman (1966), pp. 12–24. Note his discussion of how we can feel something like "empathy" for a murderer. See n. 11: "Perhaps . . . we need a new term like 'consentience' to suggest more than 'sympathy' but less than 'identification' or 'empathy,' which suffer from popular overuse."

his own integrity. In terms of his ability to be a king, there is something to be said for his having a clear knowledge of what evil is, down to some very fine details, but being able to imagine it in himself and not having to live it out.

Macduff's struggles with conscience represent still another grade, even less dramatic and therefore more mature and stable. He feels enormous remorse for having left his family without his protection and blames himself:

> Did heaven look on,
> And not take their part? Sinful Macduff,
> They were all struck for thee! Naught that I am,
> Not for their own demerits but for mine
> Fell slaughter on their souls. Heaven rest them now.   (4.3.223–27)

Macduff's guilty conscience is associated with remorse for the consequences for his loved ones and is not only a form of severe self-reproach. Note his fear that he will be haunted by the ghosts of his wife and children if he is not the one to slay Macbeth (5.7.15–16). (Macbeth of course is haunted by the ghosts of those he has slain.) Macduff has a finite debt, and he sees some way to discharge it at least partially. Again, for purposes of our discussion of conscience and narrative, Macduff is much less conflicted than Macbeth about his relationship to his loved ones. He mourns and rages at the loss but presents a less interesting and less formed "narrative voice" of conscience.[38]

In developmental terms, guilty conscience appears and becomes powerful in relation to our families, our evil thoughts, and the *deeds* we do (every child actually hurts parents, siblings, grandparents in his/her behavior, not just in his/her fantasies and wishes). At the same time, self-awareness, self-consciousness, and the capacity for introspection and self-knowledge are intimately connected with the operations of conscience, or of a "guilty conscience." Thus there is a tragic dimension to self-awareness and to maturity, including mature responsibility: it can be attained only at the price of feeling, wishing to do, and doing hurtful things to loved ones, experiencing pangs of conscience and other metaphorical kinds of pain (e.g., being stung, bitten, or struck), and thereby growing. The genre of tragic drama nourishes this aspect of the relationship between maturing self-

---

38. Jekel's (1952) emphasis on Macduff's purported ambivalence toward his family—leaving them unprotected in Scotland while he flees—is excessive. In the dramatic structure, Macduff is needed to demonstrate what real affection looks like, and real affection is never completely free of conflict or ambivalence. His grief and focused revenge are consonant with the portrait of love and tendence as his dominant attitudes toward the family.

awareness and guilty conscience by showing us characters going through one or another aspect of the torments of struggling to "be themselves," to fulfill what they have to do, and living with the guilty implications of their deeds. Tragic heroes, in trying to live up to their "ego ideals," hurt others, including others they might want to help or protect, and they suffer from the attendant guilt.

Epic telling intensifies our awareness of ego ideals but deals with failures or lapses in attaining these ideals in large part by projecting guilt and invoking shame. Tragic telling, by describing terrible things done within the family, confirms our sense of the inevitability of guilt but also suggests that we can alchemically transform guilt into self-awareness. Such awareness might ultimately benefit those we have hurt—unless, as in tragic drama, they are no longer alive.

Tragic drama specializes in showing us extreme expressions of guilt and guilty conscience—the Furies, the punishing gods, hallucinated personages (often ghosts) and punishments, derivative deeds that clearly represent the operations of self-punishment (as with Othello's suicide). Ironically, these guilt-ridden representations also serve an "object-relation" function—they produce offspring, as it were, to people our inner worlds. The less able the hero is to produce the deeds, the songs, or the heroic children to fight off the external enemy, the more he replaces great progeny and great tales with the personages associated with guilt-ridden accusation.

We must include guilt in our consideration of how the gifted playwright manages to tell and get us to listen to a story about the inability to tell a story. He or she contrives this effect in part by showing us the operations of guilt in narrative and story form. By portraying the gradations from primitive but dramatic guilt to more mature but quieter guilt, he or she helps persuade us that we can give up some part of the pleasure and gratification of storytelling and story-listening without losing interest in the story (Binstock, 1973). The "new story" that tragedy tells is that one becomes a full person and a hero not merely by struggling with powerful external enemies but also by struggling within.[39]

NARCISSISM AND THE FAILURE TO PROCREATE

As a prelude to our discussion of two modern tragedies that deal with the problem of the killing of progeny and the failure or refusal to procreate, let us briefly compare *Macbeth* with Yeats's *On Baile's Strand* (1903), a modern play that was obviously written with an eye on *Macbeth*. Yeats's

39. For a fuller account of the processes of maturation in Shakespeare's characters, see Garber (1981).

play is Celtic in setting, though Irish, not Scottish.[40] It includes witches, the yearning and fear of powerful women, and struggles of authority between a subject lord and his king.

On Baile's Strand is intermediate between classical (e.g., Shakespearean) and modern or modernist dramas by playwrights like Beckett and Pinter. In terms of affect, it is very much in the classical mold, portraying passion and its vicissitudes rather than the "anesthetized" affective quality characterizing much of modern drama. What is modern in the play is a new reason not to procreate.

The Irish mythological hero Cuchulain refuses to have a child, claiming that he could not bear to see a pale, inadequate copy of himself, a son who did not exactly duplicate his virtues. Another hero, Conchubar, disputes Cuchulain's refusal to procreate, and knows that his explanation is not the whole story.

> Cuchulain:
>   I think myself most lucky that I leave
>   No pallid ghost or mockery of a man
>   To drift and mutter in the corridors
>   Where I have laughed and sung. . . .
> Conchubar: . . . I know you to the bone,
>   I have heard you cry, aye, in your very sleep,
>   "I have no son," and with such bitterness
>   That I have gone upon my knees and prayed
>   That it might be amended.   (pp. 26–27)

Macbeth exhibits a particular aspect of narcissistic injury and outrage: he refuses to accept the limitations of linear, sequential time. His narcissistic injury around not being able to transmit the crown to his progeny is associated with this global attack on one of the primary natural limits to human grandiosity. But we do not see explicit in Shakespeare's portrait a man who cannot accept the risks of imperfect children, who cites this as a reason for not reproducing. The seeds of such an attitude may be inherent in Macbeth's form of narcissism but it is definitely not explicit. Rage at producing offspring whom you cannot control is prominent in King Lear, but still there is not the anticipatory dread of imperfection.

In On Baile's Strand, both narcissistic and patricidal issues are quite explicit. Cuchulain is challenged by a young man who turns out to be his son; he kills the son and then commits suicide by going out to fight the

---

40. Ruth Nevo (pers. comm. 1985) pointed out the relevance of this play to my thesis about Macbeth. The text is in Yeats (1964). On the narcissistic themes in Yeats' play, see Lynch (1979), pp. 140–182.

waves, which he delusionally sees as his enemy, Conchubar. As we leave the Shakespearean setting, we will move into one in which the dread of imperfection becomes a more primal motive for avoiding the risks of being part of the generational chain. One way of describing Yeats's play in psychodynamic terms is to say that "classical" overt Oedipal conflicts and "pre-Oedipal" (Blum 1986) or narcissistic issues coexist. *Macbeth* only begins to portray an important narcissistic mode of functioning. We might anticipate, then, that in our study of modern playwrights, as destructive as *Macbeth* may be, worse forms of annihilative sterility await us.

REFERENCES

Adelman, Janet. 1987. "Born of Woman": Fantasies of Maternal Power in *Macbeth*. In *Cannibals, Witches, and Divorce: Estranging the Renaissance*, ed. Marjorie Garber, pp. 90–121. Baltimore: Johns Hopkins University Press.

Baudry, Francis. 1984. An Essay on Method in Applied Psychoanalysis. *Psychoanalytic Quarterly* 53:551–581.

Binstock, William A. 1973. Purgation through Pity and Terror. *International Journal of Psycho-Analysis* 54:499–504.

Blum, Harold P. 1986. Psychoanalytic Studies and *Macbeth*: Shared Fantasy and Reciprocal Identification. *Psychoanalytic Study of the Child* 41:585–599.

Clarke, Mary Cowden. 1893. *The Girlhood of Shakespeare's Heroines*. London: Bickers.

Driver, Tom F. 1960. *The Sense of History in Greek and Shakespearean Drama*. New York: Columbia University Press.

Eccles, Audrey. 1982. *Obstetrics and Gynecology in Tudor and Stuart England*. Kent, Oh.: Kent State University Press.

Ewbank, Inga-Stina. 1966. The Fiend-like Queen: A Note on *Macbeth* and Seneca's *Medea. Shakespeare Survey* 19:82–94.

Fenichel, Otto. 1954. The Misapprehended Oracle. In *Collected Papers of Otto Fenichel: Second Series*, pp. 228–236. New York: Norton. Originally published 1942.

Forbes, Thomas Rogers. 1966. *The Midwife and the Witch*. New Haven: Yale University Press.

Freud, Sigmund. 1955. Those Wrecked by Success. In *Some Character-Types Met with in Psycho-Analytic Work*. In *Standard Edition*, trans. James Strachey, vol. 14, pp. 316–331. London: Hogarth Press. Originally published 1916.

Furness, H. H., ed. 1873. *A New Variorum Edition of Shakespeare: Macbeth*. Philadelphia: Lippincott.

Garber, Marjorie. 1981. *Coming of Age in Shakespeare*. London: Methuen.

Goodfellow, Peter. 1983. *Shakespeare's Birds*. Harmondsworth: Penguin.

Heilman, Robert B. 1966. The Criminal as Tragic Hero: Dramatic Methods. *Shakespeare Survey* 19:12–24.

Holland, Norman. 1966. *Psychoanalysis and Shakespeare*. New York: McGraw Hill.

Jekels, Ludwig. 1952. *Selected Papers by Ludwig Jekels, M.D.* London: Imago. Includes The Riddle of Shakespeare's *Macbeth*, pp. 105–130, and The Problem of the Duplicated Expression of Psychic Themes, pp. 131–141.

Kahn, Coppélia. 1981. *Man's Estate: Masculine Identity in Shakespeare*. Berkeley: University of California Press.

Knights, L. C. 1933. *How Many Children Had Lady Macbeth? An Essay in the Theory and Practice of Shakespeare Criticism*. Cambridge, Engl.: Gordon Fraser, Minority Press.

Lynch, David. 1979. *Yeats: The Poetics of the Self*. Chicago: University of Chicago Press.

Nevo, Ruth. 1972. *Tragic Form in Shakespeare*. Princeton: Princeton University Press.

Shaheen, Naseeb. 1987. *Biblical References in Shakespeare's Tragedies*. Newark: University of Delaware Press.

Shakespeare, William. 1963. *Macbeth*. Ed. Sylvan Barnet. Signet Classic ed. New York: New American Library.

Simon, Bennett. 1978. *Mind and Madness in Ancient Greece: The Classical Roots of Modern Psychiatry*. Ithaca: Cornell University Press.

Turner, Frederick. 1971. *Shakespeare and the Nature of Time: Moral and Philosophical Themes in Some Plays and Poems of William Shakespeare*. Oxford: Clarendon Press.

Willbern, David. 1980. Shakespeare's Nothing. In *Representing Shakespeare: New Psychoanalytic Essays*, ed. Murray M. Schwartz and Coppélia Kahn. Baltimore: Johns Hopkins University Press.

Yeats, William Butler. 1964. *W. B. Yeats: Selected Plays*. Ed. N. Jeffares. London: Macmillan.

Young, J. H. 1944. *Ceasarean Section: The History and Development*. London: H. K. Lewis.

CHAPTER 6

A Mistake My Being
Born a Man: O'Neill's
Long Day's Journey into Night

Eugene O'Neill (1888–1953) is widely regarded as the greatest of American playwrights and one of the best modern tragedians. He was a tortured and torturing man, abandoning and rejecting children, both his own and those of his third wife, Carlotta, and his second wife, Agnes. He stipulated that *Long Day's Journey into Night*, written in 1940–41, not be performed for twenty-five years, so that any relatives who might be offended by the representation therein of his parents and brother would be dead. The play was finally performed in 1956, a few years after O'Neill's death.[1]

O'Neill seems to have felt that writing *Long Day's Journey into Night* was an effort, and a successful one, to surmount and come to terms with his past. He dedicated the play to Carlotta: "your love and tenderness . . . gave me the faith in love that enabled me to face my dead at last and write this play; write it with deep pity and understanding and forgiveness for *all* the four haunted Tyrones" (June 1941).[2] If the play and the act of writing it served to help him work through his conflicts with his parents and his brother (all of whom were dead at the time of the writing), it did not help him with his conflicts with his children and stepchildren. His relations with them were disastrous, though there was evidence of a deep ambivalence, with love somewhat underrepresented. *Long Day's Journey into Night* presents parents who are murderously destructive toward children. O'Neill's

1. The main sources of the facts of O'Neill's life are the two major biographies, Gelb and Gelb (1973) and Sheaffer (1968).

2. O'Neill, 1955, the standard text of *Long Day's Journey into Night*, is the source of all the quotations and pagination of the play used in this chapter. For a history of the successive drafts and revisions of the final version of the play, see Barlow (1985).

relationship with his son by his first marriage, Eugene Jr., was marked first by years of his not acknowledging the son as his own and the son not knowing who his father was. There were periods when father and son did achieve some degree of intimacy, principally around their shared interests in Greek tragedy (Eugene Jr. was trained as a classicist and was co-editor of a distinguished edition of Greek dramas) and in acting. But Eugene Jr. went on the skids in the late 1940s, in his thirties, and committed suicide in September 1950. O'Neill is reported to have said little on learning about the suicide, but it apparently included the astonishing statement that, now that Eugene Jr. was dead, *Long Day's Journey into Night* could be performed: that is, he had been sparing his son by not producing the play that manifested the most extreme forms of parental destructiveness toward children (Gelb and Gelb 1973, p. 896; Barlow, 1985. p. 741).

O'Neill's other two children, Shane and Oona, born of his second marriage (to Agnes Boulton), had considerable difficulties with their father. He never seemed to make sustained loving contact. Shane was in deep trouble as an adolescent and his life was disastrous as an adult. He (like Eugene Jr.) was depressed and heavily involved in drugs and alcohol. Shane sired an infant (named Eugene O'Neill III!) who died at two months of age, probably of gross neglect or perhaps even abuse. O'Neill did not see Shane for long periods of time, and never again after the death of the baby. Shane and his wife had several more children (whom O'Neill never saw), but Shane was unable to support the family. He was arrested for heroin possession and spent two years in prison in Lexington, Kentucky, for drug abuse. His family was supported by money his wife inherited as a result of her stepfather's murdering her mother.

Oona was abruptly disowned by her father when she married Charlie Chaplin (June 16, 1943) at age seventeen (he was fifty-five, a year younger than O'Neill). O'Neill never saw her again despite some efforts on her part to resume contact. In addition to the devastation he wrought on his own children, O'Neill was implicated in his second wife's partial alienation from her children by a previous marriage. The pattern was repeated with Carlotta's children. O'Neill always regarded himself as the victim of his children's terrible behavior and, in the words of his third wife: "His children hurt him and when he was hurt, he never said a word. He just sat there and died. He knew I'd stick and he'd take it out on me" (Gelb and Gelb 1973, p. 896). In sum, O'Neill's family history is a tragic drama, and his tragic drama is family history.

In this discussion, I do not refer primarily to the play as autobiography, studying the relationship between the characters and/or the action in the play and the life of O'Neill. Rather I do what has been termed endopoetic criticism, studying the characters as if they were living people.[3] I move from this to an examination of the relationship between the play and literature and then to some connections between play and playwright. In particular, I consider the way the play portrays characters desperately involved in questions about life and death, life and birth, and questions about who in the family has a right to be alive, let alone the right to a life of his or her own. The killing (literally and figuratively) of children is crucial, and "killing" is not only manifested in past history and in future action but takes place on the stage, accomplished by a certain kind of dialogue. It is a commonplace to say that characters in tragedy continually destroy one another, but it is not trivial to examine specifically how the dialogue wounds and murders. In my study of the nature of the dialogue, I invoke some clinical analogies, particularly to kinds of unsuccessful therapeutic dialogues and to interpretations that tend to make things worse rather than better.

I consider the efforts of the characters to undo some of the damage they have done to one another: in particular, the effort to build bridges between father and sons by means of their common interest in and love for poetry and drama. In this setting the characters attempt to transform destructive impulses and depressive moods by means of creativity, especially poetic creativity. The effort does not succeed, or, rather, it succeeds only tran-siently. In particular I examine Shakespeare's role in the play as the master poet, dramatist, and student of life who briefly binds father and sons together. The play's question becomes whether killing dialogue can be transformed into creative and procreative dialogue. The characters can be seen as attempting to build a new family in the world of poetry—a family, incidentally, that both replicates and improves upon the family within the play. After examining how the characters turn to art as a way to stop killing themselves and each other, I look briefly at the life of the playwright and the role of poetry as therapy, successful or not, for O'Neill's conflicts.

RÉSUMÉ

Long Day's Journey into Night, a four-act play, is set in the summer home of James Tyrone, a once highly successful actor-entrepreneur, in a town on the Connecticut shore. It takes place on one day in August, 1912. The action

3. There are several excellent psychoanalytic studies on the relationship between O'Neill's life and his plays, supplementing the observations in the two biographies cited above. See Hamilton (1976), Lichtenberg (1978), esp. pp. 416–24, and Rothenburg (1969). See also Chabrowe (1976), p. 206, n. 13. *Endopoetic criticism* is a term coined by Kurt Eissler in his study on *Hamlet* (1971).

revolves around the recent return of Mary Tyrone, James's wife and mother of the family, who has (again) completed a course of treatment in a sanatorium for her morphine addiction. Her husband, James (called Tyrone as well), and their two sons, James ("Jamie"), the elder, and Edmund, the younger, hope that the cure will be permanent. But it becomes clear as the play unfolds that Mary has already become addicted again. She is unable to tolerate life within the family, a life marked by continuous recrimination, in which each family member in turn both denies the past and uses it as a vicious weapon against the others.

Jamie is a failed Broadway actor, severely addicted to drinking and whoring. Edmund has some talent as a writer but has been unable to focus his life, is on his way to alcoholism, and (we see as the play unfolds) has active tuberculosis. The mother denies Edmund's illness, and the husband and sons to one degree or another try to hide it from her, lest it push her back into addiction (which has already taken place). There is a good deal of argument about whether Tyrone will pay for Edmund to go to a decent sanatorium or will consign him to the "State Farm." The father lies about his intentions until he is forcefully confronted; he finally, grudgingly, agrees to provide the best possible care for his son.

Part of the history that emerges from the dialogue is that Edmund, who has "the makings of a poet," is a replacement child for a son, Eugene, who died of measles at the age of two. The mother's version of the death is that Jamie, then seven, "deliberately" went into Eugene's room when he had been forbidden to do so and infected his baby brother with the germs he had. Mary also blames her addiction on the quack doctor who took care of her when she gave birth to Edmund. (Tyrone is also at fault for hiring this cheap doctor.) Gradually the histories of both mother and father emerge, by way of self-justification or recriminating another member of the family. In the last act, the three men attempt some sort of reconciliation, barely achieved with the assistance of alcohol and the shared inescapable awareness of the mother's hopeless addiction. The play closes as Mary drifts onstage in a fog of morphine, reliving her last year in the convent school, praying to the Blessed Mother for guidance because she has fallen in love with James Tyrone.

PSYCHODYNAMIC THEMES

Any psychoanalytically oriented reader of this play will at once discern several important psycho-dynamic issues among and within the characters. Before I present my own schema of the nature of the communicative disturbances among the characters, I want to summarize these more obvious psychodynamic themes.

The play deals with *frozen introjects*, for each character has a relatively fixed and fixated view of both the past and other family members. The characters are haunted by "ghosts"—ancestors and past events, or views of past events—that rule them. No one seems to profit or change by looking at the past, and the past is hardly ever brought up in the service of increasing love and understanding.

Oral ambivalence and profound oral deprivation are recurrent leitmotifs. There is an atmosphere of deep need, of deep yearning to be fed and nurtured. There are also constantly frustrated needs to feed. All are needy, and all are deprived and kept hungry. Much of the action of the play takes place around eating, and there are recurrent arguments about its timing—who keeps whom waiting for lunch or dinner. There is much concern about whether the mother is fat (healthy) or thin (addicted). Alcohol—its allure, its dangers, its ability to soothe, its potency (the maid and the sons water the whiskey so the father won't know they have been drinking)—is one of the primary actors, as it were, in the play. Alcohol and morphine seem to be the only ways to satisfy, even briefly, these deep cravings and the sense of deprivation. There is also reference to the father's habit of giving whiskey to the children when they were having nightmares—nightmares clearly induced by the highly traumatizing nature of the parental relationships. Insofar as merging, fog, and drowning have an oral component, these recurrent images help "thicken" the atmosphere of oral craving and deprivation.

Rivalry is quite prominent in the play, but it is not the rivalry among men for a woman as sexual object. Rather, the rivalry is around who supplies and controls the alcohol and the food, and who will get the most care from the severely impaired mother. The sons claim that the father is unable to bear the mother's spending time with them, as he needs the babying and coddling for himself. There is scarcely any sexual banter or even allusions to sexuality in regard to the young maid, Cathleen. The only sexuality in the play is in Jamie's relations to whores, especially Fat Violet.

There is a rivalry not only for mothering but also for fathering, which is also in short supply. Tyrone's own father (i.e., the boys' grandfather) abandoned his large family when Tyrone was ten, returned to Ireland, and probably commited suicide. Jamie and Edmund seem to have had just enough fathering to recognize and yearn for it, but they receive nowhere near a reliable amount from their own father. Oedipal conflicts do not seem to gel in this family, for lack of the sense of a father who is strong enough and consistent enough to compete with. The competition is with the father as older sibling. The mother's history also seems to be marked by rather thin fathering—she idealizes her father, but he seems to have killed himself with alcohol when relatively young.

Rivalry between the two boys is of murderous proportions. Mary accuses Jamie of having deliberately infected his younger brother, Eugene, and Edmund is the replacement child for the dead Eugene. Jamie himself at several points warns Edmund that he feels murderous toward him, and both parents warn Edmund of Jamie's deep-seated animosity. Tyrone expresses his murderous feelings toward Edmund by planning not to pay for proper medical treatment for him: Tyrone is preoccupied with his own fears of dying penniless and must hoard the limited supplies. There is thus a mixture and confusion of sibling rivalry and parent–child rivalry.

The Harker–Shaughnessy story, told early in the play by Edmund, is about territoriality, the rivalry between rich Standard Oil millionaire Harker, and the poor Irishman Shaughnessy (pp. 22–26). In this story, the poor man accuses the rich man of having enticed his pigs into cold water so that they will catch pneumonia and die. This story also describes a form of sibling rivalry. Dramatically, it is told early in the play in an attempt to unite father, mother, and sons against a common enemy. The attempt fails: the father becomes enraged at the possibility that the sons have been egging Shaughnessy on in such a way as to damage the father's interests. The story also alludes to, and is a version of, the death of baby Eugene by what the mother claims was deliberate exposure. Thus, the rivalry is marked by seduction, betrayal, and murder.[4]

There is also a cluster of images combining oral deprivation and sibling rivalry. The theme of merging and its attendant oblivion signals both orality and sibling rivalry, as Bertram Lewin has argued. In his view, fantasies (as well as experiences) of merging may serve as defenses against murderous rage (Lewin 1950, 1968, p. 43). He proposes an elaborate theory of the *oral triad*, a constellation of wishes that the older sibling, the "knee child," attributes to the mind of the infant at the mother's breast. This oral triad constitutes both an expression of and a defense against murderous sibling rivalry. In *Long Day's Journey* the wish to merge and the creation of situations in which one can merge—especially the use of alcohol and drugs—can be seen as protecting the characters against murder and suicide. The mother could obviously kill Tyrone in her rage at him, or she could kill Edmund, who she wishes had never been born. He is an inadequate substitute for the dead baby Eugene, and her addiction serves to drown her sorrow and ward off her rage. We can also see her behavior as an important stimulus to sibling rivalry—Jamie and Tyrone are acting out her wishes for her in their attempts to destroy Edmund.

The men also seek oblivion from their murderous rage, especially in

4. A theme echoed again in a reference to the murderous rivalry of Richard III toward his brother Clarence in Shakespeare's *Richard III*, when Jamie (p. 168) quotes Clarence's nightmare at 1.4.53–55.

alcohol. Jamie in addition seeks oblivion and merging with his whores, and Edmund with the sea and the fog. Edmund talks of becoming a ghost (p. 131), losing his flesh-and-blood identity, thereby obliterating both pain and rage.

These experiences of merging are not only defenses but also attempts at rebirth and restoration. Thus, Edmund not only wards off hatred of living and his rage at and disappointment with his family, he also hopes to create a new identity.

Alcohol, morphine, words, and poetry also serve as transitional objects—they are things that the characters cling to, encompassing an illusion of security and closeness. These "objects" tend to isolate the characters and enable them to ward off the pain of full communication with another person. Words, insofar as they are banal and repetitive, serve not to communicate but to soothe the speaker, forming a protective envelope around him or her. Some of the poetry in the play, however—especially that of Shakespeare—has the potential to promote closeness and bonding among the characters. But it is only with great difficulty that the characters manage to use words to communicate with each other rather than to generate or undermine illusions.

COMMUNICATIVE STYLE, MISCONSTRUING, AND MISINTERPRETING

Mary: It's no use finding fault with Bridget. She doesn't listen. I can't threaten her, or she'd threaten she'd leave. And she does do her best at times. It's too bad they seem to be just the times you're sure to be late, James. Well, there's this consolation: it's difficult to tell from her cooking whether she's doing her best or her worst. (pp. 71–72)

The sentiment that you can't tell when someone is doing her best or her worst clearly conveys the tone of the dramatic dialogue of *Long Day's Journey*. Helping and hurting are almost hopelessly intertwined, and at best they are continually confused with each other. Attempts at communication are typically exercises in frustration or even futility. There is a special quality to this frustration: namely, it often seems as if a thought, an effort to help or repair, an honest statement, does get articulated, expressed, and a character makes some effort to sustain and keep alive the communication, insisting that the other person hear and acknowledge it. But typically the communication is conceived, born, breathes, lives for a while, then dies.[5]

5. My analysis of the family's communicative style and difficulties owes much to my colleagues in family therapy, who over the years have taught me to listen for such derailments of dialogue. The work of Sanders (1979) on family therapy includes studies of drama. However, the methods I use are devised for this play; hence I cannot cite any one study or method in family therapy I specifically apply.

Affect, like currency, either is withheld and countermanded or flows so freely and so easily that it is inflated and debased, hardly worth very much. Rage and recrimination are particularly plentiful and cheap, as are shame and apologies. Genuine remorse, with the intention to change one's ways, is scarce. Tears appear only occasionally, such as the scene where Edmund strikes Jamie for calling their mother a "hophead," and Edmund is intensely pained by the sudden realization that, in effect, he has no mother (pp. 161–62). Jamie then cries, admitting how much he has yearned for her to be well, to be a real mother to all of them, and how sad and disappointed he is for himself and for the others, including her. Edmund blinks back tears. (Tyrone cries on p. 148, and Jamie again cries on pp. 170–71, all in act 4.)

Interchanges are marked by wild, almost instant alterations of love and hate, respect and disdain. One critic has usefully contrasted Shakespeare's style of portraying mixed feelings with O'Neill's—Shakespeare is more modulated, the contradictory affects are more smoothly blended, the audience is inducted gently into the sense of painful ambivalence (Myers 1956, pp. 98–109). In *Long Day's Journey* affects are not sustained long enough to become part of a blend of feeling. It is only in the last act that one can feel a sincere and sustained effort on the part of the father and sons to maintain and communicate intense feeling. However inadequately, the men in the family are making some attempt to come closer around their common loss of a mother. This act contains by far the largest number of long and sustained speeches, speeches in which characters are granted an opportunity to tell their stories with deep feeling and at some length, and are allowed the complementary sense that the other might actually listen and be moved.

Overall, speech has little novelty and does not seem to communicate anything that genuinely interests or arrests the listeners. The characters habitually accuse each other of repeating the same old stuff, whether a complaint, a story, or a hackneyed quotation of poetry. In act 1 Tyrone accuses Jamie of having no talent except for egging others on to be insulting. Edmund exclaims, "Oh, for God's sake, Papa! If you're starting that stuff again, I'll beat it. . . . God, Papa, I should think you'd get sick of hearing yourself" (p. 26). Later in the act, Tyrone again attacks Jamie, mechanically quoting, "Ingratitude, the vilest weed that grows!" and Jamie moans, "I could see that line coming! God, how many thousand times—!" (p. 33). Thus, banal, repetitive, and stereotyped use of language is a reflection of how stuck the characters are, unable to move forward or shift their perspectives. Another manifestation of this "stuckness" is that each character has difficulty imagining that the other can have anything other than one fixed, repetitive, and malicious motive for doing or saying anything. For example, as Jamie voices his apprehension that Mary is already addicted again, Tyrone is not content with rebutting him but is compelled to add, "By God, how you can live with a mind that sees nothing but the worst motives behind everything is beyond me!" (p. 38).

Concomitantly, there are moments in the play when a character is *aching* to be heard or understood differently, not in the same repetitive mold. However, either that character has great difficulty expressing himself differently and/or a second character misses an important opportunity to respond with a different kind of understanding. In a tiresome argument about Jamie's continual leeching, his father, Tyrone, slips into a "weary complaint": "I wouldn't give a damn if you ever displayed the slightest sign of gratitude. The only thanks is to have you sneer at me for a dirty miser, sneer at my profession, sneer at every damned thing in the world—except yourself." Jamie responds wryly, "That's not true, Papa. You can't hear me talking to myself, that's all" (p. 32). At this juncture, the father might stop, consider Jamie's statement, and ask, what it is that Jamie says to himself? I believe O'Neill suggests several possibilities. One is that Jamie is grateful to his father but has a hard time expressing his gratitude. Another possibility (which does not exclude the first) is that Jamie does sneer at himself and this self-hatred is manifested in his sneering at others. Either or both understandings would allow the father to move the dialogue out of the rut it is in. But the chance goes by, as the father quotes mechanically, "Ingratitude, the vilest weed that grows!"

In a rare moment when one character does hear the need of the other and responds to the plea beneath the surface, the dialogue does shift into a register other than recrimination. In act 1, Mary attacks Dr. Hardy as a quack, attempting to discredit his intimations that Edmund in fact has an advanced case of consumption. She suddenly becomes uncomfortably self-conscious, needs some reassurance, and Tyrone offers it by kissing her and turning on the blarney.

> Mary: You mustn't be so silly, James. Right in front of Jamie!
>
> Tyrone: On, he's on to you, too. He knows this fuss about eyes and hair is only fishing for compliments. Eh, Jamie?
>
> Jamie: (*His face has cleared, too, and there is an old boyish charm in his loving smile at his mother.*) Yes. You can't kid us, Mama.
>
> Mary: (*Laughs and an Irish lilt comes into her voice.*) Go along with both of you! (*Then she speaks with a girlish gravity.*) But I did truly have beautiful hair once, didn't I, James? (p. 28).

Thus, in the midst of anger, fear, and a bitter exchange that was the occasion for Edmund to stomp out of the room, the remaining characters are able to experience something different, something positive, because of a timely and tactful intervention on the part of the father. Unfortunately, the positive feeling is a frail reed; it cannot sustain family unity for long, and, tragically, even this moment of loving feeling is purchased at the price of extruding one member of the family.

At this point, I want to introduce a perspective on tragic dialogue, drawn from ideas about therapeutic dialogue, that will enlarge our picture of the communicative disturbances among these characters. This perspective posits that important human communication is, in psychoanalytic terms, *overdetermined* and serves *multiple functions*. A number of wishes, motives, and needs go into forming any significant communication, including some that are contradictory—this is part of what is implied by overdetermination. Similarly, the communication serves several needs, several "masters," and its receiver can construe such communication in a number of ways. In some contemporary disciplines, such as semiotics, and in some schools of literary criticism, the term *polysemous* is used to convey the encoding of multiple meanings in a communication. The "decoder" can choose among several possible interpretations of "what is really meant." Some sense of the inevitable ambiguity in human communication informs various disciplines that deal with patterned, emotionally meaningful dialogue.

In clinical psychoanalytic discourse, these ideas imply, for example, the awareness that on any given interpretation the analyst makes to the patient, several other meanings or implications ride "piggyback" (Loewenstein 1957). Therapeutically intended interventions typically deliver more than the analyst intends or knows, and not all of what is delivered is necessarily something he or she wishes to have delivered. In this sense, it is not realistic to think of "exact" as opposed to "inexact interpretation"; rather, all interpretation is inexact, though some communications strike a point of urgency in the patient and as such may be "on target." Exact interpretation, at best, does not mean interpretation that is totally correct, but rather that which comes at exactly the right point in terms of the patient's affect and receptivity.[6]

If there are always a number of ways to construe the analyst's interpretation, of course there are numerous ways to misconstrue. Good analytic dialogue, then, cannot be free of misconstrual, but rather is characterized by the ability to negotiate, understand, and ultimately make therapeutic "hay" of the misconstruals, which are assumed to be patterned, significant, and shaped by desire and conflict. Neither in life nor in psychoanalysis does

6. See Glover (1931) for the first exposition of exact and inexact interpretation; he argues for the desirability of and assumes the possibility of exact interpretation.

the process of correction take place perfectly, calmly, and in a smooth, linear manner. Often there must be an opportunity to express painful and injured feelings in order to "clear the air," to enable the participants to clarify the misunderstandings. Under optimal conditions in the development of each individual and in the life of a family, the inevitable destructive misunderstandings are counterbalanced by constructive and creative understandings, and even creative misunderstandings. Comedy exploits the more benign and creative misunderstandings; tragedy exploits the destructive misconstruals.

What are described in psychodynamic language as mechanisms of defense can also be characterized as typical and common ways of misconstruing and misperceiving. In successful human dialogue, whether in life or in therapy, one sees shifts and changes in the defenses that are invoked and evoked, shifts from more primitive methods of misconstruing and failing to respond, (such as projection and denial) to more mature and ultimately more negotiable modes (such as reaction formation and repression). Obviously each person uses the whole gamut of defenses at one time or another, but the overall balance and optimal blending of primitive and mature defenses, as well as the ability to avoid being frozen in one mode, differentiate the "mature" from the "primitive" personality.

What we see in tragic drama in general, and with extraordinarily painful clarity in O'Neill, are countless examples of both the preponderance of destructive misunderstandings of ambiguous communications and the deficiency or paralysis of means whereby misunderstandings might be corrected. Within this framework, I believe, we can achieve a fresh way of looking at the web of inexorability that characterizes and helps define tragic drama.

In act 2, Tyrone responds to Mary's plaint that she has no friends and no place to visit by reminding her that he has taken pains to provide her with a car and a chauffeur so she can get out of the house. After explaining that he had hoped to help her by providing this car, he rapidly shifts to venting his bitterness at how much money it costs and repeats his fear of ending his life in the poorhouse. She responds with pseudo-agreement that he's thrown out good money. By condemning the cheap second-hand car and the second-rate chauffeur, she further infuriates her husband. She continues with a denial (only partly sincere) of any wish to offend him.

> Mary: I wasn't offended when you gave me the automobile. I knew you didn't mean to humiliate me. I knew that was the way you had to do everything. . . . it proved how much you loved me, in your way, especially when you couldn't really believe it would do me any good.
> Tyrone: Mary! (*He suddenly hugs her to him—brokenly.*) Dear Mary! for the

love of God, for my sake and the boys' sake and your own, won't you stop now?

Mary: (*Stammers in guilty confusion for a second.*) I—James, please! (*Her strange stubborn defense comes back instantly.*) Stop what? What are you talking about? (*He lets his arm fall to his side brokenly. She impulsively puts her arm around him.*) James! We've loved each other! We always will! Let's remember only that, and not try to understand what we cannot understand, or help things that cannot be helped—the things life has done to us we cannot excuse or explain.

Tyrone: (*As if he hadn't heard—bitterly.*) You won't even try?

Mary: (*Her arms drop hopelessly and she turns away—with detachment.*) Try to go for a drive this afternoon, you mean?   (p. 85)

The reader or the audience has no difficulty experiencing frustration, anger, disappointment, and a degree of empathy for Tyrone and for Mary ("the things life has done to us we cannot excuse or explain" has a definite appeal for most of us). Yet it is difficult to characterize precisely what are the communication problems in this sequence. Our difficulty in cutting through the fog of the derailed dialogue mirrors the experience of the characters. We may begin by asking what, at this point in the dialogue, stimulates or reinforces Mary's refusal to recognize her addiction. It is, I believe, her resentment—unarticulated but present in the preceding sequence about the car—that adds impetus to her denial. James, in buying the car, has acted out of a mixture of motives—a desire to help Mary, to get her out into the world for her good and for his, and, at the same time, a need or habit of infantilizing her. He also reveals his resentment of spending money on her. Her rage at him for again bringing up money is such that she cannot really forgive him. The accusation of stinginess, in turn, is enmeshed in a larger network of accusations about Edmund's birth and how Tyrone has provided inadequate medical care and inadequate conditions for rearing children.

Thus, she asks for forgiveness at a time when she is not ready to practice it herself (though it does not seem that she can acknowledge her inability to forgive). Her refusal to forgive is part and parcel of her refusal to face Tyrone's demand that she try to stop taking the drug. At the same time, we can note several instances in which each character fails to seize an opportunity to respond in a novel or surprising way and thus escape the repetitively frustrating pleas and recriminations. Mary's plea that they focus on their mutual love and "not try to understand what we cannot understand, or help things that cannot be helped" does not evoke an empathic resonance in Tyrone. Such a resonance might help reduce the atmosphere of guilt and recrimination, affects which clearly provoke Mary to further drug use. Or consider Mary's reflection that Tyrone's behavior "proved how much you loved me, in your way." This thought might allow Mary to respond affirmatively to his love—understanding that *his* understanding of precisely how she needs to be shown love might be limited, but that there might be room for negotiation. Instead, she seems to focus on the limitations of his love, caring, and understanding, and uses them to excuse her resistance to change.

The two characters continue to perform a bizarre dance characterized by requests for forgiveness and understanding, interspersed with pleas to forget the past—when each request in fact fuels the bitter memories and unforgiving revival of a tortured past. (Consider how the arm and hand gestures indicated in the stage directions mime the theme of missed understanding and consequent despair.) Over the next few pages of the script (pp. 86–88), Mary brings up memories of attempts at friendship and the memories are stamped with resentment of both her husband and her putative friends. Tyrone ("with guilty resentment") himself pleads, "For God's sake, don't dig up what's long forgotten." But Mary responds by indicating that she intends to get some more narcotic, and this time Tyrone brings up the past—the night Mary screamed for the narcotic, ran out of the house in her nightdress, and tried to throw herself off the dock. She pleads, "You musn't remember! You musn't humiliate me so!" Tyrone asks for forgiveness, and Mary, in her turn, denies that the incident ever happened. She then proceeds to bring up the past again, assaulting Tyrone, and he begs her, "Mary! For God's sake, forget the past." Mary responds, "(with strange objective calm), 'Why? How can I? The past is the present, isn't it? It's the future too. We all try to lie out of that but life won't let us.'"

We have considered briefly the role of an inadequately articulated affect—that is, resentment—in promoting further failures of the characters to understand one another. Empathic identification with the plight of an another, even an adversary (and these characters are all adversaries to each other), is one way destructive misunderstandings can be minimized or resolved. In tragedy, generally, such understanding is deficient or comes too late to change things. Importantly, the very failure among the characters to achieve such understanding enhances our awareness of its necessity in resolving conflict. In *Long Day's Journey* we hear repeated pleas for this kind of empathic identification, an identification equivalent to "putting yourself in my shoes."

But somehow, such identification is constantly being thwarted. In the latter part of act 3, Mary, in one of her unpredictable swings toward defending her husband, urges her son Edmund not to feel contempt for his father just because he is so closefisted. For, she goes on to explain, Tyrone's father deserted his mother when James was ten, leaving six young children. The ten-year-old James Tyrone had to go to work in a machine shop to help keep the family alive.

> Edmund: Oh for Pete's sake, Mama. I've heard Papa tell that machine shop story ten thousand times.
> Mary: Yes dear, you've had to listen, but I don't think you've ever tried to understand.   (p. 117)

Within the play, we can see several methods by which such *listening to understand* is thwarted, as well as several motives for the thwarting. One such method has been mentioned here: introducing a plea to understand and forgive at the wrong moment. Another method is to evoke the past not as a vehicle of understanding and increasing empathy, but as a weapon of assaultive self-justification. This pattern is so regular in *Long Day's Journey* that the exceptions cry out for explanation. Instances of constructive use of the past are almost all found in the last act (they are later considered as a group).

In this play an important motive for blocking empathic identification might be termed "political"—the wish to block the formation of alliances and coalitions. Mary pleads with Edmund to understand his father, but it is clear that she sees the possibility of such genuine understanding as a threat to the bond between Edmund and herself. This alliance is portrayed most vividly in act 1, where Mary coddles and plays nurse to Edmund, and in act 4, when Edmund strikes Jamie for stating bluntly and sarcastically that their mother is a dope fiend. But the alliance between Edmund and his mother is a fragile one, especially in view of Mary's wish that he had never been born.

Understanding is so closely intertwined with the making and breaking of alliances that even ordinary empathy can become a weapon in the politics of the family. Two people understanding one another by definition exclude a third, and three coming together inevitably exclude the fourth. All four Tyrones can be united, even momentarily, only if their aggression is directed against an outsider, a common enemy. At another level, the failures of empathy can be seen as part of the intense sibling conflicts discussed earlier. To understand would mean to include the other, and that would mean one more mouth to feed, one more sibling with whom to share limited and meager resources.

RESOLUTION OF CONFLICTS

If there is any resolution of the malignant conflicts between or within the characters in *Long Day's Journey*, it takes place in the fourth and final act. Critics, readers, and audiences have differed in their judgment of how much resolution, understanding, and sustained honesty are achieved in this act. The three men are all quite drunk, Jamie most noticeably and most abusively. All three are desperately trying to deny the hideous fact of the mother's total relapse into addiction, as well as their murderous feelings toward each other. The mother, who appears only in the last pages of the script, is totally withdrawn into her world of fog and drugs, reliving a fantasy of a past, and seeking forgiveness from and union with the Blessed Virgin (a better Mary she). Even then, her last lines, which are the last lines of the play, keep open the possibility of repeating the whole cycle of bitterness and recrimination that has marked the play (Chothia, 1973, pp. 183–184). In my opinion, these lines promise far more repetition of trauma than they do of resolution: "That was in the winter of the senior year [the mother superior told her to go out and live in the world, discouraging her from becoming a nun]. Then in the spring something happened to me. Yes, I remember. I fell in love with James Tyrone and was so happy for a time" (p. 176). Mary's last words suggest that the familiar recriminative ambivalence is likely to continue to operate in her life no matter what.

To the extent that there is any solid resolution in this act, it is to be found in the rapprochement between Edmund and his father. To a limited degree, but importantly nevertheless, they come to a mutual understanding and increased caring. This understanding takes place in the context of several long speeches of Tyrone's, principally those in which he explains to Edmund his past history, and one long speech of Edmund's to his father. I believe that Edmund's appreciation of his father's difficulties is more solid than Tyrone's understanding of him. Nevertheless, something affirming of their kinship takes place between them. What allows this affirmation to happen?

What makes the difference is, first, an angry but sustained and direct confrontation between Edmund and his father. Edmund charges Tyrone with being destructively tight-fisted by refusing to pay for a decent sanatorium for his son, and he claims that his father has lied about his intentions. Edmund accuses Tyrone of valuing his money more than the life of his son. He drives home the point that Tyrone's stinginess is not just ancient history that allegedly played a role in the genesis of his mother's addiction (Tyrone can, of course, dispute the accuracy of that story and claim that it is Mary's self-serving version). Edmund insists that Tyrone's stinginess is alive and active and continues to be both lethal and the subject of lying and denial. In part by shaming the father, Edmund finally gets Tyrone to admit that he had been planning to send his son to the cheap, shoddy State Farm. With this, he actually gets the father to settle something, to change his behavior: they agree on a sanatorium that is intermediate in cost and promises to be of decent quality.

With the resolution of this conflict, the son can give more credibility to his father's recital of his own past: the pain, aspirations, joys, defeats, and self-defeats. The son can now listen, learn, understand, and say, "I'm glad you've told me this, Papa. I know you a lot better now." The proof of Edward's increased empathy is that when he sees still another instance of the father's stinginess—Tyrone asks him not to turn on the lights in order to save on the electric bill—Edmund no longer reacts with rage. He controls an impulse to laugh and consents. In sum, Edmund's insistence that his father be honest, coupled with his staying in the room (he usually walks out of fights), allows for a measure of increased compassion between father and son.

Unfortunately, tragically, the entrance of Jamie, dead drunk, reveals that the alliance between Tyrone and Edmund seems still to depend on turning against Jamie as a common enemy. Jamie, however, is not completely dismissed, for there is also a greater rapprochement than usual between him and Edmund. Jamie confesses great love for Edmund, and the honesty of the confession permits some increased closeness and understanding. This rapprochement is less successful than that between Tyrone and Edmund, however, both because it takes place when Jamie is quite drunk (as is Edmund) and because Jamie also confesses his bitterness toward Edmund. A confession of hatred can go only so far toward bringing two people together.

Again, a prior exchange marked by spontaneous, unhackneyed, unrehearsed emotion allows a degree of rapprochement between the brothers. Jamie, after coming home drunk and relating maudlin tales of painful encounters at the whorehouse, recites:

> "If I were hanged on the highest hill,
> Mother o' mine, O mother o' mine!
> I know whose love would follow me still . . . "   (p. 161)

Edmund reacts violently to Jamie's stirring up feelings of deep maternal love, feelings that have been so painfully absent in the household. He tells Jamie to shut up. Jamie, "in a cruel, sneering tone with hatred in it," asks, "Where's the hophead? Gone to sleep?" Edmund jerks back as if struck, becomes furious, and punches Jamie in the face. The blow turns out to be salutary and sobering, allowing Jamie to realize his own deep pain:

> Jamie: (*Huskily.*) It's all right. Glad you did [hit me]. My dirty tongue. Like to cut it out. (*He hides his face in his hands—dully.*) I suppose it's because I feel so damned sunk. Because this time Mama had me fooled. I really believed she had it licked. She thinks I always believe the worst, but this time I believed the best. (*His voice flutters.*) I suppose I can't forgive her—yet. It meant so much. I'd begun to hope, if she'd beaten the game, I could, too. (*He begins to sob, and*

the horrible part of his weeping is that it appears sober, not the maudlin tears of drunkenness.)

Edmund: (*Blinking back tears himself.*) God, don't I know how you feel! Stop it, Jamie!

Jamie: (*Trying to control his sobs.*) I've known about Mama so much longer than you. Never forget the first time I got wise. Caught her in the act with a hypo. Christ, I'd never dreamed before that any women but whores took dope!

Edmund: (*Reaches out and pats his arm.*) I know that, Jamie.   (pp. 162–63)

However, this powerful and affecting interchange quickly switches into the more familiar, familial mode—Jamie attacking Edmund. Edmund tries to minimize his brother's hostility, but Jamie continues with a series of speeches in which he warns Edmund that he has always wanted him to fail or die:

Mama and Papa are right. I've been a rotten bad influence. And worst of it is, I did it on purpose. . . .

Did it on purpose to make a bum of you. Or part of me did. A big part. That part that's been dead so long. That hates life. . . . Never wanted you to succeed and make me look even worse by comparison. Wanted you to fail. Always jealous of you. Mama's baby, Papa's pet! (*He stares at Edmund with increasing enmity.*) And it was your being born that started Mama on dope. I know that's not your fault, but all the same, God damn you, I can't help hating your guts—! . . .

But don't get the wrong idea, Kid. I love you more than I hate you. My saying what I'm telling you now proves it. I run the risk you'll hate me—and you're all I've got left. . . . Can't help it. I hate myself. Got to take revenge. On everyone else. Especially you. Oscar Wilde's "Reading Gaol" has the dope twisted. The man was dead and so he had to kill the thing he loved. . . . The dead part of me hopes you won't get well. Maybe he's even glad the game has got Mama again! He wants company, he doesn't want to be the only corpse around the house! . . .

Think it over when you're away from me in the sanatorium. Make up your mind you've got to tie a can to me—get me out of your life—think of me as dead—tell people, "I had a brother, but he's dead."   (pp. 165–66)

This is honest confession, and, simultaneously, fratricidal and suicidal. How can and should Edmund sort it out, how shall he respond? The playwright does not give the audience much opportunity to see how Edmund utilizes these truths, whether they only make him hate Jamie more or lead to a more honest basis for kinship. Again, as is typical in the play, a move toward sustained love and caring, an attempt to work through long-standing enmity, is doomed to failure, and the action shifts to argument between Edmund and Tyrone, or Jamie and Tyrone. The last interchanges between Edmund and Jamie before the mother enters in her drugged fugue state ("The Mad Scene. Enter Ophelia!"), and the exchanges after she has appeared, do not allow us to become especially hopeful for a profound change in the relationship between the two brothers. Edmund's and Tyrone's needs to defend an idealized image of the mother subtly reassert themselves, and they are furious at Jamie for speaking the truth.

I have discussed primarily interactions among the characters and resolution of conflict (or failure of resolution) among them. What about resolution of conflict *within* the characters? In brief, it is clear that O'Neill, as both a dramatist and a "naturalist" observer of families, here portrays a family in which there is virtually no possibility of one member's reaching a meaningful solution to his or her internal conflicts without some radical change in the family interactions. The enmeshing of the family members precludes any one individual's growing away or maturing. Walking out, running away, "spacing out" on drugs and alcohol, staying out late—these are all ways of striking out or striking back, but they are not ways of actually leaving the family, let alone changing other members. It seems that transient changes can take place within the male characters, but no one steadily or reliably grows toward maturity. Even more basic than a "right to be mature," it appears that within the play there is a fundamental doubt about whether there is a right to be alive.

THE RIGHT TO BE ALIVE

In act 4, Jamie confesses his deep-seated resentment to his brother, telling him that even now, he might still want Edmund to die. Jamie also makes the profound observation that there is a part of himself that is dead, and this dead part "wants company." Such admissions help create an atmosphere of fundamental doubt about whether each character in the play really wants the other (or others) to exist and to continue existing. The doubt is most profound regarding Edmund; in one degree or another, each character expresses the feeling that Edmund's birth was a disaster and that it might have been better had he never been born. The unfolding of this terrible state of affairs begins in act 2, hinted at in scene 1 and made painfully explicit in scene 2. In this sequence, where Mary and Tyrone alternately urge each other to forget the past and bring it up to hurt, Mary claims, "I was so healthy before Edmund was born."

> Mary: But bearing Edmund was the last straw. I was so sick afterwards, and that ignorant quack of a cheap hotel doctor—All he knew was I was in pain. It was easy for him to stop the pain. . . .
> I blame only myself. I swore after Eugene died I would never have another baby. I was to blame for his death. If I hadn't left him with my mother to join

you on the road, because you . . . missed me and were so lonely, Jamie would never have been allowed, when he still had measles, to go in the baby's room. (*Her face hardening.*) I've always believed Jamie did it on purpose. He was jealous of the baby. He hated him. (*As Tyrone starts to protest.*) Oh I know Jamie was only seven, but he was never stupid. He'd been warned it might kill the baby. He knew. I've never been able to forgive him for that.

Tyrone: (*With bitter sadness.*) Are you back with Eugene now? Can't you let our dead baby rest in peace?[7]

Mary: (*As if she hadn't heard him.*) It was my fault. I should have insisted on staying with Eugene. . . . Above all, I shouldn't have let you insist I have another baby to take Eugene's place, because you thought that would make me forget his death. . . . I was afraid all the time I carried Edmund. I knew something terrible would happen. I knew I'd proved by the way I'd left Eugene that I wasn't worthy to have another baby, and that God would punish me if I did. I never should have borne Edmund.

Tyrone: (*With an uneasy glance through the front parlor.*) Mary! Be careful with your talk. If he heard you he might think you never wanted him. He's feeling bad enough already without—   (pp. 87–88)

In this and the subsequent speech, Mary unfolds the guilt-ridden history that is the background of her present fears about Edmund's illness. Clearly a primitive form of guilt has led her to project hostile wishes onto Edmund even from before his birth, and primitive guilt drives her to deny the likelihood that he now has consumption and could die from it. Undoubtedly guilt also plays a part in her blaming Jamie—then a seven-year-old child—and Tyrone as well as herself for the death of Eugene. She also blames Tyrone for providing her only with a cheap doctor at the time of Edmund's birth; she holds her husband responsible for her addiction. These speeches suggest that Edmund is not important in his own right, but only as a replacement child.[8]

The term replacement child denotes a child who was conceived more or less deliberately to replace a child or infant who died. It connotes that the new child bears the burden of parental guilt, shame, and ambivalence that attended the death of the previous child. In some instances, the dead child is

7. This whole sequence can also be viewed from the perspective of pathological or frozen grief (discussed in relation to *The Oresteia*). Mary cannot fully mourn the dead child but keeps seeking unconscious ways to keep him alive, as if he were a vengeful ghost, destroying her and the rest of the family.

8. Clinical literature on the replacement child is extensive. Some important pieces are Cain and Cain (1964), Nagera (1967) on Vincent Van Gogh as a replacement child, and Pollock (1970). The theme "best is never to have born and next best to die as quickly as possible" is certainly part and parcel of the theme of not having a right to a life. We know O'Neill was enamored of this ancient saying; he alludes to it in his program notes for *The Great God Brown* (Chabrowe 1976, pp. 98–99).

idealized and the replacement child becomes the bad one, who does not deserve to live or be happy. Often the replacement child becomes the object both of parental anger and of guilty oversolicitousness—a combination depicted in this play.

Mary accuses Tyrone as if *he* were a quack doctor who prescribed bearing Edmund as a narcotic for the pain of losing Eugene. Later in the play, we realize the hypocrisy in Tyrone's plea not to let Edmund overhear this story of his birth and of his not being wanted, lest the shock make him sicker. The hypocrisy, of course, is that Tyrone is planning, with the collusion of the family doctor, to spend the least amount of money possible for Edmund's treatment. In the eyes of both his sons, the father is guilty of trying to hasten Edmund's death by being his usual stingy self.

The father's behavior around the choice of a sanatorium is the most explicit example of the *continuing* effort to get rid of Edmund. Slightly more subtle examples are the way both Jamie and Tyrone (and even Mary) urge Edmund not to drink while literally providing him with the drink as well as with rationalizations for drinking. Jamie warns Edmund that when he returns from the sanatorium, Jamie's hostility might again surface. Further, Edmund is figuratively killed, or dies, within the play, when he disappears from the stage—he is virtually driven away (or so he sees it).

Edmund, for his part, has also acted as if convinced he is not worthy of living, for he made a suicide attempt. In a number of ways, he conveys that he is in love with the idea of oblivion. In his flight from the house in act 3, he goes off to be at one with the beach, the fog, and the sea:

> The fog was where I wanted to be. . . . you can't see this house. You'd never know it was here. . . . That's what I wanted—to be alone with myself in another world where truth is untrue and life can hide from itself. . . . I even lost the feeling of being on land. The fog and the sea seemed part of each other. It was like walking on the bottom of the sea. As if I had drowned long ago. As if I was a ghost belonging to the fog, and the fog was the ghost of the sea. It felt damned peaceful to be nothing more than a ghost within a ghost. . . . Who wants to see life as it is, if they can help it? It's the three Gorgons in one. You look in their faces and turn to stone. Or it's Pan. You see him and you die—that is, inside you—and have to go on living as a ghost. (p. 131)

Here is the most poignant expression of what it is to be a replacement child, to live as if you are someone else, to "go on living as a ghost." In a later address to his father, Edmund poetically recounts his experiences as a sailor of merging with the sea and the feeling of freedom and beatitude that was part of those experiences. He concludes, "It was a great mistake, my being born a man, I would have been much more successful as a sea gull or a fish. As it is, I will always be a stranger who never feels at home, who does not really want and is not really wanted, who can never belong, who must always be a little in love with death!" (pp. 153–54)

What we have here is the portrait of a man who was, is, and will continue to be wished out of his existence by his family. Another aspect of the feeling that he should not have been born is that the child he replaces is the beloved one; accordingly, it makes sense that Edmund, in order to be loved, must always be at least "a little in love with death," if not actually dead.

This question, "is Edmund entitled to be alive?" can be looked upon as the central, painful, traumatic issue of the play. It is closely tied up with the family's failure to resolve grief at the death of the baby Eugene. It also connects with the more basic failure portrayed in the play: that characters are more valuable and idealized in their absence, when dead, than they are in their presence. Ghosts are more powerful and even more beloved. Ghosts, paradoxically, by their "presence" in this play, help mitigate the rage at abandonment (best exemplified by Tyrone's feelings about his past); there is hence additional adaptive value in their "survival."

Implied in doubt about one's right to a life is the assumption that life and happiness, especially within the family, are available only in limited amounts. If one member has more, another has less. Patients sometimes live out this fantasy or assumption, that the well-being of one member of the family entails the misery or destruction of another. In *Long Day's Journey* this calculus of life and death seems to obtain, making all the rivalries, including the sibling rivalry, especially intense. Such an assumption also radically interferes with separation from the family and with any efforts to change one's own life. One person's growth entails robbing from another. The characters in this play remain fixated and frozen, in large measure to preserve one another from the lethal consequences of change in any one of them. Paradoxically, this kind of fixation is at the same time lethal to the others.

Modell, in "On Having the Right to a Life: An Aspect of the Superego's Development" (1965), outlines a vicious cycle in some patients, a primitive form of guilt-ridden bookkeeping that is fed by inadequate separation between self and other and that simultaneously interferes with any attempts at separation. I alluded earlier to the politics of the play, the shifting coalitions that always seem to exclude at least one family member. This pattern of exclusion in order to maintain equilibrium within the family can also be seen as part of the bookkeeping based on primitive guilt described by Modell. Introducing here the terms *sacrifice* and *scapegoat*, we can see a relationship between the need to scapegoat or sacrifice one member of the family and the politics of excluding one member. As in earlier tragedies involving literal or figurative sacrifice, so in this play the stability and harmony achieved by such a sacrifice are indeed fragile. If one member is sacrificed, each other member in turn, prompted by guilt, may feel obligated to sacrifice a part of him- or herself.

The death of baby Eugene, the first member of the family to be sacrificed, did not suffice, and Edmund became in effect the next designated sacrificial victim. Mary's version is that Eugene's death was a sacrifice to Tyrone's greed, ambition, and neediness. The father and mother both believed that they had sacrificed a good deal of themselves. In this play, each character has offered and continues to offer a portion of his or her life as both atonement and a form of further hostile enmeshment. Rage, resentment, and desire for revenge, along with guilt, fuel the sacrifices. Another way of sacrificing a portion of oneself is to remain inhibited, fixated, unable to make use of one's talents. There is both a terrible competition for who can sacrifice what part of him- or herself and a hostile and destructive race for each person to sacrifice someone other than himself.

Modell points out that the patients he discusses lacked an adequate parental presence during the Oedipal period, a presence that might have helped mitigate some of the disastrous effects of the earlier problems in separation and individuation. Such a parent can be viewed as one who can make a limited sacrifice that is truly for the greater good, not a masochistic surrender. Part of the tragic background of Long Day's Journey is the futile search for a father who can help lead the sons out of the morass of their ambivalence and inability to separate. For brief periods, especially in the last act, the sons get Tyrone to become such a parent. As we shall see in the next section, they attempt to create an idealized father who might lead both father and sons out of the wilderness. Alas, there is scarcely a hint of the mother's being included in this impoverished vision of salvation.

Do these themes—the question of the right to a life of one's own and the assumption that one person's happiness must destroy that of another— relate to the style of communication in the play? That style involves (1) oscillating and unstable affect; (2) inability to insist on, and persist in, making a clear point to another; and (3) responding to communications in the least affirming and most destructive manner possible. This communicative style can be usefully viewed as the implementation in dialogue of fantasies doubting one's right to a separate existence. Consider for a moment Edmund's version of his style of talking, as it were. Just after his cri de coeur that he is not really wanted and must always be a little in love with death, his father says he has "the makings of a poet." Edmund replies, "The *makings* of a poet. No, I'm afraid I'm like the guy who is always panhandling for a smoke. He hasn't even got the makings. He's only got the habit. I couldn't touch what I tried to tell you just now. I just stammered. That is the best I'll ever do, I mean, if I live. Well, it will be faithful realism, at least. Stammering is the native eloquence of us fog people" (p. 154).

The last sentence sums up much of the communicative disorder of the dialogue. All the speakers in the play, not just Edmund, are "fog people," uncertain about their status as separate, living entities, uncertain about their value as persons or as ghosts. If attempts to get at the truth, to set things straight, to get oneself or another family member to change, are spoken by characters as uncertain of their position as speakers as they are uncertain of the status of the listeners, what else can speech be but "stammering"? Edmund, I believe, speaks in some measure for the entire family, and even this attempt to articulate his own difficulties in articulation is interrupted by Jamie, *stumbling* up the stairs, drunk. Stammering is a metaphor suitable to everyone's speech in this play: Edmund's, who, supposed to be a bird or a fish or dead, is neither alive nor dead; Mary's drugged speech; Jamie's, the speech of a man unable to trust his own positive feelings; and Tyrone's faltering attempts to express effective and consistent love.[9]

Stammering is also a metaphor for the way affects, intentions, focused thoughts, and caring insistence are never allowed to live for very long. They are killed soon after birth, or perhaps even strangled and mangled in the womb before they can fully emerge. The disturbed communicative patterns are thus an instantiation of the underlying fantasy shaping the play, that no one has an unquestioned, guiltless, and God-given right to be alive.

POETRY, ACTING, AND SHAKESPEARE

Early in the final act, after Edmund has described his experience of leaving the house and wandering in the fog, "as if I had drowned long ago. As if I was a ghost," we find the father, "impressed and at the same time revolted," exclaiming:

> Tyrone: You have a poet in you but it's a damned morbid one! . . . Devil take your pessimism. I feel low-spirited enough. (*He sighs.*) Why can't you remember your Shakespeare and forget the third-raters. You'll find what you're trying to say in him—as you'll find everything else worth saying. (*He quotes, using his fine voice.*) "We are such stuff as dreams are made on, and our little life is rounded with a sleep."
> Edmund: (*Ironically.*) Fine! That's beautiful. But I wasn't trying to say that. We

9. See Chothia (1979, pp. 143–84) for detailed analyses of the speech patterns of the four characters, their style, language, simplicity, complexity, and individuality. I believe my analyses of the failures of communication and blocked empathy complement hers.

are such stuff as manure is made on, so let's drink up and forget it. That's more my idea.

There are several observations to be made here. This sequence, beginning with Edmund's quoting from Dowson, a "third-rater" of a poet (1867–1900), is the first use of poetry in this last act. Poetry as a subject, quotations from poetry, and discussions of Shakespeare pervade the last act. (Other than a few famous quotations from Shakespeare, there is no use of poetry in the earlier acts.) In act 4, virtually every other page of the script quotes poetry, often extensively.[10]

These lines allude to the three kinds of poetry that are important in *Long Day's Journey*. The first is the poetry of Shakespeare, who is the idol of the father; he is admired by the boys as well, if a bit grudgingly. Shakespeare is touted as the supreme poet, and even the supreme civilizer and teacher of morality. Tyrone declares that he came to be educated, acculturated to the larger world, when as a teenager he began the study of Shakespeare: "I read all the plays ever written. I studied Shakespeare as you'd study the Bible. I educated myself. I got rid of an Irish brogue you could cut with a knife. I loved Shakespeare. I would have acted in any of his plays for nothing, for the joy of being alive in his great poetry. And I acted well in him. I felt inspired by him. I could have been a great Shakespearean actor if I'd kept on. I know that!" (p. 150).

Tyrone clearly comes alive with Shakespeare. This is one of the few moments in the play of any feeling of exaltation, excitement, pride, and joy. Note the language: "being alive *in* his great poetry . . . I acted well *in* him." It is close to the language of religious inspiration, of prayer: "*In* Jesus Christ are we reborn." As the father goes on to narrate his history of acting Shakespeare, he details that he was acknowledged by Edwin Booth as a greater Shakespearean actor than Booth had ever been. Booth, mentioned only briefly, was clearly for Tyrone an admiring and admired father figure, in contrast to Tyrone's own father, who had abandoned the family and was degraded in his son's eyes.

The second kind of poetry is the modern poetry admired by Jamie and Edmund. The list of these poets includes some greats, some good poets, and some once popular but now unknown or considered trashy: Baudelaire, Kipling, Oscar Wilde, Swinburne, and Dowson (p. 135). Their volumes are, according to the stage directions at the opening of the play, kept in a

10. See Chothia (1979), pp. 43–52, "O'Neill's Literary Biography," and Appendix 1, pp. 198–206, for details on what O'Neill was reading, studying, and seeing on stage in relation to the writing of various plays, including *Long Day's Journey*. See pp. 178–79 for detailed examination of the way poetic quotations are used, especially the Swinburne poem.

bookcase separate from the father's, which holds three sets of Shakespeare. Nietzsche is also a favorite of the boys, and Edmund quotes from him: "God is dead: of His pity for man hath God died." (p. 78)[11] This brand of pessimism typifies for the father what he fears and hates in these modern writers. He is repeatedly driven to despair by his sons' taste for this "degraded nonsense." The third type of poetry is that written by Edmund, who has in fact earned a bit of money from his writing (we discuss his poetry in greater detail shortly).

The differences between the father's love of Shakespeare and the boys' taste for the moderns also encodes a deep difference in the views each articulates (or consciously professes) about life and the world. The line from Nietzsche conveys the sons' view—obviously grounded in their experience of the family—that traditional values are dead, and that they are dead because it is too painful to sustain the hopes that accompany the system of values the father seems to profess. Tyrone, while hardly a systematic thinker, believer, or practitioner of religious values, clings pathetically to the position that there are durable values and that we need merely open ourselves up to receive them. The two most formalized sets of values he professes are those of Catholicism and those he finds in Shakespeare. In fact, he blends the two, by claiming (much to the ridicule of his sons) that Shakespeare was a Catholic. In act 4, Edmund recites a poem by Baudelaire claiming that it is a good description of Jamie's dissipated life on Broadway:

Edmund: "as from a tower,
  Hospital, brothel, prison, and such hells

  . . . .

  Whether thou sleep, with heavy vapours full,
  Sodden with day, or, new apparelled, stand
  In gold-laced veils of evening beautiful,

  I love thee, infamous city! Harlots and
  Hunted have pleasures of their own to give,
  The vulgar herd can never understand."
Tyrone: (*With irritable disgust.*) Morbid filth! Where the hell do you get
  your taste in literature? Filth and despair and pessimism! Another atheist,
  I suppose. When you deny God, you deny hope. That's the trouble with
  you. If you'd get down on your knees— . . .
  When you deny God, you deny sanity.   (pp. 133–34)

In general, there is no rapprochement between father and son around this "morbid filth" even though the father admits a bit tentatively that there

11. On Nietzsche's importance for O'Neill, see Sheaffer (1968, index) and esp. Chabrowe (1976).

may be some good poetry there. There is at first no rapprochement around Shakespeare either, but a small measure of closeness does appear to develop later in the scene. Edmund, trying to forestall another argument, reminds the father that he too has an attachment to Shakespeare.

> Edmund: Didn't I win five dollars from you once when you bet me I couldn't learn a leading part of his in a week, as you used to do in stock in the old days? I learned Macbeth and recited it letter perfect, with you giving me the cues.
> Tyrone: (*Approvingly.*) That's true. So you did. (*He smiles teasingly and sighs.*) It was a terrible ordeal, I remember, hearing you murder the lines. I kept wishing I'd paid over the bet without making you prove it.   (p. 136)

There is an extra irony, of course, in that the play in question is *Macbeth*, and the son "murders" the lines. The irony, I believe, involves the fact that Shakespeare's play is not just about murder but about the murder of *dynastic* "lines," while Macbeth himself is doomed not to have any lines of descendants. This small detail inserted at this point in the dialogue is a painful subliminal reminder of how fragile is this father–son rapprochement and how much stronger a connection would be needed were the son ever to be able to carry on the family line. It is a pointer to the nature of the family as the "end of the line"—neither Jamie nor Edmund seems likely to be fruitful and multiply.

I discussed in the chapter on *King Lear* Barber's ideas about the kind of reciprocal mirroring, found in the sonnets, that is associated with the expectation of reproduction and a chain of intergenerational connection. The possibility of that chain is assumed in the great tragedies, and its destruction and continuity constitutes part of the tragedy. Tyrone's relationship with Booth promised to be one of such transmission of virtues from father to son—but the son, Tyrone, disappointed the father. The skill and passion for acting similarly promised to be transmitted from Tyrone to his son Jamie—but once again, the son disappointed and failed to carry on the tradition. The tradition that Jamie does continue is that of fathers and sons disappointing each other.

What is lacking in this play—the kind of continuity and intergenerational mutual identification that Shakespeare connotes—may be illustrated by an interchange in *Henry IV, Part II*. This play paints a picture of intense father–son rivalry, especially from the side of the son, and simultaneously provides some of the most moving instances of the son's learning to identify constructively with the father.

In 5.2, soon after the death of Henry IV, there is a meeting between the newly crowned Henry V and the chief justice appointed by his father—the chief justice who had once jailed the young Hal for his unruly behavior.

This man, sensing that the new king may wish to take revenge for his past jailing, mounts several arguments for Henry to uphold both him and his office as chief justice. There is the law, which not only protects the nation but also protects fathers against rebellious or dissolute sons:

> Chief Justice: Be now the father and propose a son
>   Hear your own dignity so much profaned,
>   See your most dreadful laws so loosely slighted,
>   Behold yourself so by a son disdain'd;
>   And then imagine me taking your part,
>   And in your power soft silencing your son;
>
> . . . .
> Henry V: You are right, justice; and you weigh this well;
>
> . . . .
> And I do wish your honours may increase
> Till you do live to see a son of mine
> Offend you and obey you, as I did.   (5.2.92–106)

It is just this combination of focused antagonism and focused affection that makes up intergenerational, Oedipal struggles. Identifications and cross-identifications provide a major resource for resolution of these struggles. These mutual identifications also allow for a vision of the chain of continuity, of future generations who will have their intergenerational rivalries and resolutions as well. Shakespeare, then, is needed in the Tyrone family, as a kind of "chief justice" who can facilitate the resolution of father–son enmity. He is needed as the poet who acknowledges the possibility, and indeed the reality, of the destructive transmission of trauma from father to son, but who shows in poetry and plot that there are creative compromises based on empathic identification. In contrast to *Long Day's Journey*, the assumption underlying the method of resolution in the Henry plays is that, while there is a struggle for power between father and son, the capacity of each for an affirming, empathic identification with the other leads to a net increase in love, affiliation, and even power. It is not the "zero sum game" of O'Neill's characters. Shakespeare conveys this not merely through the deeds and sentiments of father and son but by means of an elevated language, a poetry of both intensity and reciprocity. The language, by injunction and example, invites the characters (and the audience) to imagine, to envision something beyond the immediate situation. (In the speech of the Chief Justice: "*Behold* yourself so by a son disdain'd . . . *imagine* me . . . ")

The language of Shakespeare, then, is the language of kinship, with all the joys and sorrows that kinship involves. It is also the language of kinship in its invocation of the continuity of generations and the value of such continuity. Propagating the family, including its dignity, affection, and power, is an extraordinarily important virtue in Shakespeare's plays.

In *Long Day's Journey* there is kinship and there is a language of kinship.[12] But it is fragmented, inconstant, and torn by wildly ambivalent swings, lacking the smooth blending of emotions so striking in Shakespeare. It is a shorthand, pre-Oedipal rather than Oedipal language. In O'Neill, the sacredness of the family is not a background assumption but rather a cliché, a shabby idealization. If there is a sense of the deep and enduring value of kinship and of a love that binds the family together while leaving its members free to live and breathe, it is conveyed only implicitly by absence. In depicting the processes of family disintegration and annihilative enmeshment and in showing the seeds of attempts to build a kinship without hypocrisy, O'Neill reaffirms the *need* for a family that can truly care and nourish, but he *shows* all too convincingly a family in which such wishes to build and rebuild are too little and too late.

There is a sadness in the play that surfaces when the shouting and recriminations are temporarily stilled. A father and his sons who share a love for poetry (especially Edmund) and a passion for acting (Jamie) achieve little closeness or even shared consolation from poetry and drama. Even the poetry that both brothers seem to love and admire fails to bring the two of them together. Jamie arrogantly asserts that he put Edmund onto all this good poetry—converting a shared love into an occasion for putting down his brother. On several occasions in this last act, Jamie's quoting a line of poetry is the immediate provocation for Edmund's anger. Referring to tastes in poetry, Jamie makes the sweeping and damning assertion, "Hell, you're more than my brother. I made you! You're my Frankenstein!" (p. 164).[13]

There is no possibility in the play that poetry or drama may bring the mother any closer to her husband or sons. The last scene of the last act highlights how poetry can be used only to depict the hideous abyss between the mother and the men in the family. As Mary finishes playing her ghostly Chopin exercises and enters the room dragging her wedding gown, Jamie is reciting Swinburne's "A Leave-taking," a despairing counterpoint to the mother's mime show:

12. See esp. Manheim (1982) for a detailed discussion of O'Neill's creation of a new language, a new set of connections and relationships. Manheim has a more optimistic view than I do of the success of the restitutive fantasies and language in creating a new family, with more durable bonds. I see the effort, as in this scene invoking Shakespeare, but see it as unsuccessful even as a sustained fantasy, let alone as a reality.

13. This reflects a common confusion of Frankenstein, the creator, and his product, the monster, but it is significant here, as confusion about who is responsible for whom is rampant in this scene.

> "... she will not know.

. . . .

There is no help . . .

. . . .

And how these things are, though ye strove to show,
She would not know." (p. 173)

The recitation continues with excerpts around "she will not hear":

> "She loves not you nor me as all we love her.
> Yea, though we sang as angels in her ear,
> She would not hear." (p. 173)

And as Edmund's last attempt to reach her also proves futile, Jamie, as Greek chorus, continues with "she will not see":

> "Nay, and though all men seeing had pity on me,
> She would not see." (p. 173)

She will not know, hear, or see, no matter how beautifully, beseechingly, or mournfully we sing, write, or recite our poetry. Swinburne affords the small consolation of knowing that others before have experienced painful abandonment. Poetry itself is drawn into the battles among the family members and its power to bind and heal is diminished. Poetry is also debased by being assimilated to the state of drunkenness, becoming part of the futile attempt to blot out awareness of the mother's addiction, her desertion of the family.

Consider now the importance of the third form of poetry in the play, Edmund's poetry. It consists of poems written for the local newspaper and more generally the poetry that infuses certain of his speeches and pleas for understanding. The published poems are on occasion admired by both Tyrone and Jamie, though we get the impression that Edmund himself does not regard them very highly. The poetry that emerges in Edmund's long speeches in act 4 is highly significant dramatically, for it is a poetry that holds out some hope of transformation, both of himself and of the disastrous family situation. Edmund does not believe that his work can be poetic and elevated in the manner of Shakespeare. It is not just that Edmund does not have Shakespeare's talent: the family is too crazy and too destructive for anyone within it to aspire to write Shakespearean poetry. The family members, to each other, are "such stuff as manure is made on." But Edmund's poetry, though imperfect and stammering, can at least be "faithful realism" (p. 154). An example of the transformation of manure into dreams can be seen in Edmund's speech about his life as a sailor, which he concludes with, "It was a great mistake my being born a man, I would have been much more successful as a sea gull or a fish." (p. 153)

The transformation begins with a hostile death wish, originating in the wishes of others toward Edmund, but thoroughly internalized in his experience of himself as less than a full person, a ghost, a person not worthy of having been born. The process continues by taking this "manure" and mixing it with poetic imagination, so as to make it less hostile, less grim, and more moving.

It is in this kind of transformation that the play becomes autobiographical in a way that transcends the concrete biographical representation of O'Neill's family that appear on the stage. O'Neill presents us with a piece of inner autobiography, a glimpse of his own creative process, a description of how he has managed to create a poetry that contains both excrement and dreams. The creation of great poetry, great writing, the emulation of Shakespeare, the great ancestor of writers and actors, is articulated as an ideal within the play. Though dimly and feebly represented, it is present and, as an ideal, it is also a piece of O'Neill's autobiography.

What was the outcome of O'Neill's struggle to transform his pain and suffering—suffering he both endured and inflicted—into poetry and drama? O'Neill's writing—that is, *Long Day's Journey*—is more elaborated and successful than is Edmund's poetry (within the play). One way of measuring the success of the writing, of the drama, is to see how O'Neill's style begins to mediate between and synthesize the two kinds of poetry described in the play, the great and elevated poetry of Shakespeare and the "morbid filth" of the modern poets.

In a quite literal way, O'Neill refers, through Edmund and his period of wandering and seafaring, to his own earlier life as a wanderer and seafarer and to his early efforts at writing poetry (O'Neill 1980). Edmund's ecstatic descriptions of merging on and near the sea convey something of what we know O'Neill experienced. Edmund suffers from consumption and will go to a TB sanatorium, as did O'Neill. But we need to examine the figure of Jamie as well, especially his language, for a fuller representation within the play of the creative struggles of its author. As is so often the case in studying the relationship between created characters and an author's inner life, we need to combine and superimpose two or more characters within the created work to get to something like a portrait of the author.

Jamie, by his own account, is a failed writer, and yet we find that his language comes closer to O'Neill's successful artistic synthesis, his own blending of the language of manure and the language of dreams. Jamie's speech combines a keen awareness of literature—including Shakespeare, but especially the nineteenth- and early twentieth-century "morbid poets"—with the language of the streets, of the racetracks, and the slang of Broadway (Manheim 1982, pp. 184ff). Thus, "the dope" in this play condenses the slang for drugs and the slang for "the real story." "The game has got Mama again" follows a rendition of Oscar Wilde's "The Ballad of Reading Gaol." And consider Jamie's last words before passing out: "That last drink—the old K.O." (p. 167)—his first words when awakening a few moments later (after the father has denounced him as "a waste . . . a drunken hulk") are quotations from Shakespeare and Rossetti. This juxtaposition and fusion of elevated and street language, classical and nineteenth-century decadent poetry, is the hallmark of O'Neill's style. This particular synthesis can be seen both microscopically in the language and style of his major later plays (from the early 1930s on) and in the larger content and setting of the plays. *Mourning Becomes Electra* (1931) combines the structure of the Greek tragedy *The Oresteia*, the American grandeur of a post–civil war Northern aristocracy, and the "ordinary" language of small-town New England. Such a synthesis, even if not totally successful, reflects O'Neill's attempt to create a solid, meaningful tradition and sustaining values. In his chaotic personal life as well as within his tragedies, O'Neill repeatedly sought out enduring values and tried to resurrect or create good ancestors. This quest took place alongside a despair that the possibility of grounding in enduring values may already have been lost. Sometimes the feeling that such values can be found is in the foreground and the despair is in the background, and sometimes the reverse, as in Gestalt puzzles.

The search for values can be seen both in O'Neill's conception of himself as a playwright and in his struggles as a son, father, and brother. As for the first, in a famous letter to George Jean Nathan, O'Neill wrote, "The playwright of today must dig at the roots of the sickness today as he feels it—the death of the old God and the failure of science and materialism to give any satisfactory new one for the surviving primitive religious instinct to find a meaning for life in, and to comfort its fear of death with" (Nathan 1932, p. 10). In the course of "digging at the roots," the playwright struggles to construct a new basis and to try out possible new bases, thereby affirming for us the need for and value of such a sustaining meaning.[14] Among these roots, two intertwined ones for O'Neill are his literary and poetic forebears, and his own families, both family of origin and family of procreation. As for his poetic ancestors, we can sense something of O'Neill's ambivalence toward poetic authority, particularly the overwhelming authority of Shakespeare. If hints within the play do correspond to O'Neill's poetic autobiography, he needed both to rebel against and to

14. Chabrowe (1976, esp. pp. 14 ff.) has a detailed discussion of O'Neill's quest for values and also describes the sense of competition O'Neill felt toward psychotherapists.

admire Shakespeare. Within the play, as we have seen, Shakespeare has several functions, including standing in for a good and worthy father, a personage substantial enough to sustain his sons and to permit growth-fostering identifications. But both for the characters within the play and for O'Neill, Shakespeare is a kind of tease, because in some ways he is unattainable. In *Long Day's Journey*, Tyrone has literally sold out Shakespeare, giving up a career as a brilliant Shakespearean actor for a successful but hack commercial theatrical venture (as the Count of Monte Cristo). This is also the story of O'Neill's father's acting career.

O'Neill, I believe, viewed this "selling out," both in life and in the play, as a more subtle kind of murder, the child that is allowed to be born, but that dies or is killed in infancy. O'Neill did not see himself as having sold out; he had plenty of passion and sustained intentionality, but it was an excluding passion, requiring the sacrifice of one loved one or another for his own survival.

In the letter to Nathan cited above, O'Neill claims that the playwright must help find the meaning for life. There is reason to believe that O'Neill saw this as a competitive, not a cooperative, venture, and that among his competitors were the psychotherapists. In a 1930 proposal for a play that he never wrote, O'Neill outlined this competition and also the theme of sacrificing one or another of the seekers, as well as the personal dangers of trying to confront the darker side of human nature:[15]

> Play of the psycho-therapeutist to whom a creative artist—genius or of great talent—man or woman comes in torture and half-pleads, half-challenges to have his devils cast out—the haunting ghosts of his past. He is about to give up, about to commit suicide. . . . the doctor fights with his demons and him until finally the artist transfers them one by one to him, as he is freed he enslaves the doctor with his horrible bitterness, his blasphemies against life, his sins of lust and cruelty. It breaks the doctor. And the final scene is where the artist has mercy on the doctor and kills him to free him (as he wished to do with himself) and all his ghosts come back, the ghost of the doctor added. And the artist goes to give himself up for murder, to let the State cure him of his life and his ghosts. (Floyd 1981, p. 214)

This is an extraordinarily painful portrayal, not only of psychotherapy, but also, I believe, of O'Neill's view of writing and producing a play.[16] One

15. See also his proposal for a play, "Life of Aeschylus" (Floyd 1981, pp. 211–13), which might have become a "poetic autobiography," perhaps emphasizing the grandiosity and immortality of the playwright O'Neill-Aeschylus.

16. O'Neill never had formal psychotherapy, let alone analysis, and was suspicious of the whole enterprise. He had a brief course of "treatment" with Dr. G. Hamilton that led to a permanent abstinence from alcohol. For this intriguing story see Sheaffer (1968), under "Hamilton, G."

man's exorcism of his own demons leads to the demise of another; the exorcist is at great risk. O'Neill saw the writing of *Long Day's Journey* as a way of coming to terms with his own ghosts, but I have suggested that it also transferred the ghosts onto his children.[17]

O'Neill's poetic biography and his family relations converged around his son, Eugene Jr., who committed suicide. Shane, the half-brother of Eugene Jr., recorded that he watched his father and Eugene Jr., the literateur and classicist, become deeply immersed in discussions around the classics, particularly Greek tragedy. Shane yearned to be included in these discussions, but he was too young, felt inadequate, and concluded that he could never reach his father in that way. Tragically, it appears that Eugene Jr. could get close to his father *only* in that way. I believe that reverberations of those attempts to build father–son closeness around shared love for the great passionate plays and poets are felt in *Long Day's Journey*. The failure and inadequacy of poetry to bind and hold together are also reflected there. The failure of poetry and playwriting as exorcism or as therapy is documented in the relationship of the author to his children.

To conclude, the "curse of the misbegotten"—the title of a biography of O'Neill based on the title of one of his last plays, *A Moon for the Misbegotten*" (Bowen 1961)—sums up much of the sadness and tragedy recorded in *Long Day's Journey*. The children, whether they are parents, children, or both, are misbegotten, and the play's dialogue is the language of the misbegotten. Neither a child nor an intense verbal communication can count on being valued for itself—it is liable to be quickly replaced or told there was another and better one before. In O'Neill we encounter the futility of the characters' struggle to surmount this curse, and thereby we learn something of the deep, sustaining value of kin and kinship. In chapter 7 we see in the work of Samuel Beckett, especially *Endgame*, the parallelism between the death of children and the death of language carried a step further. In Beckett, the old is only a very faint memory, not even a ghost, perhaps an occasional recrimination. The new has nothing sustaining, and nothing sustaining will be born. Best is not only never to have been born, but everything that exists should shrink back to the smallest possible state of concentrated non-existence. In Beckett we find a language that documents and implements surrender in the struggle to find any meaningful and sustaining connections, whether between the generations or between words themselves.

17. Chabrowe (1976, e.g., pp. 164–65) argues cogently that O'Neill had the explicit idea that the essence of tragedy includes the transgenerational repetition of trauma, which he works out in detail in *Mourning Becomes Electra*. Chabrowe contends that the repetition of trauma was brought to perfection in *Long Day's Journey*.

REFERENCES

Barlow, Judith E. 1985. *Final Acts: The Creation of Three Late O'Neill Plays.* Athens: University of Georgia Press.

Bowen, Croswell. 1959. *The Curse of the Misbegotten: A Tale of the House of O'Neill.* New York: McGraw-Hill.

Cain, Arthur C. and B. S. Cain. 1964. On Replacing A Child. *Journal of the American Academy of Child Psychiatry* 3:443–456.

Chabrowe, Leonard. 1976. *Ritual and Pathos: The Theater of O'Neill.* Lewisburg: Bucknell University Press.

Chothia, Jean. 1979. *Forging a Language: A Study of the Plays of Eugene O'Neill.* Cambridge: Cambridge University Press.

Eissler, Kurt. 1971. *Discourse on Hamlet and "Hamlet": A Psychoanalytic Inquiry.* New York: International Universities Press.

Floyd, Virginia, ed. 1981. *Eugene O'Neill at Work: Newly Released Ideas for Plays.* New York: Ungar.

Gelb, Arthur and Barbara Gelb. 1973. *O'Neill.* 2d ed. New York: Harper and Row.

Glover, Edward. 1931. The Therapeutic Effect of Inexact Interpretation. *International Journal of Psycho-Analysis.* 12:397–411.

Hamilton, James W. 1976. Early Trauma, Dreaming and Creativity: The Works of Eugene O'Neill. *International Review of Psycho-Analysis* 3:341–364.

Lewin, Bertram. 1950. *The Psychoanalysis of Elation.* New York: Norton.

———. 1968. *The Image and the Past.* New York: International Universities Press.

Lichtenberg, Joseph. 1978. Psychoanalysis and Biography. *The Annual of Psychoanalysis* 6:397–427.

Loewenstein, Rudolph M. 1957. Some Thoughts on Interpretation in the Theory and Practice of Psychoanalysis. *Psychoanalytic Study of the Child* 12:127–150.

Manheim, Michael. 1982. *Eugene O'Neill's New Language of Kinship.* Syracuse: Syracuse University Press.

Myers, Henry A. 1956. *Macbeth* and *The Iceman Cometh:* Equivalence and Ambivalence in Tragedy. In *Tragedy: A View of Life,* pp. 98–109. Ithaca: Cornell University Press.

Modell, Arnold H. 1965. On Having a Right to a Life: An Aspect of the Superego's Development. *International Journal of Psycho-Analysis* 46:323–331.

———. 1971. The Origin of Certain Forms of Preoedipal Guilt and the Implications for a Psychoanalytic Theory of Affects. *International Journal of Psycho-Analysis* 52:337–346.

Nagera, Humberto. 1967. *Vincent Van Gogh: A Psychological Study.* London: Allen and Unwin.

Nathan, George J. 1932. *The Intimate Notebooks of George Jean Nathan.* New York: Knopf.

O'Neill, Eugene. 1955. *Long Day's Journey into Night.* Paperback reprint. New Haven: Yale University Press.

————. 1980. *Poems 1912–1942*. Ed. Donald Gallup. New York: Ticknor and Fields.

Pollock, George. 1970. Anniversary Reactions, Trauma and Mourning. *Psychoanalytic Quarterly* 39: 347–371.

Rothenburg, Albert. 1969. The Iceman Changeth: Toward an Empirical Approach to Creativity. *Journal of the American Psychoanalytic Association* 17:549–607.

Sander, Fred M. 1979. *Individual and Family Therapy: An Integration*. New York: Jason Aronson.

Sheaffer, Louis. 1968. *O'Neill: Son and Playwright*. Boston: Little, Brown.

————. 1973. *O'Neill: Son and Artist*. Boston: Little, Brown.

CHAPTER 7

Beckett's *Endgame* and the Abortion of Desire

If the plot, as Aristotle claims, is "the soul of the tragedy," then the reader of a Beckett play could easily conclude that the play has little soul. To summarize the plot of a Beckett play is to enter into the experience of the characters in his plays: it is an exercise in impasse and futility. The plot of Beckett's play in one act, *Endgame* (*Fin de Partie*), is indeed bare. Beckett once described it, while still it was in statu nascendi, as a three-legged giraffe that "leaves me in doubt whether to take a leg off or add one on" (Beckett 1984b, p. 106). The reader is hard pressed to divine what in fact happened, especially since in the play itself there is a three-legged dog!

There are four characters: Hamm, a man of unspecified age but hardly young, sitting in a chair on wheels, covered with an old sheet and wearing dark glasses; Clov, younger, who somehow came as a small child to Hamm's house; Nagg, Hamm's father, and Nell, probably, though again not certainly, Hamm's mother, who are both quite old and in ashcans. The mise-en-scène implies some end-of-the-world catastrophe, a grouping of perhaps the only survivors, a state of impending destruction of all life on earth.

In terms of action, one could list the following: Hamm wants to die, more or less, and more or less requests pills to end his misery. Clov wants to leave, more or less, and perhaps does so at the end. Nagg and Nell get fed a biscuit, reminisce a bit about old times; Nagg curses Hamm; Nell dies, Nagg weeps, more or less for her; Hamm needs Clov to move him and take care of him—Hamm cannot get up—and Clov somehow needs Hamm, and Clov can never sit down. Hamm is interminably telling a story, carrying on aborted theatrical scripts with himself. He ends with an apostrophe to his bloody handkerchief:

Old stancher! (*Pause.*) You remain. (*Pause. He covers his face with hand-kerchief, lowers his arms to armrests, remains motionless.*) (p. 84)[1]

These, and a few other kindred undramatic acts, constitute the "action" of the play. If *Waiting for Godot* is a two-act play "in which nothing happens, twice" (Mercier 1977), then *Endgame* is a play in which nothing happens once.[2]

Endgame, then, at once poses a number of problems for audiences, readers, and critics. First, what does the play mean? At a cognitive level, audiences, readers, and literary critics seem to strive, indeed yearn, to find a pattern and a meaning to Beckett's plays. There is the hope—repeatedly disappointed—that the play has a recognizable underlying plot or allegorical correspondence. Is *Waiting for Godot* a story about the second coming of Christ, or a perversion of some identifiable Old Testament tale? Tantalizingly close, but not really. Critics of *Endgame* have variously found a story of the Biblical apocalypse, a tale of postatomic holocaust, Noah's ark, a chess game, a parody of *Hamlet*, a tale of nailing, as to the cross (the names of all of the characters seem to have to do with hammers and nails), and an existentialist parable. Other interpretations describe the play as an intrapsychic drama in which each character represents a portion of the psyche; an intrauterine fantasy; and a representation of the relationship between the blind James Joyce and his disciple, Samuel Beckett. Each such construction has some justification, each is built on clues probably "planted" by Beckett, but none is totally satisfactory. Beckett himself belittles exegetical efforts. His attitude is exemplified in a 1957 letter to his director, Alan Schneider: "My work is a matter of fundamental sounds (no joke intended) made as fully as possible and I accept responsibility for nothing else. If people want to have headaches among the overtones, let them. And provide their own aspirin. Hamm as stated, and Clov as stated, together stated, *nec tecum nec sine te* [neither with you nor without you], in such a place, and in such a world, that's all I can manage, more than I could" (Beckett 1984, p. 109; cf. p. 114).

Even in this rebuttal of all attempts to find an exegesis of his texts, Beckett teases with "fundamental sounds (no joke intended)" and again revives a bit of hope that his work has hidden meanings. But just as we are repeatedly frustrated in our efforts to find "the meaning," "meaning," or

1. These are page numbers in Beckett (1958), the standard edition of *Endgame*.

2. I draw heavily on the wealth of critical writing that has appeared about Beckett, especially Adorno 1969; Bair 1978; Ben-Zvi 1986; Cavell 1976; Cohn 1962, 1966, 1967, 1973; Chevigny 1969; Esslin 1965, 1980; Friedman 1970; Kenner 1968, 1973, 1974; Harvey 1970; McNeece 1976; Mercier 1969, 1977; Morrison 1983.

to make a "meaningful connection" with the play, so the characters in the play are repeatedly thwarted in their half-hearted attempts to make a "meaningful connection" with other characters, or even between one thought and another.

Frustrated in its search for meaning in *Endgame*, the audience typically experiences thwarted and poorly articulated affective responses while watching the play. Beckett, whose name is virtually synonymous with the "Theater of the Absurd" (Esslin 1980), has developed a style that induces in the audience a mixture of boredom, numbness, and a kind of nearly continuous frustration. There is an intermittent feeling of hopeful anticipation that is repeatedly disappointed. It is clear that Beckett has carefully crafted and patterned dialogue and action so that the frustration is diluted with just enough gratification or promise of it to seduce the audience into staying or, better, "waiting."

Among the characters on stage, there is a blunting of sensation, a blunting of caring, that may be interspersed with annoyance or even anger. There is rarely any sense of discharge or culmination. In Beckett's two major plays, *Waiting for Godot* and *Endgame*, there is some physical violence (e.g., Lucky beats Estragon in *Waiting for Godot*), but it is inconclusive, seeming to come from nowhere and leading nowhere. Sexual intercourse is virtually nonexistent in the world of these plays, and certainly an experience of sexual arousal in watching or reading them would be quite unusual. Nothing is consummated, whether sexual or aggressive.

The style of communication or, rather, noncommunication in Beckett is typically one in which the characters hardly seem to be listening to each other. If they seem to listen, then neither the message sent nor the message received has much potency, effectiveness, or purpose. The discourse can be broadly characterized as one of poorly articulated desire. Each character's speech in turns elicits poorly articulated counter-desire, not a focused, directed sense of "I want" or "I resist" or "I desire exactly the opposite." The style conveys a despair about being understood and, even more devastating, a despair about being able to clarify and articulate what one wishes, desires, or intends. Thus, to speak of the characters in Beckett as "tantalizing" each other or of the play (and playwright) as tantalizing the audience is not quite accurate.

The myth of Tantalus portrays a god who committed crimes of desire against the other gods (attempting to seduce Hera; murdering his children and serving them up as food to the gods). His punishment in Hades is perpetual torment by being proffered food and drink and then having them withdrawn out of his reach. The myth and the word based on the myth imply articulated desire and its frustration. But in Beckett, characters do not desire sharply enough to be keenly frustrated. The combination of blunted desire and muted frustration is best conveyed in a mime-show, written as a companion piece for *Endgame,* entitled *Act Without Words.* The action consists entirely of one person in a desert being presented with, and then deprived of, various comforts, including a carafe of water. He is not portrayed as a man who is tormented but rather as one who is already numbed and does not desire (though perhaps needs). He is jerked, diddled, pulled around, but he does not seem to experience clear will or counterwill. Students of developmental psychology, especially the psychology of infants reared in various traumatizing and deprived situations, might well use such terms as "hospitalism," "infants in institutions," "anaclitic depression," and the like to begin to characterize the quality of apathy and resignation. We shall return later to this stream of associations, because in *Endgame* there are numerous references to childrearing and the problems of relationships between infants and caretakers.

Greek tragedy and Shakespeare presuppose well-defined desires and passions. These may become clarified, further differentiated, or transformed as the play proceeds. Fears and consequences are associated with these passions and desires; actions and counteractions are intense and focused. When Aristotle speaks of a catharsis of pity and terror, he takes it for granted that neither the characters in the play nor members of the audience will have any difficulty recognizing and experiencing these states. Language in classical tragedy is crisp and sharp—it is also overdetermined, many-layered, rich, and nuanced. Tension builds and comes to a head. If one compares, for example, "waiting" in the opening scenes of two classical plays, Aeschylus' *Agamemnon* and Shakespeare's *Hamlet,* with the opening scene of *Waiting for Godot,* one finds the difference between intense, anxious waiting with some endpoint in sight and endless, poorly defined expectation with no culmination. Affects and intentions are not sharp or focused, messages are neither clearly sent nor clearly received, neither directly accepted nor directly rebutted. Overall, any account of the experience of the characters on stage comes very close to an account of the experience of the majority of the audience. The main exception is that members of the audience can walk out, an option never open to Beckett characters.

What kind of man wrote such plays as *Waiting for Godot* and *Endgame*? How does he experience the world, and what of the world has he experienced? Difficult, creative, sick, stubborn, durable (eighty years old in 1986 and still writing), schizoid, generous and generative—all these characterizations can be found in various biographical and critical accounts of Beckett. Later I address the relationship between Beckett's personal psychology and psychopathology and his plays, including the creatures depicted within.

Beckett's work obviously belongs in several larger twentieth-century contexts, as part of the literature of "the absurd," "modernism," or "postmodernism." Later I discuss a few aspects of the questions raised by these terms. The chapter concludes with an examination of one of the main issues of this book—"what is tragedy?"—by considering the sense in which *Endgame* is tragic. This question involves a further elaboration of such terms as schizoid and narcissistic and the implications of certain psychiatric disorders of infancy. These disorders, I argue, have a true tragic dimension. Defining it will help us understand the nature of tragedy in Beckett's works.

The unifying thesis in the various parts of the chapter is suggested in its title. In *Endgame*, and in Beckett's works in general, there is a pervasive concern with the terrible implications of desiring to procreate, procreating, being born, and needing to kill off the products of procreation. The "products of procreation" are, at the most literal level, children, but—in terms of metaphorical and symbolic equivalences—passions, intentions, meanings, stories, and any experience of intimacy are all at grave risk in this play. If they cannot be prevented, aborted in utero, or killed, then they must be shrunk back into nonexistence. Let us proceed to a more detailed study of how these processes of aborting, thwarting, killing, and "unbirthing" are instantiated in the text of *Endgame*.

HOW TO IGNORE A CRYING BABY

The setting of *Endgame* at once communicates the mood of bleak noncommunication:

> *Bare interior.*
> *Grey light.*
> *Left and right back, high up, two small windows, curtains drawn.*
> *Front right, a door. Hanging near door, its face to wall, a picture.*
> *Front left, touching each other, covered with an old sheet, two ashbins.*
> *Center, in an armchair on castors, covered with an old sheet, Hamm.*
> *Motionless by the door, his eyes fixed on Hamm, Clov. Very red face.*
> *Brief tableau.* (p. 1)

Frozen motion, frozen affect, frozen memory—all of these are conveyed by the stage setting. There is no sense of contact except for the two ashbins touching. It will turn out that the people inside the ashbins never touch in the course of the play; at most they allude to having touched, "yesterday . . . Ah, yesterday!" (p. 20). One can examine any sequence of lines in the text and demonstrate one form or other of inability to sustain or consummate intimacy, but always combined with a clear sense of the characters' inability to separate from each other. Difficulty in making contact goes hand in glove with continuous effort on the part of each character to prevent any strong emotion from being conceived, gestated, delivered, or allowed to remain alive.

Early in the play, Clov, who can stand and walk but not sit, is waiting on Hamm, who is blind and cannot walk. Clov refuses Hamm's requests to move him, and finally Hamm threatens:

Hamm: I'll give you nothing more to eat.
Clov: Then we'll die.
Hamm: I'll give you just enough to keep you from dying. You'll be hungry all
   the time.   (p. 5)

Hamm thus begrudges Clov his existence when Clov refuses him, but his threat to extinguish him is quickly blunted to a threat to keep him continuously hungry. These images of food and of continuous hunger also begin to capture something of the audience's state of inadequate nourishment while watching the play.

A bit later in the play, there is a near-poignant moment, an expectation of some feeling beginning to gel between Hamm and Clov. But consider how this development is regarded:

Hamm: (*Pause.*) Last night I saw inside my breast. There was a big sore.
Clov: Pah! you saw your heart.
Hamm: No, it was living. (*Pause, anguished.*) Clov!
Clov: Yes.
Hamm: What's happening?
Clov: Something is taking its course. (*Pause.*)
Hamm: Clov!
Clov (*impatiently*): What is it?
Hamm: We're not beginning to . . . to . . . mean something?
Clov: Mean something! You and I, mean something! (*Brief laugh.*) Ah, that's a
   good one!   (p. 32–33)

The dialogue continues and culminates (if that word can be applied at all to Beckett) in a plea to capture and quickly kill a flea, who could turn out to be the progenitor of the human race and start the whole damn thing all over again! Thus, the first attempt is to kill any nascent strong feeling and any attempt to ascribe significance to their relationship or their existence. This kind of murder by scorn is quickly followed by an even stronger exterminative frenzy to kill off anything that might procreate any life, especially human life. The equation of the life of the flea with human life does not serve as a plea for the sanctity of all life but reduces human life to the status of insect or animal life. It also further numbs the sense of the distinction between life and death. This passage may well be intended as a perverse commentary on Lear's cri de coeur about Cordelia dead: "Why should a dog, a horse, a rat, have life, / And thou no breath at all?" (5.3.308–09), a wail that underlines the privileged place of human life.

A later passage links the imagery of semistarvation, noncaring, nonaffective communication, and the treatment of children. Hamm is telling his story, his "chronicle," the story of a starving man who came begging for bread for his child. The setting of the tale is the end-of-the-world, such as after a flood, or the Flood. Hamm disdainfully and contemptuously narrates how he dealt with the man: "In the end he asked me would I consent to take in the child as well—if he were still alive. (*Pause.*) It was the moment I was waiting for. (*Pause.*) Would I consent to take in the child . . . (*Pause.*) I can see him still, down on his knees, his hands flat on the ground, glaring at me with his mad eyes, in defiance of my wishes. (*Pause. Normal tone.*) I'll soon have finished with this story" (p. 53).

The story implies a father deeply affected by his son's suffering and trying everything in his power to save the boy. Hamm mocks the father's concern and is quite prepared to see the child die and or continue suffering or to see the father continue to beg on his behalf. The story is supposed to have taken place on Christmas Eve, and as such is a degradation of the stories of Christ's birth, a mockery of the compassion, love, and joy in those accounts, a perverse *Christmas Carol.*

This same Hamm is the one who first addresses his father, Nagg, as "accursed progenitor" (p. 9). In the sequence following the first narration of this story, Nagg, the "Noah" of this desolate ark, demands that Hamm, his son, give him his sugar-plum. "Me sugar-plum!" is the striking condensation of a request, infantile babble, and a loss of the boundary between the desiring agent and the object of desire. Hamm first puts him off with an admonition to pray, and after a futile attempt at prayer by Nagg, Hamm, and Clov, Hamm exclaims (about God), "The bastard, he doesn't exist!" Hamm then informs his father that there are no more sugar-plums. After a pause, Nagg, as if replying to Hamm's "accursed progenitor" and also injured by his son's failure to provide a sugar-plum, mutters:

> It's natural. After all I'm your father. It's true if it hadn't been me it would have been someone else. But that's no excuse.
> (*Pause*)
> Turkish Delight, for example, which no longer exists, we all know that, there is

nothing in the world I love more. And one day I'll ask you for some, in return for a kindness, and you'll promise it to me. One must live with the times.   (p. 56)

The first stage of the father's revenge on the son, then, is the disavowal that there is anything personal in the relationship, especially in the begetting. Nagg attempts to reestablish the fragile bond of feeding and obligation around "Turkish Delight," which "no longer exists." Hence even the hypothetical kindness and promise are impossible. But the imprecation continues:

Whom did you call when you were a tiny boy, and were frightened in the dark? Your mother? No. Me. We let you cry. Then we moved you out of earshot, so that we might sleep in peace.
(*Pause*)
I was asleep, as happy as a king, and you woke me up to have me listen to you. It wasn't indispensable, you didn't really need to have me listen to you.
(*Pause*)
I hope the day will come when you'll really need to have me listen to you, and need to hear my voice, any voice.
(*Pause*)
Yes, I hope I'll live till then, to hear you calling me like when you were a tiny boy, and were frightened, in the dark, and I was your only hope.   (p. 56)

In this extraordinary perversion of parent–infant relationships, we see a glimpse of the "genetic" or "developmental" aspects of the characters in the play and their characteristic ways of nonrelating. The child does not need the parent, and the parent hopes that—out of revenge on the child— the grown-up child will sometime need the parent! Even at that point, there will be nothing personal, for Hamm will need to hear "any voice." Father gets nothing from the son, can give only curses, and has not given much in the past. God, or Jesus, whether as father or as son, is a bastard and, besides, doesn't exist.[3] The reciprocity of nongiving and noncaring is indeed the major act of sharing in the play.

After Nagg speaks, he knocks for Nell on her ashcan, receives no reply, and sinks back into his can, closing the lid behind him. Nell is dead, probably. Hamm parodies "our revels now are ended," the end of Shakespeare's *Tempest*, which affirms the reconciliation of generations and kin, forgiveness, and the wonderful liberating power of the imagination. The

3. See Cavell (1976) for the insight that the biblical tales of Noah and Christ are used here as parent–child stories. The biblical tales, especially Noah and the rest of Genesis, are replete with seed, fertility, birth, and multiplication. The Noah story combines the theme of total destruction of life and birth with a tremendous urge to reproduce and proliferate.

dialogue now reverts to the frustration and aimlessness typical of most of the play.

> Hamm: Our revels now are ended. (*He gropes for the dog.*) The dog's gone.
> Clov: He's not a real dog, he can't go.
> Hamm (*groping*): He's not there.
> Clov: He's lain down.
> Hamm: Give him up to me. (*Clov picks up the dog and gives it to Hamm. Hamm holds it in his arms. Pause. Hamm throws away the dog.*)
> Dirty brute!   (pp. 56–57)

This interchange, about Hamm's toy dog, replays the mutual parent–child rejection, now using Clov and the dog as props. The precise form of the rejection is again stated as a paradox: the dog's gone, but he can't go—he's there, he's not there. Rage at rejection, but no satisfaction. I can't live with you, and I can't live without you. Children's usual objects of affection—toys, blankets, animals (transitional objects, in Winnicott's terms)—fail to soothe and provide companionship. The object is too closely tied up with the destructiveness of its owner and of Clov to serve its consolatory role. The only physical object that seems to console is Hamm's bloody handkerchief, "old stancher."[4]

Another curse and set of images of loneliness are presented earlier in the play. These images set the stage for and amplify the affects in the picture of the crying baby, a baby destructively ignored by its parents. In this scene, Clov refuses a request of Hamm's, and Hamm curses him with the prediction that one day Clov will be as unable to walk as Hamm cannot now. He will be blind and paralyzed:

> Infinite emptiness will be all around you, all the resurrected dead of all ages wouldn't fill it, and there you'll be like a little bit of grit in the middle of the steppe.
> (*Pause*)
> Yes, one day you'll know what it is, you'll be like me, except that you won't have anyone with you, because you won't have had pity on anyone and because there won't be anyone left to have pity on.   (p. 36)

Thus, conflating these two sets of images—Nagg's curse and his description of Hamm's infancy, and Hamm's curse on Clov—we can imagine the experience of the child crying, unanswered. After a while, it would be an experience of "infinite emptiness." Even if the parents eventually awakened and responded, they would at best be like "the resurrected dead of all ages,"

---

4. See Morrison (1983, p. 40) for commentary on the failure of "blood" as relationship and the role of the handkerchief. Cf. *Macbeth*, 2.3.142–43, "The near in blood / The nearer bloody."

who could not fill the void. The curse continues with a further gloss on the experience of loneliness—there will not only be no one to pity Clov, but Clov will have no one left to pity. Beckett captures here one of the crueler forms of parental deprivation: robbing the child of the opportunity to feel pity for another person. The child must become as blocked and thwarted in his ability to express love, caring, and pity as are his parents. In these lines too is replicated an aspect of the audience's experience while watching the play: there is no opportunity to feel for, to sympathize, to pity. No catharsis of pity and terror, for there is no pity—it has been choked in the cradle.

But something does save the characters from complete nonrelatedness to each other, just as Beckett manages to spare the audience the experience of total nonrelating to the play and to the characters. The characters' ability to torture each other by their paradoxical rejections seems to imply that somewhere each of them has known enough of response that he can recognize its absence or its being withheld. They have had just enough of "presence" to be able to describe "absence." Therefore, they are still in conflict. They must ward off the pain of knowing that there is an alternative, but one no longer available to them—"Turkish Delight, for example, which no longer exists." The tragic conflict for the characters is stimulated by the awareness of the existence of love and caring and the massive defenses that must be erected against the pain that accompanies hoping to achieve such closeness.

Instances of the capacity to relate and care deeply are limited. Most important is Hamm's story of the father who pleads with him for food for his child. Hamm's last mention of the child, in his closing soliloquy, hints that even Hamm's sadism toward father and child may contain a microscopic amount of pity: the child should be allowed to die because the earth is too terrible now (p. 83). Then there is the fact, perhaps related to the chronicle, that Clov arrived as a small child and Hamm somehow or other took him in.

The story of Nell and Nagg rowing on Lake Como, fraught as it is with sarcasm and put-down, nevertheless hints at a past in which the characters felt something for each other. Caring and affection are also preserved in an interchange early in the play: Nagg offers Nell a biscuit, she doesn't want it, and he offers to save it for her. Crumbs of pity and caring—Beckett doles them out to the audience at just the right pace and timing to keep us at the table, but always hungry!

Thus, the images and associations to childhood are those of isolation, ignoring, allowing to wither and die, even killing. One can view that picture of childhood as Beckett's "genetic explanation" of how the characters came to be the way they are, or one can say that the bleak atmosphere of the current situation is consistently projected forward and backward in time to all other situations. It is clear that childhood is hardly a state devoutly to be desired; there is no lost paradise, and children are a threat to the scheme of things. That scheme in the play is forever trying to bring things to an end, and never quite able to consummate even an ending. The state of not being able to end is itself represented in the penultimate image of a child in the play:

> Clov: Let's see. (*He moves the telescope.*) Nothing . . . nothing . . . good . . . good . . . nothing . . . goo—(*He starts, lowers the telescope, examines it, turns it again on the without. Pause.*)
> Bad luck to it!
> Hamm: More complications! (*Clov gets down.*)
> Not an underplot, I trust.
> (*Clov moves ladder nearer window, gets up on it, turns telescope on the without.*)
> Clov (*dismayed*): Looks like a small boy!
> Hamm (*sarcastic*): A small . . . boy!
> Clov: I'll go and see. (*He gets down, drops the telescope, goes towards door, turns.*) I'll take the gaff. (*He looks for the gaff, sees it, picks it up, hastens towards door.*)
> Hamm: No! (*Clov halts.*)
> Clov: No? A potential procreator?
> Hamm: If he exists he'll die there or he'll come here. And if he doesn't . . . (*Pause.*)
> Clov: You don't believe me? You think I'm inventing? (*Pause.*)   (pp. 78–79)

Does the boy exist or not? Is he a figment of the imagination? Worse still, is he a potential procreator, like the flea and the rat, who must be exterminated lest he begin the human race anew? In the ambiguity about the boy's existence and about his future, there is both a reiteration of the obliterative mode in relation to children, and at the same time a possibility, a hope, however teasing and frustrating, left open.

This scene is significantly shortened in the English version, and a number of commentators have addressed the difference between it and the more detailed French version. Hamm supposes Clov must be looking at the house with the eyes of the dying Moses. There is an allusion to Christ resurrected—"the stone is lifted"—and Clov says he's contemplating his own navel (Buddha-like). I believe that in the transition between the French and English versions Beckett has done a further bit of "extermination." He has shrunk a character into a smaller and smaller sphere of existence. In the comparative barrenness of the English version, he has considerably diminished the child and eliminated allusions to traditions and ideals.

Thus, the constant state in this play of inability to give birth or to sustain, let alone allow to culminate, any passion, intention, or significance is intimately tied up with images of the neglect or destruction of children. In order to understand further the link between these kinds of prevention of procreation, let us turn to the representation of storytelling, acting, and playwriting in *Endgame*.

STORYTELLING AND STAGE-ACTING

In *Endgame* we witness the progressive degradation and dissolution of the fundamental human activity of telling a story. The motives to tell a story are gradually eroded as it becomes clearer that there is no audience interested in hearing and that the storyteller must increasingly talk to himself. The existing progeny do not care to hear their parents' stories; the parents do not wish to hear stories from their children; the parents scarcely care to hear each other's stories; and there will be no progeny to hear any future stories. The very existence of a past worth telling about is in question, with the remote past perhaps having some value ("We too were bonny—once"; p. 42) and the recent past being unspeakable ("Yesterday! . . . that bloody awful day, long ago, before this bloody awful day; pp. 47–48). The stories principally turn on mutilation and death, the destruction of creation and of procreation; they also involve the destruction of strong positive feelings, such as love and tenderness. Tears are belittled or interdicted (e.g., pp. 51, 62, 81). The stories themselves are endless and repetitive, lack any major communicative impetus, and at times are almost reduced to the babble implied by Beckett's comment that this play is a "matter of fundamental sounds." As we shall see, there is one major function left for the storytelling—Morrison (1983) makes this point most elegantly—the function of substituting narrative for soliloquy. Storytelling, especially Hamm's chronicle, is a way of both revealing and concealing painful knowledge about oneself in relation to oneself, to other characters, and to the audience. What is both most deeply yearned for and most deeply dreaded—love and tenderness—is represented in storytelling, but represented at a safe distance and overlaid with enough cynicism, indifference, and nastiness to be almost completely disguised.

The first story within the play is told by Nagg to Nell:

> When we crashed on our tandem and lost our shanks. (*They laugh heartily.*) It was in the Ardennes. (*They laugh less heartily.*) On the road to Sedan. (*They laugh still less heartily.*) (p. 16)

It explains in part their present plight, that they are in ashbins, without legs. At the same time, the story alludes to terrible battles of World War I, in which many thousands lost their limbs or their lives. Thus the first story told is one of mutilation. It is told and heard in such a way as to gradually degrade a clear emotional response, that of laughter, a response that is not altogether appropriate in the first place.[5]

The next story, Nell's tale, is one of physical mishap, but it conveys in its contents and in its telling the mutilation of happiness and of any possible shared joyful feeling. "Nothing is funnier than unhappiness," she asserts and, brushing aside Nagg's shocked response, continues, "Yes, it's funny like the funny story we have heard too often, we still find it funny, but we don't laugh any more" (p. 19). After a few more lines of semi-futile interchange Nagg asks Nell, "What does that mean? (*Pause.*) That means nothing. (*Pause.*) Will I tell you the story of the tailor?" Nell replies "No . . . It's not funny" (p. 20). They proceed to narrate, alternately. Nagg insists that the first time he told the tailor story, it was very funny. It was on Lake Como, the day after they had gotten engaged: "It always made you laugh. (*Pause.*) The first time I thought you'd die . . . " "Not because the story was funny, but I was happy," Nell says (p. 21).

Nagg insists it was his story that made her laugh, and Nell dwells on the total experience, her happiness, the vision of the bottom of the lake. The two accounts of the experience are as separated from each other as are Nell and Nagg in their bins. In itself the interchange is rather like an ordinary marital quarrel in which a piece of past history again becomes an occasion for disagreement (Cavell 1976, p. 117). The ridicule of any shared happiness is all the more distressing by being both commonplace and so much of a piece with the more monumental destruction of shared positive affects in the play.

When Nagg finally does retell his story, it turns out to be a joke about creation—a tailor who takes forever to make a botched pair of pants and claims that still he did better than God, who made such a botched job of the universe (pp. 22–23). Thus, the main joke in the play is one about the fundamental rottenness of the whole of creation—a comic version of God's repenting that he had made man and destroying all humankind except for Noah and his seed.

The next story is Hamm's tale of an artist-madman he knew, a man who was convinced that the world had come to an end (p. 44). He could not be convinced by seeing the green earth outside the window; he saw only ashes and was convinced he was the only one left on earth. The tale is presented as an example of a delusion, but of course it anticipates and replicates the setting and frame of the play. It is also an accurate rendering of a delusion sometimes found in psychotically depressed people or schizophrenics.[6]

5. See Ruby Cohn (1962).

6. See Bair (1978, pp. 169–70) for Beckett's observations of psychotic patients in a mental hospital as part of his relationship with the psychiatrist Geoffrey Thompson. On this delusion, especially in connection with the Schreber case discussed by Freud, see Frosch (1983, pp. 123–30) and McAlpine and Hunter (1953).

The main story told in the play is Hamm's narrative of the man who came pleading for food and lodging for his son. The "chronicle" begins about halfway into the play, and its narration constitutes a major piece of the "action." The bulk of the narration concerns how Hamm made the man grovel, ridiculed him for wanting to save his son, though perhaps he eventually did take in the son (who might be Clov):

> Well, what ill wind blows you my way? He raised his face to me, black with mingled dirt and tears. . . .
> I'm a busy man, you know, the final touches, before the festivities, you know what it is. . . .
> It was then he took the plunge. It's my little one, he said. Tsstss, a little one, that's bad. My little boy, he said, as if the sex mattered. Where did he come from? He named the hole. A good half-day, on horse. What are you insinuating? That the place is still inhabited? No no, not a soul, except himself and the child— assuming he existed. . . . Come now. . . .
> what he wanted from me was . . . bread for his brat? Bread? But I have no bread, it doesn't agree with me . . .
> if he's still alive—a nice pot of porridge . . .
> And then?
> (*Pause.*)
> I lost patience.
> (*Violently.*)
> Use your head, can't you, use your head, you're on earth, there's no cure for that! . . .
> . . . I finally offered to take him into my service. He had touched a chord. And then I imagined already that I wasn't much longer for this world.   (pp. 51–53)

This is indeed a grim tale, not just about the destruction of the earth, but also of the destruction of pity (by ridicule), caring, parental affection for children, and any sense of purpose in living on earth. Hamm's act of pity, his resonance with a deep human need and his taking in the man and his son, is an act that Hamm says marks his own demise.

Let us turn now to the methods of telling stories, focusing especially on the relationship between the storyteller and his audience. In brief, the method of storytelling, especially Hamm's method, progressively drives away, numbs, frustrates, and throttles whatever audience interest and passion there once may have been. The stories are repetitious, they have no end, no climax; if there is an ending (as in Nagg's joke), the story is repeated endlessly whether or not anyone wants to hear it.

Further, we see that the storyteller must either bribe or coerce someone to hear his tale:

> Hamm: It's time for my story. Do you want to listen to my story?
> Clov: No.
> Hamm: Ask my father if he wants to listen to my story . . .

Clov: He's asleep.
Hamm: Wake him.
Clov: He doesn't want to listen to your story.
Hamm: I'll give him a bon-bon . . .   (p. 48)

Storytelling is thus set in the frame of failed father–son relationships. It is also placed in proximity to the issue of procreation.

Nagg: I'm listening.
Hamm: Scoundrel! Why did you engender me?   (p. 49)

Hamm starts to tell the story as if he is almost finished, or perhaps as if in medias res, as a caricature of epic storytelling (p. 50). Hamm is a Homer seemingly unaware of his audience, unaware of any emotional impact of the story he is about to tell (or has somehow finished telling). He is also unaware of the full emotional import of this story for himself. By concentrating on nuances of style, language, and delivery, he can avoid the pain of realizing that his chronicle is, in fact, his own childhood history, the history that Nagg has told (p. 56). Hamm can also avoid the dread of experiencing his yearnings for tenderness between father and son, tenderness such as is evinced by the father toward his son in the chronicle (Morrison 1983, p. 39). In fact, instead of an affect, Hamm seems to have a somatic sensation: "Something dripping in my head, ever since the fontanelles" (p. 50).

Hamm, it becomes clear, has no great need of an audience—he can tell the tale to himself. As both teller and listener, he can be excited, pleased, bored, or exhausted. He comments throughout on his own storytelling: "That should do it. . . . Nicely put, that. . . . There's English for you. Ah well . . . " (p. 51). Nor does Hamm's story help forge any link between teller and listener, one of the traditional functions of storytelling. It scarcely functions to connect the teller to himself:

Clov: What is there to keep me here?
Hamm: The dialogue. (*Pause.*) I've got to go on with my story. (*Pause.*) I've got on with it well. (*Pause. Irritably.*) Ask me where I've got to.
Clov: Oh, by the way, your story?
Hamm (*surprised*): What story?
Clov: The one you've been telling yourself all your days.   (p. 58)

Clov: Keep going, can't you keep going!
Hamm: That's all. I stopped there. (*Pause.*)
Clov: Do you see how it goes on.
Hamm: More or less.
Clov: Will it not soon be the end?
Hamm: I'm afraid it will.

Clov: Pah! You'll make up another.

Hamm: I don't know. (*Pause.*) I feel rather drained. (*Pause.*) The prolonged creative effort. (*Pause.*)   (p. 61)

As Hamm becomes more and more deprived of an audience, including himself, he invokes a powerful image of loneliness, the child who must talk to himself: "All kinds of fantasies! That I'm being watched! A rat! Steps! Breath held and then . . . (*He breathes out.*) The babble, babble, words, like the solitary child who turns himself into children, two, three, so as to be together, and whisper together in the dark" (p. 70).

As Clov makes one more attempt, ambivalently, to relate to Hamm, his story, and his storytelling, Hamm pushes him away:

Hamm: And me? Did anyone ever have pity on me?

Clov (*lowering the telescope, turning towards Hamm*): What? (*Pause.*) Is it me you're referring to?

Hamm: An aside, ape! Did you never hear an aside before? (*Pause.*)
I'm warming up for my last soliloquy.   (p. 77)

Hamm is thus ambivalent about whether he wants to speak to an audience; he mostly prefers and trusts his own soliloquy, either with an audience overhearing or, better yet, with no audience. But some need for the minimal relatedness that is involved in inventing and telling a story persists. He makes up a story about Clov's departure, even while Clov is still there. Is this also a way of mastering, or minimizing, the pain of departure and loss? "Clov. . . . He never spoke to me. Then, in the end, before he went, without my having asked him, he spoke to me. He said . . . " (p. 80). Clov and Hamm, though speaking alternately, are not speaking to each other. Clov, telling his story about what happened to him, reports conversations to himself (as on pp. 80–81). Not only does the audience for the narratives disappear, but even the characters in the story disappear. Hamm stops the narrative with:

I'll soon have finished with this story. (*Pause.*) Unless I bring in other characters. (*Pause.*) But where would I find them? (*Pause.*) Where would I look for them? (*Pause. He whistles. Enter Clov.*)   (p. 54)

The fundamental triangular relationship of storytelling—the interdependence of storyteller, audience, and characters within the story—is destroyed by the fact of an indifferent teller and an indifferent audience. The ability to generate characters within a tale is clearly dependent upon the existence of an audience who cares about them. It is analogous to the necessity of adequate caring for generating and sustaining the life of a child.

In storytelling, there is also the perennial issue of control between teller and audience. The optimal condition is one in which there is some sharing of the control, a negotiation, so that the storyteller is a "spellbinder," but the audience agrees to be spellbound. There is a failed negotiation here, and the storyteller can scarcely even retain his own interest. The story Hamm is telling, his chronicle, is about control: he controls the man and his son and holds the man as a captive audience. The counterpoint to Hamm's controlling the story and the audience is Clov's wish for complete order, his desire to get all the fragments of physical objects in place. Hamm, for his part, wishes to get all the fragments of the story in place.

> Hamm: Dirty brute! (*Clov begins to pick up the objects lying on the ground.*) What are you doing?
> Clov: Putting things in order. (*He straightens up. Fervently.*) I'm going to clear everything away! (*He starts picking up again.*)
> Hamm: Order!
> Clov (*straightening up*): I love order. It's my dream. A world where all would be silent and still and each thing in its last place, under the last dust. (*He starts picking up again.*)   (p. 57)

Clov's passion for order is also a desire for death and constitutes another attack on procreation, a disorderly process that leads to further disorder. In order to survive and propagate itself, storytelling requires a certain amount of disorder or "play," both as fun and as "give" in a system. In *Endgame* that combination of imaginative freedom within a certain amount of constraint is not available to the characters. Similarly, within the vision of the play, procreation is a process that involves too much risk, too much play, and the danger of things getting out of control. The attendant passion seems too dangerous. Thus, the "endgame" is also an "end of games," an end to that elasticity that allows for the creative disorder of procreating children and stories.

When all is said and done, however, there is a kind of begetting and reproduction that takes place between the play (or its characters) and the audience. The frustration, impotence, and thwarted yearnings of the characters are replicated, cloned, "Xeroxed" within the audience. There is also some replication of the limited capacity for play that exists among the characters, but it is not engendered in the audience in any deeply gratifying, pleasurable, or "cathartic" mode. It is almost as if the play works like a virus invading a cell and converting (or subverting) the cell's molecular apparatus to the task of replicating the virus rather than the cell.

An aspect of the form of the dialogue helps transmit these various "maimed" affects to the audience: the use of the pause. *Pause* is the most frequently used word in the script, and its importance to Beckett is indicated by the lawsuit he brought in 1984 against a production of *Endgame* that eliminated the pauses.[7] These pauses do not mark "pregnant silences"; rather, they are a means of cutting short or interrupting the full development of a feeling. The frequent pauses are also of a piece with the thematic content—the break in continuity of generations. The pauses concretize the fatigue of the characters but also convey the vague hope that there will be a continuation—"I can't go on, I do go on."

Beckett tries to ensure that anything born is shrunk down again to the smallest possible state of existence. However, while Beckett's characters slouch toward absolute zero, the complete end, it is important that they never get there. When a person or story within Beckett's work is shrunken down and reduced, it still continues to exist and replicate, as if within a shrunken womb—it replicates the elements of the world it has abandoned or destroyed.

THE CURE FOR "YOU'RE ON EARTH"

In *Endgame* and other works of Beckett, being conceived, gestated, born, and alive are terrible. These states either contribute to or constitute a disease for which the cure is extermination; or, if that is not possible, next best is to shrink back into the smallest possible size or space.

References to birth in *Endgame* are hardly flattering, such as Clov's "I'm trying . . . Ever since I was whelped" (p. 14), or the punning allusion to the vagina, "where did he come from? He named the hole" (p. 52), or "If he was laying we'd be bitched" (p. 34). There are the efforts to stamp out all potential generative life, be it a boy or a flea or a rat. In a brief interchange about Clov's seeds, there is a violent nihilism: Clov cries, "If they were going to sprout they would have sprouted. (*Violently.*) They'll never sprout!" (p. 13).

What we might term an "obliterative mode" is also recurrently found in the play. Every begetting is already a destruction—"The end is in the beginning and yet you go on" (p. 69). Even in a very brief sequence we can find "Nothing doing," "The bastard [i.e., God], he doesn't exist!" and "There are no more sugar-plums!" (p. 55). There is the frequent repetition of "Zero" (pp. 29, 51). The penultimate lines of the play include: "and speak no more about it . . . speak no more" (p. 84). In Hamm's long final soliloquy he announces: "Moments for nothing, now as always, time was

7. The American Repertory Theater in Cambridge, Mass., produced a version of *Endgame* in December, 1984, that outraged Beckett and prompted a suit. In the compromise that was reached, the theater produced its version but agreed not to bill it or advertise it as Beckett's play, *Endgame*.

never and time is over, reckoning closed and story ended" (p. 84). People become smaller, as Nagg and Nell, legless as they are, must be even further compressed in their ashbins. "Have you bottled her? . . . Are they both bottled?" (p. 24).

Motion also becomes more and more constrained and restricted. Clov, it is true, is in motion; he moves himself and pushes Hamm around (literally and metaphorically). But the play opens with Clov motionless, and after his many abortive efforts to leave we find him, according to the stage directions, "impassive and motionless, his eyes fixed on Hamm, till the end" (p. 82). Hamm ends the play by covering his face with his "old stancher," lowering his arms to armrests, and remaining motionless. His movements throughout the play are highly patterned and exacting, punctuated by occasional throwing of things. But the end of his motion too is immobility.[8]

Thus, in terms of this play, we see that the cure for the disease called being alive, having been conceived, having been born, is to refuse to further that process. The movement is contraction in time, in motion, in size, in contact with other human beings, in affective depth and reach, and toward zero. Storytelling, affect, and progeny all end together. And yet there is a constant urge, even if sluglike in intensity, to start again, to try to regenerate. It is an effort that is doomed to fail but, Sisyphus-like, doomed to start all over again. Thus, if one were to graph the rhythm of the play, it would be a slow, pulsating contraction-expansion-contraction-expansion. One might imagine such a rhythm as characteristic of the bladder or bowel sensations in certain neurologically impaired persons, whose intense sensations of fullness and intense pleasures of emptying are blunted while some sensation remains. If this were the rhythm of a birth process, it would indeed be a very sluggish labor, with no final culminative push or expulsion of the baby at the end. Perhaps the infant is born with significant damage as a result of such a prolonged experience inside the contracting uterus and birth canal.

After coming to these conclusions from the study of Beckett's plays, I became curious about the man who was writing such material. Turning to the plethora of available biographical material, especially the 1978 biography by Deirdre Bair, I was astonished to find that what one could read in Beckett's two main plays was indeed the stuff of the author's recurrent personal preoccupations. I believe my astonishment was a tribute to the artist's nearly successful effort to expunge anything remotely "personal" from his writings.

Beckett, in his late twenties, came to conceptualize his own (rather

8. In *Words and Music* (Beckett 1984, p. 127), written a few years after *Endgame*, Beckett has an ode to *sloth* as the most urgent movement and passion within the soul.

extensive) personal difficulties as the result of terrible experiences in the womb, or of having been born improperly or incompletely, or of having been born at all. According to his friend and sometime lover, Peggy Guggenheim, Beckett was haunted by a prenatal memory. "Ever since his birth he had retained a terrible memory of life in his mother's womb. He was constantly suffering from this and had awful crises, when he felt he was suffocating" (Chevigny 1969, p. 3).

Chevigny goes on to cite one reviewer's assessment of the core situation in *Endgame.* "Imagine a foetus, doomed to be stillborn, suspended in darkness in the amniotic fluid, its life-not-to-be leaking away through the fontanelle—the membraneous gap at the top of the skull of every human embryo." She points out the allusions in Hamm's lines: "Something dripping in my head, ever since the fontanelles. . . . Splash, splash, always on the same spot" (p. 50). There is another related image in his "There's something dripping in my head. . . . A heart, a heart in my head" (p. 18).

The story of how Beckett came to "realize" how much he had been "damaged" by being born is unfolded by Bair; it involves an account of Beckett's brief encounter with intensive psychotherapy or psychoanalysis.[9] From February 1934 to Christmas 1935 he was in treatment with Dr. Wilfred Bion in London. He sought treatment because of a combination of long-standing interpersonal difficulties in close relationships—he had to be absolutely in control of the relationship—and crippling, puzzling somatic symptoms. These included terrible sleep disturbances, immobilizing lethargy that kept him in bed for extended periods, and severe recurrent cysts, including a painful anal cyst. In 1935, the analysis seemed stalemated and Bion suggested that he and Beckett go to hear a lecture by Jung, the third in a series of five that Jung delivered at the Tavistock Clinic on "Analytic Psychology: Its Theory and Practice." In the course of that lecture a number of points important to Beckett about psychopathology and literary creativity were raised. But it seemed that one of Jung's comments during the question-and-answer period struck a deep chord. Jung mentioned that a ten-year-old girl brought to him for consultation had reported dreams that he found very worrisome, for they seemed to be a premonition of her death (she died only a year later). Jung concluded from these dreams that "she had never been born entirely."

9. Bair gathered the information, with Beckett's permission, from interviews with his friends and from his contemporaneous correspondence to them. Bair refers to the treatment as "analysis" and at times I follow her usage. Strictly speaking, it was more likely intensive psychotherapy, though we do not know how often sessions took place or whether Beckett used the couch. See Simon (1988) for more detailed discussion of this and related issues about the treatment.

Beckett seized upon this remark as the keystone of his entire analysis. It was just the statement he needed to hear. He was able to furnish detailed examples of his own womb fixation, arguing forcefully that all his behavior, from the simple inclination to stay in bed to his deep-seated need to pay frequent visits to his (extremely difficult) mother, were all aspects of an improper birth. . . . With Jung's words, Beckett finally found a reasonable explanation of his relationship with his mother. If he had not been entirely born, if he did indeed have prenatal memories and remembered birth as "painful," it seemed only logical to him that the aborted, flawed process had resulted in the improper and incomplete development of his own personality.   (Bair 1978, pp. 209–10)

Bair goes on to discuss briefly the appearance of this theme in several of Beckett's later works. *All That Fall* (1956), which includes references to Jung's lecture, is much more "realistic" than *Endgame* and was written while he was trying to get the latter play produced. It too is full of childlessness, dead children, wishes to kill children, and perhaps—the play leaves it ambiguous—the actual murder of a child.

Beckett's ambivalence about having been born is further reflected in the well-known confusion about his birthdate. Bair begins her biography with this issue: "He insists that he was born on Good Friday, April 13, 1906, a date to which he has not discouraged scholars of his writing from attaching undue importance, but his birth certificate gives the date as May 13, 1906. . . . born in the Dublin district of Stillorgan, a name he links casually with a line from the play that made him famous, *Waiting for Godot*: 'They gave birth astride of a grave' " (p. 1). Beckett's concerns with the terrors of being born and being in the womb, the killing of children, and stopping procreation or being impotent to procreate can be seen in his earliest works (e.g., the poem *Whoroscope*, which deals with Descartes' reaction to the birth and death of his daughter) to the most recent. These themes around birth and children are also repetitively interwoven with themes of storytelling, its difficulty or impossibility, and the gradual contraction of the audience into few people or only one person, the speaker dialoguing with some part of himself. Alternatively, especially in plays written in the past twenty years, and most strikingly in some of his radio scripts, the speakers are disembodied voices, mouths, and disconnected "ghosts."

Conceiving and birthing tend to be joyless and loveless projects in the universe of Beckett's writings. In *Not I* (1984d, p. 216), a stage play, relating the lonely death of a lonely old woman, Beckett's "Mouth" begins:

. . . out . . . into this world . . . this world . . . tiny little thing . . . before its time . . . in a godfor- . . . what? . . . girl? . . . yes . . . tiny little girl . . . into this . . . out into this . . . before her time . . . godforsaken hole called . . . no matter . . . parents unknown . . . unheard of . . . he having vanished . . . thin air . . . no sooner buttoned up his breeches . . . she similarly . . . eight months later . . . almost to the tick . . . so no love . . . spared that . . . no love such as normally vented on the . . . speechless infant . . . in the home . . . no . . .

How and why did Beckett come to this grim view of himself and project that view into his writings? A few comments about his background and temperament may help flesh out and frame this preoccupation with issues about conception, abortion, and birth. First, as far as can be told, in his own case there was no special problem about the process of being born. He was a sickly infant for a few months but was never in any danger. Difficulties about bearing him were not part of his mother's discourse with or about him. A crucial issue, however, according to Beckett himself and all who knew or know him, was his relationship with his mother, May. She was, by all accounts, an extremely difficult woman, prone to extended periods of depressive withdrawal and/or extreme rages at her children (Sam and his older brother, Frank). She was intent on exerting absolute control over her sons. Beckett entered treatment at age twenty-eight in the setting of a desperate attempt to escape from her, and over the two or so years of his work with Bion, he struggled continuously with the pain of separation from her. While realizing that disaster awaited him if he returned to her in Dublin, return he did, breaking off his analysis. He encountered the predicted disaster and had to flee back to London and Bion.

One might speculate, then, that Beckett's fantasy-memory of his terrible life in the womb and of being incompletely born reflects a continuous struggle over individuation, an expression of the fear that too much closeness means suffocation while not enough means the risk of isolation and starvation. In short, this is the classic schizoid dilemma—"nec tecum, nec sine te," in Beckett's own words. His "memory" of the claustrophobic experience of being in the uterus is a projection backward in time of the long-standing feeling of being suffocated by the very person he needs in order to sustain his life.[10]

Beckett's mother died in August 1950 after a period of illness and confinement to a nursing home, just as Beckett was trying to get Roger Blin to produce *Waiting for Godot* (as he eventually did). Beckett returned to Dublin to be with her and his brother at the end. His life-long ambivalence

10. Most psychoanalysts do not believe it is possible to retrieve an experience of birth or life in the womb. Rather, there are fantasies, often not conscious, about these experiences. It is not clear to me from Bion's writings whether he took the experience of birth as a retrievable memory, but in his later years he was definitely most interested in the psychology of the embryo and fetus. I myself have not heard from a patient a conscious fantasy of being in the womb, let alone the conviction that this is a memory. See Guntrip (1969), pp. 51–54. See Simon (1988) on Bion and the psychology of intrauterine life as well as Bion 1977c.

was again enacted as he tried to rid himself of all memory of her. The previous year, he had disposed of all his personal effects that remained in her home, and at her death he took absolutely none of her possessions. Bair writes, "He was sure he would never set foot in Ireland again, and there was nothing from his past that he wanted to save. With this rejection of May's effects, he had finally, symbolically killed her" (p. 406).

Endgame, written and rewritten from 1954 to 1956, marked the end of the writing block that had plagued Beckett since *Waiting for Godot* (1950). It seems likely that his previous writing blocks were deeply involved with conflicted feelings about separation from his mother. Her death and his attempt to be symbolically rid of her must have again been a large part of his difficulty in new creation. Strikingly, he was able to conceive, gestate, labor, and deliver a play about the need to exterminate all conception and procreation! Further, it is a play about the inability to be with *or* to depart from. It ends with both an ambiguity about departure and the act of discarding all personal possession. Hamm rips off his whistle, throws it to the audience, tosses away the dog, and holds onto only one personal possession, his bloody handkerchief—all that he wants of his "blood." It is also a play with two mothers: Nell, on stage, who dies, and "Mother Pegg," mentioned, who died as a result of Hamm's cruelty.[11]

From a psychoanalytic perspective, Beckett's own life "drama" can be seen as a series of unconsciously generated impasses and prolonged experiences of impotence and sterility. Frustration and rage at a powerful and unpredictably devastating mother, projected onto women and female sexuality more generally, may well be important dynamic issues.

An important aspect of his sense of impasse may be dread of the separation that accompanies lack of complete control over what he generates and produces—for example, control over the meanings people will ascribe to his work (Bair 1978, pp. 407–08). He proceeds to overcome such a state by producing writings that describe and even extol the virtues of sloth, impotence and indifference to generativity. As evidence that Beckett managed some partial resolution of his conflicts, we can cite his biographers (e.g., Bair 1978; Ben-Zvi 1986), who suggest that the writing of plays was of major importance in bringing Beckett into more intensive contact with other people. While he apparently has never relinquished his powerful need for privacy and for close control over the quality and quantity of his relationships with friends and with the public, those who knew him for many years observed a change with his success as a playwright. Bair

11. Beckett's sadness at the loss of his beloved brother, Frank, who died of cancer in 1953, does not seem to be represented in the play. His death, though painful, was probably much less in the realm of conflict than his mother's.

suggests that the necessities of the world of theater—getting plays produced, directed, and publicized—and, eventually, the attendant success—"propelled" Beckett out of his relatively limited, "womblike" existence into more intensive contact with more people than he had been willing or able to deal with for years.

It is always of interest and at times quite exciting to glimpse how an artist has converted his own recurrent conflicts and dilemmas into the stuff of art. Trauma transformed—by all accounts an important aspect of the still unsolved mystery of artistic creativity—is a wonder to behold and a moving tribute to the human spirit. Beckett, a man struggling with his own schizoid dilemmas, was able to create and present to the world works of literature, particularly drama, that articulate major psychological issues of his era. His great dramas appeared on the world stage at a time when issues of the isolation and fragmentation of the self, the breakdown of community, the dangers of obliteration of both self and the world of other selves—these and kindred issues are vital concerns of contemporary mankind. It is important, then, to examine some aspects of the relationship between Beckett's portrayal of schizoid issues and the interest of psychoanalytic theoreticians and practitioners in these issues. The connection between Beckett the playwright and the psychoanalyst Bion allows us to consider the similarity between problems articulated by playwrights and those identified by psychoanalysts.

THE AGE OF THE SCHIZOID: THE ATTACK ON MEANINGFUL CONNECTION

Psychoanalysis in the past few decades, both in clinical practice and in theory, has become particularly concerned with issues about the wholeness of the self and the attendant problems of intimate relationships with others. Pari passu, there has been interest in the fact that patients with disorders of the self are prone to difficulties around meaningful affective communication. Whole theories and schools have arisen around such issues, notably the so-called British object-relations theorists and self psychology, associated with the work of Heinz Kohut (Layton and Schapiro 1986). Along with clinical and theoretical interest in states involving the self there is the growing suspicion that there has been a historical shift in the nature of the dominant psychopathology of our time, from the classic psychoneuroses and their related character types (phobia, hysteria, and obsessional neurosis) to character styles reflecting fundamental issues about the integrity and functioning of the self and the ability to relate to others in the most elemental ways. The classic neurotic suffers from conflicts surrounding his or her passions; patients with issues about the self frequently appear to be suffering from a deficiency of passion.

A variety of diagnostic terms and categories, none of them totally satisfactory, have arisen in the attempt to describe and classify these disorders, which appear somewhat more amorphous than the classic neuroses and associated character types. Some of the terms in current use are *schizoid*, *narcissistic*, and *borderline*. I shall focus on the term schizoid, in large part because that term eventually became important in the British psychoanalytic world, where Beckett was a patient.[12]

Schizoid denotes the character style of a person who has difficulty forming close and emotionally warm bonds with others, seeming in fact to dread such intimacy. Such a person gives the outer impression of being cold and aloof, self-preoccupied, but he or she may be engaged in a great deal of inner struggle about his or her yearnings and dread of intimacy. There may be an impression of distractedness, affective nonengagement, and frequent retreat into a world of daydreaming. Such patients frequently come for treatment complaining of feeling unreal or "out of touch" and suffering from diffuse unhappiness.

Several quarters within clinical psychiatry and psychoanalysis have paid increased attention to disorders of blocked or ineffective communication and the inability to experience or express strong affect. For decades, inappropriate or blocked affect was associated with full-blown schizophrenia. Clinicians who developed the term schizoid paid attention to the affect block in cases of people who were not obviously psychotic. Several clinicians working with patients who suffered from severe psychosomatic diseases noted that some of them had difficulty with ordinary affective and symbolic communication; the clinicians coined the term *alexithymia* (inability to speak of feelings) to capture this aspect of several different kinds of difficulties. Similarly, clinicians working with victims of overwhelming trauma, especially war and torture, have described *post-traumatic stress syndrome*, which is frequently marked by numbness, depersonalization, inability to feel, and a state somehow beyond despair. This condition is commonly associated with nightmares, affect storms, and, in the case of some Vietnam war veterans, sudden aggressive outbursts. What is important here is that numbed and blocked affect may be a protective layer against enormous underlying vulnerability.

Another area in which clinicians, especially since the beginning of World War II, have been studying states of apathy, giving up, and emotional nonresponsiveness is that of infant psychiatry. The emotional deficiency diseases of childhood have been described by René Spitz, John Bowlby, and

12. See Beckett's brief admiring paean to "the higher schizoids" in *Murphy* (1957, p. 180).

other psychoanalytically oriented child-observers. These states, in which the infant seems apathetic and limp and fails to develop properly, are related to failures in basic parental or adult nurturance. Absent, sick, depressed, or schizophrenic mothers, and parents who have difficulty providing adequate emotional care because of overwhelming external trauma, seem to be the main etiological factors. While some of the traumatic situations described in this body of research are those of ordinary living, the disruptions of the war and the immediate postwar years provided all too many opportunities to see infants and older children in these categories.

In Beckett's plays, especially *Endgame*, we can see the same combination of concerns that emerges from the clinical and theoretical psychoanalytic literature of the past forty years or so. The play, via mood, setting, characterization, and the frustrated attempts at dialogue, depicts a situation in which the very existence of a self is at stake. Especially at risk in the world of Beckett's drama is the feeling, wishing, willing, and communicating self. In *Endgame* these states of blocked affect and the refusal to make meaningful connections are juxtaposed to images of abandoned and sadistically treated children. I propose that Beckett presents us with "the age of the schizoid"[13] complete with the equivalent of a childhood history of his characters, a portrait of the care and rearing of blocked and numbed adults.

One can argue that both artists and psychoanalytic clinicians are expressing issues arising from the zeitgeist. This brings up the fascinating question of the interaction between Beckett and his analyst, Wilfred Bion. Bion, as it happens, was one of the most important psychoanalytic thinkers and writers on patients with difficulty in communication and patients who cannot or will not allow the establishment of meaningful connections. Although his interest in these areas may well have dated to his early years as a clinician, when he was working with Beckett, his writing, both theoretical and case-oriented, did not appear until around 1950 and was published largely during the next decade, many years after his encounter with Beckett. Yet the congruences between the work of the artist and work of this psychoanalyst are so singular and striking that one must consider the nature of their interaction over many years.

Wilfred R. Bion (1897–1979) was thirty-three in 1930 when he finished his medical training (having started at a later age than usual) and began his psychotherapeutic work and training. He had probably become interested in psychoanalysis while still in medical school.[14] In 1932 Bion began working at the Tavistock Clinic, a strongly independent and eclectic center for

---

13. This term was coined by Guntrip (1969, p. 47) to describe the modern world.

14. These facts are excerpted from James Grotstein's memoir, in Grotstein, ed. (1983). Autobiographical material (although substantially edited after his death) is found in Bion (1982, 1985).

psychotherapy and research that straddled the fence between British academic psychiatry (descriptive and organic) and psychoanalysis, which was a small and much controverted profession at that time in England. Bion began formal psychoanalytic training in 1937, but we do not know who were the main influences on his thinking in the early 1930s.

Bion was perhaps then, and definitely in the late 1930s and 1940s, influenced by the work of Melanie Klein, who had come to England from Berlin in 1929. He became her patient in 1946, his second experience in psychoanalysis. She had already begun to spell out her theories about the earliest stages of the infant's mental life, theories that posited a rather well-developed inner mental life, with the paranoid position of early infancy yielding to a depressive position in the second half of the first year of life. At first her theories seemed to differ only in emphasis from Freud's (especially from Anna Freud's view of his theories), but later they came to be regarded by Klein herself and other analysts as sufficiently divergent to warrant the labeling of a Kleinian school, eventually embodied in a separate training track within the British Psychoanalytic Society.[15]

According to Bion's account of his life (a two-volume autobiography written toward the end of his life, published posthumously), he himself struggled with schizoid issues, especially schizoid defenses against strong affect. It is likely that Bion personally understood the experience of having a very difficult mother from whom separation was difficult and with whom closeness was dangerous. His autobiography suggests that he was enough in touch with the schizoid style to understand and empathize with someone like Beckett, and that he also had enough mastery to help Beckett make some movement. Representative of these trends are several statements from his autobiography:

> One night when I was lying on my bed with pyjamas on waiting for Dudley [his school chum—age ten or so] to get into his bed, he suddenly discarded the towel he had round his waist and jumped astride me as if challenging me to wrestle. "*Now* how do you feel?" he said. I felt nothing physically, mentally a sense of boredom and anticlimax, which soon communicated itself to Dudley, who, after a few futile attempts to provoke a struggle, got off. . . . Dudley and I continued to duel and wrestle with a growing sense of pointlessness. The only overt and unmistakable emotional experience was when futility flared into mutual dislike or more correctly hate.   (Bion 1982, p. 74)

Speaking of his loneliness and missing his mother after he went to preparatory school in England, Bion wrote, "I learned to treasure that blessed hour

15. Melanie Klein is said to have regarded herself as "a Freudian, but not an Anna Freudian." (Grosskurth 1985).

when I could get into bed, pull the bed-clothes over my head and weep. As my powers of deception grew, I learned to weep silently till at last I became more like my mother who was *not* laughing, and was *not* crying" (pp. 33–34). Bion, about to enlist in the army in 1916, described himself as "a chitinous semblance of a boy from whom a person had escaped" (p. 104).

The most striking examples of reactions that involve schizoid defenses, including extreme depersonalization, are Bion's accounts of tank and trench warfare in France, accounts that consume more space in the first volume of his autobiography than any other experiences. He was a tank commander at age twenty and was decorated for bravery, but he felt that it was a most dehumanizing experience. He knew, both from observation of his men and his fellow officers and from his own direct experience, the terror, the loneliness and isolation, and the defensive numbness and depersonalization that came with mechanized warfare. He was relieved to be shot at by a German soldier, a discrete human being, rather than a machine. He describes the defensive withdrawal from caring too much about another soldier, who may well be killed. In sum, he depicts traumatic and post-traumatic states that overlap considerably with schizoid defenses. This was a man for whom the experience of the war elicited schizoid trends and defenses that had been available earlier in his development.

There is a palpable "Beckettian flavor," a theater-of-the-absurd quality to some of Bion's accounts of war casualties. Of a fellow officer he wrote:

> He has lost both eyes, his right arm and both legs. He didn't know who I was though the nurse told him. He's simply—just has a silly grin. The nurse told me afterwards that every now and then he becomes terrified, cowers down in a corner of the room and sucks his thumb. Once he told his doctor that at these times he could see a patch of lawn open up, his mother rise out of her grave and walk slowly towards him. Otherwise he told no one—just went into a corner, scuttling on his stumps with astonishing speed, stuffed his left thumb into his mouth and waited trembling. When the fit was over he would go back to his silly giggling.   (p. 186)[16]

After reading Bion's accounts of the incredible destructiveness of the war, one can see irony in the technical psychoanalytic terms—part objects, splitting, fragmentation, and projection—that he himself used and amplified.[17] It seems to me that Bion's understanding of psychotic inner catastro-

16. For another example of the overlap between the disasters of war and the theater of the absurd see Bion (1985), pp. 47–48.

17. Bion's account of World War I, in its emphasis on detachment, depersonalization and grotesque absurdity, resembles in literary terms some of the post–World War II writing about war, e.g., Jerzy Kosinski's *The Painted Bird*, more than it does the great World War I classics, such as *All's Quiet on the Western Front*.

phe must have formed in connection with his perception of the war as a
psychic as well as a physical catastrophe.

For Beckett, too, war, especially World War II and perhaps more unconsciously World War I, played a major part in his perception of the world and
has influenced his writings. Beckett's family was astonishingly apolitical in
the midst of the Irish rebellion against England and World War I. Several
informants have told me that after the war the streets of Dublin were, in
effect, one massive veterans' hospital, the war-wounded very visible. The
gates of Trinity College, Dublin, where Beckett attended school in the
1920s, were a gathering place for crippled beggars, including impaired war
veterans. Allusions to the destructiveness of the war pepper Beckett's
writings.

Beckett was importantly involved in France during and shortly after
World War II. As an agent for the French underground, he had to escape
from the Gestapo and hide out in the small town of Roussillon in Provence.
(*Waiting for Godot* seems to have its origins in this period; see Bair 1978,
pp. 385–89.) He did relief work with the Irish Red Cross in France immediately following the war, and subsequently he was cited by De Gaulle for
his heroism.[18] By all accounts, Beckett was deeply affected by what he did
and saw during the war. There is one incident, however, that to me suggests
a connection between the horrors of war and the necessity for schizoid defenses against such horror and pain. Bair describes Beckett, his aunt, and his
cousins touring around Chalons, in the south of France:

> When they paused in the busy town square to search for a restaurant, Ann
> Beckett was upset by Beckett's unaccustomed emotion. He shook tears from his
> eyes and said, "You should have seen this place the last time I was here—there
> were bodies in the square, shot by the Germans in retaliation . . . " His voice
> drifted off, and he could say no more. It was the only time his family had heard
> him mention the war since it had ended, and they were embarrassed by not
> knowing how to change the mood. Lunch was a series of awkward silences
> punctuated by too much chatter, and the afternoon seemed cloudy and sad from
> that point on.   (p. 520)

In the course of studying and formulating the nature of the communicative disorder represented in *Endgame*, I became aware that I was drawing on
a common fund of clinical and theoretical knowledge about the psychotherapy of severaly withdrawn and psychotic patients. Much of this "common fund" had accumulated during the years after World War II, in both
America and England. It was not until I learned that Beckett had been in

---

18. See a recently published address by Beckett (1946) on the war delivered on Irish radio
in June 1946, and the discussion by Alan Jenkins (TLS, Nov. 14, 1986, 1281–82).

treatment with Bion that I recalled Bion was a major contributor to the understanding of primitive states of communication and noncommunication. A 1959 paper, "Attacks on Linking," is one of the most commonly cited (although little read) psychoanalytic papers on patients who refuse to make "links"—that is, who dread meaningful connections. Bion presents material from patients who strenuously objected to the analyst's act of interpretation, more than to the content of the interpretation. "Linking" of one thought, feeling, or situation to another is viewed as a profound threat by these patients because it implies the possibility that the patient and the analyst mean something to each other and have some connections. In one instance, Bion's interpretation threatens to link patient and analyst in a creative and fecund relationship; the patient cannot tolerate this. Bion closes with:

> The main conclusions of this paper relate to that state of mind in which the patient's psyche contains an internal object which is opposed to, and destructive of, all links whatsoever from the most primitive (which I have suggested is a normal degree of projective identification) to the most sophisticated forms of verbal communication and the arts. . . . These attacks on the linking function of emotion lead to an overprominence in the psychotic part of the personality of links which appear to be logical, almost mathematical, but never emotionally reasonable. Consequently the links surviving are perverse, cruel and sterile. (p. 315)

Reading this paper brought home to me the extent to which I had been interpreting Beckett's plays, especially *Endgame*, implicitly using models that Bion makes explicit. Each of his clinical vignettes or commentaries suggests a character or situation or dynamic in a Beckett work.

I conjecture that reverberations from Bion's treatment of Beckett are present in his post–World War II clinical papers, though Beckett's case material is never directly presented (e.g., Bion 1974). Bion probably could not write up material from his treatment of Beckett, not only for reasons of confidentiality, but also because it took many years to find a framework for conceptualizing this difficult and torturing clinical material. Bion must have been struggling both to articulate his personal issues and to understand the nature of early defects in object-relations—early issues around closeness and its dangers—at the time he encountered Beckett, who probably presented such issues in "pure culture." Bion became able to articulate these issues more fully only in the years after World War II, as a result of personal analysis and growth and/or through further clinical experience and exposure to other psychoanalytic viewpoints (especially those of Melanie Klein and Fairbairn).

Bion, I surmise, spent many years consciously and unconsciously trying to assimilate the impact of the incomplete, but quite powerful, treatment of Beckett. Beckett's verbal and artistic gifts must have allowed him to articulate more vividly than most other patients the nature of his disturbed and disturbing inner experiences. He touched something personal in Bion's inner struggles and left Bion with clinical and theoretical puzzles that formed an important part of the subsequent program of Bion's writing. Bion did not lack passion, impetus, strong desires, or will—he was not a character from a Beckett play—but he clearly could mobilize stances and defenses cut from the same cloth as those of Beckett's stage characters. It is my speculation that in the analysis Beckett and Bion profoundly influenced each other.[19]

Another aspect of the similarity between Bion's clinical and Beckett's artistic work resides in the paradox that along with or even despite the push to break all meaningful links, there is a persistent urge to keep trying, to keep communicating. To read either Bion's case studies or Beckett's texts only as efforts at thwarting communication is to comply in the defenses used by the patient and by the "texts" (Cavell 1976).

In sum, I claim that there is an important gestalt of form and content common to Beckett and Bion. I also suggest that in their encounter during 1934–35, each intuitively apprehended the presence of that gestalt in the other, though neither could conceptualize or formalize it. What is that gestalt, that complex? First, a view of the difficulties of human communication and yet a deep regard for the struggle to maintain that communication; as well as an insistence on owning up to the implications of a profound unwillingness, inability, or dread of making deep connections with another human being. At a somewhat more cognitive level, this gestalt involves a view of the problematic nature of language and the necessity of exploring the implications of those problems. It includes, or subsumes, a capacity to utilize and blend two seemingly contrasting styles—the construction of primitive dialogue among primitive objects and part objects (Bion 1979), "names without words and words without names" (a Beckettian phrase), and the construction of highly ordered mathematical grids and algebraic combinations (see Bion 1977a). The *style* implicit in the gestalt includes a willingness to experiment, to "play," to outrage, to push to the limit, and a deep conviction of the absolute necessity to spell out and play out all the implications of ideas.

Obviously this complex of ideas and approaches overlaps considerably with what is implied by the term *modernism*, designating those artistic and

19. As for subsequent contact between the two men, Beckett did not follow Bion's career, nor did he read any of his works. Bion did read and see some of Beckett's works, though I do not know the details and doubt they can be learned at this date. (My correspondence with Beckett, July 1985, and with Francesca Bion, July 1985.)

literary expressions so prominent in the twentieth century where form is fragmented, rearranged, abstracted, and re-presented in novel ways. The motives for such works are complex but clearly include the attempt to identify and characterize the "elementary particles" of sensation, perception, matter, and, in the case of literary works, the "elementary particles" of affect and human relatedness. An important characteristic of modernist literature seems to be an alteration in the representation and experience of the I or the self. The I is somehow more passive, more continuously self-reflective, and numbed—lying "etherized upon a table." This self-reflection is qualitatively different from classical soliloquy—it is paralytic rather than a prelude to action.[20]

Works in the modernist style are typically difficult to comprehend at first and difficult to respond to without excessive hostility and/or boredom. Some hostility and boredom seem to be requisite for grasping the aesthetic, psychological, and historical significance of these works more fully, but too much can block empathic involvement. Over the past few decades a number of psychoanalytically informed critics of culture (e.g., Adorno, who has written an important essay on *Endgame*, 1969) have attempted to characterize and explain aspects of modernism. Features of the twentieth century invoked in discussions about the nature of form and feeling in modern cultural products include mass production, the conquests of technology, the conceptual revolution in modern physics about the constitution of matter, the incredibly destructive wars of this century, and the potential for global nuclear holocaust. Changes in the structure of the family, particularly those that undermine the authority of parents and elders, are also frequently mentioned in such discussions (e.g., Lasch 1978). The developments in the technology of reproduction must also play a major role in the modern and modernist consciousness. The ability to control reproduction—to detect and abort genetically damaged fetuses, to create "test-tube babies," to use surrogate mothers, and related developments—actualizes what for millennia was only the subject of humankind's fearful and wish-fulfilling fantasies.[21] Any one of these features of twentieth-century life merits detailed consideration of its impact both on art and on psychology.

20. Bradbury and McFarlane (1976, chap. 7), "Modernist Drama," is especially helpful. See, e.g., pp. 505–11 on problems of communication; 534–35 on monologue. Also helpful is Sass (1985) and his bibliography. Sass uses the term *hyper-reflexivity* to designate the extremity of self-awareness and self-consciousness found in modernist works. Also useful in characterizing modernist and modern conceptions of the self is Christopher Lasch, *The Minimal Self* (1984). See also Kermode (1968a, b).

21. See, e.g., Aldous Huxley's *Brave New World* and Margaret Atwood's *The Handmaid's Tale* (1985). For a provocative discussion of the implications of these technologies for family continuity, see Kass (1985), esp. chap. 2, "Making Babies: The New Biology and the 'Old' Morality," pp. 43–79.

Here I can only suggest the ways these forces are reflected in literature and clinical practice.

THE SCHIZOID AND THE TRAGIC:
ENDGAME AS TRAGEDY

Is *Endgame* a tragedy? I would like to spell out the implications of this question by considering what Ronald Fairbairn has called the "tragic situation" of the schizoid. Fairbairn was the psychoanalyst who brought the descriptive term *schizoid* into psychoanalytic discourse, and his works remain the richest source of description and theorizing about the nature of this state. He further argued that there is a schizoid core in each person, a contention by no means universally accepted among psychoanalysts, but compatible with the spirit of modernism. I believe there is an important overlap between the tragedies written by Beckett and the tragedies formulated by a psychoanalytic clinician. An examination of this overlap will take us back to the question "what is tragedy?" and in particular to the relationship between tragedy and the family.

Fairbairn's 1940 essay "Schizoid Factors in the Personality" defines the *schizoid position* as one in which the individual feels that his love is bad because it appears destructive toward his libidinal objects.

> It represents an essentially tragic situation; and it provides the theme of many of the great tragedies of literature, as well as providing a favourite theme for poetry (as in the "Lucy" poems of Wordsworth). It is small wonder then that individuals with any considerable schizoid tendency experience such difficulty in falling in love; for they always entertain the deep anxiety expressed by Oscar Wilde in *The Ballad of Reading Gaol* when he wrote, "Each man kills the thing he loves." It is small wonder too that they experience difficulty in emotional giving; for they can never entirely escape the fear that their gifts are deadly, like the gifts of a Borgian. Hence the remark of a patient of mine, who, after bringing me a present of some fruit, opened the next day's session with the question, "Have you been poisoned?" (pp. 25–26)

Another of Fairbairn's schizoid patients said to him, "Whatever you do, you must never like me." Among the protective devices used to avoid the dangers of love, a schizoid individual may mobilize aggression and hatred toward others who either do or might love him. He may eventually induce those others to hate him, and he is skilled in doing so, for in some sense his survival depends on that skill. This is the second great tragedy of the schizoid.

There is a third great tragedy for the schizoid person. Since love is so dangerous, and the joy of loving therefore so unattainable, "he may as well deliver himself over to the joy of hating and obtain what satisfaction he can out of that." Similarly, since loving seems to involve destroying, the schizoid person may attempt to *spare love*, to preserve secretly somewhere the capacity to love, or to preserve an awareness of the virtues of loving, by dint of "it is better to destroy by hate, which is overtly destructive and bad, than to destroy by love, which is by rights creative and good." Not attempting to love avoids the risk of love's becoming contaminated by hatred; hence it is safer to hate, thereby preserving an illusion that love still exists somewhere.

These tragic dilemmas are unconsciously enacted by schizoid individuals. When such persons seek treatment, they complain of feelings of emptiness, boredom, or unhappiness ensuing from repeated failures in love; frequently somatic complaints are intertwined. It is the work of psychoanalysis to help show the patient that in fact "unhappiness" or "boredom" is the surface manifestation of a drama within, a tragic drama with protagonists and heroes and villains. His or her diffuse "chest pain" represents the drama of a heart that is too terrified to bear the pain of disappointment of love again.

Beckett, in his dramas, portrays something between a description and an explanation of the workings of the schizoid person and his or her dilemmas. One might usefully conceptualize these plays as occupying an intermediate space between literature and psychopathology. It is as if they were written midstream in the psychoanalysis of a schizoid person or are the partially interpreted dreams of such a person. The psychoanalyst must help the schizoid patient understand the nature of the classic tragedy that underlies his or her life, a life that is on the surface enacted as theater of the absurd.

The analyst must be aware of the patient's perspective that it is dangerous to experience his or her problems as struggles among strong passions and intentions. The analyst's very attempt to help "translate" is itself a potential assault on the necessary defenses of the patient. Here lies the crux of an important theoretical and clinical debate in the treatment of schizoid and narcissistic personalities, a debate that has some implications for audience response to Beckett's works. Some theorists view blocked affect and blocked communication as defenses against the eruption of powerful impulses, destructive toward self and others, toward the person's world of inner objects. Others view these affective and communicative states as "holding operations," warding off the dreaded experience of the lack of any relatedness, an existential emptiness, the anxiety of not being a person. The situation may differ, of course, from patient to patient, but my own sense is that both theoretical approaches are needed and are relevant in different instances. On the whole, the view that the blocked affects are a defense against powerful destructive urges tends to be that of the therapist, who longs to find a conventional drama beneath the weird and absurd surface. The view that what is central is the dread of nonbeing and non-relatedness tends to be close to the patient's experience. Each of these theories, while potentially valid, can be used defensively to avoid the implications of the other. For such an analysis to work, the analyst must develop more respect for the schizoid stance and the patient more tolerance for the "passionate" stance of the analyst.

We can speculate that Beckett, in effect, wrote his great plays in the setting of a partially successful analysis. By *analysis* I mean not just the psychoanalytic work done with Bion, but also the process of self-analysis and "working through" ongoing in subsequent years. The analysis was successful enough to allow Beckett to portray these schizoid dilemmas accurately and yet with both compassion and some detachment. His analysis was incomplete in the sense that, as some critics and audiences experience his work, he monotonously and obsessively works and reworks the same themes with little expansion or innovation. His work has been experienced both as profound and artful analysis of terrible human states and as pure psychopathology dumped onto the stage or the printed page.[22]

Now let us return to tragedy. Insofar as the audience can resonate with the underlying "deep structure" of a Beckett play, it can be experienced as belonging to the genre tragedy. Insofar as the playwrights' style and the audience's defenses cause more of the manifest schizoid material to be the main experience, the play will be experienced as absurd, outrageous, pathetic, or boring. I believe the more theatrically successful of Beckett's works have struck just the right balance between the classical and the schizoid. Some of his more recent short plays, which have left even ardent supporters at a loss, I believe fail to evoke enough of the classical.

Among the artistic devices or effects that help achieve that balance is the limited but "evocative" allusion to a classical past, a past with some traditions. Literary references to biblical and Shakespearean themes, especially if they are muted, help achieve this effect. The curtailment and "aborting" of the characters' and audience's attempts to pin a clear meaning onto the story is the other side of achieving that proper balance. There is a game of hide and seek—Beckett's own words are, "I hid and you sook" (*Whoroscope*)—a game of whether or not he put the meaning in his work and how one must search for it.

22. The old Dublin friendship between Beckett and Geoffrey Thompson, the psychiatrist (and later psychoanalyst) who referred Beckett to Bion, began to cool when Thompson told Beckett that he did not like *Endgame* and that he was "unable to see Beckett's plays as anything other than manifestations of severe depression and possibly psychosis" (Bair 1978, p. 457).

In characterizing tragic dialogue, I have utilized the model of "partially correct interpretation," a model drawn from the clinical psychoanalytic setting. One character understands and communicates just enough understanding to the other to maintain an impassioned involvement, but also just enough misunderstanding, or missing empathy, to drive a further wedge between the two. Such dialogue can be considered typical of developed wish, intention, and passion, whether in everyday life, in psychoanalysis, or onstage in tragic drama. Tragic drama exploits and magnifies this aspect of human communication in order to achieve its artistic and emotive ends. The kind of drama constructed by Beckett and the kind of affective communication characteristic of schizoid individuals present us with blunted and stunted passions, intentions, and meanings. The characters do not engage enough with each other to sustain the dialogue of "partially correct interpretation." They do not remain intimate enough with each other to do the "copulatory" acts that "engender" great tragic deeds and great tragic outcomes.

The schizoid issues portrayed in Beckett's characters interfere in the most fundamental ways with maintaining a family. The "family" of *Endgame* is far more of a blasted and hollow shell than the worst of the families of Greek tragedy or Shakespeare. Further, the processes of propagation and procreation are not just problematic, but virtually banished from existence. Procreation, from the schizoid perspective, entails too much closeness, both with the partner and with the progeny. At the same time, such closeness and mutual interdependence may threaten loss of control of the situation. Both the processes of procreation and the rearing of progeny involve too much anarchy. (Cf. Clov's dream of absolute order in *Endgame*.)

The theme of the "hidden self" in schizoid patients, a self that is hiding out in an air-raid shelter, as it were, is connected, I believe, with the belief that emergence would risk repeating the transmission of trauma. I have argued throughout that one of the core problems posed by tragic drama is how to avoid or end the transmission of trauma from one generation to the next. Beckett's dramas, then, present us with another "solution" ("final solution") to this problem—stopping all procreation, bringing an end to the awful chain of parents damaging children in the same way they were damaged when they were children. The perpetration of intergenerational trauma presented so graphically at the beginning of tragic drama, as in Aeschylus' *Oresteia*, is finally brought to a halt. No longer to have progeny is to spare the progeny from uncontrollable parental rage and despair and to spare oneself from reliving one's own childhood traumas. Therefore, in the world of *Endgame* children must be "bottled," eliminated, in an attempt to kill off the raging and despairing traumatized child within the adult (Morrison 1983; Schapiro, pers. comm., 1985). We must not only stop the progeny, we must even stop stories about progeny, or else render those stories so dull and unengaging that we are not affected by them—for stories are about progeny and for progeny.

Without progeny, however, there can be the most profound loneliness and despair, a total thwarting of yearnings to express love and tenderness, yearnings buried but preserved deep within. One's own self, the hypothetical progeny, and the internalized parents may all be saved from one kind of destruction but are then prone to another kind—death by attrition or the claustrophobic nightmare, death by being buried alive. The schizoid world then demands some terrible compromises. These include setting up a pattern of neither staying nor leaving, neither copulating nor not copulating, making neither a strong beginning nor a strong ending. Another such compromise is to clone oneself in imaginary dialogues, in plays within the play, such as Hamm's endless soliloquy in *Endgame*.

Classical and Shakespearean tragedies evoke lofty and significant ideals that are part of what sustains the hope of, and the motive for, procreation and continuity. Aristotle's definition of tragedy includes the requirement that the play be a mimesis—a representation of an action, a praxis, that is serious and complete. The characters must have an important self-ideal, much pride, both self-importance or injured pride and pride in what they represent for the community and for the world in which they live. Such pride must involve the major ideals and values of the culture presumed in the play (and in some sense presumed in the audience). These are the bonds that hold the community and the family together, the community of ancestors and the community of posterity. At the same time, it is the essence of tragedy to explore and at times expose these ideals as containing contradictory directives that can tear the hero and the family apart. The theme of sacrifice—some must die that others can live—often actualizes these contradictions (see Little 1981, pp. 64–76). The classical tragedies refine and purify our appreciation of certain core values, and our appreciation of the difficulty of being human. Even the profound pessimism implied in some choruses of the Sophoclean Oedipus plays—"Oh ye generations of men, I count you as zero" (*Oedipus Rex*), or "Best is never to have been born, and second best is to go through life as quickly as possible" (*Oedipus at Colonus*)—convey a sense of the preciousness of human life, a preciousness enhanced by our appreciation of deep human suffering. The ideals and values conveyed by the tragic process ultimately serve as the fundamental ones that hold families and communities together and allow life and procreation to continue by establishing the virtue of deep caring for the human condition.

In contrast, much of modern tragedy, beginning probably with some of Ibsen's plays, struggles with the problem of constructing ideals or of trying to resurrect and inflate dying and crumpled ideals. In Ibsen's *Wild Duck* or *Master Builder*, deep and destructive intrafamilial rivalries are combined with shabby and failed attempts to construct mobilizing and uplifting ideals. O'Neill, especially in the later plays (e.g., *The Iceman Cometh, Long Day's Journey into Night*), cruelly dissects the failure of ideals and of durable, life-sustaining illusions. O'Neill succeeds, for much though not all of his audience, in evoking a kind of deep pity for his characters that can be associated with a sense of tragic catharsis and fulfillment. In Beckett, however, ideals are shadowy; artifacts of a remote and almost forgotten past (perhaps even a nonexistent past) can occasionally be constructed, but they have a very short half-life, as it were, and ultimately serve only as a further source of frustration and difficulty. Ideals threaten to remind us of the depth of our buried longings, our profound disappointments; they thereby threaten to mobilize extraordinary rage at those who seem to dangle them before us. Ideals interfere with the business of getting down to the end.

In *Endgame*, then, Beckett has written a kind of commentary on the history of Western tragic drama. If the play were in the form of an extended prose argument, it would run something as follows:[23] Tragedy began with the Greeks and portrayed how conflicting values about what is important for the house, for the family, can lead to the destruction of the house and its progeny. Tragedy has continued to explore this problem from antiquity to the present, and though different resolutions have been tried, tragedians have never been able to satisfactorily solve the intractable conflicts inherent in the family. The old Greek said, "Best is never to have been born," and we have not been able to get beyond that.

I, Sam Beckett, will try one more solution: portray what it is like to eliminate ideals, eliminate a past, eliminate deep human connection, eliminate generational continuity and generation, and, of course, eliminate writing plays. For better or for worse, this solution doesn't work either, because the more relentlessly and repeatedly I draw this portrait, the more people think I must have something up my sleeve, some secret meaning. You might be thinking that somewhere, deep in my own bomb shelter, I cherish hopes of a rebirth from the debris. If that's your hope, then that's your headache, not mine. I'll just go on writing plays.

---

23. While Beckett would probably disclaim any such intent, I think my view of the play as a commentary on tragedy is bolstered by consideration of the works of Beckett's younger fellow dramatist and friend Eugene Ionesco. His *Victims of Duty* (1958) contains his analysis of the problem with tragic drama up to his day. He has a character suggest, tongue in cheek, that the plays of Ionesco have corrected all the problems and should suffice for all drama lovers.

REFERENCES

Adorno, Theodore W. 1969. Towards an Understanding of *Endgame*. In *Twentieth Century Interpretations of Endgame: A Collection of Critical Essays*, ed. Bell Gale Chevigny, pp. 82–114. Englewood Cliffs: Prentice-Hall.

Atwood, Margaret, 1985. *The Handmaid's Tale*. New York: Ballantine.

Bair, Deirdre, 1978. *Samuel Beckett: A Biography*. New York: Harcourt, Brace Jovanovich.

Beckett, Samuel. 1946. The Capital of the Ruins. In *As No Other Dare Fail: For Samuel Beckett on His 80th Birthday*, John Calder, Martin Esslin, Billie Whitlaw, David Warrilow et al., pp. 73–76. London: Calder, 1986.

———. 1957. *Murphy*. New York: Grove Press. Originally published 1938.

———. 1958. *Endgame, Followed by Act Without Words*. New York: Grove Press.

———. 1984a. *The Collected Shorter Plays of Samuel Beckett*. New York: Grove Press.

———. 1984b. *Disjecta*. Ed. Ruby Cohn. New York: Grove Press.

———. 1984c. *Words and Music*. In *The Collected Shorter Plays of Samuel Beckett*. New York: Grove Press. Originally published 1961.

———. 1984d. *Not I*. In *The Collected Shorter Plays of Samuel Beckett*. New York: Grove Press. Originally published 1972.

Ben-Zvi, Linda. 1986. *Samuel Beckett*. Boston: Twayne Publishers.

Bion, W. R. 1959. Attacks on Linking. *International Journal of Psycho-Analysis* 40:308–315.

———. 1974. The Imaginary Twin. In *Second Thoughts*, pp. 3–23. New York: Jason Aronson.

———. 1977a. *Learning from Experience*. In *Seven Servants: Four Works by Wilfred R. Bion*. New York: Jason Aronson. Originally published 1962.

———. 1977b. *Seven Servants: Four Works by Wilfred R. Bion*. New York: Jason Aronson.

———. 1977c. On a Quotation from Freud. In *Borderline Personality Disorders*, ed. P. Hartocollis, pp. 511–515. New York: International Universities Press.

———. 1979. *Memoir of the Future: Book Three: The Dawn of Oblivion*. Perthshire: Clunie Press.

———. 1982. *The Long Week-End, 1897–1919: Part of a Life*. Abingdon: Fleetwood Press.

———. 1985. *All My Sins Remembered: Another Part of a Life and The Other Side of Genius: Family Letters*. Ed. Francesca Bion. Abingdon: Fleetwood Press.

Bradbury, Malcolm and James McFarlane, eds. 1976. *Modernism 1890–1930*. Harmondsworth: Penguin.

Cavell, Stanley. 1976. Ending the Waiting Game. In *Must We Mean What We Say?*, pp. 115–162. Cambridge: Cambridge University Press.

Chevigny, Bell Gale, ed. 1969. *Twentieth-Century Interpretations of Endgame: A Collection of Critical Essays*. Englewood Cliffs: Prentice-Hall.

Cohn, Ruby. 1962. *Samuel Beckett: The Comic Gamut*. New Brunswick: Rutgers University Press.

————. 1966. The Beginning of *Endgame*. *Modern Drama* 9:319–23.

————. 1967. *Casebook on Waiting for Godot*. New York: Grove Press.

————. 1973. *Back to Beckett*. Princeton: Princeton University Press.

Esslin, Martin, ed. 1965. *Samuel Beckett: A Collection of Critical Essays*. Englewood Cliffs: Prentice-Hall.

————. 1980. *The Theatre of the Absurd*. 3d ed. Harmondsworth: Penguin Books.

Fairbairn, W. Ronald D. 1952. Schizoid Factors in the Personality. In W. Ronald D. Fairbairn, *Psychoanalytic Studies of the Personality*, pp. 1–27. London: Routledge and Kegan Paul. Originally published 1940.

Friedman, Melvin J., ed. 1970. *Samuel Beckett Now*. Chicago: University of Chicago Press.

Frosch, John. 1983. *The Psychotic Process*. New York: International Universities Press.

Grosskurth, Phyllis. 1986. *Melanie Klein: Her World and Her Work*. New York: Knopf.

Grotstein, James. 1983. Wilfred R. Bion: The Man, the Psychoanalyst, the Mystic. A Perspective on His Life and Work. In *Do I Dare Disturb the Universe? A Memorial to Wilfred R. Bion*, ed. James Grotstein, pp. 1–36. London: Karnac.

Guntrip, Harry. 1969. *Schizoid Phenomena, Object-Relations and the Self*. New York: International Universities Press.

Harvey, Lawrence E. 1970. *Samuel Beckett: Poet and Critic*. Princeton: Princeton University Press.

Huxley, Aldous. 1960. *Brave New World* and *Brave New World Revisited*. New York: Harper and Row.

Ionesco, Eugene. 1958. *Three Plays: Amédee; The New Tenant; Victims of Duty*. Trans. Donald Watson. New York: Grove Press.

Jenkins, Alan. 1986. A Lifelong Fidelity to Failure. *Times Literary Supplement*, November 14, 1986, pp. 1281–82.

Kass, Leon R. 1985. *Toward a More Natural Science: Biology and Human Affairs*. New York: Free Press.

Kenner, Hugh. 1968. *Samuel Beckett: A Critical Study*. Expanded ed. Berkeley: University of California Press. Originally published 1961.

————. 1973. *A Reader's Guide to Samuel Beckett*. New York: Farrar, Straus, Giroux.

————. 1974. *The Stoic Comedians: Flaubert, Joyce and Beckett*. Berkeley: University of California Press. Paperback reprint.

Kermode, Frank. 1968a. Modernisms. In *Continuities*. London: Routledge and Kegan Paul.

————. 1968b. Samuel Beckett. In *Continuities*, pp. 167–175. London: Routledge and Kegan Paul.

Kern, Edith. 1970. *Existential Thought and Fictional Technique: Kierkegaard, Sartre, Beckett*. New Haven: Yale University Press.

Khan, Masud. 1974. Clinical Aspects of the Schizoid Personality: Affects and Technique. *The Privacy of the Self: Papers on Psychoanalytic Theory and Technique*, pp. 13–25. New York: International Universities Press. Essay originally published 1960.

Kott, Jan. 1964. *King Lear* or *Endgame*. In *Shakespeare Our Contemporary*, trans. B. Taborski, pp. 87–124. Garden City, N.Y.: Doubleday.

Langs, Robert J. 1978. Some Communicative Properties of the Bipersonal Field. *International Journal of Psychoanalytic Psychotherapy* 7:89–136.

Lasch, Christopher. 1978. *The Culture of Narcissism*. New York: Norton.

———. 1984. *The Minimal Self: Psychic Survival in Troubled Time*. New York: Norton.

Layton, Lynne, and Barbara A. Schapiro, eds. 1986. *Narcissism and the Text: Studies in Literature and the Psychology of the Self*. New York: New York University Press.

Little, J. P. 1981. *Beckett: En attendant Godot* and *Fin de partie*. London: Grant and Cutler.

Macalpine, Ida, and Richard A. Hunter. 1953. The Schreber Case: A Contribution to Schizophrenia, Hypochondria, and Psychosomatic Symptom-formation. *Psychoanalytic Quarterly* 22:328–371.

McNeece, Lucy Stone. 1976. Theatrics of Being: The Comic Mask: A Study of Samuel Beckett's *Fin de Partie*. B.A. thesis, Bennington College.

Mercier, Vivian. 1969. *The Irish Comic Tradition*. London: Oxford University Press.

———. 1977. *Beckett, /Beckett*. Oxford: Oxford University Press.

Morrison, Kristin. 1983. *Canters and Chronicles: The Use of Narrative in the Plays of Samuel Beckett and Harold Pinter*. Chicago: University of Chicago Press.

Sass, Louis A. 1985. Time, Space, and Symbol: A Study of Narrative Form and Representational Structure in Madness and Modernism. *Psychoanalysis and Contemporary Thought* 8:45–86.

Simon, Bennett. 1988. The Imaginary Twins: The Case of Beckett and Bion. *International Review of Psycho-Analysis*, in press.

Sontag, Susan. 1967. The Aesthetics of Silence. In *Styles of Radical Will*, ed. Susan Sontag. New York: Dell.

Spender, Stephen. 1963. *The Struggle of the Modern*. London: Hamilton.

Sypher, W. 1962. *Loss of the Self in Modern Literature and Art*. New York: Vintage.

Tobin, Patricia Drechsel. 1978. *Time and the Novel: The Genealogical Imperative*. Princeton: Princeton University Press.

CHAPTER 8

Psychoanalytic Theories
and Tragic Drama

T ragic drama from antiquity to the present has tried out various solutions and resolutions of the "problem" of living among one's own kind, the problem of the survival of the family. Psychoanalytic theory, though considerably younger, in its less than a century of existence has also examined various formulations and "solutions" to the same problematic.

From its inception, psychoanalysis has been intertwined with the study of tragic drama (Simon 1984). Freud's self-analysis and his clinical work, as well as his discovery of the Oedipus complex, were substantially augmented by his study of *Oedipus Rex* and *Hamlet*. Over the years, along with a prodigious number of psychoanalytically based studies of particular dramas, there have been a few tentative approaches toward formulating a psychoanalytic view of tragedy and the tragic. At the same time, several authors have tried to illuminate aspects of psychoanalysis by tracing the tragic dimensions of the analytic situation and of the development of the individual (e.g., Schaefer, 1976, pp. 22–56). The most extended and impressive treatments of the tragic and tragedy from psychoanalytic perspectives are Kurt Eissler's book on *Hamlet* (1971) and André Green's *Tragic Effect* (1979), works based on detailed study of particular plays. Green pays close attention to the role of the family in tragedy and discusses "whether kinship relations constitute the tragic or whether the tragic elucidates these kinship relations" (p. 37).

Several authors in the past few decades have sketched out theories about the relationship between theater, especially tragic drama, and the nature of the mind, especially in the psychoanalytic situation. Particularly important are the works of Devereux (1970) relating the structure of Greek tragedy to the structure of the mind-in-conflict, Hans Loewald (1975) on the theatrical nature of fantasy and transference, and Joyce McDougall's *Theaters of the Mind* (1985). The writings of Donald Kaplan, exploring the meanings theater accrues in relation to early childhood experiences and assaying various approaches to understanding audience–performance interactions, are also crucial (1968, 1969, 1971, 1972).

My focus, however, is on three "sketchy" psychoanalytic views of the nature of tragedy, ones not necessarily developed in the course of detailed study of particular dramas, but also not developed independently of their authors' favorite plays. The theories are Sigmund Freud's, especially his speculations on the origins of Greek tragedy; Heinz Kohut's distinction between Guilty Man and Tragic Man; and Erik Erikson's view of the relationship between tragic drama and the cycle of generations. These theories represent three clinically relevant views of human nature and human culture, which briefly alight on the terrain of tragic drama.[1]

Freud constructed a view of *human civilization* as a tragic drama, as having originated in a tragic crime, the murder of the primal father by the primal band of sons (see chap. 1). Civilization is a continuing tragic story, requiring for its success the control, renunciation, and repression of instinctual forces, especially aggression and sexuality, and thereby generating increasing amounts of guilt (Holmes 1983). The generation of guilt, of conscience, can itself lead to new aggression, variants of either suicide or homicide, in the effort to avoid, displace, and deny the power of conscience. Culture requires renunciation, but itself is a form of substitute gratification and at times a successful sublimation of instinctual drives.

Following leads from Frazer, Nietzsche, and a distinguished contemporary classicist, Salomon Reinach, Freud claimed that tragic drama originated in a ritual or dramatic representation of the primal crime:

> A company of individuals, named and dressed alike, surrounded a single figure, all hanging upon his words and deeds: they were the Chorus and the impersonator of the hero. He was originally the only actor. Later, a second and third actor were added, to play as counterpart to the Hero and as characters split off from him. . . . The Hero of tragedy must suffer; to this day that remains the essence of tragedy. He had to bear the burden of what was known as "tragic guilt"; the basis of that fault is not always easy to find, for in the light of our everyday life it is often no guilt at all. As a rule it lay in rebellion against some divine or human authority; and the Chorus accompanied the Hero with feelings of sympathy, sought to hold him back, to warn him and to sober him, and mourned over him when he had met with what was felt as the merited punishment for his rash undertaking.

1. A fourth such perspective, that of Lacan, remains to be elaborated elsewhere. Shoshana Felman's discussion (1987), especially "Beyond Oedipus," pp. 99–159, provides a basis for expounding a Lacanian view of tragedy.

But why had the Hero of tragedy to suffer? and what was the meaning of his "tragic guilt"? . . . because he was the primal father, the Hero of the great primaeval tragedy which was being re-enacted with a tendentious twist; and the tragic guilt was the guilt which he had to take on himself in order to relieve the Chorus from theirs. . . . Thus the tragic Hero became, though it might be against his will, the redeemer of the Chorus.   (Freud 1955, pp. 155–56)

With all this theory's flaws (e.g., it presumes the primacy of actor over chorus and fails to describe many existing Greek tragedies, such as those with a heroine or those with no central hero), the emphases are nevertheless of importance. First, tragic drama recapitulates something critical in human development—a repressed historical trauma and drama, the origin of the Oedipus complex. Second, tragic drama presents a story of the community, or, more specifically, the tortured and complex relationship between the individual and the community. Third, tragic drama involves suffering, violence, sacrifice, and scapegoating and is inextricably imbued with "tragic guilt."

I do not provide a complete survey of Freud on tragic drama here. In his detailed studies of particular plays, he pursued the analysis of Oedipal themes as far as he could, but he actually cast a wider net than his theory here would allow. He did not systematically develop the implications of these studies, though over time many others did. The history of psychoanalytic study of *Oedipus Rex* shows that analysts and literary critics have found not only, or perhaps not even primarily, the Oedipus complex in that play. Studies argue for the presence and/or primacy of pre-Oedipal themes, adoption fantasies, infanticidal impulses of the parent, narcissistic issues, and more (Edmunds and Ingber 1977; Caldwell 1974). However, Freud's "theory" of tragedy involves the Oedipus complex, a constellation of violation of a taboo, rebellion, suffering, sacrifice, collectivity, and tragic guilt.[2]

It was with some amazement, then, that I discovered that the psychoanalyst Heinz Kohut, the founder of self psychology, had begun to argue for a critical distinction between Tragic Man and Guilty Man, in effect to decompose "tragic guilt" into two oppositional terms. Guilty Man, according to Kohut, is the subject of classical psychoanalytic theory and treatment, the person suffering from an unresolved Oedipus complex, while Tragic Man, belonging to the late twentieth century, requires a theory and a praxis based on self psychology. Kohut's most extensive discussions of this distinction are found in two papers written in the 1970s: "On Courage"

2. See Figes (1976, pp. 137–45) for an important discussion of the role of taboo in tragedy, including a theory of why woman can still constitute, by her very existence, a tragic situation.

(Kohut 1985) and "Remarks about the Formation of the Self" (Kohut, 1978). In the former, he writes:

> Analysts, beginning with Freud, have felt strongly attracted by the mystery of tragedy, which they have explained largely in terms of a psychology of passions (drives), inner conflicts concerning these passions (structural conflicts), and punishment for transgressions motivated by passions (the victory of the self-punitive forces in the superego and the ascendancy of the death instinct). In this view of tragedy, which sees man as striving for happiness through love and work, man comes to grief because he cannot master his unruly passions and must ultimately bow to the inevitable victory of the life-destructive forces as embodied in his aggressions, in his guilt, and in the inevitable end of his biological existence. . . .
>
> . . . The art of the tragic . . . is concerned with man's attempt to live out the pattern of his nuclear self. And the tragic hero who is the protagonist of the great tragedies . . . is a man who, despite the breakdown of his physical and mental powers (e.g., Oedipus) and even despite his biological death (e.g., Hamlet) is triumphant because his nuclear self achieved an ascendancy which never will, indeed which never can, be undone.
>
> . . . man comes closest to narcissistic fulfillment when he is able to realize the pattern of his most central self. The effacement or the death of the tragic hero is thus not an incidental occurrence. Its essential meaning is not to be seen as punishment for a code-transgressing deed, which sets in motion the pattern of guilt and retribution. It is instead a necessary component of the hero's achievement, for it is only in death the hero's narcissistic fulfillment attains permanence. The survivors weep about the hero's fate, but the raised body of the hero as it is carried to the funeral pyre is not lamented as the remains of defeat would be. It is admired as the symbol of the hero's narcissistic triumph which, through his death, has now become absolute.   (Strozier 1982, pp. 37–38)

In "Remarks about the Formation of the Self," Kohut writes, "Tragic Man does not fear death as a symbolic punishment (castration) for forbidden pleasure aims (as does Guilty Man); he fears premature death, a death which prevents the realization of the aims of his nuclear self. And, unlike Guilty Man, he accepts death as part of the curve of his fulfilled and fulfilling life" (1978, pp. 753–54).

My own view is that Kohut's position affords a partial and one-sided account both of the nature of tragic drama and of audience reaction to such drama, including its reaction to the tragic hero. First, a view that declares that Guilty Man is not an essential part of tragic drama misses something absolutely critical. Second, this definition of Tragic Man bypasses or ignores the intense sense of community and generational consciousness that pervades tragic drama. Importantly, Kohut focuses on the tragic *hero*, rather than on the tragic *drama*.

I argue that it is a *tragic error* to divide humanity either psychologically or historically into the two polarized categories of "guilty" and "tragic," for that theoretical split actually replicates the problematic of tragic drama. Tragedy asks how one can both maintain one's integrity *and* take the risk of uniting with another to bear offspring and continue the line, that is, how one can define oneself as part of the line, not only as a being in splendid isolation and disconnection. The tragic hero, or tragic heroism, as I define it, entails a sense of community and continuity, not merely self-fulfillment. The "self-fulfillment" of the tragic hero is deeply involved in the problem of the collective. The problem in tragedy is a conflict between different views of what it is that fosters intergenerational continuity: is taking revenge on the fratricidal king, Claudius, a way of preserving the house of Hamlet, or is buying into Claudius' deals and offers of "sonship" a better method of preservation? Hamlet is not just discovering and carrying out his own ambitions and ideals—Kohut's emphasis (1985)—he is gradually working through and working out inner issues, conflicts of loyalty and duty, that eventuate in a view of what, to him, is absolutely necessary to preserve the larger entity. The tragic hero, in my view, is carrying a burden for all of upholding and fulfilling an ideal in order to preserve a larger entity. It is tragic that the task of preserving a larger whole entails death and destruction to both the upholders and the destroyers (or usurpers).

As for a theory of audience response to the hero (Kohut does not discuss audience response to the *play*), we find:

> Tragedy . . . has another function: It gives the spectator, reader, listener or beholder the opportunity to experience, in temporary identification with the tragic hero, the unfolding, expansion and triumph of his nuclear self. . . . [Great tragedy] allows us, therefore, to participate in the emotional development of the tragic hero from doubt to decision and from dejection to triumph as his nuclear self attains realization and is made permanent through death. Paradoxically, the spectator participating in the ultimate self-realization of the tragic hero, experiences his own self as more vigorous and cohesive than he even can in his real life. (Kohut 1985, p. 39)

Again, Kohut's account of our relationship to the tragic hero is not wrong, but he presents a lopsided and partial view. The sentiments he ascribes to the audience are undoubtedly often there, but if they are the main or only responses, then the audience has been caught up on one of the horns of the tragic dilemma—namely, seeing or experiencing the self *outside* the context of the communal. Experiencing, conversely, *only* the communal would similarly be a very partial response to the complexity of the tragic situation. Thus, Kohut more or less accurately renders one stage in the response to tragic drama or, better, to the tragic hero. But his account misses the possibility of a larger integration that can but does not always occur: an enlarged understanding and empathy for the tragic situation. Kohut's theory, for better and for worse, is a "self-centered" view of the hero.

Does Kohut, in his distinction between Tragic Man and Guilty Man, describe something veridical apart from tragic drama? He is right to pick up on the uniqueness of representation of the human condition in much of twentieth-century literature, from the works of Kafka to Beckett. He captures the spirit of characters and situations that are in large part illuminated within the framework of self psychology, that is, deeply damaged characters whose core sense of self is devastated or almost nonexistent. In this sense, Kohut's work overlaps with, for example, Fairbairn's and Guntrip's observations on the schizoid in modern times. But even here—whether this is a limitation of self psychology or of what Kohut thought and wrote about literature—he slights the communal aspects of the fictional worlds of these characters, overlooking the repression or suppression of the role of the other. He captures and conveys much of the experiential world of the characters, but his explanations do not go as far as they might. Kohut (1977, p. 287) cites Eugene O'Neill's play, *The Great God Brown*: "Man is born broken. He lives by mending. The grace of God is glue." What I have written about O'Neill, however, suggests that our appreciation of his work is limited if we only respond to the broken self and not to the community and the communication in which that self exists. There is no doubt that O'Neill's characters have problems with their "selves" and their right to an existence, but there is a constant interpersonal and intrapsychic conflict as well. O'Neill's characters are driven by instinctual forces; they suffer from various forms of guilt and are warding off intense instinctual wishes. Kohut's larger theory would have it that disorders of drives and defense arise from disturbed development of the self—instinctual drives are, as it were, radioactive disintegration products of the breakdown of the self. From the perspective of tragic drama, however, we see a two-way interaction— selves are broken because of the disastrous ways the characters handle their impulses and instincts, whether in direct expression of murderous and incestuous impulses or in the destructive defenses erected against the drives. But the account Kohut gives is correct in that defects in the sense of a coherent self—failure to experience a self that has a right to be alive and to feel—contribute to difficulties in managing and expressing the impulses.

Overall, Kohut appears reluctant to admit an unavoidable conflictual dimension to human development within family and society. In his last paper, "Introspection, Empathy, and the Semi-Circle of Mental Health" (1982), he states emphatically:

Healthy man experiences, and with deepest joy, the next generation as an extension of his own self. It is the primacy of the support for the succeeding generation, therefore, which is normal and human, and not intergenerational strife and mutual wishes to kill. . . . And it is in response to . . . a flawed parental self which cannot resonate with the child's experience in empathic identification that the newly constituted assertive-affectionate self of the child disintegrates and that the break-up of products of hostility and lust of the Oedipus complex make their appearance.

In my view, Kohut's reluctance to admit to the inevitability of conflict and imperfect relationships between the generations creates false expectations. The search for perfection can indeed lead to tragic consequences. Resolution of difficulties in development is possible, but not without some pain, sacrifice, guilt, and some diminution of either the self or the other.

Kohut's idea that conflict and damage from conflict is avoidable stands at the opposite extreme to the picture presented in much of the twentieth-century literature he describes: a portrait of a world beyond conflict, because it is already numbed, destroyed, murdered in its soul. Both extremes are illusional worlds, of either perfection or unmovable devastation. I argue in my discussion of Beckett's work that the world of his plays and novels is not prescriptive and does not insist that all is at an end. Rather, it presents one end of a painful dialectic of exploring the implications of humanity as we understand it, an "end" that contains the seeds, however blighted, of continuation, of "going on."

My critique of Kohut may be perceived as part of a "family quarrel" within psychoanalysis, and that perception may have some truth to it. I slight the full complexity of Kohut's thinking here, in part because I wish to highlight the problems rather than to lay out all of its virtues. Not the least of Kohut's virtues is an insight into modern intergenerational issues around the problem of conceiving, begetting, and rearing children. One of his students, for example, describes how Kohut's clinical formulations helped her to understand that her patient was unconsciously sparing his unborn child from repetition of the same trauma and deficiencies he experienced (White 1985, p. 229).

The third viewpoint on tragic drama that I will discuss is laid out in Erik Erikson's work on intergenerational continuity (1980), and in his discussion of Sophocles' Oedipus Rex. Like Kohut, Erikson does not study particular tragedies in detail, nor does he attempt a systematic study of what tragedy is. His brief comments on Oedipus Rex are situated in a larger body of work about human development and the life cycle.

Each individual human life, with its developmental lines, is embedded in "life cycles" of others. Erikson quotes Freud's Civilization and Its Discon-

tents—a work that takes the "tragic" view of human civilization: "Just as a planet revolves around a central body as well as rotating on its own axis, so the human individual takes part in the course of development of mankind at the same time as he pursues his own path in life" (quoted in Erikson 1980, p. 213). Erikson's discussion of *Oedipus Rex* utilizes the framework of tragedy as a representation of these interlocking cycles between the life of an individual and the lives of generations. He argues, implicitly, that the play portrays adolescent and adult life stages more than it does early infancy. Erikson presents his views on the stage of generativity versus stagnation as part of midlife:

> Within the life cycle I have postulated a psychosocial stage of *Generativity* which is concerned with new beings as well as new products and new ideas and which, as link between the generations, is as indispensable for the renewal of the adult generation's own life as it is for that of the next generation. . . . this sounds rather idealized . . . I can only say that we are here concerned with human potentials without which we would not exist. We must . . . claim for generativity a *procreative drive*, whether we wish to consider it an extension of genitality or a further stage. . . . it . . . is rooted back in the pregenital stages when the experience of parental care, in addition to a certain degree of instinctual gratification, also leads to an anticipatory identification with parenthood.
>
> . . . it may seem paradoxical to emphasize procreativity at a time when the technological triumph of birth control at last permits the safe prevention of undesirable procreative involvement. But there is today also a real danger that in the very name of genitality a new kind of repression may become a mark of adult life. We, with our generative profession, can easily underestimate how much some modern persons practising systematic birth control may need enlightenment in regard to what they are *not* doing. For new generations joining in planned parenthood must sublimate some of their procreativity in such active pursuits as will universally improve the conditions of every child chosen to be born. . . . [There are some who] in their undiagnosed aggravation of a sense of stagnation and self-absorption—the dystonic counterparts to generativity— need help.   (1980, pp. 215–16)

Erikson goes on to discuss the generational and intergenerational implications of the story of *Oedipus Rex*. The sphinx's riddle is about the life cycle of man. The play's storyline involves intergenerational transactions. From Oedipus' parents' trying to kill him to spare themselves (and him!) to Oedipus' concerns for his own children with Jocasta, the play portrays the ways in which parents' terrible deeds harm children. The impact of each generation on the others is an important part of the play and enters into the behavior of all the characters. Erikson emphasizes the community context of Oedipus' deeds. "In the end, the sinner-saviour has to mutilate and expel himself in order to renew the generational process in the *polis*" (p. 219).

Among Erikson's concluding points is that the "complex," the Oedipus complex, is presented as a stage play. He "plays" with these words, reminding us that the "play age" (presumably three to five) "is a combination of the incestuous tendencies most dangerous to social evolution, on the one hand, with affective and cognitive intensification of human *playfulness* on the other" (p. 220). He reviews the "play" characteristics and contents of that age, comments on play in adolescence, and goes on to discuss aspects of play in adult life. Public performances of rituals, including theater, "enable adults to revive and keep in touch with the abandoned imagination of childhood—and, of course, to become generative partners in the *interplay* of generations" (p. 220).

This account of intergenerational development is very much of a piece with what I have outlined as Shakespeare's model, at least as Barber describes it in relation to intergenerational mirroring in the *Sonnets* (see chap. 4). It is also as Kohut would wish it. However, Erikson, by using the "classical" drama of psychoanalysis, *Oedipus Rex*, as his exemplar, makes it clear that such development does not take place easily, free of conflict and without cost. His model, however, is of a system that has a good deal of resiliency and flexibility, both in the possibility to go sour, to stagnate, and in the ability to go right, to generate, to procreate.

Erikson concludes with a plea for clinicians to keep in mind, indeed to study, the dynamics surrounding the clinical enounter of the generations that takes place in analysis.[3] The patient, he suggests, comes to the analyst in "an attempt . . . to involve the analyst as a generative being in the repetition of selected life crises in order to restore the *developmental dialogue*" (p. 220). The analyst also experiences something of a restoration of his own blocked or inhibited developmental issues and, optimally, can find creative ways to utilize his or her own reawakened issues.

It should be obvious to the reader that I sympathize with Erikson's sense of the communal and intergenerational aspects of tragic drama, and that I believe it crucial for psychoanalysis to include those dimensions in an account of tragic drama. It is important to note (and Erikson has some awareness of this) that his is by no means a complete account of the nature of tragedy or of audience response. Like Freud and Kohut, he presents some important partial truths in the psychoanalytic interpretation of tragedy. Among the limitations of Erikson's understanding is that it falls short of conveying the pain, pessimism, and grimness of tragic drama. I return

---

3. Boszormenyi-Nagy's theory of family therapy complements Erikson's views on individual therapy in emphasizing the mutual obligations of the generations (e.g., Boszormenyi-Nagy and Krassner, 1980).

shortly to the implications of a plurality of psychoanalytic views on tragic drama.

Erikson's language suggests to me a further formulation of the way tragic drama works its effects on audiences. I propose that tragedy works by restoring a developmental dialogue for the members of the audience. The "development" has two aspects: audience members are simultaneously reshuffling their own relationships between self and the community, especially the family, and reworking their own lives in reference to earlier and subsequent life stages. The dialogue is usually experiential, rarely literal or verbal dialogue, unless the experience is elaborated by further thought, discussion, self-analysis, or critical study of the play. Thus the play, the performance, acts as a kind of transferential presence, a transient analyst, evoking feelings and images of different developmental stages, especially of stages that were only partially or imperfectly negotiated.

There reside in the structure, in the poetry, in the plot, as well as in other features, particular invitations to reenter a "developmental dialogue." One small example: many years ago, Caroline Spurgeon in her classic study of imagery in Shakespeare showed that, compared to other Elizabethan playwrights, Shakespeare's plays contained many more sensory references, in every modality, including smell! (Spurgeon 1935, pp. 12–85; Singer 1974, pp. 21–23). It seems as if Shakespeare himself was able to keep open and alive the pansensory and coenesthetic sensitivities of the child under the age of five, sensitivities which for most people are dulled in later development. His ability to enliven his plays with sound, touch, smell, and vertiginous sensations invites and helps us touch something vital that is partially cut off in our own development. Under optimal conditions, the experience allows growth and movement forward; under adverse psychic and social conditions, the experience may threaten us by reviving repressed or unbearable traumatic memories.

I also believe something in the *imperfect and incomplete* match between characters and audience allows for a renewal of developmental dialogue. As I describe in chapter 6, there is something incomplete and imperfect in the dialogues among the characters. Partial inaccuracies or failures of empathy mark tragic dialogues, and the great playwrights have discovered how to craft such "partially correct interpretations." In all, it is as if we encounter in the play a partially closed gestalt, or some ambiguous figure, and each of us in his or her own way makes some closure. The play is enough of a gestalt to invite an engagement and an attempt to "make sense" or "achieve closure," but it is open enough that there is room for a variety of closures; it is even possible to avoid further engagement. Some of what I call the "partially closed gestalt" resides in the formal features of the play, and some in the eye of the beholder.

The tragic dialogue and plot act for the audience like partially correct interpretations, and members of an audience, reacting and explicating what they think and feel about the play, *give partially correct interpretations.* Any given interpretation must possess and convey a measure of certainty and conviction that "this is what the play means" but it must still allow or admit that there is an unexplained residuum. "Explanation without remainder," in literature and in life, is a dream, not a reality.

There are then, in my view, no exact interpretations of the meaning of a play; there is only a process of interpreting. That process can be one that opens possibilities or one that prematurely forecloses. The process of criticism and interpretation of tragic drama involves a continuing dialectic between conviction and ignorance.

In this sense, recall my earlier discussions, in relation to *King Lear* for instance, of how tragedy deals with the tension between creative and deconstructive tendencies. (Recall Calderwood's 1986 essay, "Creative Uncreation in *King Lear*.") *Endgame* "plays" with meaning and meaninglessness, meaningful connections versus meaningless disconnections. *The Oresteia* resolves intractable male–female tensions, but only through a fiction, a "perverse solution" that in turn reinstates those tensions. *Macbeth* ends with the death of the overambitious former hero turned villain, while setting the stage for a further tragedy of hypertrophied male ambition, spurred by dread of the female. In providing a resolution based on a man "not of woman born," the play (like *The Oresteia*) denies and minimizes the role of woman in life of man. While different idioms may apply more aptly to one play or another, the model of tragic drama as providing some sort of closure—but incomplete closure—is useful for constructing larger theories about its effects.

Similarly, psychoanalytic dialogue at its best, by virtue of its dialectic between closure and nonclosure, knowing and not knowing, can generate new perspectives for the patient and new clinical sensibilities for the analyst. The proper ratio of "open-ended" to "formulated" dialogue is absolutely critical, though it is impossible to tell in advance what that optimal ratio will be in any given psychoanalysis. The same is true for psychoanalytic theory: it is at its best and most generative when it knows and shows a great deal, but not everything and not perfectly. Theory is best when it informs but also fails to inform; as such it generates puzzles that in turn can lead to new observations, new constructions, new theories. I am not at all dismayed by the plurality of theories in psychoanalysis; I view the situation as an inevitable and useful process. Psychoanalytic theories about tragic drama are, then, as unfinished and incomplete as psychoanalytic theories about development or about clinical work. Under proper circumstances, such a plurality can be fructifying and procreative.

At the beginning of this chapter, I suggested that both tragic drama and psychoanalysis have tried to deal with the intertwined human problems of death and kinship, and that both drama and theory have experimented with different possibilities of resolving these ineluctable human issues. I believe that these two developments of the human imagination have been associated with an opening of new possibilities and new outlooks and not only with pessimism and a sense of the terrible limitation of the human condition. This is the amazement and paradox—that the psyche can articulate how awful and awesome is the human predicament and emerge enriched and ennobled by that process. It is fitting, then, to recall that *Hamlet* is not only the play that spells out the pain of kinship—"more than kin and less than kind"—but also the play that defines the nobility of the creature capable of expressing and exploring its own pain.

> What a piece of work is a man! How noble in reason, how infinite in faculties, in form and moving how express and admirable, in action how like an angel, in apprehension how like a god!

REFERENCES

Boszormenyi-Nagy, Ivan, and Barbara R. Krasner. 1980. Trust-Based Therapy: A Contextual Approach. *American Journal of Psychiatry* 137:767–775.

Calderwood, J. L. 1986. Creative Uncreation in *King Lear*. *Shakespeare Quarterly* 37:5–19.

Caldwell, Richard S. 1974. The Blindness of Oedipus. *International Review of Psycho-Analysis* 1:207–218.

Devereux, George. 1970. The Structure of Tragedy and the Structure of the Psyche in Aristotle's *Poetics*. In *Psychoanalysis and Philosophy*, ed. C. Hanly and M. Lazerowitz, pp. 46–75. New York: International Universities Press.

Edmunds, Lowell, and R. Ingber. 1977. Psychoanalytical Writings on the Oedipus Legend: A Bibliography. *American Imago* 34:374–386.

Eissler, Kurt, 1971. *Discourse on Hamlet and "Hamlet": A Psychoanalytic Inquiry*. New York: International Universities Press.

Erikson, Erik H. 1980. On the Generational Cycle: An Address. *International Journal of Psycho-Analysis* 61:213–223.

Felman, Shoshana. 1987. *Jacques Lacan and the Adventure of Insight: Psychoanalysis in Contemporary Culture*. Cambridge: Harvard University Press.

Figes, Eva. 1976. *Tragedy and Social Evolution*. London: Calder.

Freud, Sigmund. 1955. *Totem and Taboo*. In *Standard Edition*, trans. James Strachey, vol. 13, pp. 155–156. London: Hogarth Press. Originally published 1913.

———. 1961. *Civilization and Its Discontents*. In *Standard Edition*, trans. James Strachey, vol. 21, pp. 57–145. London: Hogarth Press. Originally published 1930.

Green, André. 1979. *The Tragic Effect: The Oedipus Complex in Tragedy*. Trans. Alan Sheridan. Cambridge: Cambridge University Press.

Holmes, Kim R. 1983. Freud, Evolution, and the Tragedy of Man. *Journal of the American Psychoanalytic Association* 31:187–210.

Kaplan, Donald M. 1968. Theatre Architecture: A Derivation of the Primal Cavity. *The Drama Review* 12:105–116.

———. 1969. On Stage Fright. *The Drama Review* 14:60–83.

———. 1971. Gestures, Sensibilities, Scripts: Further Reflections on Performance–Audience Interactions. *Performance* 1:31–46.

———. 1972. Reflections on Eissler's Concept of the Doxalethetic Function. *American Imago* 29:353–376.

Kohut, Heinz. 1977. *The Restoration of the Self*. New York: International Universities Press.

———. 1978. Remarks about the Formation of the Self. In *The Search for the Self: Selected Writings of Heinz Kohut, 1950–1978*, ed. Paul Ornstein, vol. 2, pp. 737–770. New York: International Universities Press. Essay originally published 1974.

———. 1982. Introspection, Empathy and the Semi-Circle of Mental Health. *International Journal of Psycho-Analysis* 63:395–407.

———. 1985. On Courage. In *Self Psychology and the Humanities: Reflections on a New Psychoanalytic Approach*, ed. Charles B. Strozier, pp. 5–50. New York: Norton.

Loewald, Hans W. 1975. Psychoanalysis as an Art and the Fantasy Character of the Psychoanalytic Situation. *Journal of the American Psychoanalytic Association* 23:277–299.

McDougall, Joyce. 1985. *Theaters of the Mind: Illusion and Truth on the Psychoanalytic Stage*. New York: Basic Books.

Simon, Bennett. 1984. "With Cunnings Delays and Ever-Mounting Excitement" or, What Thickens the Plot in Tragedy and Psychoanalysis. In *Psychoanalysis: The Vital Issues*, ed. George H. Pollock and John E. Gedo, vol. 2, pp. 387–436. New York: International Universities Press.

Singer, Jerome L. 1974. *Imagery and Daydream Methods in Psychotherapy and Behavior Modification*. New York: Academic Press.

Spurgeon, Caroline F. E. 1935. *Shakespeare's Imagery and What It Tells Us*. New York: Macmillan.

White, Marjorie Taggart. 1985. The Rediscovery of Intergenerational Continuity and Mutuality. In *Progress in Self-Psychology*, ed. Arnold Goldberg, vol. 1, pp. 228–239. New York: Guilford Press.

INDEX

Absurd, the, 216
Achilles, 14–15, 61
Adoption, 156
Adultery, 19–20, 31, 116. See also *Medea*
Aegeus, 85–87
Aelptós (unexpected), 70
Aeschylus. See *Danaids, The; Oresteia, The*
Affect: blocked, 109–10, 167*n*, 236, 245–46; in *Endgame*, 216–17; in *King Lear*, 109–10; in *Long Day's Journey into Night*, 184
Agamemnon (Aeschylus). See *Oresteia, The*
Agamemnon (character): continuity of family and, 3; as father, 53–54; murder of, 44, 46; sacrifice and, 17, 25; as tragic hero, 58–59. *See also* Iphigenia, sacrifice of
Albee, E., 86
Alexithymia, 236
Ambivalence, 24–25, 184
Amphisbaina, 18, 46
Anagnorisis. See Recognition
Anouilh, Jean, 82
Antigone (Sophocles), 6
Anti-tragic (term), 6
Apaides (children), 69*n*
Aristophanes, 61
Aristotle, 1, 5, 13, 14, 16
Atreus, House of, 29–30, 32, 38

Audience response: and Aeschylus vs. Euripides, 69–71; and Beckett's works, 213–14, 217, 221, 225–29, 245–46; developmental dialogue for, 262–63; empathetic, 126, 133–34, 188, 221; Euripides' [pro]creativity and, 96–101; form and, 123, 225–29; generational differences in, 126; Kohut's theory of, 257–58; to sacrifice, 25–26

Bair, Deirdre, 230–32
Barber, C. L., 127, 202, 261; "Family in Shakespeare's Development," 127–29, 134–36
Baudelaire, Charles, 201
Beckett, Samuel: *Act Without Words*, 215; *All That Fall*, 232; *Not I*, 232–33; psychology of, 215–16, 229–30, 232–34, 237, 246; *Waiting for Godot*, 4, 213; war in writings of, 240; *Whoroscope*, 232, 246; *Words and Music*, 230. See also *Endgame*
Begetting: caring forms of, 119–23; in *King Lear*, 113, 117, 119–23; Kohut's insights into, 259; in *Macbeth*, 148–49, 151–56; of narrative, meaning, and children, 60–66; of play, 97–101, 228; without women, 49, 83–84. *See also* Birth; Procreation
Biblical tales, 219*n*
Bion, Wilfred, 10, 231, 235, 237–42